UNDERSTANDING A CHANGING CHINA

Key Issues for Business

Howard Davies and Matevz Raskovic

LONDON AND NEW YORK

First published 2018
by Routledge
2 Park Square, Milton Park, Abingdon, Oxon OX14 4RN

and by Routledge
711 Third Avenue, New York, NY 10017

Routledge is an imprint of the Taylor & Francis Group, an informa business

British Library Cataloguing-in-Publication Data
A catalogue record for this book is available from the British Library

Library of Congress Cataloging-in-Publication Data
A catalog record for this book has been requested

ISBN: 978-1-138-20374-7 (hbk)
ISBN: 978-1-138-20375-4 (pbk)
ISBN: 978-1-315-47093-1 (ebk)

Typeset in Goudy
by Swales & Willis Ltd, Exeter, Devon, UK

Visit the Companion Website: www.routledge.com/cw/davies

UNDERSTANDING A CHANGING CHINA

As China becomes the world's largest economy, so it becomes important to understand the key issues shaping the country's business environment and the behaviour of Chinese businesspeople.

This is difficult because those issues are contested. Is China growing at 3% or 8%? Is the Chinese consumer going to save the world? Are state-owned enterprises national champions or zombies? Have we reached the end of "Cheap China"? Can China innovate? Is business still dominated by personal connections? Are markets or the state in control? Does Chinese culture impede or support organizational effectiveness? Are Chinese dragons at your door? Will the finance and property sectors implode? Is the Chinese model sustainable, or will it end in tears?

On all these issues there is ill-informed "noise", and an abundance of partisan interpretations. The purpose of this book, therefore, is to provide an even-handed analysis of the key issues that will shape the threats and opportunities arising from China's development in the next decade. It cannot resolve the competing claims made. However, it does provide the reader with the ideas and the sources of evidence needed to understand and to make well thought-out judgments as China continues to evolve.

Howard Davies is Adjunct Professor at Hong Kong Polytechnic University. He served in the Faculty of Business from 1990 to 2013, as Professor, Dean, and Associate Dean. His publications on China business include papers in *Strategic Management Journal, Journal of International Business Studies* and *Organization Studies*.

Matevz Raskovic is Assistant Professor of International Business at the University of Ljubljana, Faculty of Economics, Visiting Professor at Shanghai University of International Business and Economics and 2017 Fulbright Visiting Scholar at Harvard University, FAS Sociology.

TO OUR STUDENTS AND VISITORS, WHO ASKED THE QUESTIONS, AND TO OUR FAMILIES AND FRIENDS WHO SUPPORTED US.

MATEVZ RASKOVIC WOULD ALSO LIKE TO ACKNOWLEDGE THE SUPPORT OF THE FULBRIGHT PROGRAM AND THANK HARVARD UNIVERSITY, FAS SOCIOLOGY, IN PARTICULAR CHRIS WINSHIP.

CONTENTS

FIGURES

TABLES

1

FROM ANCIENT CIVILIZATION THROUGH HUMILIATION TO POWERHOUSE

Howard Davies

Doing business with China involves engaging with the modern manifestations of an ancient civilization. This chapter reviews the historical background and the impact it has on the attitudes and perspectives of Chinese people today.

The ancient power

It is a commonplace that China is an ancient country, whose wealth and achievements outshone contemporary Western societies for millennia. However, an appreciation of the sheer scale of that phenomenon is less common.

The Han majority refer to themselves as the "sons of the Yellow Emperor" in deference to Huang Di, born in 2704 BCE. He is revered as an ancestor but also as the patron of the *Huang Di Nei Jing* or "Yellow Emperor's Internal Canon" which is a compilation of Chinese traditional medical practices, still in use today. In reality, the *Huang Di Nei Jing* was probably compiled between the period of the Warring States (475–221 BC) to the early part of the Han period (206 BC–AD 220). However, even if the latest of those dates is taken as the reference point, modern Chinese doctors and their patients still refer extensively to a text that is nearly 1,800 years old. The Western equivalent would be if CNN's health programmes today featured medical advice from the days of the Roman Empire, not as historical curiosities but as remedies for today's ailments.

The Yellow Emperor is relevant today because contemporary Chinese perceive themselves as direct inheritors of an ancient set of traditions and practices that retain their value. Of course, the narrative of a homogeneous "Chinese" identity does not rest easily with the fact that the country has more than 50 recognized ethnic minorities, and that important ruling dynasties – the Mongol Yuan (1271–1368) and the Manchu Qing (1664–1911) – were initially foreign invaders. However, the minorities (almost) all consider themselves Chinese first and the alien rulers were absorbed into Han culture. Mongols and Manchus wielded sovereignty, but their scripts never replaced Chinese characters.

While the Yellow Emperor is probably mythical, the Emperor Qin Shi Huang, who reigned from 221 to 210 BC, was not. His accession followed the "Warring States" period (475–221 BC) during which seven dynasties fought for control of the territories stretching from Hangzhou in the East to Xi'an in the West and Beijing in the North. The devastation was immense and Qin general Bai Qi alone is said to have been responsible for more than 890,000 enemy deaths. However, the Warring States period was also one of achievement. There were significant military innovations and Sun Tzu's *Art of War*, recently re-discovered by business strategists (McNeilly, 2012), was probably compiled at that time. The period saw also seminal intellectual developments as the major schools of Legalism, Confucianism and Daoism contested for superiority.

Having prevailed over his enemies and united the country, Qin Shi Huang became forever associated with it, his name providing the basis for referring to the country as "China". Despite reigning for just 11 years, and being followed by an incompetent son who lost control, his achievements were staggering. His armies had more than a million men, with the most up-to-date technologies, supported by a logistical system that brought them to action with rapid effect. Qin Shi Huang understood the value of standardization and decreed a fixed axle width for carts, so that roads could have a standard width. He standardized weights and measures, and he provided the greatest unifier and carrier of culture by standardizing the Chinese script. (Even today, the languages spoken across China are mutually incomprehensible. Hence, television programmes carry sub-titles that can be read by everyone.) In the North, Qin Shi Huang began the construction of a great wall, designed to keep out the hostile Xiongnu. In the South, he began work on a canal linking the river systems of the Yangtze and the Pearl, to facilitate the movement of supplies.

Despite his greatness, Qin Shi Huang has also entered history as a ruthless taker of lives and a cultural vandal. In particular, the Han dynasty historian Sima Qian described him as having buried Confucian scholars alive and burned books of poetry, history and philosophy. Such actions fit with his behaviour in war, and his determination to impose the Qin vision. However, the Han were the immediate successors to the Qin, with an interest in slandering their predecessors, and Qian's accusations are now regarded as largely unsupported (Nylan, 2001). Nevertheless, Qin Shi Huang's ruthlessness remains a part of his image, and was openly emulated by Mao Zedong at important points in his career.

Qin Shi Huang was obsessed with mortality, after assassination attempts which provide extensive material for modern Chinese cinema. He sought the elixir of life, ingested unusual substances, and passed away in 210 BC, perhaps as a result of taking pills containing mercury.

Qin Shi Huang's death provided him with real immortality through his mausoleum in Xi'an, known as the "Terracotta Army" (Man, 2007), which stands as testimony to the sophistication of Chinese technology and culture in the years around 200 BC. Built to protect the Emperor in the afterlife, those parts of the tomb that have been excavated contain more than 8,000 life-size warriors in terracotta, including cavalrymen with their (real) horses and every type of warrior from generals to halberdiers and crossbowmen, all equipped for action.

The warriors are imposing but there is more to the Qin Mausoleum. The section that has been excavated probably accounts for only 25% of the total. Folklore has it that somewhere in the complex there is a detailed map of Qin China, with the seas and rivers filled with mercury, and mercury levels in the soil at some points are unusually high. Particularly impressive technologically is a sword that is 2,000 years old and has been chrome-plated. In the West, the technology for such a process was invented in Germany in the 1930s, to be replaced by a more efficient technique in the US in the 1950s. The question of how such a difficult task could have been completed at the time remains a mystery.

From greatness to stagnation

By the time of the Qin, Chinese technology far surpassed the West. Little is known about the level of national income, although estimates for around AD 50 (Maddison, 1998) are that China then had the same per capita GDP as Europe, dominated by the Roman Empire. The Qin were succeeded by the Han (206 BC to AD 220), followed by the Six Dynasties (220–589) and the Sui (581–618) who were succeeded by the Tang (618–906). While there had been significant accomplishments throughout that time – the Han piped natural gas to power saltworks, and had bamboo gas cylinders (Temple, 1986) – the Tang era is often seen as China's Golden Age (Benn, 2002). Emperor Xuanzong had a room air-conditioned by rotary fans and fountains, and the world's first widely printed books were produced. Maps were improved and building standards introduced. The first escapement for a clock was made, porcelain was invented and the upper classes had scented toilet paper. The walls of the capital Chang An (modern day Xi'an) measured nearly 40 km in total (the Ming walls, which stand today, measure 14 km). Tang poetry and the magnificent coloured pottery horses still impress as emblems for a society which was rich in culture, cosmopolitan, and tolerant of different religions.

While the period of the Han, Sui and Tang saw progress in culture and technology, income per capita hardly grew at all between the years 50 and 960. However, during the Song dynasty (AD 959–1279) it grew by approximately one third, to a level in 1270 that had not been exceeded 500 years later (Maddison, 1998). Just as the Tang had seen important technological improvements, so did the Song, with the first use of gunpowder, the compass, national banknotes, movable type printing and a permanent navy, amongst a host of mathematical, engineering, and administrative innovations.

When the Song collapsed, they were followed by three dynasties which take the Imperial period to its close in 1911. The Mongol Kublai Khan, grandson of Genghis, declared himself Emperor in 1271 and defeated the Song. He promoted the Silk Road to the Middle East, expanded the Grand Canal, and (possibly) hosted Marco Polo. While the Yuan dynasty saw progress in culture, the arts and science, it lasted less than 100 years. Natural disasters and ineffective government fuelled unrest, so that in 1368 the forces of the Ming, ethnically Han and based in the South, were able to prevail, ushering in the era of the Great Ming, which was to last 276 years.

The Ming era was another of Chinese greatness, not least in respect of sheer size. The population was between 160 to 200 million, twice that of the whole of Europe (Kirk, 1946), its growth stimulated by crops from the Americas, including corn, potatoes and chili peppers. The standing army had more than one million troops and the Muslim eunuch admiral Zheng He completed sea voyages with a fleet of ships whose size challenges the imagination even today. Admiral Zheng's five fleets each comprised more than 100 ships, carrying around 25,000 men and women. His largest treasure ship was 140 metres long and 50 metres wide and his voyages between 1421 and 1423 certainly took the treasure fleets to Indonesia, India and around Africa. According to Menzies (2002), he also sailed to South America, the Western seaboard of North America, Japan, the Arctic, Iceland, Greenland and even the Eastern coast of North America. Historians dispute the full extent of Zheng's expeditions but even conservative interpretations are impressive and stones inscribed with Chinese characters are still found on distant shores, perhaps where Zheng hauled his ships onto beaches for maintenance.

While the Ming era was one of Chinese pre-eminence, it also saw the beginnings of decline. Innovations were made, but historians see it as a period in which technological progress slowed down and per capita income did not rise at all. Despite the greatness of the Ming fleets, Emperor Hongwu had banned maritime trade as early as 1371 in order to deter piracy. The ban had been ignored by Emperor Yongle, which allowed Zheng He's voyages to take place, but it was re-instated in 1550, and the great expeditions were over. The Ming were under pressure from the Mongols in the North, the resources needed for expeditions were not available and the great shipyards of Nanjing fell into disuse.

By the early seventeenth century, the Ming were in a difficult position, which they were incompetent to handle. A rise in the price of silver (in which taxes were paid) was a disaster for the peasantry, who rebelled. Unusually bad weather, natural disasters and a court rife with in-fighting meant that the state lacked both resources and the ability to allocate them appropriately. In the Chinese way of thinking about the legitimacy of their rulers, the Mandate of Heaven had been withdrawn from the Ming, as they were unable to provide livelihoods and stability for their people. In 1644 a rebel army led by Li Zicheng seized Beijing and the last Ming Emperor hung himself behind the Forbidden City.

While the Ming capital fell to Li Zicheng, the real victory went to the Manchus from the North. Assisted by turncoat Ming general Wu Sangui they defeated Li, founding the last of the Chinese dynasties, the Great Qing. Han officers and officials defected to the Qing en masse, making possible the rule of a huge country by a small, though warlike, minority

The Qing ruled from 1644 until 1911, corresponding to the reigns of Charles I to George V in England or Louis XIV to the Third Republic in France. While the earlier part of the Qing reign saw continued Chinese pre-eminence, the disappearance of the technological progress that had characterized Chinese history prior to the fifteenth century contributed to the gradual weakening of the regime's authority, hastened by its overconfidence and steadfast belief in its own superiority.

The first century of Qing rule gave warning of what was to come. By 1683 Emperor Kangxi had unified the country politically but done little to improve administration or life for the peasantry. His successor, Yongzheng, understood the need for reform and tried to free the "mean people" of China from servitude. However, his reign was too short (1723–1735) to accomplish reform in the face of court opposition, rebellions, and charges that he had usurped the throne. Ominously, during Yongzheng's reign, the use of opium, which played a significant role in China's humiliation, extended beyond medicinal use to become widespread.

Yongzheng was succeeded by Qianlong who reigned from 1736 to 1799. It was another period of prosperity, when the population grew to around 300 million, after falling drastically during the late Ming. Huge areas to the West were conquered and the Dzungar Mongols and Jinchuan Tibetans were wiped out. In the cultural arena, Qianlong compiled a huge anthology of literary and historical works, collected paintings and calligraphy, and drew on the Jesuits to design and build a European style summer palace – the *Yuan Ming Yuan* – which was later burned down by European troops. China's greatest novel, *The Dream of the Red Chamber*, was completed in 1792, after the author Cao Xueqin's death in 1763.

While the Qianlong era was the apogee of prosperity and Imperial control, it was also the beginning of the decline. There was little growth in per capita income, which allowed Western countries to catch up in that respect. When the British King George III sent his emissary Lord Macartney to Beijing in 1793, with a mandate to persuade the Emperor to open China to trade, Qianlong sidelined the mission and wrote to the King that "we have never valued ingenious articles, nor do we have the slightest need of your country's manufactures". Macartney used a naval metaphor to describe the Chinese Empire of the time as:

> An old, crazy, first-rate Man of War, which a fortunate succession of able and vigilant officers have contrived to keep afloat for these hundred and fifty years past, and to overawe their neighbours merely by her bulk and appearance. But whenever an insufficient man happens to have the command on deck, adieu to the principles and safety of the ship. She may, perhaps, not sink outright; she may drift some time as a wreck, and then will be dashed to pieces on the shore; but she can never be re-built on the old bottom.
>
> (Spence, 1990, p.123)

Macartney was right. The crazy warship was torn apart by a combination of internal failings and external predation by Western powers whose technological and military prowess had overtaken the now sleeping dragon.

Qianlong was succeeded by Emperors Jiaqing, Daoguang and Xianfeng, none of whom were "sufficient" to save the ship of state. Daoguang tried to eliminate the opium trade and in 1838 appointed scholar-official Lin Zexu as imperial commissioner to carry out that task. To this day, Lin is a symbol of the rare incorruptible Chinese official and he went about his task with competence. However, his destruction of British-owned opium provided the trigger for the First Opium War, 1839–42, in which technologically superior British warships, weaponry and tactics quickly overcame the Qing troops. The Treaty of Nanjing in 1842 (referred to by the Chinese as the first of the "unequal treaties") ceded the island of Hong Kong to the British in perpetuity. It also forced the Qing to open Canton (Guangzhou) and four additional "Treaty Ports" to trade – Xiamen, Fuzhou, Ningbo and Shanghai.

In the 1850s, Britain sought to expand its privileges in China, while the Chinese kept out as many foreigners as they could, triggering the Second Opium War. France joined with Britain and they took Guangzhou, before concluding the 1858 Treaties of Tianjin, which gave further concessions, and to which Russia and the US were also party. Despite the evidence of the Western powers' superiority, the Emperor Xianfeng was persuaded to resist further encroachment and British troops were beaten off at the Dagu forts near Tianjin in June 1859. While that encouraged anti-foreigner sentiment in the Qing court, the affront to British prestige guaranteed that they would return in force and in September 1860 the Chinese troops who had imposed the Dagu defeat were wiped out by the British and French, who entered Beijing that October.

The Opium Wars marked the beginning of the Century of Humiliation, which lasted until Mao Zedong stood on the Gate of Heavenly Peace in 1949 and declared "the Chinese people now stand up". The combination of foreign intervention and domestic upheaval, most notably the Taiping Rebellion (1850–1864) in which at least 20 million people died, ensured that the country's pre-eminence was lost. While China accounted for as much as 32% of the world's GDP (Maddison, 1998, p.40) as late as 1820, that figure fell precipitously. China was reduced to the status of a backward country, technologically backward, dismembered by foreign predators, and incapable of maintaining sovereignty over its own territory.

The Needham Question: why did China fall behind?

Technology is a key determinant of power and prosperity and China had been technologically superior to the West for millennia. Joseph Needham, a British biochemist turned polymath, discovered in the 1940s and 1950s that the country had hundreds of inventions to its credit, including those considered most important by Francis Bacon – paper and printing, gunpowder and the compass (Winchester, 2008). However, that lead had been lost and technological backwardness rendered the country helpless in the face of superior ships and weaponry. Needham therefore sought to answer the question, "why did modern science not develop in China?" The answers help to explain why China lost its position in the world and raise important questions today.

Several hypotheses have been put forward in answer to the "Needham Question" (Lu, 2011). Elvin (1973) suggested that population growth meant that labour was too cheap to provide incentives for labour-saving inventions, and the need to feed the population limited the surpluses available to support technology development. However, as Lin (1995, p.274) points out, the evidence is of labour shortages rather than labour abundance and the surplus available in the stagnant Ming era was probably larger than in the preceding more inventive centuries.

An alternative argument, put forward by Fung (1922), is that the philosophies of Confucianism, Daoism and Buddhism, which underlie Chinese patterns of thought, inhibit the development of science. In Daoism, a central principle is *wu wei* or action through non-action, the idea that to exert one's will against the world is disruptive of the harmony that is in place. From that perspective, Nature works by "doing nothing", not by following knowable laws, whose pursuit is irrelevant. Confucian thinking also emphasizes the importance of harmony, while Buddhism treats the external world as an illusion. Those philosophies therefore share a disdain for activities designed to harness nature, which are a distraction from the real pursuit of meaning and happiness.

While Needham was drawn to that argument, it suffers from the basic problem that the schools of thought in question had been in place throughout the period of technological fecundity. If they were inhibitive of innovation, why had they not prevented technological development in ancient times? One answer concerns the place occupied by Confucian thinking in the civil service examination system and in the incentives facing the most able people.

One of China's greatest innovations, in the Sui dynasty (580–618), was to introduce a system of meritocratic appointments to the civil service through fair and impartial examinations. Of course, those with more resources had a greater chance of success through their ability to spend time studying. Nevertheless, the examination system did provide a path by which those of limited means but great intellectual ability could, and did, rise above their birth prospects to acquire power and status. The incentives to pass the examinations were intense (and Chinese today retain a belief in the value of examinations which is incomprehensible to many Westerners). In the period before 1313, the examinations included mathematics, astronomy and the "laws of nature" which were well suited to the development of science. However, those subjects were eliminated and from 1313 until 1904 the core of the syllabus was made up of the Confucian classics. The impact was to divert the best minds away from investigation, and experimentation and towards philosophy. When the Ming scholar Song Yingxing wrote a review of science and technology to date, he commented (Ho, 1962, p.16)

> An ambitious scholar will undoubtedly toss this book onto his desk and give it no further thought: it is a work that is in no way concerned with the art of advancement in officialdom.

Sivin (1995) pointed out that Western universities placed a similar emphasis on philosophy and divinity. However, that was replaced from the mid-1600s onwards with an increasing emphasis on technology related subjects, and the timing of the curriculum changes in China and the West seems to be consistent with the "examination hypothesis". In China, technological development slowed after its intellectual underpinnings were deleted from the curriculum while in the West the Industrial Revolution was preceded by a shift towards them.

Lin (1995) offers another explanation. In the pre-modern era innovations occurred as the result of trial and error, within the normal production process. There was some use of systematic methods but most innovations arose randomly. In that case, the key factor in determining the rate of technological progress was the size of the population. As China's population was much larger than Europe's, China inevitably produced more innovations. However, in the absence of a method for inventing inventions, the productivity of that innovation-generating process was limited and diminishing returns set in. As China's innovation slowed, the Western shift to invention based on deduction, hypotheses and experiment meant that population size was no longer the key determinant. The West invented the method of invention, and its brightest minds were engaged in innovation, while China remained indifferent to the ability to change the world and its Confucian intellectual elite focused on the 430,000 characters of the classics.

While these are the major hypotheses on the Needham puzzle, there are others. One concerns the lack of competition within the Chinese system and between China and its neighbours. Europe was made up of small states (Italy and Germany only became single nations in the nineteenth century) who warred with each other continuously, providing incentives for innovation. On the other hand, before 1840, China faced no technologically competent rival on its borders and struggles for power largely took place within the court, between rival factions of the nobility and the eunuchs. Complacency was more evident than competition and no one needed to improve technology in order to maintain their power and influence.

The key point about these answers to the Needham puzzle is that they highlight issues that remain significant today. Is China now capable of significant "indigenous innovation" or is it locked in the role of "copycat" (Rein, 2014)? Are the incentives and capabilities needed for invention now in place? Does the examination system still stifle creativity and technological progress? Chapter 6 examines those questions.

China's Century of Humiliation

The Opium Wars marked the beginning of China's collapse and dismemberment at the hands of foreign powers. In the 1890s, Germany occupied Qingdao and claimed rights in the province of Shandong. Britain extended its territory in Hong Kong through a forced lease of the Kowloon peninsula and the New Territories. Russia occupied Lushun, the French claimed privileges in the South West, and the Japanese extended their influence from Taiwan into the North. Under the principle of "extra-territoriality", treaty-state foreigners involved in criminal cases on Chinese soil were exempt from prosecution under the Chinese legal system and had the right to be tried under their own national laws. The Chinese state therefore lost sovereignty within large parts of its own territory.

One response was an upsurge in nationalism. The Boxer Uprising of 1898–1900 was an inchoate movement of fanatics who killed foreigners, Christian converts, engineers and those in possession of foreign objects. When the Boxers had a degree of success against a small army sent by the Western powers to relieve the besieged foreign legations in Beijing the Empress Dowager Cixi praised them and in effect declared war on the foreigners, in a foolish move reminiscent of the Emperor Xianfeng in 1859. The outcome was the same as the foreign powers sent a contingent of 20,000 troops, which routed the Boxers, relieved the foreign legations and occupied Beijing, forcing Cixi to flee.

The failings of the Qing regime also led to less irrational forms of nationalistic response. One of them, led by Sun Yat-sen, was to portray the Qing as Manchu tyrants who had enslaved the Han and should be overthrown. In the words of Zou Rong (1903) "our sacred Han race, descendants of the Yellow Emperor, should support revolutionary independence". It took time, and there were as many defeats as victories, but the anti-Qing forces eventually overthrew the dynasty in 1911.

The other form of nationalistic response came from the Qing government itself. Recognizing that the West was much stronger, and that Japan had strengthened itself by learning from the West, officials tried to institute long overdue reforms. In 1908, just before both Cixi and the Emperor Guangxu died, it was announced that constitutional government would be in place within nine years. Superstitious opposition to railway building was overcome and the network expanded, financed through foreign investment. The military was re-organized and the "New Army" adopted modern weapons, uniforms and drills.

Despite these attempts to reform, the Qing were unable to maintain control. The New Army was too weak. As in the last days of the Ming, disastrous harvests impoverished millions of peasants who became enemies of the state. Nationalism of the anti-Manchu variety combined with socialist, Marxist and anarchist ideas to fuel uprisings that were suppressed without eliminating their root causes. By 1911, the revolutionaries had recruited about one third of the New Army troops in the Wuhan area, and in October they mutinied. The revolt spread across the country, Manchus were massacred, and the Qing were forced to comply with demands for immediate establishment of a parliament, a constitution and a premier, the banning of the Imperial family from office and restriction of the Emperor's powers. While the reforms seemed to lead to a constitutional monarchy, rather than the republic proposed by Sun Yat-sen, Sun had so much support that when he returned from France delegates from 16 provincial assemblies elected him provisional president of a new republic, which was declared on 1 January 1912. At that point, the "republic" also had a Manchu emperor. However, after negotiation with General Yuan Shikai, to whom Sun offered the presidency, the child emperor Pu Yi abdicated on 12 February 1912. Thousands of years of imperial rule had ended and China faced an uncertain future.

In February 1913, the first month of the new republic, Sun Yat-sen handed the presidency to Yuan Shikai, but by May Yuan had fallen out with the leaders of the *Guomindang* political party, which had won elections in January. He forced the parliament to elect him president for five years and declared the *Guomindang* a seditious organization. He began to take the emperor's place in the Confucian rituals held in the Temple of Heaven and in 1915 had himself declared emperor. The country erupted, several provinces declared independence, and then Yuan Shikai died in 1916.

From this point until 1949, China was divided, chaotic and occupied by foreign powers. In the period 1916 to 1928 regional strongmen, usually referred to as "warlords", held sway over their own territories, collecting taxes, equipping their own armies and ruling with varying degrees of competence and brutality or benevolence. In 1928, three years after Sun Yat-sen died, *Guomindang* General Chiang Kai-shek completed the Northern Expedition, which destroyed the power of the three most important warlords.

While Chiang Kai-shek attempted to build a national political and economic structure, the following 20 years were dominated by a complex set of rivalries between three competing interests. These were the *Guomindang* (GMD) under Chiang Kai-shek, the Chinese Communist Party (CCP), and the Japanese military, dominated by the almost autonomous Kwantung Army.

While the GMD and the Communists worked together in the Northern Expedition, their relationship was undermined by their rivalry. Some elements of the GMD, led by Wang Jingwei in Wuhan, emphasized the need for a social revolution and the ending of foreign concessions, while taking military advice from the Russian agent of the Communist International, Borodin, who had cemented the alliance between them and the CCP. The others, including Chiang Kai-shek, were more conservative, and had links with wealthy interests and the secret societies that protected them. In April 1927, when Russian leader Stalin was still insisting that the CCP cooperate with Chiang, the latter collaborated with the Green Gang and wealthy industrialists in Shanghai to turn violently on the CCP. Hundreds of Communists were killed in the city, and thousands arrested. At first, the Wuhan faction of the GMD denounced Chiang as a traitor, but they reversed course when they found out that Borodin had secretly been ordered to use the CCP to move the Wuhan GMD to the left, while pretending to support it. The Chinese Civil War, between the CCP and the GMD, had begun. It lasted from 1927 until 1950, was responsible for millions of deaths and a significant proportion of the devastation visited on the country in that time.

The GMD's nemesis, the Chinese Communist Party, had been founded in 1921 in Shanghai. It originally formed the left wing of the GMD, until the schism of 1927, at which point it formed the Red Army as its own military wing. In August 1927, General Zhu De led an abortive attack on Nanchang while Mao Zedong (supposedly) led an equally unsuccessful Autumn Harvest Uprising (Chang & Halliday, 2005). In the face of those defeats, the Red Army developed the guerrilla tactics described by Mao and Zhu as:

> The enemy advances, we retreat; the enemy camps, we harass; the enemy tires we attack; the enemy retreats, we pursue.
>
> (Spence, 1990, p.375)

Alongside its military effort, the CCP established rural "Soviets" – areas of CCP control in which social and land reforms were introduced. While these provided bases for the Red Army, encirclement by the GMD threatened their survival, leading to the retreat known as The Long March. Between October 1934 and October 1935, the Red Army covered more than 6,000 miles on foot, taking a circuitous route from its base in Jiangxi to Yan'an in Shaanxi. The terrain was terrible and of 80,000 troops who began the March, only 8,000 to 9,000 reached the end, the others having been killed, died of illness and cold, or deserted.

While the Long March was a defeat, it provided a symbol and rallying point that far outweighed the loss of troops and materiel. The CCP base in Yan'an provided a platform for social reform and, in CCP mythology, the beginnings of a new society free from the constraints of the traditional past. It became a place of pilgrimage for left-leaning Westerners like Edgar Snow, whose *Red Star over China*, published in 1937, did more to advocate the Communist cause abroad than any military victories could have done.

The battles between the GMD and the CCP continued, with serious doubt about the Communists' ability to survive. However, the situation became more complex with the opening of full-scale war with Japan in 1937, which rapidly deprived the GMD of its industrial centres and fertile land in the South. For a few years, it seemed possible that the two sides could form a united front against the common enemy. However, when the USA entered the war with Japan in 1941, the GMD was the recognized government and hence began to receive American financial aid, military advice and weapons. As Chiang Kai-shek regarded the Japanese as a "disease of the skin" while the CCP was a "disease of the heart", there was no further co-operation.

The struggle against Japan

While the GMD and CCP were the domestic participants in China's struggles, the involvement of Japan was just as important and even more destructive. Having modernized under the Meiji from the 1870s onward, the resource-poor Empire of the Sun had long been interested in China's minerals and markets. In 1894 the Japanese army had invaded Lushun in Liaoning province and the forts of Weihaiwei in Shandong. Turning the guns at Weihaiwei onto the ships they were supposed to defend, the Japanese sank most of the Chinese fleet. The Treaty of Shimonoseki in 1895 imposed reparations payments, ceded Taiwan and parts of Manchuria to Japan, and opened up additional treaty ports, including Chongqing on the Yangzi River. In 1914 and 1915, during the First World War, Japan seized Germany's concessions in Shandong province.

Japan's involvement deepened in 1931 when militarists took matters into their own hands, going further than the Japanese government intended. Before an order from Tokyo to behave with "prudence and patience" could be received, officers of the Kwantung Army provoked a violent incident in Shenyang, after which they took control of Manchuria. A puppet state, titled "Manchukuo" or the "Country of the Manchus" was established with the last Qing Emperor, Pu Yi, as its Chief Executive (he would not agree to the title Emperor). The establishment of a Japanese-controlled state within China's borders was bitterly resented, Japanese goods were boycotted and there were concerns that the Japanese concession in Shanghai might be overrun by protesters. When Japanese marines, landed to protect business interests in Shanghai, exchanged shots with GMD troops, the Japanese bombed and then attacked the city with three divisions, beginning the orgy of destruction that they were to visit on civilians and soldiers.

Despite attempts by the Japanese government to rein it in, the Kwantung Army continued to strengthen its hold. In 1937 an incident at the Marco Polo Bridge, close to Beijing, led to the first battle of the Second World War. While the GMD armies had improved, they were no match for the Japanese. Chiang Kai-shek ordered the bombing of Japanese ships in Shanghai but his air force missed and killed hundreds of Chinese civilians. The Japanese outflanked the GMD, who retreated towards Nanjing, only to be over-run. In December 1937, Japanese soldiers inflicted one of the most shameful episodes in military history on the unprotected inhabitants of the city. In the course of the "Nanjing Massacre" more than 200,000 Chinese were killed. Thousands of women were raped and often mutilated while men of military age were executed for no other reason. Japanese newspapers reported a competition between two young officers for the "glory" of being first to kill 100 Chinese with their swords, noting that as the outcome was inconclusive the second lieutenants had opted to go in for a "second innings" where the aim was to kill 150 Chinese. (Toshiaki Mukai and Tsuyoshi Noda were found guilty of these crimes and executed by firing squad in Nanjing after the war.)

The Massacre at Nanjing remains a searing wound in the memory of Chinese people, made worse by the fact that some leading Japanese still deny that it happened. In 2007

Liberal Democratic Party lawmakers argued that there was no evidence for the events and the mayors of Nagoya and Tokyo both made similar denials in 2012. Anger at the event, and disgust at its continuing denial, forms a significant part of the modern Chinese identity.

Victory for the CCP, land reform, the command economy and policy disasters

By 1938 China was split into ten parts, controlled by the CCP, the GMD, the Japanese and remnant warlords, all battling for pre-eminence. America's entry into the war in 1941 gave some relief to the GMD, as they received financial and military aid. However, Japanese attacks significantly damaged their armies, who were suffering from poor conditions, malnutrition and the depredations of a corrupt officer class. Chiang Kai-shek lost territory and the behaviour of his troops turned the peasantry against them. While the CCP continued to call for a coalition government, they worked on their support in the countryside, and by summer 1945 they controlled "liberated areas" with a population of 95 million people. When the Japanese surrendered on 14 August 1945 the CCP had far fewer troops than the GMD, with 1 million facing 2.7 million, but their enemy was in decline. Communities that had been devastated by the Japanese and by the looting of the GMD took enthusiastically to the CCP's programme of land reform. Inflation in GMD territories took prices to 30 times the 1945 level by 1947 and then a further 60-fold by 1948. The Chinese republic became a barter economy.

As the economy was collapsing, the People's Liberation Army (PLA) was gaining strength. Having captured vast quantities of weapons, Mao Zedong and Lin Biao re-organized the PLA as a conventional fighting force. Two hundred thousand troops were thrown against the GMD at Kaifeng, inflicting 90,000 casualties. Jinan fell, followed by Changchun, putting Manchuria in the hands of the CCP. Having lost the North, Chiang Kai-shek hoped to take a stand to the south of the Yangzi river, but that was a military impossibility, and he retreated to the island of Taiwan. The GMD was unwelcome there, but opposition amongst the native Taiwanese was ruthlessly put down, and many of China's imperial treasures were shipped there as loot, or in preservation of Chinese culture, depending on one's point of view.

On 1 October 1949, Mao Zedong stood atop the Gate of Heavenly Peace – *Tiananmen* – in Beijing and announced the founding of the People's Republic of China.

The first years saw land reforms in which as many as 2 million "landlords" were liquidated, many hardly richer than their neighbours (Dikotter, 2013). When China came to the aid of North Korea in 1950, foreigners were denounced, and most left. A mass campaign in 1951, to root out "counter-revolutionaries", led to the murder of another 2 million citizens, and soon after that, the "Five Antis" campaign of 1951–2 encouraged workers to seek out wrong-doing by their employers. Denunciations poured in, businessmen were subjected to "struggle sessions" in which they were vilified before being fined, often on baseless charges. At this point, it became clear that the CCP was fundamentally an anti-business organization.

Consistent with that orientation, the CCP adopted the Soviet model for economic development, based around a command economy and a series of Five Year Plans focused on the development of heavy industry. The First Plan, 1953–1957, was dramatically successful in increasing industrial production, albeit from a very low base, and the Plan's targets were exceeded (Spence, 1990, p.543). However, the growth it brought was significantly unbalanced, with nearly 20% growth in industrial output but less than 4% growth in agriculture, below the growth in population. In the face of that challenge the leadership set off on the disastrous "Great Leap Forward". Mass campaigns, mobilizing perhaps 100 million peasants, were used to open up and irrigate vast areas of land. In the belief that scale could increase productivity, peasant households were organized into huge "communes" with public kindergartens, baths and dining halls.

Catastrophically, the belief had no basis in reality. With no incentive to work on collectively held land, peasants worked less and grain production fell. However, the officials in charge of grain procurement were afraid to report failure, for fear of being executed as "rightists or defeatists". Some even believed the propaganda that grain production had increased tenfold. They concluded that peasants were hiding food and confiscated everything they could find, leaving whole villages to starve (Becker, 1998). At the same time, the communes were encouraged to establish their own steel smelters, in order to overtake Britain in steel production. More than one million homemade smelters were set up, including some in primary schools. But as the iron for making steel was not available, cooking pots and agricultural implements were used as raw material, turning useful objects and forests into totally unusable pig iron. Overall, China's economy shrank between 1958 and 1962 and estimates of the death toll range from 18 to 45 million. Meanwhile, China and the Soviet Union had fallen into disagreement in 1960 and the Soviet advisers left, taking with them their knowledge of heavy industrial technology.

The Great Leap Forward was too much of a disaster even for Mao Zedong and he took a backseat in politics, until his next disastrous initiative. The "Great Proletarian Cultural Revolution" lasted from 1966 to 1976. It began with Mao's return to the centre when he declared that the CCP had been infiltrated at the highest levels by bourgeois who sought to overthrow the "dictatorship of the proletariat". To counter that threat he encouraged youngsters to become "Red Guards" and in a "big character poster" he encouraged them to "Bombard the Headquarters". The CCP Central Committee, under Mao's direction, then promulgated a "Decision Concerning the Great Proletarian Cultural Revolution", which called for the proletariat to "crush those in authority who are taking the capitalist road" and "repudiate the reactionary bourgeois academic 'authorities' in order to transform education, literature and art and all other parts of the superstructure".

This was a call for students to take the country by force and it was met with adolescent enthusiasm. More than a million Red Guards descended on Beijing to see Mao, as they were allowed free travel. Schools and universities were closed and teachers were humiliated, tortured, murdered and even eaten by their students. Cultural treasures were vandalized on the grounds that they represented old customs, culture, habits and ideas, and the police did not intervene. Senior officials were targeted by subordinates, and Deng Xiaoping was sent to work in a rural tractor factory, after his son had been rendered paraplegic by Red Guard violence.

In some respects, the Cultural Revolution destroyed China. The education system was closed until 1972. Family and friends betrayed each other and suicides were common. In a country that had always been one of low trust between strangers, social life became fraught with fear. Hysterical teenage bullies were given full rein to their fantasies and tens of millions of people, who make up the middle-aged population today, were traumatized.

The full story of the Cultural Revolution is Byzantine in its complexity (MacFarquhar & Schoenhals, 2006). A simple summary is that the "Gang of Four", led by Mao's wife, Jiang Qing, headed a radical clique, which wielded significant power in the name of the Cultural Revolution, while Vice-Premier Zhou Enlai attempted to restore some kind of order and progress to the economy. When Zhou fell ill, Deng Xiaoping returned as Vice-Premier, with Mao's approval, and the champion of reform began to regain influence.

The dragon awakes: China's re-ascent

In 1976, Mao died, at the end of a reign in which he had behaved much like an emperor. Without his support, the Gang of Four were unable to hold on to power and they were arrested amid national rejoicing. The country began to regain an element of stability and then in December 1978 the Third Plenum of the CCP announced the beginnings of the momentous change that was to bring the country back to greatness.

In 1978 China's per capita GDP was US$210 and the country accounted for 5% of world GDP (World Bank, 1992). By 2013 GDP per capita reached almost US$7,000 on a nominal basis, or nearly US$12,000 at purchasing power parity. Japan had been overtaken as the world's second largest economy and China was on the verge of once again becoming the largest. That astounding progress arose as a result of the radical shift in economic policy described as "reform and opening up" (*gaige kaifang*). In the first years, progress was slow and it was not clear that the policy swings of the Mao era were a thing of the past. However, in the spring of 1992 "paramount leader" Deng Xiaoping made a tour of southern China which outflanked those who sought a return to the past and confirmed the direction of reform. The rest is the subject of this book.

The relevance of China's past for today

Chinese people are deeply aware of their history. "Chinatowns" across the world are known in Chinese as *Tang Ren Jie* or "the street of the Tang people" in reference to that long-gone dynasty's global reach. Many of the most popular films and television programmes are costume dramas based upon Imperial history or the struggle between the PLA, the Japanese and the *Guomindang*. At all levels of society, the awareness of extreme violence from the Warring States through the Taiping rebellion, the warlord era and the Civil War to the Cultural Revolution has led to a deep fear of *da luan* or "great chaos". Chinese born in the 1950s, in particular, have traumatic personal experiences of being afraid for their lives – or of having been responsible for the nightmares of others. Small wonder that the absolute priority of the authorities is to maintain stability, and that priority is shared by most of the populace. China does not have democracy to provide a source of legitimacy for the rule of the CCP and Western commentators see that as a weakness (Hutton, 2007). However, the thinking behind the Mandate of Heaven forms the basis for an implicit agreement that if the rulers take good care of (most of) the ruled they will be accepted to have earned the right to their authority and power. At the same time, the right to rule is matched by the right of rebellion against a ruler whose mandate has been withdrawn. China's growing middle classes are quick to make their views known and to take action when their material interests are threatened, although there is little evidence of a desire for democracy itself, perhaps because of the implicit contract.

In government policy, the past is drawn upon as a source of inspiration and legitimacy. When the authorities sought to develop China's "soft power" by establishing organizations overseas that teach Chinese language and culture, they named them "Confucius Institutes". In 2014 President Xi and Premier Li invoked the Silk Road, and Zheng He's voyages as the backdrop to the "One Belt One Road" foreign policy initiatives designed to re-create ancient economic links between China and Central Asia and to promote Asia-centric trade policy regimes. In November 2015 when President Xi met Taiwan's leader Ma Ying Jeoh, they expressed their common ground as "we are all descendants of the Yellow Emperor".

Xi Jinping's emphasis on "The China Dream" may have been influenced by the "American Dream" but the posters articulating that dream were of pre-Liberation style images in woodblock prints celebrating plump children and elderly grandparents' wearing traditional Chinese clothes and living out the Confucian lifestyle.

These references to the past form a part of the modern Chinese sense of self, which is ambivalent in itself and in its relationship with foreigners. On the one hand, being part of an ancient and superior culture, held together for millennia by the writing system, produces what Winchester (2008, p.256) describes as:

> A Chinese state of mind, and one that outsiders – and all who are non-Chinese are very much outsiders here – may occasionally find infuriating and insufferable, but which certainly exists, and at no great depth beneath the Chinese skin. It is an attitude, one might argue, that has been born of the very achievement which Joseph Needham attempted to catalogue and describe in his series of books. It is an attitude of ineluctable and self-knowing Chinese superiority, and it results from the antiquity and the longevity of the Chinese people's endeavours.

At the same time, the Chinese are deeply conscious that their society collapsed as much through its internal flaws as through outside pressure. Mao described his people as "grains of sand", incapable of adhering into social structures of great strength. Corruption, malpractice in office, and a general lack of civility have dogged Chinese society for as long as there has been recorded history. In what Hall (1976) calls a "high context" society, promises and contracts are taken less literally than in the West, causing difficulties for literal-minded foreigners and leading to the view, even amongst themselves, that the Chinese are inherently dishonest. In 1860, asked why a small country like Britain was more powerful than a large country like China, the Chinese scholar sent to find out concluded that the British were better able to secure the "necessary accord of the word with the deed" (Spence, 1990, p.197).

This ambivalence about themselves is reflected in Chinese attitudes towards "foreigners", a term used without recognition that it might be offensive. Ancient history saw foreigners as inferior to the Chinese, to whom they should be grateful for the gifts of civilization. But then the great civilization was brought down by small "outside" countries that proved more powerful. Novelist Lu Xun (1881–1936) captured the ambivalence when he noted that "the Chinese always consider themselves to be inferior or superior to foreigners, never equal" (Crozier, 2001, p.1). Mixed feelings towards foreigners are particularly powerful in respect of the Japanese, whose products are admired and sought after, but whose depredations are not forgotten. As tensions rise over resource-rich islands in the South China Sea, episodes of "aggression" by the Japanese lead to anti-Japanese rioting, which the authorities do not attempt to prevent, unless they threaten to spill over into more domestic complaints. In 2012, in sophisticated Shenzhen, Guangzhou and Qingdao, Japanese businesses and cars were attacked and burned.

Business people seeking to work with China, therefore need to appreciate the sensibilities of a proud people whose way of life was superior to that of the rest of the world for millennia, but who stumbled, causing them unthinkable suffering, in which foreigners played no small role. They believe that it was a temporary setback, and they were probably right.

References

Becker, J., 1998. *Hungry ghosts: Mao's secret famine*. London: Holt.

Benn, C., 2002. *China's golden age: Everyday life in the Tang dynasty*. Oxford: Oxford University Press.

Chang, J. and Halliday, J., 2005. *Mao: The unknown story*. London: Jonathan Cape.

Crozier, J., 2001. 5,000 years of history. *China in Focus*, Issue 10, London: Society for Anglo Chinese Understanding.

Dikotter, F., 2013. *The tragedy of liberation*. London: Bloomsbury.

Elvin, M., 1973. *The pattern of the Chinese past*. Stanford, CA: Stanford University Press.

Fung, Y-L., 1922. Why China has no science – an interpretation of the history and consequences of Chinese philosophy. *International Journal of Ethics*, 32, April, pp.237–263.

Hall, E.T., 1976. *Beyond culture*. New York: Doubleday.

Ho, P-T., 1962. *The ladder of success in Imperial China: Aspects of social mobility 1369–1911*. New York: Columbia University Press.

Hutton, W., 2007. *The writing on the wall: China and the West in the 21st century*. London: Little, Brown.

Kirk, D., 1946. *Europe's population in the interwar years*. New York: Gordon and Breach.

Lin, J., 1995. The Needham puzzle: Why the Industrial Revolution did not originate in China. *Economic Development and Cultural Change*, 43 (2) January, pp.269–292.

Lu, J., 2011. Reassessing the Needham Question: What forces impeded the development of modern science in China after the 15th century? *The Concord Review*, 21 (4), pp.209–254.

MacFarquhar, R. and Schoenhals, M., 2006. *Mao's last revolution*. Cambridge, MA: Harvard University Press.

Maddison, A., 1998. *Chinese economic performance in the long run*. Paris: OECD.

Man, J., 2007. *The terracotta army*. London: Bantam Press.

McNeilly, M., 2012. *Sun Tzu and the art of business*. New York: Oxford University Press.

Menzies, G., 2002. *1421: The year China discovered the world*. London: Bantam Press.

Nylan, M., 2001. *The five "Confucian" classics*. New Haven, CT: Yale University Press.

Rein, S., 2014. *The end of copycat China*. Hoboken, NJ: Wiley.

Sivin, N., 1995. *Science in ancient China*. Aldershot: Variorum.

Snow, E., 1937. *Red star over China*. London: Left Book Club, Victor Gollanz.

Spence, J. D., 1990. *The search for modern China*. London: Hutchison.

Temple, R., 1986. *The genius of China: 3,000 years of science, discovery and invention*. New York: Simon and Schuster.

Winchester, S., 2008. *The man who loved China*. New York: Harper.

World Bank., 2017. Available at: data.worldbank.org/country/china [Accessed 12 May 2017].

Zou, R., 1903. *The revolutionary army: A Chinese nationalist tract of 1903*. Translated by John Lust. The Hague, 1968. p.122.

2

CHINA'S MIRACLE, CHINA'S TENSIONS – THE FOUR "*IZATIONS*"

Howard Davies

In 1949, 90% of China's 550 million population lived in the countryside and 80% of employment was in agriculture (Ash, 2006). Manufacturing accounted for 7.4% of employment and international trade (imports plus exports) added up to less than 2% of national income.

By 2016 economy and society had been transformed. Less than 50% of the 1.3 billion population lived in the countryside and "primary industry" accounted for 10% of employment. China had become the world's manufacturing base, with 31.4% of the workforce, or 230 million people, in the secondary sector, producing 43.9% of the nation's output, much of which was exported as trade has expanded to the point where exports plus imports equal 45% of national income.

That transformation has four components – industrialization, urbanization, marketization and globalization – examined in this chapter.

Industrialization and its consequences

Industry has two main sectors. Primary industries – agriculture, fishing, mining and quarrying – extract resources for conversion into other products. Secondary, or manufacturing, industries convert the output of the primary industries into components or final products. Manufacturing can be divided into "heavy industry" like steel, power generation equipment, and construction equipment and "light industry" including garments, and electronic products. Manufacturing can also be divided into "upstream" sectors, which produce components for the "downstream" sectors that produce final products.

The starting point

Although the *Guomindang* had a plan for state-led industry (Wu, 2011), they were unable to fulfil its targets and in 1949 heavy industry was very undeveloped. The Japanese had built steel plants after the First World War but the facilities were either damaged or seized by the Soviets. The chemical industry was negligible and the automotive sector consisted of a plant set up by warlord Zhang Xueliang to produce a truck, another that produced vehicles running on charcoal, and an automobile powered by tung oil, made by the China Automotive Company. Shanghai had a significant light industrial sector, with foreign direct investment from Japan and using British machinery. However, it was an island of industry in an agricultural ocean.

Two industrial revolutions

With the victory of the Communist Party, industrial development became key to the Plan, modelled on the Soviet Union. Rural consumption was restricted (Ash, 2006) to finance heavy industry in the North East and the First Five Year Plan was very successful in meeting its targets. However, progress was halted in the 1960s and 70s by the disastrous impact of the Great Leap Forward and the Cultural Revolution.

On the eve of reform, China remained agricultural. Mao's policy of moving industrial plants away from the coastal areas meant that Shanghai lost its importance, and the re-located industries were often ill-suited to their new locations, inefficient and slow-growing.

That industrial structure changed rapidly once reform began. Opening to foreign investment brought an influx of manufacturing companies, mostly from Hong Kong (Tracy, 1995). Around 100,000 firms crossed the border, transforming China's industrial landscape. They were concentrated in the light manufacturing sectors that had grown up in Hong Kong – garments, toys, jewellery, assembly of electronics, wigs – and they were located in the agricultural province of Guangdong, adjacent to the British colony. Even before the legality of foreign investment was confirmed, Hong Kong entrepreneurs drove their operations across the border, working with local governments to establish joint ventures in the form of "township and village enterprises". The governments provided infrastructure, utilities, the labour force, and political protection, while Hong Kong firms provided the (limited) equipment and technological knowledge and (crucial) commercial information needed to access export markets.

These industries were labour-intensive, hence aligned with China's comparative advantage in cheap labour and capable of exporting and competing internationally. As Lin, Cai and Li (1996) pointed out, that "comparative advantage-following" development strategy marked a transformative shift away from the previous "comparative-advantage denying" approach and it kick-started growth for the next three decades.

While foreign investment and alignment with comparative advantage were key to industrialization, other factors were at work. The initial stage took place in the countryside, and Wen (2015) points out that rural industrialization was made possible by the extension of rural markets, which was the result of road and bridge-building, most of which took place during the Mao era. China was fortunate in that the command economy had provided the initial public infrastructure, which then allowed the market economy to do what it does well – managing resources for the production of private goods.

China's initial industrial revolution was based on consumer goods, especially garments. However, that produced increased demand for energy, vehicles, infrastructure, and equipment, which triggered a second industrial revolution, in which "upstream" goods were produced. China's manufacturing industry is therefore no longer limited to light goods, as industries like automobile manufacture, chemicals, steel, cement and heavy electricals have developed (with continued heavy involvement of foreign companies).

The consequences of industrialization

The most general effect of industrialization was to re-allocate resources in several directions. First, shifting hundreds of millions of peasants from agriculture into light industry allowed easily achievable increases in output and incomes. Although the peasants were working hard, the inefficiency of agriculture meant that their marginal productivity was close to zero.

Shifting the equivalent of the entire US population from the production of nothing to the production of something provided major gains.

Secondly, the sectoral balance of manufacturing industry changed. In the first phase, it shifted from heavy industry into garments, the assembly of electronic components sourced from elsewhere, and other light goods, largely for export. In the second phase, more capital- and technology-intensive industries grew, to serve the domestic market for machinery and components that developed from the first phase and the need to meet demand from a higher-income population.

These developments were accompanied by geographical shifts. Before 1978 heavy industry was focused in the North East and the West. The first post-reform industrial revolution shifted that pattern so that Guangdong in the South, and the Pearl River Delta in particular, became the manufacturing centre, exporting goods made in China by Hong Kong firms through Hong Kong's port. As the second phase developed, other coastal areas, in outward-looking Fujian, Zhejiang, Shanghai and Jiangsu, first became involved and then manufacturing gradually spread across the country, with Western cities like Chengdu, Chongqing and Xi'an becoming major centres of production.

Industrialization raised incomes, stimulated investment in infrastructure, and provided employment for millions. At the same time, it has contributed to China's most intractable problems. Foremost amongst those has been the damage done to the environment. Factories pollute, as does construction, and China is a very dirty place. The air is a danger to health in virtually every city. Supplies of potable tap water are generally not available and rivers and lakes are heavily polluted. The authorities recognize the problem, understand its significance and are mobilizing significant resources to deal with it. Nevertheless, pollution is hazardous to health, and with a middle class which is increasingly conscious of that risk, it poses a real threat to China's future and the authorities' maintenance of control. It also provides business opportunities in environmental control, the management of sustainability and consumer products like air quality monitors, air and water filters for homes and offices.

Industrialization has other negative effects. Shifts in employment have led to mass migrations, away from the North and the West, towards the South and East. The numbers are enormous, with almost 300 million migrant workers making up almost one third of the working population. As the *hukou* household registration system limits migrant workers' access to public services, this has created huge inequalities between the holders of rural *hukou* living in the cities and their locally registered neighbours. Migrant workers leave their children behind, as they are not entitled to education in their parents' work location, and families are separated for long periods of time. Village populations consist solely of children and the elderly who care for them while their parents work far away, and communities cease to be viable.

Urbanization

In 1978, less than 20% of Chinese lived in cities. By 2012, that had risen to 52% – around 700 million – as the urban population increased by more than 500 million. Those numbers are huge but proportionately less than Korea or Japan in their "take-off" periods. As high income countries have urbanization rates above 70% it is clear that the process is far from complete and official estimates are that China's cities will house around 1 billion people by 2030, a further increase of around 250 million (World Bank/DRC, 2014).

Chinese cities are huge by European or North American standards. Population statistics are difficult to interpret, because the boundaries of Chinese cities often include part of their (rapidly disappearing) rural surroundings, and there are huge differences between formally resident populations – those holding city *hukou* – and the actual number of residents, which also includes migrant workers, who retain the *hukou* of their birthplace. However, the *World Population Review* (2016) reports population figures for Beijing of 21–22 million, with a forecast of possibly 50 million by 2050. Shanghai is larger, with 22–23 million in 2013, Guangzhou has 14 million and Shenzhen nearly 11 million. The corresponding figures for London and New York are less than 9 million, Berlin 3.4 million and Paris 2.4 million. China has 42 cities with more than 2 million residents.

This development of the urban setting has taken place at breakneck speed, and there are many ugly and dirty places in Chinese cities. There is, however, nothing approaching the murder-ridden favelas of South America, or the blighted slums of Africa and India.

China's cities have grown in three ways. First, the natural increase in urban populations accounts for about 15% of urban growth. Second, around 40% has come from the 260 million people who have moved from rural areas in search of better opportunities. Third, about 40% of new urban residents did not move at all (World Bank/DRC, 2014, p.5)! The city came to them as the urban areas expanded into rural settings. As the need for dwellings, workspaces and infrastructure has burgeoned, local governments have expanded existing cities, and built new ones, some of the largest being Zhengdong in Zhengzhou, Zhujiang in Guangzhou, and Longgang in Shenzhen.

Urbanization is transforming China, for good and ill. On the positive side, it promotes spending, increases incomes and is helping to shift the Chinese growth model in the required direction. On the negative side, it imposes significant economic and social costs.

Urbanization as a catalyst for economic growth

Urbanization promotes growth through four mechanisms. First, the need for housing, transport and services has led to spending on residential construction and infrastructure on a gargantuan scale. In the years from 2009 to 2013 a total of 46.5 million new residential apartments were built and residential construction accounted for around 10% of Gross National Product. In 1993 the Shanghai subway had 4.4 km of track and 4 stations. By 2015 it had 588 km of tracks, 14 lines, 364 stations and 8 million daily users. The Beijing subway expanded from 3 lines in 2000 to 18 lines in 2015 with more than 9 million daily users. Bus services are extensive and access to electricity, gas and running water is close to universal. The Beijing Olympics of 2008 and the government's response to the World Financial Crisis both increased spending significantly, but it was urbanization which drove the development.

The second mechanism through which urbanization promotes growth is through consumer spending. Urban residents have higher incomes. They enjoy increasing wealth as around 80% own their own homes, and growth in urban residential prices has averaged 17% for more than ten years (Chen & Wen, 2015). Urban residents enjoy greater "consumption amenities" with a wider variety of products and services on offer and they can observe and emulate the lifestyles of the wealthy. Hence they spend more. In the Party magazine *Qiushi* in 2012, Premier Li Keqiang noted that urban residents spent 3.6 times more per capita than rural dwellers, implying that for each rural resident who moves to the city, consumption increases by more than 10,000 RMB per year. On that calculation, a 1% increase in the urbanization rate leads to an increase in consumption of around US$15.9 billion.

As China's urbanization rate is around 50%, compared with more than 70% for developed countries, the potential for further increases in consumption is large indeed.

The third benefit of urbanization is efficiency improvements which arise through "agglomeration economies", both static and dynamic. Agglomeration economies were first analysed by the British economist Alfred Marshall (1890) who identified three reasons why costs fall when economic activities are located closer together (Duranton & Puga, 2004). The first is that fixed costs can be spread across a larger number of users. In a rural location, providing public transport is expensive, compared with a heavily used urban underground and bus system. Providing education, libraries, roads, electricity, water and gas to a concentrated population takes less resources per resident than in areas where the population is widely spread.

The second source of agglomeration economies is through specialization and matching in the labour market. The larger the local labour market, the larger the market for specialist skills and the easier it becomes to match supply with demand. For example, Chinese urban housing developments are supremely efficient at the provision of services like plumbing, electrical work, and decoration. Outside the gate to every development sit migrant workers, displaying signs advertising their expertise and their telephone numbers. When a resident requires their services, they call the number and work will be started immediately. The workers can be trusted to provide a quality service because if they do not, word spreads in the customer base, and they will be denied further entry by the security personnel. Such instant matching is impossible in less densely populated areas, because the local market is not large enough to support the specialist functions.

Sharing and matching are "static" economies, which accrue without any improvement in technology. However, urbanization also leads to "dynamic" agglomeration economies, as improved opportunities for innovation occur when a wider variety of people live closer together. Individuals having different knowledge bases, values and attitudes discuss and communicate, learn from each other and become more efficient. New ideas arise and are disseminated better in an "agglomerated" environment. Hence, productivity increases more quickly and activities that depend on knowledge, information and technology are concentrated in cities (Ciccone & Hall, 1996).

The impact of urbanization on the quality of life in China

While urbanization is central to the drive towards a "moderately prosperous" economy, it also affects the quality of life through its impact on the environment, peoples' health, happiness and "social capital".

China's cities are not like Third World slums, strewn with garbage and criss-crossed by open sewers. Nevertheless, they are highly polluted. Urbanization contributes to that pollution in several ways. Building millions of homes, factories and offices is dirty in itself. Cities need energy and China's major source of energy is coal, accounting for 77% of electricity production in 2014. Less than 15% of coal-fired power stations are fitted with desulphurization systems, and those are not always used. Urban residents in older housing still use coal for cooking and heating. In the North, where it becomes very cold in winter, districts have central heating which provides for thousands of apartments. They are a good example of agglomeration economies, as such heating is efficient, but they contribute significantly to pollution.

In addition to environmental degradation from the production of electricity and heating, factories emit pollutants, especially in the cement and steel industries, and China used more cement in 2011–2013 than the US used in the whole of the twentieth century (Smil, 2013). The massively increased number of motor vehicles on the roads has also contributed (Feng & Li, 2013), and congestion has been added to pollution as an additional cost.

The full impact of urban pollution will take time to reveal itself (Economist, 2015), and awareness of its health implications is only now becoming widespread. Residents of Chinese cities walk around without masks in levels of pollution that are dangerous. Masks sold in stores and medicine shops often have little more than cosmetic value and pollution-related illness is increasing. As better-educated urban residents understand the effects that pollution can have on their health, so they spend more on air monitors, air filters and water purification devices. They are also becoming much more demanding on the authorities to take action.

The adverse effect of pollution on health caused 800 billion RMB in damage by 2010 (World Bank/DRC, 2014, p.26) but urbanization triggers other mechanisms, working in both directions. Urban levels of obesity and diabetes have soared as the opportunities to emulate Western lifestyles with junk food become more available. On the other hand, exercise habits like jogging, gym-going and marathon running have all become popular in China's cities, as have the purchase of home treadmills and exercise bicycles, to the benefit of residents' health.

In addition to its effects on physical health, urbanization changes lifestyles, which affects general well-being, psychological health and social relations. Chinese cities are generally more sociable than their European and American counterparts. In every communal space, people gather to dance, play music, walk birds in cages, write poetry on the pavement with water, and exercise in all manner of ways. Strangers are welcome and the atmosphere is delightful. At the same time, urban life implies moving away from traditional villages, social structures and customs, and for the migrant workers who do not possess urban *hukou*, city life is a matter of long hours, hard work, and separation from family. For them, city lights are preferable to the poverty of the countryside but the balance is much less favourable than for urban *hukou* holders.

Given the costs and the benefits of urbanization, and the differences between city *hukou*-holding urban residents and their migrant co-citizens, an overall judgment is impossible. One observation is useful, concerning the difference between "top-down" and "bottom-up" urbanization. "Top-down" is where the authorities develop an area with housing, shops, hospitals and universities, and move rural residents into those developments. As might be expected, that type of urbanization has been shown to have a positive impact on "social capital" – residents' feeling of community (Zhang, Wang & Yu, 2014). On the other hand, "bottom-up" urbanization is where villages around cities absorb rural migrants, with the local population adding (often illegal) structures to their homes and then renting them to migrants. Guangzhou, for instance, is surrounded by 138 such villages. The result is the closest China comes to slums and their residents have much less "social capital". There is resentment between locals and migrants, sometimes going as far as public disorder.

This observation on "top-down" urbanization is relevant to a common misunderstanding of China's property market. For years, pundits have pointed to China's "ghost cities" where there are millions of square metres of empty residential buildings, and they predict a collapse in property prices, with consequences for the economy as a whole. There certainly are many empty apartments, and "ghost cities" do exist. However, what is being observed is often the early stage of "top-down" urbanization. The local government plans to house several hundred thousand residents in a new town. They build the apartments, and shopping malls, which remain empty for some time, as the rest of the urban structure is put in place. Then state-owned firms move their offices into the area, universities build campuses and thousands of students move in. Hospitals, schools and libraries follow and the "ghost city" becomes alive. In many cases, they were simply work-in-progress.

Marketization: from iron rice bowl and the plan to markets for everything

Market and command economies

An economy is an enormous set of transactions amongst individuals and organizations. Goods and services are produced by suppliers who deliver them through intermediaries to those who want them. In a market economy, the choice of products, production techniques, wages paid, prices, and the distribution of products to users are decided by a decentralized "invisible hand" working through the interaction of supply and demand. Firms are formed by entrepreneurs in response to opportunities for profit, signalled by the prices which buyers are prepared to pay, in comparison with the costs of production. Firms who identify profitable opportunities survive, while those who make mistakes do not. Market economies have major weaknesses in respect of inequality and when public goods, like clean air and water, are not properly costed. In general, however, provided markets are competitive and open to new entry, they are efficient, flexible and supportive of innovation,

In a command economy, by contrast, there is a central authority which decides how resources are used. What should be produced, how, where, by whom, for what wages, and for whom, are decided by the authorities. The economy is a single "firm" with multiple departments and prices are an instrument for internal administration, not the basis for decision-making. In the Maoist economy, there were no "profit opportunities" or "job opportunities", just assigned tasks to be carried out.

Dismantling such a system and replacing it with markets is a huge task. Nevertheless, it has been largely completed (Lardy, 2014). To understand that process it is helpful to consider marketization in two domains, markets for products and markets for factors of production.

Product markets: agriculture, industry and housing

In the Maoist economy, agriculture was carried out by collectives who grew the crops determined by the authorities, in quantities determined by them, and delivered to them at "administrative" prices. Prices set by the State Price Commission bore no resemblance to the levels that would balance supply and demand, because their key role was to "squeeze" the peasants (Ash, 2006) to finance heavy industrial development.

In the industrial sectors, decisions on what to produce, how to produce it, and who should receive it were taken though a planning system developed under Soviet tutelage (Nolan & Ash, 1995). Prices were set by the State Price Commission, and their purpose was to divert resources to the state's preferred activities. Low prices were set for coal, and industrial raw materials, to ensure that the firms producing final goods would be profitable, turning over their profits to the authorities for use in "big push" industrialization (Lardy, 2014).

Replacing this system through "marketization" (*shichang hua*) proceeded gradually, in line with Deng Xiaoping's concept of "crossing the river by feeling for the stones" (*mozhe shitou guo he*) (Nolan, 1994). There was no "big bang" privatization. Instead, market activities were allowed to grow around the state sector, which remained intact. In agriculture, the household responsibility system (HRS or *jiating lianchan chengbao ze renzhi*) began with an experiment in Anhui province whereby local cadres entrusted production to individual households, who made contracts with them for the use (but not ownership) of land. The households agreed to deliver quotas of produce to government, but were free to sell other outputs for whatever price they could get. This "great invention of Chinese farmers" as Deng Xiaoping described it, was the catalyst for the whole economy. By 1983 more than 90% of agricultural "production teams" had adopted the system, farm output grew and huge numbers of peasants not required on the land manned the "township and village enterprises".

As agriculture powered the development of rural light industry, market forces gradually came to bear on other parts of the economy. In 1983 the basic concept of the HRS was extended to industry with the introduction of two-track pricing (Wu & Zhao, 1987) and the "contract responsibility system". State enterprises were contracted to deliver quotas at administrative prices, but were free to make additional products and sell them at market prices. Quotas were kept roughly constant, and the economy grew, so the proportion of output delivered to the state fell. By 1993 the material allocation plan had been abolished and by 2001 the only consumer goods subject to price controls were salt and pharmaceuticals. Government controls remain on the prices of fuel, electricity, water and utilities, railway freight, postal and telecommunications service, but every other price is set by the market (Lardy, 2014).

Of all the changes in product markets, perhaps the most important, which has transformed the financial position of Chinese households (Hu, 2011) and provided a major driver for growth, is that for housing. In the command economy, housing was owned by the state and collective enterprises, and the cost of providing accommodation for workers was a barrier to marketization. Hence in 1998 the State Council abolished the provision of employer-allocated housing (Yang & Chen, 2014). Workers were encouraged to purchase their homes, at prices which turned out to represent significant discounts. Given that urban home prices have risen by an average of 17% per year for a decade (Chen & Wen, 2015) the transfer of wealth to households has been enormous. In Beijing, for instance, a professor who purchased his apartment from the university in the late 1990s, for perhaps RMB 90,000, had an asset worth around RMB 8 million by 2016. The rise in prices creates problems for young professionals seeking homes in first line cities. However, 80–90% of urban households own their own homes and that financial security supports the lower saving and higher consumption which the country's growth needs, while giving the population a major stake in stability.

Marketizing Chinese housing has been described as "probably the largest neo-liberal reform project ever implemented in the world" (Wang, Shao, Murie & Cheng, 2012, p.356) and its implications spread beyond the provision of accommodation and the distribution of wealth. The quality of housing has improved, in terms of living area per person, and the nature of its construction (D'Arcy & Veroude, 2014). Chinese apartments are generally delivered unfinished to their owners, who provide kitchens, bathrooms, floor coverings and air-conditioners themselves. As owner-occupiers tend to be more interested than tenants in the maintenance and upkeep of their homes, so the demand for furniture, household appliances, decoration and maintenance has soared, providing major business opportunities.

The privatization of housing changed the financial landscape in other ways. The (dangerous) confidence that property prices never fall, coupled with a traditional belief in the value of tangible assets, means that property has become a favoured asset class with the wealthy and nearly 40% of households in the top 10% of the income distribution hold empty properties (Chen & Wen, 2015). That could portend trouble if returns to other assets rise, and households try to dump their empty properties onto the market. However, as Chapter 14 points out, several factors mitigate that danger. Property is a (literally) concrete asset which feels less likely to evaporate, in a country whose financial system is riddled with instability and corruption. The nature of Chinese housing – high-rise apartments made of concrete and steel – makes it suffer less from depreciation if left empty, when compared with homes with their own roofs, gardens and ground-level entry points. As the gender imbalance shifts bargaining power towards girls, a middle-class boy who does not own an apartment has little chance of finding a socially equal mate. Several million apartments therefore stand empty, owned by young men whose parents have bought them a reverse "dowry", but who currently prefer to live with Mum.

Overall, the marketization of product markets is close to complete. They do not function optimally because that would require full property rights, and an absence of monopoly power. It would also require that the markets which determine the prices of inputs to product markets are fully functional. Nevertheless, as the basis on which product-related transactions are co-ordinated, the market has become the dominant mechanism in China.

Factor markets: labour, land and capital

If markets for inputs to the production process are ineffective, the cost/price signals which guide de-centralized decision-making will be inappropriate. Hence the development of markets for labour, land and capital are as important as those for products.

In the command era, China did not have a labour market. Work units (*danwei*) were "total institutions" (Goffman, 1961) within which whole lives were lived. Workers were borne, fed, housed, educated, played, treated for illnesses, retired, and died in the *danwei* to which they belonged. Workers were allocated to *danwei* by the authorities, and wages were paid partly in cash, partly in accommodation and medical care, and partly in coupons for rationed goods, made necessary by endemic shortages. The "iron rice bowl" (*tie fan wan*) meant that everyone received similar rewards, regardless of ability or effort, and no one need fear unemployment. Chinese workers were poor by world standards but there was a very high level of equality. School leavers and university graduates were assigned to *danwei* by labour bureaux and job mobility was non-existent. The government set wage levels using a system of grades (Cai, Park & Zhao, 2008) and wage increases came with seniority, not performance.

As with other aspects of reform, labour market changes were gradual. The reform of agriculture generated millions of industrial jobs in the countryside, and wages were not set by the authorities. Initially, farmers had to remain in their home villages; they could not respond to market signals telling them of higher wages elsewhere and the market could not fulfil its function. However, restrictions were relaxed; by the mid-1980s farmers were allowed to seek jobs in nearby towns, and the migrant worker phenomenon began. In 1982 7 million were working outside their native county, rising to 22 million, 79 million and 163 million in 1990, 2000 and 2012 respectively. (Another 99 million had moved from their home village but within the same county (Lardy, 2014)). Demand for these workers was determined by business opportunities, their supply was effectively infinite, and the resulting low wages were set by the market.

In the cities and state-owned enterprises, lifetime jobs were abandoned and workers were taken on through five-year contracts. Fewer graduate jobs were assigned by the Ministry of Education and that was abandoned in 2002. The most dramatic development came in 1995 when Premier Zhu Rongji culled the state-owned sector through a policy of "seize the large and let go the small" (*zhua da fang xiao*). Large firms were retained by the state but small and medium-sized state firms and collectives were closed or privatized, in a process that led to an estimated 30 million job losses. Those who lost their jobs were absorbed by the rapidly growing private economy and the command economy labour system was effectively demolished.

In 2017, Chinese workers, managers and professionals find jobs and receive pay and benefits in a largely market economy fashion. The *hukou* system imposes costs on workers who move away from their place of registration, so distortions remain, but that system is gradually changing. Workers can move to occupations with better wages and conditions, and they can earn more by improving their skills, as their increased productivity is rewarded by the market.

Marketization of land and capital is less complete than for products and labour. For land, "ownership by the people" has deep ideological roots and to privatize land ownership would be seen as a regression to the days before Liberation. Nevertheless, there have been significant reforms. The Household Responsibility System introduced in 1978 involved contracting farmland to individual households, initially for 5 years but then for 30 years under the Land Management Law of 1998. Ownership remained with the collective, but land-use rights went to the farmers for the contracted period. Rights could be transferred between private users, allowing farmers to re-arrange plots of land or to sell their interests. In 2008 the Central Committee of the Party pointed to the future direction by declaring that farmers' land rights should be "long term without change", implying that the 30-year period would be extended to perpetuity.

In the cities, the direction of policy is clearly towards the definition of property rights and the establishment of a market-oriented framework. Marketable land-use rights, granted for 70 years, were established with the *Interim Regulations* in 1990. However, as the World Bank and Development Research Centre of the State Council (2013) point out, the system is not fully established or effective. Local governments own land and they need land sales to meet their obligations. Hence, they often expropriate farmland in order to sell the rights for industrial or residential development. Farmers find their land has been taken in return for poor compensation, and they lose their livelihoods, which has led to public disorder. Cities use more land than is efficient as governments sell as much as they can to raise revenue. "Industrial development zones" proliferate, urban boundaries expand, and China's land has been urbanized more than its people. Furthermore, the secondary market – where those who have purchased land-use rights from the state rent or lease them to other parties – is still largely invisible. If an effective system for the transfer of land-use rights is to be in place, further reforms are needed. First, China needs to remove the complexities that arise from the distinction between state-owned urban land and collectively owned rural land. Second, property rights to land-use need better protection. Third, public finance needs to change so that local governments are less dependent on land sales. These needs are recognized by the authorities, but constitute a difficult and complex agenda.

The third factor of production being marketized is capital, and the financial system is examined in Chapter 8. In any economy, capital can be raised from domestic savings, government taxes and borrowing from abroad. In the command economy, the key sources were state enterprise profits, which were kept high through administrative pricing. The peasants were "squeezed" so that consumption was low and savings accrued to the authorities. The banking system consisted of a single bank – the People's Bank of China – which was essentially part of the Ministry of Finance, and played no part in channelling savings into investment because long-term projects were funded through grants from the state budget. The government saved and the government funded investments, with no need for a system of financial intermediation linking multitudes of savers/lenders to spenders/borrowers.

In a market economy, most savings accrue to households and companies according to their individual circumstances and decisions. When capital is needed, it can be raised from many different sources, and savings need to have channels through which they can be directed into productive investments. The first such channel is the banking system, where savers deposit income they do not wish to spend and others can borrow. The second is financial markets, where companies sell equities or issue bonds and use the proceeds for their projects. The third is "non-intermediated investment" where individuals or companies use their own savings or retained earnings to fund their own development. In a fully functioning market economy the best investment projects provide the highest returns, and those projects would be most easily funded as lenders to them could be offered the highest returns on their savings.

In one sense, access to capital in China, and its allocation to projects, is already marketized because "non-intermediated" investment makes up a large proportion of the total. Retained earnings have become the source of around 70% of China's total fixed asset investment (Li, 2006) and the private sector's share of those earnings have been increasing (Lardy, 2014). If private sector firms take more disciplined and market-based decisions on the use of capital raised from themselves, this should mean that capital is being better allocated.

On the other hand, non-intermediated investment cannot provide the means by which all of China's savings can be put to effective use. The need for intermediation arises from the fact that those who save and those who spend on investment projects are not usually the same people. Most households do not invest in business projects, but they save. If a company has retained earnings, there is no reason to suppose that they perfectly match their investment requirements, and they usually need to be a net lender or borrower. Furthermore, by using their own funds for their own projects they are making risky bets on a single asset, when by using retained earnings to buy a portfolio of assets, and borrowing to cover their own project, they could reduce that risk.

Marketization of capital therefore needs an effective system of financial intermediation, which is not yet in place. Financial markets are riddled with corruption, poor regulation and a lack of transparency, as the share price panic of July 2015 demonstrated. Banking is dominated by the big four banks – Bank of China, Industrial and Commercial Bank of China, China Construction Bank and Agricultural Bank of China – all of whom are state-owned and the banking system remains a creature of the state, operating to a great extent on non-market principles. Until 2015 the government enforced a deposit rates "ceiling" low enough in some years to constitute "financial repression" where returns to savers are lower than inflation, providing a transfer of wealth from households to the government. While interest rates have been liberalized, the authorities still announce "benchmark rates" which do not correspond to market rates and at which local governments and state-owned enterprises can borrow cheaply. When the government stimulates the economy, as it did in the international financial crisis of 2008, it directs the banks to increase lending, largely to the state sector.

China's factor markets have seen considerable development, but its extent varies from factor to factor. For labour, marketization is close to complete, *hukou* reform being the final hurdle. For land and capital considerable institution-building and regulatory reforms need to be in place before the objective of "putting market forces in charge" is fully realized.

Globalization: everything in Walmart comes from China!

Giddens (1991, p.64) defined globalization as:

> The intensification of worldwide social relations which link distant localities in such a way that local happenings are shaped by events occurring many miles away, and vice versa.

In the Mao era, China was an insignificant participant in world trade and its relationship with other countries was defined in terms of geo-politics and support for Communist-backed "national liberation movements". Isolated by policy and distance, "local happenings" had very little impact on the developed world, and vice versa.

By 2011 the world had changed. Around 90% of the world's laptop computers were made in China, alongside 80% of the air-conditioners and 70% of the mobile phones. Walmart sourced 70% of its products from China, and it would be difficult to find a Westerner who was not using something Chinese-made. In summer 2015 a decline of one third in stock prices on the Shanghai and Shenzhen Stock Exchanges (after gains of more than 150% in one year) caused so much concern that the US Federal Reserve delayed a rise in US interest rates over concern for global financial stability. The reduction in China's rate of growth, from around 10% per annum for three decades to a still handsome 6–7% for 2015–2020, led to almost hysterical Western media coverage on the impact of China's "slowdown" on everything from commodity prices, to growth in trading partner nations, to currency rates and the financial situation of governments worldwide. China has come to the world, and the world to China, so that domestic events reverberate around the global economy, and China's own economic situation depends upon happenings elsewhere.

Globalization has four components (IMF, 2000) namely: trade; investment; migration, and; the dissemination of information. In the Mao era China practised autarky where goods were only imported if they were needed to implement the Plan, and other goods (largely primary products) were exported in order to pay for those imports. International trade was a monopoly of state-run foreign trade corporations. Inward foreign investment was not allowed, being seen as an instrument through which rich countries exploit the poor. Chinese people were not allowed to travel abroad so that migration was largely limited to those illegally entering the British colony of Hong Kong, which would allow them to stay if they could cross the controlled border and reach the urban area undetected. Dissemination of information was tightly controlled by the authorities for whom even mundane statistics constituted "state secrets" whose revelation was punished. All four components of globalization have changed significantly, though migration of people and the dissemination of information lag behind trade and investment.

One of the most important changes brought about in 1978 was opening up the country to trade and foreign investment, whose development has been intimately linked. The *Joint Venture Law of 1979* allowed foreign investors to set up production in China, provided it was in collaboration with local partners. In line with the gradualist approach to reform, four "special economic zones" were set up in Shantou, Shenzhen, Xiamen and Zhuhai, where foreign investors were less constrained by rules and regulations. When those proved to be successful, the experiment was extended to allow all of the coastal regions to participate in foreign trade (Yang, 1991).

The key drivers in this initial stage of globalization were Hong Kong firms, seeking to maintain competitiveness when wages and rents in the city were making it difficult to compete on cost (Sung, 1992). As explained above, they loaded their machinery onto trucks and drove over the border into Guangdong province, to establish joint ventures with local governments, often in the towns from which they or their parents had emigrated to Hong Kong. That wave of inward foreign investment coincided with the rural reforms that were freeing workers from the land, and the companies were an excellent match for China's requirements. They were generally small, and concentrated in the industries that had developed as a survival response to China's isolation from world trade after 1950 – garments, watches, cheap jewellery, wigs, toys, assembly of electronic products (Whitla & Davies, 1995). They employed simple technologies, suitable for peasant workers, well aligned with China's comparative advantage (Lin, Cai and Li, 1996). Perhaps most important, Hong Kong manufacturing firms had been "born global". The lack of a local market and the closed border with China meant that they had been forced from their inception in the 1950s to serve markets overseas. Hence, despite their small size, they were able to export to developed country markets by using the business model known as "original equipment manufacturing" (OEM). That consists of manufacturing products to designs provided by brand-owning customers, thereby avoiding the costs of technology or brand development, buying inputs from wherever they are cheapest, and monitoring and controlling low quality labour to produce decent quality products.

By 1993, there were more than 100,000 Hong Kong-based "foreign-invested enterprises" in China (Tracy, 1995, p.3). Low technology, family-based and cost-competitive, they were focused on production for export through Hong Kong, and they drove China's exports from less than $US10 billion in 1978 to $US121 billion in 1994 (National Bureau of Statistics of China, 2015). Without their commercial acumen and knowledge of foreign markets and customers, China's export-led development could never have taken place.

While the contribution of Hong Kong firms was crucial in kick-starting export-led development, they were in a very narrow range of light industries, and had little contribution to make in respect of heavier industries and technological development. However, as explained above, the development of light industry led to growing demands for machinery, and equipment, which stimulated a second round of industrialization. Again, inward foreign investment was a key contributor, but the second generation of foreign investors was very different. They originated in the developed countries of Europe, North America and Japan, they were more capital and technology-intensive, and they were not solely focused on China as a base for exports, becoming increasingly interested in the Chinese market itself.

The result of these developments has been an enormous inflow of foreign direct investment. In the early years of reform, Hong Kong, Taiwan and Macau firms were pioneers, because the rest of world was not convinced that China would stay on the path to reform. In 1986, inflows were only $US2.24 bn. However, in early 1992 Deng Xiaoping made a tour of Southern China, extolling the virtues of the Special Economic Zone in Shenzhen. His hold on policy was confirmed, and investors became more confident. Hence by 1993, the inflow had risen to $US27.5 bn. In 2001 China joined the World Trade Organization (WTO), significantly stimulating inward investment, which soared to $US113.3 bn in 2012. By 2010 the estimated stock of foreign direct investment was $US579 bn (Davies, 2013). There are no reliable figures on the distribution of that investment by source country because a large proportion of it is routed through Hong Kong (which is treated as "foreign" for statistical purposes). Nevertheless, it is safe to say that almost every major company involved in international business now has a presence in China.

This influx of foreign investment has helped the country become the manufacturing centre of the world, producing 22% of world manufacturing output in 2012, displacing the US in first place. About 27% of that output is attributed to foreign-invested enterprises (FIEs) and they account for more than 50% of China's manufactured exports. Involvement in the global economy and WTO membership has contributed significantly to China's rising incomes. Perhaps more important, however, FIEs have brought superior technology, management and manufacturing expertise to China, whose local firms have learned from the in-comers, making productivity gains of their own through knowledge "spill-overs".

Until recently, foreign investment in China has been inward, with minor exceptions. That changed in 2000 when the authorities included a "go global" strategy in the 10th Five Year Plan (2001–2005) and followed it up in the subsequent 11th, 12th and 13th Plans. Companies are encouraged to invest directly overseas through incentives and government support, assisted by government loans to other countries for investment projects that can be implemented by Chinese firms. The amounts invested abroad increased significantly after the financial crisis of 2008 when many Western competitors faced financial difficulties, rising from $US60 bn in 2005–2007 to $US181.2 bn for 2008–2010. Chinese companies have made high profile acquisitions of foreign firms including Lenovo's purchase of IBM's computer business, Geely's purchase of Volvo, and Shuanghui's acquisition of Smithfield Foods. They have also become major investors in "trophy" assets, like football clubs, and French vineyards. At the same time, some of their attempts have failed because of suspicions about perceived Chinese state involvement, which prevented Huawei's part-acquisition of 3Com in the US, or concerns over Chinese ownership of natural resources, which blocked Chinalco's Australian investment in Rio Tinto. Cognisant of that, government policy has moved from simply encouraging firms to "go out" to helping them manage the risks in involved (Davies, 2013).

Integration with the global economy has contributed to China's export-based growth and has changed life-styles and consumption patterns across the world. Global brands are ever-present in Chinese cities from KFC, McDonalds and Pizza Hut to Uniqlo, Carrefour and Walmart to Armani, Gucci, Prada, and Patek Phillipe. On the other side of the transaction, in every developed nation, almost every manufactured product imaginable, from iPhones and ThinkPads to sports shoes, furniture and table lamps, carries a "made in China" label and is significantly cheaper for the consumer. There have been gains for both sides from globalization. At the same time, it is clear that the gains have not been equally distributed. Developed country workers in manufacturing industries, who do not have skills superior to workers in China, have "lost their jobs to China". As a small group (estimated at 1 million in the US) that loses significantly is more likely to take political action than a larger group that benefits marginally (300 million US citizens gain an estimated $US250 per year (Economist, 2016, p. 31)), it is not surprising that policy regimes are moving away from globalization, which would make China's shift away from growth based on exports even more urgent.

Globalization has two other components. The first is the migration of workers in pursuit of better opportunities. China has seen some significant outflows and inflows in this respect. Individual Chinese workers, sometimes illegal, are found in agriculture, construction, fishing, mining and the service industries across the world. Chinese workers and managers can be found in Chinese projects from Iran, to Luanda, Mozambique, and Sudan. In Egypt, an estimated 15,000 "shanti sini" or Chinese traders sell Chinese products door to door, as in other Middle Eastern and African countries (Cardenal & Araujo, 2012). Their total numbers are unknown, small in comparison to the total population, but large in absolute terms.

In terms of inward migration to China, the expatriate population was approximately 600,000 in 2010, according to official census data, with the largest number coming from South Korea, the US and Japan. Guangzhou city has a substantial "Africa Town" with an estimated population of 16,000, many of whom are traders using tourist visas, and Jilin province is home to an unknown number of illegal North Korean immigrants. While these immigrant groups make contributions to China's economy, their numbers pale into insignificance relative to the size of the population.

The fourth component of globalization is the flow of information across borders, which remains a sensitive issue for the Chinese authorities. On the one hand, China has embraced the Internet very quickly, with 830 million mobile Internet users in 2015. Smartphones are ubiquitous, with more than 500 million users, a penetration ratio of more than 90% in tier-1 cities, and average on-line time for users reaching an average of nearly 20 hours per week. Despite the low-trust nature of Chinese culture, e-commerce has grown at exponential rates, with on-line retailers like TMall leading market growth towards an annual total of around US$600 billion. Messaging services like WeChat *(Wei Xin)* have revolutionized personal communications and (as with TMall) have successfully outcompeted their foreign rivals, with new business models and more flexible and extendable services. China overtook the US in 2013 as the biggest digital marketplace in the world.

Despite this enthusiasm for digital technology, information remains tightly constrained. The government owns the access routes to the Internet and employs censors to delete content it deems inappropriate. Any reference to the *Tiananmen* incident in 1989 will be instantly deleted, as will references to the *Falungong* religious sect, or unrest in Tibet or Xinjiang. Criticism of leaders or the Party is tolerated, provided it stays within narrow limits, and the media have become adept at sensing how far they can, and cannot go. Key foreign service providers including Google, Facebook, Twitter and YouTube are still not available in 2017.

The Chinese Internet community has become adept at finding its way around many of the barriers put in place. Newspapers, journalists and bloggers post material in the knowledge that it will be taken down, but only after it has been read many times. The Chinese language is full of homonyms, which makes it easy to substitute one phrase for another which would be "filtered", and the virtual world has become the source of a whole new comedic tradition. Any Internet user with a moderate degree of technical knowledge can install a Virtual Private Network (VPN) to get around the restrictions and the purpose of government intervention may be to intimidate users, rather than actually block content. As the censors and the censored dodge around each other, China remains less open for information, especially that coming from outside the country, than almost any other nation.

References

Ash, R., 2006. Squeezing the peasants: Grain extraction, food consumption and rural living standards in Mao's China. *The China Quarterly*, pp.959–998.

Cai, F., Park, A. and Zhao, Y., 2008. The Chinese labor market in the reform era, in Brandt, L. and Rawski, T. (eds), *China's great economic transformation*, Cambridge: Cambridge University Press, pp.167–214.

Cardenal, J. and Araujo, H., 2012. *China's silent army: The pioneers, traders, fixers and workers who are remaking the world in Beijing's image*. London: Allen Lane.
Chen, K. and Wen, Y., 2015. *The great housing boom of China*. Working Paper 2014–022B, Research Division, Federal Research Bank of St Louis, St Louis.
Ciccone, A. and Hall, R., 1996. Productivity and the density of economic activity. *American Economic Review*, 86 (1), pp.54–70.
D'Arcy, P. and Veroude, A., 2014. Housing trends in China and India, *Reserve Bank of Australia Bulletin*, March, pp.63–68.
Davies, K., 2013. *China investment policy: An update*. OECD Working Papers on International Investment 2013/01. OECD Publishing 10.1787/5k46911hmvbt-en
Duranton, G. and Puga, D., 2004. Micro-foundations of urban agglomeration economies, in Henderson, V. and Thisse, J-F. (eds), *Handbook of regional and urban economics, Volume 4: Cities and geography*. Amsterdam: Elsevier, pp.2063–2117.
Economist, 2015. Mapping the invisible scourge. 15 August. Available at: http://www.economist.com/news/china/21661053-new-study-suggests-air-pollution-even-worse-thought-mapping-invisible-scourge [Accessed 26 February 2017].
Economist, 2016. Trade at what price? 2 April. Available at: http://www.economist.com/news/united-states/21695855-americas-economy-benefits-hugely-trade-its-costs-have-been-amplified-policy [Accessed 26 February 2017].
Feng, S., and Li, Q., 2013. Car ownership control in Chinese mega cities: Shanghai, Beijing and Guangzhou, *Journeys*, September 2013, pp.40–46.
Giddens, A., 1991. *The consequences of modernity*. Cambridge: Polity Press.
Goffman, E., 1961. *Asylums: Essays on the social situation of mental patients and other inmates*. New York: Doubleday.
Hu, F., 2011. Homeownership and subjective well-being in urban China: Does owning a house make you happier? *Social Indicators Research*, February, pp.951–971.
International Monetary Fund (IMF), 2000. *Globalization: Threats or opportunity*, Washington, DC: IMF Publications, April.
Lardy, N., 2014. *Markets over Mao: The rise of private business in China*. Washington, DC: Peterson Institute for International Economics.
Li, D., 2006. *Large domestic non-intermediated investments and government liabilities – challenges facing China's financial sector reform*. Washington, DC: World Bank.
Lin, J., Cai, F. and Li, Z., 1996. *The China miracle: Development strategy and economic reform*. Hong Kong: Chinese University Press.
Marshall, A., 1890. *Principles of economics*. London: Macmillan.
National Bureau of Statistics of China, 2015. *China Statistical Yearbook*, Beijing: China Statistics Press.
Nolan, P., 1994. The China puzzle: "Touching stones to cross the rivers". *Challenge*, January–February, pp.25–31.
Nolan, P. and Ash, R., 1995. China's economy on the eve of reform, *China Quarterly*, 144, pp.980–998.
Smil, V., 2013. *Making the modern world: Materials and dematerialization*. New York: Wiley.
Sung, Y-W., 1992. *The China–Hong Kong connection: The key to China's open door policy*. Cambridge: Cambridge University Press.
Tracy, N., 1995. 'Transforming South China: The role of the Chinese diaspora in the era of reform', in Davies, H. (ed.), *China business: Context and issues*. Hong Kong: Longman Asia, pp.1–21.
Wang, Y., Shao, L., Murie, A. and Cheng, J., 2012. The maturation of the neo-liberal housing market in urban China. *Housing Studies*, 27 (3), pp.343–359.
Wen, Y., 2015. *The making of an economic superpower – unlocking China's secret of rapid industrialization*, Working Paper 2015–006B, Federal Reserve Bank of St Louis, June.
Whitla, P. and Davies, H., 1995. The competitiveness of Hong Kong's domestic manufacturing operations, in Davies, H. (ed.), *China business: Context and issues*. Hong Kong: Longman Asia, pp.37–65.
World Bank/Development Research Center of the State Council, PRC, 2013. *China 2030: Building a modern, harmonious and creative society*. Washington, DC: IBRD.

World Bank/Development Research Center of the State Council, PRC, 2014. *Urban China: Toward efficient, inclusive and sustainable urbanization*. Washington, DC: IBRD.

World Population Review (2016). Available at: worldpopulationreview.com/ [Accessed 12 May 2017].

Wu, H., 2011. *Rethinking China's path of industrialization*. Working Paper No.2011/76, United Nations University, World Institute for Development Economics Research. Helsinki.

Wu, J. and Zhao, R., 1987. The dual pricing system in China's industry. *Journal of Comparative Economics*, 11 (3), pp.309–318.

Yang, D., 1991. China adjusts to the world economy: the political economy of China's coastal development strategy. *Public Affairs*, pp.42–64.

Yang, Z. and Chen, J., 2014. *Housing affordability and housing policy in urban China*. Heidelberg: Springer.

Zhang, L. Wang, S. and Yu, L., 2014. Is social capital eroded by state-led urbanization in China? A case study on indigenous villagers in the urban fringe of Beijing. *China Economic Review*. Available at: http://dx.doi.org/10.1016/j.chieco.2014.04.005 [Accessed 26 February 2017].

3

CHINA'S STRATEGY FOR DEVELOPMENT

From "crossing the river by feeling the stones" to "revving up the consumer"

Matevz Raskovic

> China is a sleeping giant. Let her sleep, for when she wakes she will move the world.
>
> (Napoleon Bonaparte, 1817)

The interacting forces of industrialization, urbanization, marketization and globalization have transformed China's economy and society in the period since 1978, as the development indicators in Table 3.1 illustrate. However, that development did not just "happen". The structural and institutional transformation that underpins it (Tisdell, 2009) took place as the result of a complex sequence of policy decisions that began in 1978. The purpose of this chapter is to explain how that process unfolded and where it leaves China today.

Four key points can be made to frame the analysis. First, China's socio-economic transformation is still an ongoing process. Second, there has never been a "grand plan" to guide development. Instead, a patchwork of gradualist approaches and small-scale experiments have been built on to produce the outcomes seen today. Third, the process has seen several cycles of over-heating followed by cooling down, accompanied by a tug-of-war between ideology and economic reality which continues today. Fourth, the whole process has been profoundly influenced by Deng Xiaoping.

Antecedents of the 1970s reforms

Deng's vision

As Chapter 1 explained, in 1820 Chinese GDP at purchasing power parity (PPP) accounted for roughly one third of the global total (Maddison, 2001). However, the century that followed was one of severe decline caused by warlordism, feudal tensions, two world wars, Japanese colonization and civil war. While liberation in 1949 was seen as the end of China's century of humiliation, the policy disasters of the Great Leap Forward (1958–1961) and the Cultural Revolution (1966–1976) meant that China could be labelled "backward" until the end of the 1970s (Tisdell, 2009).

Table 3.1 China's selected development indicators (1976–2015)

Indicator/Year	*1976*	*1978*	*1987*	*1992*	*1997*	*2001*	*2006*	*2011*	*2015*
GDP (current, bn USD)	151.6	148.4	271.3	424.9	958.2	1,332.2	2,729.8	7,492.4	10,866.4
GDP growth (annual)	−1.6%	11.9%	11.7%	14.3%	9.2%	8.3%	12.7%	9.5%	6.9%
GDP per capita (current, USD)	162.9	155.2	250.3	364.8	778.9	1,047.5	2,082.2	5,574.2	6,991.9
GDP per capita PPP*	n/a	n/a	n/a	1,260.2	2,265.3	3,205.9	5,836.8	10,274.5	14,238.7
Population (million)	930.7	956.2	1,084.0	1,165.0	1,230.1	1,271.9	1,311.0	1,344.1	1,371.2
Urban population (% of total)	17.5%	17.9%	24.3%	28.2%	32.9%	37.1%	43.9%	50.6%	55.6%
Life expectancy at birth (years)	64.3	65.5	68.6	69.3	70.5	72.2	74.1	75.2	75.4
Agriculture value added**	32.8%	27.9%	26.5%	21.4%	18.0%	14.1%	10.7%	9.5%	9.0%
Industry value added**	45.4%	47.6%	43.2%	43.0%	47.0%	44.7%	47.4%	46.1%	40.5%
Services value added**	21.7%	24.5%	30.3%	35.6%	35.0%	41.3%	41.9%	44.3%	50.5%

Source: World Bank, Development Indicators' database, 2016.

Note: * Current prices, international USD; ** % of GDP.

When Mao died in 1976, the tenure of his appointed successor Hua Guofeng (1976–1978) was short-lived, and Deng Xiaoping emerged as the *de facto* second-generation leader, following the Third Plenary Session of the Eleventh Central Committee of the Chinese Communist Party (CCP) in December 1978. More than anyone else, Deng was the architect of China's reform and opening up policy (*gaige kaifang*) alongside Chen Yun and Zhao Ziyang (Bachman, 1986).

Deng Xiaoping himself had been the victim of political purges but his "strong visionary leadership" (Li, 2011, p.32) and "powerful, effective and efficient government" (Wang, 2011, p.51) were the catalysts for the start of the reform and opening up process. What distinguished him in particular was his pragmatism and result orientation, expressed in his most famous saying: "I don't care if the cat is black or white, as long as it catches the mice."

Drawing on Marxist and Leninist ideology, which he encountered during his stays in France and the Soviet Union in the 1920s, Deng was the main proponent of the concept of "socialism with market characteristics". It was based on the step-wise model of socialist development that underpinned Lenin's New Economic Policy, where socialist ideology did not exclude the use of market principles (Leung, 1995). Following the general principles of China's Communist Party (CCP), which emphasized material economic development (Tisdell, 2009), Deng believed that "Poverty is not socialism. To be rich is to be glorious" and that the gradual introduction of market mechanisms would not only increase prosperity, but also provide legitimacy for the CCP.

In December 1978 support for Deng meant that "economic management in China would be transformed; economic co-operation with other countries would be expanded; special efforts would be made to adopt the world's advanced technologies and equipment; and that scientific and education work would be greatly strengthened" (Tisdell, 2009, p.275). His agenda also included an end to "bureaucratic centralized management of the economy" and for politics to give way to efficiency and development (Tisdell, 2009, p.276). The failure of centralized planning was recognized and Deng saw the "Four Little Dragons" (Hong Kong, Taiwan, South Korea and Singapore), and the comparison between Western Europe and Eastern Europe as exemplars (Chow, 2004). Public support for market reforms was also strong after the devastation of the 1950s and 1960s.

Zhou Enlai's Four Modernizations

Deng's views were profoundly influenced by Zhou Enlai – China's much beloved first premier (1949–1976) – with whom he spent his youth in France. In 1975 Zhou outlined the "Four Modernizations" – a development model focusing on: agriculture; industry; science and technology; and defence (Mason, 1984). The Four Modernizations were "basic themes" rather than a "programmatic blueprint for China's future" and their implementation required political skill and wisdom because they also translated into disputes on the direction, legitimacy and speed of developmental reforms which continue today (Vogel, 2011). Deng's push for rapid reform, in which some would get richer than others, sometimes led to overheating, as in the mid-1980s (Zhu, 2013). At such times, the pace of reforms slowed and a more conservative approach advocated by Chen Yun prevailed for a while (Bachman, 1986). Those policy swings have continued, with clear differences of priority between the Jiang Zemin, Hu Jintao and Xi Jinping leadership periods.

While the Four Modernizations failed to gain support at the Fourth National People's Congress in 1975 (Gao, 2007), Deng's courage, wisdom and pragmatism provided the energy needed to bring Zhou's vision to life. As Tisdell (2009, p.272) put it:

> He was courageous in that several CCP members at the time would have viewed his approach as radical. He was wise in the sense that he could foresee the advantages to China of the reforms and opening up but was also aware that the reforms would have to be phased in at a gradual pace and systematically.

Deng's understanding that reform should be gradual and small-scale arose from the devastating consequences of the rapid and large-scale Great Leap Forward and is epitomized by another of his famous sayings: "Crossing the river by feeling for the stones" (Vogel, 2011).

The Deng reform era

Deng's gradual crossing of the river involved several stages, waves, which he presented as small-scale experiments and implemented in careful phases (Naughton, 2007). They involved four major shifts.

Shifting from politics to the economy

The period from Liberation in 1949 until 1978 was one of "politics first" where the priority was placed on consolidating China "under the banner of socialism" and on the class struggle of workers and peasants against capitalist and imperial elites (Pan, 2011, p.42).

The initiation of economic reforms in 1978 marked a profound shift away from class struggle and towards economic development. More than just a shift in ideology, it was a tectonic shift "from a revolutionary system to an institutional system" (Pan, 2011, p.42) structured around the idea of "one centre and two basic points", with economic development as the centre, supported by socialist values and the legitimacy of the CCP (Li, 2012).

Shifting from a planned economy to a "bird in a cage" market economy

> The Chinese economy is like a bird in a cage. The bird represents the free market, while the cage represents the central plan.
>
> (Chen Yun, Vice-Premier and Vice-Chairman of the CCP, quoted in Bachman, 1986, p.297)

The Great Leap Forward had illustrated the inefficiency of a planned economy, having failed to provide either agricultural advancement or rapid industrialization. Nevertheless, the transformation towards a market-based alternative was slow. While Deng pushed for the introduction of economic incentives, especially management and economic responsibility in organizational governance (Tisdell, 2009), it was Chen Yun who called for the restructuring of the Chinese economy away from its emphasis on heavy industry. Chen advocated the "three balances" (Bachman, 1986, p.298): a *balanced state budget* (avoidance of international borrowing); a *balanced financial system* (banking loans vs. repayments); and a *balance between planned supply and market-driven demand*. This was further accompanied by balancing foreign exchange inflows and expenditures. In contrast to Deng, Chen Yun was a much stronger advocate of financial centralization, more cautious regarding integration into the international economy and he believed market mechanisms should be subordinate to socialist economic planning (Bachman, 1986).

The first stage of the shift followed after the 12th CPC National Congress in 1982, with the "idea of supplementing the planned economy with market regulation" (Li, 2012, p.14). A "dual-track price system" was established, first in agriculture. State-set prices were assigned for quantities under the state plan and market-set prices were allowed for quantities above the plan (Naughton, 2007). This system was first introduced as part of agricultural reform (under the so-called "household responsibility system") and later extended to industry and commerce (Naughton, 2007). After the Third Plenary of the 12th CPC Central Committee in 1984 a "planned commodity economy on the basis of public ownership" was developed (Li, 2012, p.14) and state planned quantities became fixed in absolute terms, allowing the economy to gradually outgrow the plan (Naughton, 2007, p.92). By 1992 (as Deng withdrew from public politics) the model further developed into the "socialist market economic system" with market mechanisms implemented across most areas.

The structure of enterprise ownership provides a useful indicator of China's shift from plan to market. In 1978 state-owned enterprises (SOEs) created 77.6% of gross industrial output value but that had fallen to 28% by the mid-1990s (Chow, 2004) and around 22% today. After China's 2001 entry to the World Trade Organisation (WTO), the share of assets owned by SOEs in terms of total industrial assets declined from close to 70% to about 40%, while the share of SOEs' profits in total profits decreased from 55% to less than 30%. Accompanying this transition SOEs stopped being "cash cows" (Naughton, 2007, p.105) and the share of SOEs' profits in GDP decreased from about 15% in 1978 to less than 2% of GDP by the mid-1990s.

Shifting from a closed to an open economy

China had not been a completely closed economy prior to Deng's reforms, especially before the Great Leap Forward (Naughton, 2007). In fact, the country was quite open to trade and aid in the period 1952–1960. However, most of the trade was with other communist countries – 48% was just with the Soviet Union (Naughton, 2007). The Great Leap Forward boosted imports, but the post-Great Leap crisis resulted in no trade growth between 1959 and 1970, at which point imports and exports together accounted for only about 5% of GDP. Prior to 1978, China's foreign trade model was a typical "double air lock" Soviet-style model with international trade restricted to 12 state foreign trade companies and a non-convertible currency (Naughton, 2007).

The shift from a closed to an open economy had two phases. The first was the initial "opening up" (*kaifang*) policy under which China abandoned autarchy, participated in trade and encouraged inward direct investment. The second, was the "going out" policy where, from around 2002, Chinese firms were encouraged to invest directly overseas (Li, 2012). Another important distinction is that between the periods before and after China's accession to the WTO in 2001. This event has been described as "one of the most important events in world economic history" (Zhang, Zhang & Cui, 2013, p.70).

Deng's vision of an open China represented a profound departure from the previous closed-door policy which was influenced by China's century of humiliation and grounded in a philosophy of "strategic self-sufficiency" (Naughton, 2007, p.379). It is not difficult to understand why Deng placed a high priority on "opening up". In contrast to Mao Zedong, who had no international experience, Deng's vision was profoundly influenced by his foreign experiences – as a youth in France and the Soviet Union, and while in charge of China's foreign affairs in the 1970s. He was impressed by Japan's modernization through opening up during the Meiji period (1868–1912), and kept a close eye on the development of the "Four Little Dragons". Table 3.2 shows just how extensive the "opening up" has been.

In the initial years, small steps were taken, which Deng called "experiments" to appease sceptics (Bachman, 1986). These experiments included first opening "specialized trade channels" in the southern provinces of Guangdong and Fujian, close to Hong Kong followed by "special export processing agreements" which developed into "export processing zones" (EPZs) and thence into "special economic zones" (SEZs). These were one of Deng's most controversial experiments (Bachman, 1986) and it is noteworthy that the father of China's current president, Xi Jinping, was a key CCP official in Guangdong during that time (1978–1981) (Vogel, 2011).

SEZs were granted exceptional local autonomy and given priority in receiving state-planned resources. They also functioned outside the existing foreign trade system of state-led foreign trade companies, providing new opportunities to earn foreign currency needed for technological modernization (Naughton, 2007; Vogel, 2011).

The combination of autonomy, market incentives, and preferential access to state-managed resources brought economic success to SEZs but created tensions with other provinces, and scepticism within the CCP (particularly from Chen Yun). By the mid-1980s reports of corruption in Guangdong and Fujian were rampant (Vogel, 2011) and the juxtaposition of SEZs with the traditional centrally planned system of national trade called for a wider liberalization of foreign trade (Naughton, 2007). That process began as early as 1984, but was scaled back in 1985 following an alarming surge in imports, and a more gradual approach was adopted (Naughton, 2007, p.382). According to Naughton (2007, p.393): "Despite the [1984–1985] setbacks, policy makers maintained some flexibility, and within a few years they had transformed the rules for trade, largely dismantled the old foreign-trade monopoly, and created a framework for subsequent growth of trade and investment." That liberalization of foreign trade involved (Naughton, 2007, pp.383–386):

- Abandoning the overvalued exchange rate and setting up a dual exchange rate system (for exports outside the state plan) which further contributed to the RMB's devaluation.
- Relaxing the limits on the number of national foreign trade companies, allowing local governments to set foreign trading companies (FTCs) and *township-and-village enterprises* (TVEs) to be involved in foreign trade as suppliers to FTCs.
- Re-adjustment of pricing principles due to increased competition, profit retention and other market incentives for exporting actors.
- Support for a comprehensive "Coastal Development Strategy", opening up 14 additional coastal areas. These were granted decision-making autonomy for inward FDIs up to $US30 million and were able to encourage different types of companies to pursue export opportunities, particularly through more flexible types of export-processing contracts (Branstetter & Feenstra, 2002).

Despite these changes the system of liberalizing foreign trade after the mid-1980s still included an elaborate system of tariffs, accompanied by non-tariff barriers (particularly limitations on trading rights). Those persisted until the mid-1990s, because of fear of import spikes, exponential trade deficits and worries over foreign currency debt.

From the mid-1990s onwards, negotiations for WTO entry led to the abandonment of the dualistic trade structure distinguishing between "ordinary trade" and "export-promoting trade".

Table 3.2 China's integration with the world economy after the 1978 reforms

Indicator/Year	*1970*	*1978*	*1987*	*1992*	*1997*	*2001*	*2006*	*2011*	*2015*
Exports as % of GDP	2.5%	4.6%	12.1%	17.3%	19.1%	20.0%	35.7%	26.8%	22.4%
Imports as % of GDP	2.5%	5.1%	13.3%	16.4%	14.9%	18.3%	29.1%	24.4%	18.8%
FDI net inflows as % of GDP	n/a	n/a	0.9%	2.6%	4.6%	3.5%	4.9%	3.7%	2.3%
FDI net outflows as % of GDP	n/a	n/a	0.2%	0.9%	0.4%	0.7%	0.9%	0.6%	1.7%
Net foreign assets (in bn RMB)	n/a	0.54	65.75	278.22	1,363.4	2,640	10,083	25,097	28,001

Sources: World Bank, Development Indicators' database, 2016.

The abandonment of a "secondary swap market for foreign exchange" led to a liberalized foreign currency market and was accompanied by a gradual reduction of tariffs from 1994 to WTO accession in 2001 – the unweighted tariff mean decreased from 43% in 1992 to 17% by 1999 (Naughton, 2007). The currency reform was part of a broader "coordinated fiscal package, financial and trade reforms", which emphasized value-added taxes and gave exporters opportunities for VAT rebating (Naughton, 2007, p.389).

China's decision to join the WTO had both pre-membership and post-membership effects. In the pre-WTO period, the negotiation process provided additional external pressure which was used to leverage market liberalization (Naughton, 2007). Once membership was secured, it brought not only the elimination of the dual track trading structure, currency reform and the liberalization of trading rights, but also promoted: economic reform through market incentives for private companies, which led to the diminishing role of state-owned enterprises (SOEs); physical and human capital accumulation based on rapid growth of exports; and substantial inward foreign direct investment (Zhang, Zhang & Cui, 2013), especially from the "circle economies" of Hong Kong and Taiwan.

The success of "opening up" was followed by "going out" which began within the 10th 5-year plan (2001–2005). There had been some outward foreign direct investment (FDI) in the earlier period but it had been relatively small in scale (Ramasamy, Yeung & Laforet, 2012; Zhang & Daly, 2011). The general idea of "going out" as a policy was to "create a comparative advantage for Chinese firms by promoting multinational operations and actively develop and utilize overseas resources" (Chou, Chen & Mai, 2011, p.2154). The strategy also involved "strong, national public endorsement for an institutional environment that fosters outward FDIs" (Luo, Xue & Han, 2010, p.75), as well as:

- The relaxation of foreign exchange transaction rules and quotas.
- A supportive administrative environment with simplified procedures, an information bank, various types of insurance, and tax preferences.
- Financial resources from the Export-Import Bank of China and better access to financing through the banks.
- Monitoring rules for outward FDI shifting the "focus from amount to performance" (Luo, Xue & Han, 2010, p.75).

Shifting from an agrarian to an industrial society: China becomes the factory of the world

The importance of agriculture for China is the consequence of a simple fact: with less than 6% of the global land area (most of which is not fit for agriculture), China has to feed almost a fifth of the global population. Agriculture also played a key role in the civil war, contributing to the victory of CPC through the mobilization of the countryside (Vogel, 2011). Even today, agriculture is seen as a key strategic resource and each Five Year Plan starts with agriculture.

Following the foundation of the PRC, collective land ownership was an integral part of the socialist philosophy. However, large state-owned collective farms failed to increase agricultural output and contributed to the famine caused by the Great Leap Forward.

After 1978, the key initiative that increased agricultural efficiency was the "household responsibility system" (Vogel, 2011). This radical change in policy, accompanied by the technological progress accompanying opening-up, was the necessary precondition for rapid industrialization (see Chapter 2) which relied upon an extensive labour force from the countryside. Rapid industrialization also required additional land, particularly in the southern and coastal areas, which added to the pressure to increase agricultural efficiency. Both the rural labour force (who became migrant workers) and land were crucial antecedents of China's industrial transformation (Naughton, 2007). Only then could opening up, aimed at importing technology, attracting inward FDIs and promoting export, bear fruit.

This industrial transformation was accompanied by rapid urbanization (see Chapter 2), creating the dual urban–rural structure (Li, 2012) that persists today, with average urban income exceeding average rural income by more than 3:1. It also required significant government investment, which has been one of the key engines of the growth of the Chinese economy (Naughton, 2007). Unlike the Great Leap Forward, which focused on heavy industry (steel production), the modernization of industry under Deng's reforms focused initially on light industry and manufacturing aimed for export, followed by the development of more upstream sectors in support of manufacturing.

By 2017 the shift from an agrarian society to one based on industry (and services) could not be said to be complete, as the leadership anticipates a further reduction in the rural population of perhaps 200 million people. However, China had become the world's most important manufacturing base, overtaking the US, and agriculture accounted for less than 10% of national income.

Table 3.3 summarizes the most important features of the Deng-era reforms.

Table 3.3 Key features of the Deng-era economic reforms

Feature	*Short description*
Dual track system	State-set planned prices vs. market prices; ordinary trade vs. export-promoting trade.
Growing out of the plan	Fixed aggregate level of central-government material allocation leads to diminishing influence of central planning in a growing economy.
Particularistic contracts	Specific individual contracts with every SOE to meet production, material balance plan and for taxing.
Industry liberalization and entry	Opening in industry for new entrants from 1979; establishment of local foreign trade companies and TVEs (township-and-village enterprises).
Market price mechanism	Diminishing dual-track system and SOEs with above plan production.
Managerial reform over privatization	State-sector management replaced privatization; focus in incentives, performance and increasing management capabilities.
Gradual disarticulation from planned economy	Successive sections of economy were "disarticulated" from planned economy in gradual wave (earliest example are SEZs).
Initial macroeconomic stabilization	Using planned economy tools to alleviate macroeconomic imbalances (through reducing investments) and resource channelling.
High saving and investment	Gradual takeover of national saving by households from the government.

Source: Naughton (2007, pp.91–98).

Economic reforms as waves

The evolution of Chinese economic reform can also be broken down into distinct reform waves (Leung, 1995). Table 3.4 describes their key features.

The first reform wave (1978–1984) was aimed at addressing the inefficiency of state planning. It delegated authority to local levels, introduced economic management and responsibility to support a more effective planned economy and attracted technology and equipment imports in the form of inward FDI. The second reform wave (1984–1987) created a hybrid state-planned and commodity economy based on the gradual introduction of "economic levers" (dual-track system) (Leung, 1995, p.69). It introduced new types of enterprise and gave them a legal basis. The third reform wave (1987–1993) deepened the enterprise reforms and improved the investment environment, but also introduced the foundations of China's private sector. General Secretary Zhao Ziyang saw China's challenge not in class struggle, but in resolving "the contradiction between the growing material and cultural needs of the people and China's backward production" (Leung, 1995, p.76). In his view, the private sector could complement the planned economy based on state ownership, by promoting production, increasing efficiency and employment.

Table 3.4 Waves of Chinese economic reforms of the Deng era and their key features

1st wave (1978–1984)	
National contract system	Economic Contract Law of 1981/82 specifying ten transaction types, including: sales and purchasing, storage, rentals, loans etc. It was designed to provide "greater autonomy [to] economic management" by organizations assuming profit/loss responsibility, but "under the guidance of unified state planning".
Inwards FDIs	Industrialization and modernization of science and technology required in the first phase technology importing, which China labelled as international economic cooperation – based on: (a) mutual benefits and (b) advanced cooperation (advanced technology importing). The *Joint Ventures Law* of 1979 and the *Joint Ventures Regulations* (1983) provided the basis for the first inward FDIs in the form of joint ventures.
2nd wave (1984–1987)	
Enterprise reforms	Enterprise reform was aimed at invigorating state or collective enterprises (70% of production). The *State Industrial Enterprise Law* of 1983 introduced the dual-price system for production over the assigned state plan. The *General Principles of Civil Law* of 1986 introduced state, collective and foreign joint venture enterprises. The *State Enterprise Law* of 1988 introduced ownership and management division. This introduced the so-called "economic responsibility system "with two possible forms: (a) lease/contract management, or (b) director responsibility. Introduction of the *Bankruptcy Law* of 1988.
Wholly Foreign-Owned Enterprises	The *Foreign Enterprise Law* of 1986 allowed for the establishment of wholly foreign-owned enterprises, which used advanced technology and equipment to China's benefit and were export oriented. Foreign investors were protected against nationalization and expropriation (bad experience from the 1950s), or appropriately reimbursed. WFOEs enjoyed preferential tax treatment and/or exemptions.

Co-operative joint ventures	The *Co-operative Joint Venture Law* of 1988 aimed to attract foreign capital, technology, equipment and know-how. Preferential profit status was granted to foreign investors to offset greater risk and recover the investment. Progressive profit-sharing was allowed for the Chinese later on, which also received ownership of the assets after expiration of the relationship.
3rd wave (1987–1993)	
Private enterprises	The *Private Enterprise Regulations* of 1988 distinguished between: (a) sole proprietorship, (b) partnership and (c) limited liability companies. Eligibility among the population was limited to: rural population, urban unemployed, retirees, or people who quit their jobs. Appropriate capital, facilities and workforce were also stipulated. Also, private enterprises were obliged to reinvest 50% of their after-tax profits into a *production development fund*.
Revision of foreign equity joint ventures	The 1990 revision introduced "protection from nationalization of joint ventures, provision of foreigners to assume chairmanship [. . .], relaxation of foreign exchange banking restrictions [. . .] and elimination of the time limits on some types of joint venture" (*ibid.* 79).
Shareholding enterprises	The *Shareholding Enterprises Trial Measures* of 1992 laid the foundation for the establishment of shareholding enterprises, despite the fact that some trial experiments were already conducted in Shanghai, Xiamen and Shenzhen. In addition to already introduced separation of ownership and management, and enterprise autonomy and responsibility, this introduced also a new way of raising capital. The *Joint Stock Company Opinion* allowed for public subscription and determined minimum paid in capital (10 mn RMB; or 30 mn RMB in case of foreign equity). The *Limited Liability Company Opinion* prescribed an ownership of 2 to maximum 30, and set various paid-in capital thresholds for (a) production companies (500,000 RMB), (b) commercial/wholesale companies (500,000 RMB), (c) commercial retails companies (300,000 RMB), and (d) service, science and technology and consultancy companies (100,000 RMB).

Source: Leung (1995: 88–86).

1989 and its aftermath: the legacy of Deng and beyond

1989 was a decisive year for Deng Xiaoping and Chinese politics, as well as the economy. In the Tiananmen Square incident on 4 June, Deng ordered the use of military force on protestors in Beijing after months of protests and disobedience of martial law. Hundreds were killed, it was a dark day in Deng's leadership and it drew severe international criticism (Vogel, 2011). The protests were not just a political movement opposed to the power structure within the CCP (Naughton, 2009). They were also the result of a failure to tackle economic overheating (inflation) and anger over fiscal austerity, corruption, slow-paced economic reforms, dual structures and local experimentation. As Naughton (2009, p.10) noted, it is: "surprising that such reforms were economically successful", let alone "that they could be sustained politically for a decade". The violent response of the authorities was also the result of panic amongst a leadership that had been observing the disintegration of the Soviet Union and Eastern Europe. In Chinese eyes, that was the consequence of their "big bang" approach to market reform (Ray, 2002) and hence their conviction that gradualism would be safer was reinforced.

In the wake of the 1989 events, Jiang Zemin replaced Deng Xiaoping as the paramount third-generation leader (Vogel, 2011). With the Party's survival at stake, Jiang focused on political consolidation and re-centralization, while economic reforms were passed to Vice-Premier Zhu Rongji (who became Premier between 1998 and 2003). In political terms, Jiang re-positioned the Party as the "core" in China's socio-economic development through "The Three Represents" (*sange daibiao*). They referred to advanced economic development, advanced cultural development and political consensus to serve the interests of the people, which included greater acceptance of the private sector, producing a new type of elite within Chinese society (Narayanan, 2006).

By the early 1990s China had grown out of the planned economy. With public opinion mobilized in support of further reforms, following Deng's tour of the South in early 1992, the 3rd Plenum of the 14th CCP Central Committee introduced the "socialist market economic system" in November 1993. This created a uniform playing field through a single market, based on the co-existence of public and private ownership with political oversight. It included macroeconomic reform, financial control, and hard budget constraints for SOEs. It also continued the strengthening of market institutions and the start of the privatization process which continues today (Naughton, 2007). Jiang's leadership introduced "state-sponsored capitalism", which has been described as "reforms with losers" (Naughton, 2009, p.12). This period also included significant tax reform, which shifted tax revenue from local to central government, significantly broadened the tax base (inclusion of VAT) and re-directed government and political power towards Beijing (Naughton, 2007).

When Jiang Zemin stepped down in 2002, President Hu Jintao and Premier Wen Jiabao (2002–2012) shifted the focus from politics towards economic and social issues, and aimed at bring the Party closer to the people. Building on Jiang's Three Represents, Hu introduced his "Three Closenesses" (*sange tiejin*), emphasizing closeness to reality, the people and life. This was complemented by his vision of the "Five Overalls" *(wuge quanpan)* – corresponding to: balanced urban–rural development; regional development; economic and social development; harmonious development between man and nature, and; overall balance between open economy and domestic development (Narayanan, 2006).

Hu's leadership of China rode the wave of China's WTO membership after 2001. Double-digit growth, and high employment made China "the factory of the world" (with annual export growth above 20%) and also "the chimney of the world". China's GDP overtook Japan in 2010 to become the world's second largest economy, while GDP per capita (at PPP) more than tripled (IMF, 2016). Privatization of the housing market in the late 1990s put vast wealth into the hands of households, and caused a real-estate surge, with residential construction growing at 17% annually between 2002 and 2010 (Wall Street Journal, 2012). Favourable economic trends, a stronger RMB and an unparalleled real-estate and construction boom were accompanied by increased borrowing from the private sector. Following Jiang's tax reform, which had shifted revenues from local to central government, local governments were selling land, and borrowing extensively in an attempt to outcompete each other with success stories which would attract the attention of Beijing. The 2008 global economic crisis led to a massive decline in exports (close to 20% in 2009) but China weathered the crisis through a staggering US$586-billion fiscal stimulus package (Economist, 2008). Much of the spending went on investments in infrastructure, which prevented massive unemployment, but also contributed to the overcapacity that would become a problem. While the share of SOEs continued to decline, the state kept control over key sectors, and procrastinated on SOE reform. Ironically, despite the attempt to

Table 3.5 China's development under Hu Jintao (2002–2012)

Indicator/Year	*2002*	*2004*	*2006*	*2008*	*2009*	*2010*	*2011*	*2012*
GDP growth (annual)	9.1%	10.1%	12.7%	9.6%	9.2%	10.6%	9.5%	7.8%
CO_2 emissions (metric tons per capita)	2.9	4.1	4.9	5.3	5.8	6.2	6.7	n/a
Domestic credit to private sector (% of GDP)	118.2%	119.5%	110.1%	102.8%	125.4%	127.6%	124.1%	130.0%
Debt-to-GDP*	~ 175%	170%	170%	170%	187%	192%	204%	215%
Gini coefficient**	0.479	0.472	0.487	0.491	0.490	0.481	0.477	0.474
Gross capital formation (% of GDP)	37.7%	43.0%	42.7%	43.7%	47.6%	47.3%	47.2%	47.3%
Corruption perception rank***	#59	#71	#70	#72	#79	#78	#75	#80

Source: World Bank, Development Indicators' database, 2016.

*Edwards, 2016 (data from Chinese Academy of Social Sciences, 2015).

**Gini coefficient refers to income inequality. It is an index between 0 (complete equality) and 1 (complete inequality); data courtesy of Han, Zhao & Zhang, 2016.

***Transparency International database, 2016. Higher numbers indicate more corruption.

relate more closely to the people, this period was accompanied by a significant increase in income inequality, corruption scandals and incidents of unrest (Wall Street Journal, 2012). Table 3.5 shows some of key characteristics of the period.

In terms of "going out", the 10th Five Year Plan (2001–2005) signalled the beginning of a new externally-oriented "expansion phase" of the Chinese economy (Naughton, 2007, p.105). While some have accused China of neo-colonialism, Vendryes (2012, p.5) argues that "going out" should be seen as a "simple and natural progression matching China's current stage of economic development". The 11th Five Year Plan (2006–2010), took advantage of "fire sale" opportunities in Western economies following the 2008 global financial crisis, and China more systematically targeted specific sectors (including resources, utilities, high technology, and high-end manufacturing). The objectives included: *natural resource-seeking* (particularly among SOEs); *market-seeking* (especially for private companies); and commercial technology, or *strategic asset-seeking* (Ramasamy, Yeung & Laforet, 2012). Export strengthening has also been part of the process (Dong & Guo, 2013; Zhang & Daly, 2011). Overall, the Hu-Wen era positioned China as a leading global player, symbolized with the 2008 Summer Olympics in Beijing, and the 2010 Expo in Shanghai.

A new reality under Xi Jinping: the "new normal" and becoming a three-legged economy

In 1981 China's Gini coefficient (a measure of income inequality) was 0.29 but it increased to 0.39 by the mid-1990s (Ray, 2002). When Xi Jinping took over as the fifth-generation paramount leader in 2012, a Gini coefficient of 0.47 and rampant corruption were eroding the legitimacy of the political system (Brown, 2016a). This called for a new style of leadership, which would improve legitimacy, and adjust China to a "new normal" involving lower percentage growth rates, less dependence on exports and investment spending and more emphasis on domestic consumer spending (Brown, 2016b).

In political terms, Xi Jinping brought political centralization and the emergence of a personality cult, which hasn't been seen since the Mao era (Naughton, 2015). In comparison with Deng Xiaoping, who never "officially" occupied any leading position in the Chinese political structure (Vogel, 2011), Xi not only became CCP secretary and president of the Peoples' Republic of China, but also the chairman of the military, national security and internet security commissions, as well as the chairman of the Central Leading Group for Comprehensively Deepening Reforms. This combination of Mao-style centralization of political power with a Deng-style focus on the deepening of economic reforms makes the fifth-generation leadership unlike the previous two (Brown, 2016b; Kroeber, 2016).

In economic matters, Xi first focused on China's transition towards more sustainable and inclusive growth (Naughton, 2015; Kroeber, 2016). The sustainability aspect related to China's extreme pollution and natural environment depletion, as well as the limitations of its energy and resource model. The inclusiveness aspect sought to address growing income inequality, close the gaping urban–rural divide and restrain corruption. The rhetoric of "comprehensive and deepening reforms" is reminiscent of the Deng era and has led some Western observers to label Xi as a "real reformer" (Naughton, 2015), or China's great "CEO" (Brown, 2016b). While Xi's extensive anti-corruption campaign (see Chapter 11) is focused on boosting the Party's legitimacy, it has costs and some analysts have estimated that it contributed to a decrease in GDP growth of between 1 and 1.5 percentage points (Sudworth, 2014).

The key distinguishing feature within Xi's early stage reform rhetoric was the emphasis on China transitioning towards a "three-legged economy", which would rely most on domestic consumption by "revving up the Chinese consumer" and leveraging the

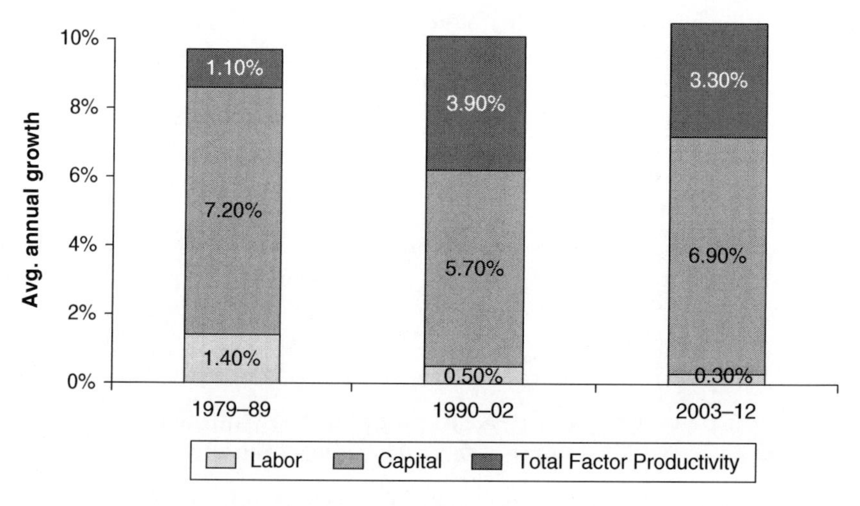

Figure 3.1a China's productivity breakdown between 1979 and 2012

Source: Purdy (2013).

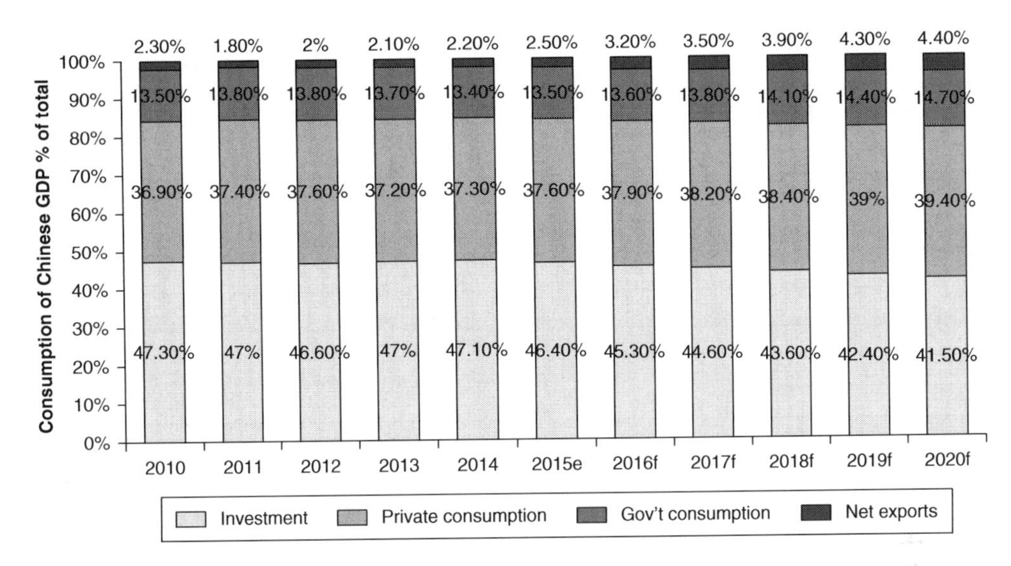

Figure 3.1b The sources of Chinese growth and the transition to a three-legged economy

Source: AT Kearney (2016).

Table 3.6 China's economic slowdown under the "new normal"

Indicator/Year	*2012*	*2013*	*2014*	*2015*
GDP growth (annual)	7.8%	7.7%	7.3%	6.9%
Exports as % of GDP	25.7%	24.8%	23.9%	22.4%
Manufacturing as % of GDP	31.0%	30.1%	> 30%	n/a
Gross capital formation as % of GDP	47.3%	47.7%	46.2%	> 46%
Investment as % of GDP*	46.4%	46.5%	45.9%	43.3%
Household final consumption expenditure as % of GDP	36.6%	36.2%	37.4%	n/a
Inflation (consumer prices, annual, %)	2.6%	2.6%	2.0%	1.4%

Source: World Bank, Development Indicators' database (2016).

* Economy watch (2016).

enormous urbanized middle class to become a middle-income society while avoiding the so-called middle-income trap. This new focus on domestic demand stemmed from China's over-reliance on exports and the negative spill-overs from the 2008 global economic and financial crisis, as well its exhaustion of surplus labour and reduced returns on fixed capital formation (Kroeber, 2016).

As Chapter 10 examines the Chinese consumer, it suffices here to point out that while consumer confidence and spending have remained strong, (McKinsey, 2016) there is little evidence yet of a major shift in the overall pattern of national expenditure, as a recent IMF review confirms (Zhang, 2016). As Figure 3.1a–b show, investment is predicted to still account for more than 40% of total spending in the year 2020.

The second stage of Xi's reforms, from 2014 to date, has clearly established that they are not merely rhetoric and seems to indicate a deeper and bolder approach. Naughton (2015) identifies three key features:

- Fiscal reforms focused on resolving the problem of growing local government debt.
- Rural land policy and agricultural rights reform, stipulating three types of agricultural land ownership (collective ownership, land contract rights from the 1980s reform, and more transferable land management rights) and creating "nationwide system of secure and transferable property rights in agricultural land" (*ibid.*, p. 5).
- Further trade reforms, including: Free Trade Agreements (FTAs) with Korea and Australia; the Hong Kong-Shanghai Stock Connect mechanisms for stock purchases; the launch of the Shanghai Free Trade Zone; commitments for deeper reform of SOEs and the financial system reform; and liberalization of the service sector.

Xi's initiative to renew the ancient Silk Road under his "One Belt One Road" project is also important. In the autumn of 2013, during a visit to Central Asia, he laid out a proposal for the new "Silk Road Economic Belt", which would be both the revival of China's ancient trade connection with Europe, and an upgrade of the 2001 Shanghai Cooperation Organization linking China with Russia and the Central Asian economies. A month later, the concept of the "21st Century Maritime Silk Road" was outlined during his tour of South-East Asia. These two ideas have converged into the "One Belt One Road" (*yi dai yi lu*) initiative launched in March 2015 with the so-called "OBOR" document. Based on a five-pillar approach of (1) policy coordination, (2) infrastructural connectivity by land and sea, (3) trade promotion, (4) financial cooperation, and (5) people-to-people dialogue, the OBOR initiative is aimed at significant infrastructural investment and extensive trade facilitation. The infrastructure investment would not only decrease transportation costs and time, but also help China to tackle its excess capacity in steel, cement and glass. The trade facilitation would not just improve market access, but would also help with the upgrading of China's value and production chain (moving Chinese-owned low

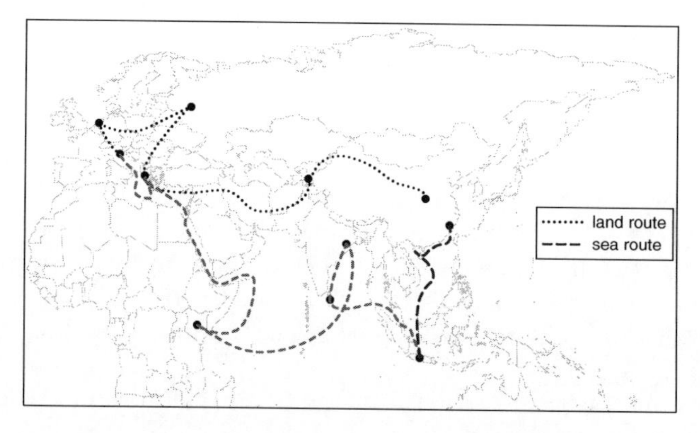

Figure 3.2 China's One Belt One Road (OBOR) initiative

Source: Own depiction, adapted from AmCham Shanghai (2015)

added-value manufacturing to other places) and the development of both investment and e-commerce. While OBOR remains to be operationalized and the appropriate mechanisms are not yet in place the establishment of the $US40-billion New Silk Road Fund in 2014 and the $US100-billion Asian Infrastructure and Investment Bank (AIIB) in 2015 suggest significant real commitment and a major extension of China's geo-political power.

In 2017 many of the trade and business reforms still remain to be seen. The 13th Five Year Plan (2016–2020) shows China's a commitment to tackle environmental issues, a greater focus on human capital (education, healthcare), innovation, financial reform and liberalization, in addition to SOE and military reform. All of those are to be based on principles of innovation, openness and coordination, as well as inclusiveness and sustainability, in order to help rejuvenate and revitalize China on its path towards a "moderately prosperous society", according to Xi (APCO, 2016).

Nevertheless, in an uncanny resemblance to aspects of both Mao and Deng, Xi's approach suggests a more centralized top-down approach with greater state control, but the lack of a unified blueprint, a focus on processes and institutions, the re-emergence of more particularized reform approaches and a new type of "going-out" strategy (Naughton, 2015). Through the latter, China seeks to climb along global value chains and address its excess capacity issues through a mixture of internal structural reforms and geo-politics.

References

AmCham Shanghai. (October 2015). *China's 'One Belt One Road' strategy*. Available at: http://insight.amcham-shanghai.org/chinas-one-belt-one-road-strategy/ [Accessed 15 May 2017].

APCO, 2016. *The 13th 5-year plan: Xi Jinping reiterates his vision for China*. Available at: http://www.apcoworldwide.com/docs/default-source/default-document-library/Thought-Leadership/13-five-year-plan-think-piece.pdf?sfvrsn=2 [Accessed 18 August 2016].

AT Kearney, 2016. *Prospects for achieving escape velocity: Global economic outlook 2016–2020*. Available at: https://www.atkearney.com/gbpc/thought-leadership/issue-deep-dives/detail/ /asset_publisher/qutCpQekuJU8/content/prospects-for-achieving-escape-velocity/10192 [Accessed 17 August 2016].

Bachman, D., 1986. Differing visions of China's post-Mao economy: The ideas of Chen Yun, Deng Xiaoping, and Zhao Ziyang. *Asian Survey*, 26 (3), pp.292–321.

Branstetter, L. G. and Feenstra, R. C., 2002. Trade and foreign direct investment in China: A political economy approach. *Journal of International Economics*, 58 (2), pp.335–358.

Brown, K., 2016a. A response to Francis Fukuyama's 'reflections on Chinese governance'. *Journal of Chinese Governance*, 1 (3), pp.392–404.

Brown, K., 2016b. *CEO China: The rise of Xi Jinping*. London: I.B. Tauris.

Chou, K-H., Chen, C-H. and Mai, C-C., 2011. The impact of third-country effects and economic integration on China's outward FDIs. *Economic Modelling*, 28, pp.2154–2163.

Chow, G. C. (2004). Economic growth and reform in China. *Annals of Economics and Finance*, 5, pp.127–152.

Dong, B. and Guo, G., 2013. A model of China's export strengthening outward FDI. *China Economic Review*, 27, pp.208–226.

Economist. (10 November 2008). China seeks stimulation: A $586 billion stimulus plan for China's economy. Available at: http://www.economist.com/node/12585407 [Accessed 13 August 2016].

Edwards, J., 2016. How China accumulated $28 trillion in debt in such a short time. *Business Insider*. Available at: http://uk.businessinsider.com/china-debt-to-gdp-statistics-2016-1 [Accessed 14 August 2016].

Gao, W., 2007. *Zhou Enlai: The last perfect revolutionary*. New York: Public Affairs.

Han, J., Zhao, Q. and Zhang, M. 2016. China's income inequality in the global context. *Perspective in Science*, 7, pp.24–29. Available at: http://dx.doi.org/10.1016/j.pisc.2015.11.006 [Accessed 31 January 2017].

Kroeber, R. A., 2016. *China's economy: What everybody needs to know*. New York, NY: Oxford University Press.

Leung, S., 1995. The implications of China's economic reforms for economic legislation, in Davies, H. (ed.), *China business: Context and issues*. Hong Kong: Longman Asia Ltd, pp.65–97.

Li, D., 2011. Prospects for the next 30 years, in Hudson, M. (ed.), *China in the next 30 years*. Beijing: Central Compilation & Translation Press, pp.30–36.

Li, Z., 2012. The Chinese economy: Transforming in development, in J. Wu & Y. Li (eds), *Economists' analysis of China's economic transformation*. Beijing: Foreign Languages Press, pp.11–17.

Luo, Y., Xue, Q. and Han, B., 2010. How emerging market governments promote outward FDI: Experience from China. *Journal of World Business*, 45 (1), pp.68–79.

Maddison, A., 2001. *Growth and interaction in the world economy: Roots of modernity*. Washington, DC: AEI Press.

Mason, D., 1984. China's four modernizations: Blueprint for development or prelude to turmoil? *Asian Affairs*, 11 (3), pp.47–70.

McKinsey., 2016. *2016 Chinese consumer report: The modernization of the Chinese consumer*. Shanghai: McKinsey & Co.

Narayanan, R., 2006. The politics of reform in China: Deng, Jiang and Hu. *Strategic Analysis*, 30 (2), pp.329–353.

Naughton, B., 2007. *The Chinese economy: Transitions and growth*. Cambridge, MA: MIT Press.

Naughton, B., 2009. *China: Economic transformation before and after 1989*. Paper presented at the conference on "1989: Twenty years after", 6–7 November 2009, University of California Irvine. Available at: http://www.democracy.uci.edu/files/docs/conferences/naughton.pdf [Accessed 11 August 2016].

Naughton, B., 2015. Is there a "Xi Model" of economic reform? Acceleration of economic reform since Fall 2014. *China Leadership Monitor*, 46, pp.1–14.

Pan, W., 2011. China in the next 30 years: A prospective future and possible pitfall, in Hudson, M. (ed.), *China in the next 30 years*. Beijing: Central Compilation & Translation Press, pp.38–47.

Purdy, M., 2013. *Chinese economy in six charts*. Harvard Business Review on-line. Available at: https://hbr.org/2013/11/chinas-economy-in-six-charts [Accessed 17 August 2016].

Ramasamy, B., Yeung, M. and Laforet, S., 2012. China's outward foreign direct investment: Location choice and firm ownership. *Journal of World Business*, 47, pp.17–25.

Ray, A., 2002. The Chinese economic miracle: Lessons to be learnt. *Economic and Political Weekly*, 37 (37), pp.3835–3837 and 3839–3848.

Sudworth, J., 2014. The real costs of China's anti-corruption crackdown. *BBC News*, 3 April. Available at: http://www.bbc.com/news/blogs-china-blog-26864134 [Accessed 1 March 2017].

Tisdell, C. A., 2009. Economic reform and openness in China: China's development policies in the last 30 years. *Economic Analysis & Policy*, 39 (2), pp.271–294.

Vendryes, T., 2012. The "going out" strategy: economic moves with political consequences, in *China analysis: Facing the risks of the going out strategy*. Paris: Asia Centre, pp.5–6.

Vogel, E. F., 2011. *Deng Xiaoping and the transformation of China*. Cambridge, MA: Belknap Press.

Wall Street Journal. (16 November 2012). Charting China's economy: 10 years under Hu. Available at: http://blogs.wsj.com/chinarealtime/2012/11/16/charting-chinas-economy-10-years-under-hu-jintao/ [Accessed 13 August 2016].

Wang, H., 2011. The characteristics, challenges and expectations of the "Chinese Models", in Hudson, M. (ed.), *China in the next 30 years*. Beijing: Central Compilation & Translation Press, pp.48–62.

World Bank., 2016. *World Bank open data: Development indicators*. Available at: http://data.worldbank.org/ [Accessed 31 January 2017].

Zhang, X. and Daly, K., 2011. The determinants of China's outward foreign direct investment. *Emerging Markets Review*, 12, pp.389–398.

Zhang, L., 2016. Re-balancing in China: Progress and prospects. *IMF Working Paper*, WP/16/183 Asia Pacific Department. Washington, DC: IMF.

Zhang, Z., Zhang, X. and Cui, R. (2013). Research on the effects of WTO accession on China's economic growth: Path analysis and empirical study. *Journal of Chinese Economic and Foreign Trade Studies*, 6 (2), pp.70–84.

Zhu, J., 2013. Chen Yun and Deng Xiaoping in the initial stage of reform and opening-up. Available at: http://www.cssn.cn/upload/2013/01/d20130111154110755.pdf [Accessed 25 August 2013].

4

CHINESE CULTURE, *GUANXI* AND THEIR CONSEQUENCES

Howard Davies

For "foreigners", engaging with Chinese people involves experiencing cultural differences that need to be understood. This chapter outlines how Chinese culture differs from others and how that affects behaviour. It then explains the cultural phenomenon of *guanxi* and its consequences.

Confucianism

Culture can be defined as "the way we do things around here", as "the collective programming of the mind, distinguishing the members of one group or category of people from another" (Hofstede, 1980) or as:

> patterned ways of thinking, feeling and reacting, acquired and transmitted mainly by symbols, constituting the distinctive achievement of human groups, including their embodiment in artefacts; the essential core of culture consists of traditional (i.e. historically derived and selected) ideas and especially their attached values.
>
> (Kluckhohn, 1961, p.89)

Cultures can be approached in several ways, the most direct being the "narrative", where each is described in its own idiosyncratic terms (Fisher, 1985). For China, the key narrative descriptor is "Confucian" (Liu, 2009), and it is important to understand the salient features of Confucian thought.

Confucius (*Kong Fu Zi* in Chinese) was a sage who was born in 551 BC in Qufu in Shandong province and died in 479 BC. While he is the key "moulder of the Chinese mind and character" (Bary, Chan & Watson, 1960, p.15) in his lifetime he was a failure who wandered across China with his followers, attempting to persuade rulers to adopt his prescriptions for government and private life, with little success. However, after his death, his followers organized his thinking into the *Analects of Confucius* and the "Five Classics" – the *Book of Change*, the *Book of Odes*, the *Book of Rites*, the *Book of History* and the *Spring and Autumn Annals*. Those form the foundation texts of the Confucian canon that have influenced Chinese thought and behaviour for more than two thousand years. Like all such texts there has been continuous debate and re-interpretation of their meaning but the key elements can be identified.

In the first place, Confucianism is not "religious" in that it is not concerned with God, with God's relationship to Man, or Man's duties to God. Nor is it concerned with an after-life. Confucius was firmly focused on life on earth, and with improving the governance of a country through a system of morals and behaviour, which should extend from a King downwards throughout society – and upwards from the family.

For Confucius, there was no need to invoke gods because he believed that the kings of the ancient Zhou dynasty (1046–771 BC) had found the proper way to conduct life. Hence, an important aspect of his teaching involved the re-imposition of their approach to social, ethical and political issues – seen as inseparable aspects of an integrated philosophy.

The central concept of Confucianism is *ren*, which translates partially into English as "benevolence", or "humanity" or "goodness". For the "gentleman" – the virtuous person to whom Confucius addresses himself in his writings – the cultivation of *ren* is the ultimate goal. However, *ren* is not simply an admirable personal objective but the key to good government, a stable society, and a happy family life.

For Confucius, the key lay in the insistence that the most effective and morally proper way to rule a kingdom and a family is through the virtuous behaviour of the superior person. He likens a ruler who governs through virtue to the North Star, which simply remains in place while the other stars turn towards it. However, while being virtuous required that a person should "not do to others what you would not wish to be done to yourself", which is the "Golden Rule" in many philosophies, Confucius introduced a "twist" to the interpretation of *ren* that is unfamiliar to Western minds. For him, being a "benevolent" and worthy person also involved "knowing one's place", being respectful and obedient to those to whom one is subordinate. The foremost example lies in the father–son relationship, where sons should display "filial piety" (*xiao*), to a degree that Westerners find ridiculous. Worthy Confucian sons should obey their fathers' every whim, however unreasonable (though it was permitted for them to "remonstrate"). On the death of a father, sons were expected to mourn for three years, and some were lionized as exemplary because they cut off pieces of their own flesh for their father to eat, or tasted their father's excrement in order to judge the extent of their illness.

This requirement for deference and obedience extended beyond the relationship between father and son to that between ruler and subject, to husband–wife relationships, and to siblings, where the younger son should obey the older. For Confucians, harmony in society is the highest objective and is to be found in this submission to hierarchy and the acceptance of what Westerners might interpret as sanctioned bullying (Parfitt, 2012). The obligations, however, are not simply one way – of inferior to superior – as the virtuous superior has an equally powerful requirement to take care of those subservient to him. An emperor who ensured that his people were fed, well governed and free from conflict would continue to hold the Mandate of Heaven (*tian ming*), legitimizing his position. On the other hand, the Mandate could be lost if the people were subject to famine, exploitative officials and civil war. In a similar way, husbands and older sons (and by extension CEOs and senior managers) are obliged to take care of those who obey them.

The other central tenet of Confucianism, is *li*, which translates as "proper conduct" but also means "adherence to the rites of propriety". As Liu (2009, p.42) puts it, "*ren* is the internal moral basis for the performance of *li*, while *li* is the external manifestation of *ren*." At one level, *li* refers to adherence to the rituals of the Zhou era, as a demonstration of commitment to the virtuous way. Hence, Confucius criticized the Ji family for having eight rows of dancers in their mansion as that was a number reserved for the King. If they could commit such an outrage, what would they not condone? The practice of *li*, however, extends beyond ritual and into moral norms that extend into every corner of society. Foremost amongst those, and the salient feature from a Western perspective, is the deference to superiors and paternalism towards subordinates already described. However, it also has other important implications. If a harmonious moral, social and political order is to be maintained through ritual and virtue, it is important to study them, and superiority is attained through learning, not through birth or wealth. Hence, the paramount importance attached to learning throughout Confucian societies. Hong Kong kindergarten students take bags of textbooks to school from the age of three. Chinese high school students study 70 hours per week for the dreaded *gao kao* university entrance examination. "Tiger Moms" take the view that A-minus is a poor grade (Chua, 2011). When Hong Kong Polytechnic University developed a thesis-based Doctor of Business Administration degree, it was described as the degree for the "scholar–leader", and students included the chairman of a mainland telecoms company having more than 200,000 employees, a Party leader of Shenzhen city and several other very senior businesspeople. It is difficult to imagine the CEOs of major Western companies signing up for Research Methods classes, or submitting to a final examination, but it sits well in a Confucian culture.

Of course, the wealthy have more opportunity to study than the poor, but in Confucian thinking it is the learning that bestows the virtue, and the right to wield power, not the wealth. As Confucianism became the state-sponsored philosophy, from the Sui dynasty onwards, the appointment of officials was determined by performance in a national examination, based on the Confucian classics, and meritocratic government by scholars, as opposed to the rule of law or "the rule of the people, by the people", was the ideal. Bell (2015) makes the case that the Chinese system today is a competitive meritocracy, having a greater claim on legitimacy than Western systems of "one man one vote" in which narrow-minded voters are seduced by the empty promises of narcissistic office-seekers.

The virtuous person of the Confucian ideal would be educated, modest and self-disciplined, deferential to those above him and authoritative but protective towards those below. This leads to behaviours that differ from those in Western cultures. The family is a much more powerful force in the life of most Chinese, compared with Anglo-American and Northern European cultures. Parents are treated with greater respect as they age, and expect to be taken care of by their children – a requirement that has been recently enshrined in Chinese law. In family-controlled companies the distinction between business and family is blurred. Senior members wield authority, not yielding it as they age. In 2008, for example, Hong Kong property developer Sun Hung Kei, controlled by the Kwok family, became embroiled in a quarrel between the brothers. The dispute was only resolved when 79-year-old matriarch Kwok Kwong Siu-hing replaced one of them with herself as Chairman.

The emphasis on the family also means that helping relatives is a powerful positive moral imperative, so that behaviours that would be considered nepotism in Western cultures – hiring relatives over better qualified outsiders, giving contracts to family-connected suppliers over better offers – are regarded as ethically good behaviour. While Confucian values are most obvious in the family setting, Cheung and Chan (2005) found that benevolence, harmony, humility, learning and loyalty were most salient in the leadership beliefs of Hong Kong CEOs.

These modes of thought have three other consequences. The first is that the emphasis on virtuous behaviour as the "right" way to organize society puts the enforcement of rules and laws in an ethically inferior position. As Confucius said,

> if you try to guide the common people with coercive regulations and keep them in line with punishments, the common people will become evasive and will have no sense of shame. If, however, you guide them with Virtue and keep them in line by means of ritual, the people will have a sense of shame and will rectify themselves.
> (Analects 2.3)

The rule of law is morally inferior to rule by virtue. The second consequence is that emphasis is placed upon social obligations, rather than individual rights. The third is that the emphasis on behaving properly is firmly set in the context of close personal ties and says little about behaviour towards those who are not involved in such relationships. Given the requirement to treat family members well and obey superiors, to treat more distant parties in the same way would not be *ren* or *li*. Hence, Chinese make sharper distinctions between "insiders" and "outsiders" than Westerners, and have less sense of civil, as opposed to familial, responsibility. (Chinese apartments are neat and clean inside but staircases and public spaces are often filthy. If the maintenance of such spaces is not covered by the service fee for the apartment block, it will not occur to anybody that they might tidy up the public approach to their private space.) The Chinese concept of self as "myself in relationship to others" is very different from the independent Western self of "me, myself, I" – to the point where some psychologists have argued that Chinese are actually different people when in different contexts (Nesbitt, 2003). The filial son is a different person from the authoritarian husband and deferential worker who inhabit the same body.

The narrative approach, then, describes a set of Confucian beliefs built around the value of harmony in hierarchy, which can be achieved through virtuous behaviour involving deference to superiors, care for the family, modesty, thrift and learning. In common with every great belief system it is honoured in the breach as much as in the observance, it has been put to ideological use by tyrants through the ages, and it is under pressure from modern life. For Mao Zedong, Confucius represented the "old China" that was to be destroyed, so that other countries, notably South Korea, are more "Confucian" today than China itself. Nevertheless, the way of looking at life that it represents is persistent and a basic knowledge of its precepts is a requirement for anyone who wishes to understand Chinese society and make sense of the behaviours encountered.

The comparative approach to culture: China's position on multiple dimensions

Describing Chinese culture in terms of Confucian influences provides important keys to understanding but the narrative approach does not allow systematic comparison across multiple cultures. An alternative is the "comparative" approach, where cultures are compared across a common set of dimensions. Two well-known frameworks for that analysis are Hall (1976) and Hofstede (1980), which together help to explain features of Chinese business behaviour that foreigners often find puzzling.

The difference between high- and low-context cultures

Sociologist E. T. Hall (1976) drew a distinction between "high context" and "low context" cultures, with countries occupying a continuum from very high to very low, with many placed in the intermediate range.

The most important difference between high- and low-context cultures lies in the nature of communication. In a low-context culture (Anglo-US, the Netherlands and Germany being the exemplars) the explicit content of the message – the words spoken, the wording of a contract, the definition of a set of standards – is the message. What you say is what you mean and it does not matter who you are or the context in which you say or write it. In a high-context culture (China, Japan and Korea being the exemplars) the explicit words spoken or written are less important. Meaning is carried by the social and power positions of the speaker and listener, non-verbal cues are more important than the actual words being spoken and speaker and listener share a common understanding that allows them to understand that which is *not* being said.

When the inhabitants of high- and low-context cultures try to communicate across the divide there will be misunderstandings. Low-context individuals mean what they say, no more and no less, but that may not be understood by high context individuals. High-context individuals pay less attention to the explicit but send implicit signals that the low-context individual will miss. Meyer (2014, pp.29–60) provides examples, noting that low-context individuals often perceive those from a high context as secretive, and poor at communication, while the high-context person will be irritated at the other's tendency to state the obvious and even patronize.

This distinction between high (China) and low (Anglo-US, Netherlands, Germany) context explains some important business misunderstandings. In a low-context culture a contract is a contract. Both parties are expected to carry out the letter of the agreement they made. But in a high-context culture, contracts are good faith statements of intent, subject to change if necessary. Chinese businesspeople are used to change; they expect the terms of a deal to change and can be offended if attempts to do so are interpreted as bad faith or breach of contract. Similar issues arise in respect of standards. In a low-context setting a standard is something to be met, as written. In a high-context setting a standard is an expectation to be met when the situation allows, but not a binding requirement.

This phenomenon is not solely attributable to the high/low-context difference, but also to the less developed Chinese legal system and the Confucian emphasis on harmony. Nevertheless, if low-context businessmen understand the nature of high context communication, they will be better equipped to understand what is happening and to develop appropriate responses.

Hofstede's dimensions

Hofstede (1980) surveyed 117,000 IBM employees in 40 different countries to identify four "dimensions" that together could be used to describe the variation in culture across nations.

The first of those dimensions, on which China occupies a relatively high position, is "power distance" defined as "the way in which power is distributed and the extent to which the less powerful accept that power is distributed". In high power distance cultures, people with less power expect to be told what to do, they do as they are told, and they are accepting of the power wielded over them. Clearly, high power distance is consistent with Confucianism. The consequences of high power distance range from strategy to human resource management. Rapid decision-making is easier when the boss can simply decree what is to be done, without consultation, and it will happen. Efficiency and flexibility are more easily achieved, and strategies built around cost reduction and the elimination of slack are culturally supported. At the same time (see Chapter 6), it is difficult to compete through innovation when workers and managers expect to be told what to do and not to debate alternatives. For the same reason, the practice of "empowering managers" to find their own way, often recommended in the West, may induce a negative response. When employees are used to being told what to do, if they are told to figure it out for themselves a natural response is that "this boss wants me to do something he does not know how to do himself". From the perspective of a Chinese boss, empowering subordinates can be seen as a violation of the natural order (Gallo, 2008, pp.99–106).

The second dimension that Hofstede (1980) identified is that which contrasts individualism and collectivism. In an individualistic culture a person's self-identity is based on their personal characteristics, whereas in a collectivist culture, self-identity is defined by the group to which the individual belongs. Again, the description of Confucianism makes it clear that Chinese culture is more collectivist than that of the West, and the difference manifests itself in several ways. When considering an action, Chinese will think in terms of the outcomes for their group, and their position in it. In an American classroom, or workplace, an open question to the room will elicit several "hands-up", eager to contribute their individual views. In a Chinese setting the result will be an embarrassed silence and close examination of the floor. Many Asian universities have installed raked, horseshoe-shaped lecture theatres on the American model, in the belief that direct sightlines of individual student to the teacher represent good practice. Lecturers then find that a huge proportion of the input they get from the room comes from international students or those who have studied abroad. However, put students into groups to discuss issues and raise questions and the outcome is very different. If responsibility is shared, individuals no longer feel exposed, lively debates ensue and groups can become as competitive with each other as individuals are in Western settings.

Differences in power distance and collectivism/individualism are the most salient of Hofstede's four original dimensions when considering differences between China and Anglo-US and Northern Europe. On the others the differences are less marked. A "Masculine" culture is one in which aggression, ambition and achievement are emphasized over the "Feminine" characteristics of nurturance and interpersonal harmony. It might be expected that Chinese culture would tend towards the feminine, given the Confucian emphasis on harmony. In fact, that is not the case and China's average score (66) is the same as that for Great Britain, and slightly higher than that for the US (62). Those scores contrast with the values for Denmark (16) Sweden (5) and Norway (8). The fourth dimension is "Uncertainty Avoidance", which refers to the extent to which a society tries to reduce uncertainty and promote stability, where China (30) is close to the UK (35) and US (46), around the middle of the scale.

These four dimensions complete Hofstede's original set, but a fifth was added later, originally titled "Confucian work dynamism" (Hofstede & Bond, 1988) and later re-named "long-term vs. short-term orientation". That reflects the values of thrift, perseverance, order and a sense of shame where, unsurprisingly, Confucian China scores very high (87) compared with the US (26) and UK (51).

Meyer's (2014) "culture map"

Meyer (2014) draws on Hall's and Hofstede's work to consider culture's practical implications for eight business activities: communicating; giving negative feedback; persuading; leading; deciding; trusting; disagreeing; and scheduling. China is one of 27 countries included in the analysis, but its specific implications for business in that nation can be highlighted

With respect to communicating, Meyer draws directly on the high- and low-context distinction. The practical recommendations for low-context individuals working with higher context colleagues are to recognize the differences, listen more carefully, paying attention to clues like body language and ask clarifying questions to determine what is meant as opposed to what is said. The judgment that higher context colleagues are being evasive, or are poor communicators, should be avoided. Maintaining a sense of humour, laughing at yourself, taking the blame for misunderstandings and describing the cultural differences in ways that are positive for the other culture, can all be helpful. Meyer (2014, pp.55–57) also recommends that in teams having members from both low- and high-context cultures, the appropriate strategy is to adopt low-context processes whereby the cultural differences are explained as a possible source of misunderstanding, and ground rules developed to ensure that at the end of meetings explicit, written, agreed recaps and summaries are provided. It may be necessary to explain to high-context individuals that putting everything in writing is not a manifestation of distrust, as they might interpret it, but a culturally appropriate procedure when low-context individuals are also involved.

The second management process in the Meyer (2014) analysis is the extent to which negative feedback is given directly or indirectly. China is towards the "indirect" end of the scale with the US, UK, Canada and Australia in the centre and Russia, Germany, Israel and the Netherlands at the "direct" end. As feedback is communication, China's high context and collective setting matters. Hence negative feedback is best given implicitly, softly and subtly. To criticize a subordinate in the presence of their peers is unacceptable, and negative feedback requires repeated low-key references in private, preferably accompanied by food and drink outside the work setting. It may be useful to praise those aspects of a colleague's work that are satisfactory, while omitting to mention those that are not. Provided the weak areas are salient, the message may be received without offence.

Similar issues arise in respect of persuasion, where Meyer draws on Nesbitt's (2003) work on the "Geography of Thought". A key theme, consistent with collectivism and the Confucian importance of position, is that Chinese think "holistically" while Westerners think "specifically". Chinese perceive situations in terms of a full description of the environment, the participants and their inter-relationships, whereas Westerners focus on what they perceive to be the key elements of the task on hand. As a result, it can be difficult to persuade Chinese to take a particular course of action if the reasoning is too specific. They will take the view that important inter-dependencies may be ignored. For the same reason, Chinese-led discussions of an issue can appear rambling and unfocused to those having a more specific mode of thought.

On leading, Meyer's analysis draws directly on Hofstede's power distance concept, where China scores at the high end of the scale. In low power distance cultures (the Netherlands, Australia) a "good leader" is an egalitarian who is "just one of the guys". He is referred to by his given name, behaves informally, does not wield power over subordinates and empowers them to make decisions and take actions without close oversight. However, as noted above, such an approach can be counter-productive in a high power distance culture, where leaders are expected to behave in a hierarchical way. The "good leader" acts as a strong director who knows what to do (in principle he will be better educated). He instructs subordinates, insists on hierarchy, and sets himself apart through the trappings of power – expensive car, a better office, and so on.

The consequences of hierarchical leadership are several. When meeting executives from other companies it is important to establish their positions in the hierarchy, and to accord due priority to the boss. "Level-hopping" is not acceptable, as a junior who takes issues to the senior of his senior is seen as disloyal to his immediate boss. A senior who asks for information directly from a junior more than one level below them is seen as exhibiting a lack of trust in the manager holding the intermediate position.

One of the most common sources of frustration for managers from more egalitarian and individualistic societies is the difficulty of eliciting honest opinions from subordinates who prefer hierarchy. If the most senior person in a meeting asks colleagues for their views, subordinates will not interpret that as a request for their input, but as a test to see if they understand how the boss himself is thinking. If they know his views they will espouse them, even if they disagree, and if they are not sure they will remain silent. Meyer (2014, p.140) suggests overcoming this by: having subordinates meet without the boss, after which they make an agreed group report; telling subordinates in advance of meetings what questions are going to be discussed, and explaining that they will be called upon; and not expecting participants to volunteer their views, but formally invite them to make their contributions.

Just as the Chinese preference for hierarchy has implications for leading, similarly for decision-styles, where Meyer (2014) contrasts "consensual" with "top-down". Consistent with high power distance, decisions in China are "top-down", often made by the boss, quickly and in advance of meetings supposed to discuss them. "Pushing back" is interpreted as disloyalty, and decisions must be followed even if they are not the best that might have been made. Bosses accustomed to more consensual decision-making processes need to be aware that to carry that style over into the Chinese context is to risk being seen as weak, indecisive and ineffective.

The sixth of Meyer's dimensions concerns the basis for trust in different cultures, where the contrast lies between "cognitive" trust based upon knowing that a person is capable of completing tasks effectively and with honesty and "affective" trust based on feelings of personal empathy and closeness. In the US, Denmark, Germany and the UK, trust in business is largely "cognitive" and built through business-related tasks. If I have done business with you and you proved reliable, I trust you. I do not need to see photographs of your family, sit around for hours together over lunch, or get drunk with you. In Chinese culture, by contrast, trust in business is built upon sharing personal time, exchanging personal details, eating and drinking (in the belief that alcohol will reveal the "real" you). If I have a good feeling for you as a person I will trust you, even if I have no experience of how you behave in business. In Confucian terms, if you are a "gentleman" (which never precluded occasional drunkeness!) I can trust you.

Clearly, these different bases for trust have implications for behaviour. Executives from "cognitive" task-based trust cultures tend to pay too little attention to the personal relationships they need to function effectively in China. From the Chinese perspective, they try to rush things, spend too much time on the details of the business and too little on the personal dynamics. Most important, they fail to appreciate the importance of *guanxi*, the personal networks of connections that make up one of the most important and characteristics aspects of day to day Chinese life.

Before turning to an analysis of the *guanxi* phenomenon, there are two more dimensions in Meyer's (2014) "culture map" that distinguish Chinese culture. The first concerns approaches to disagreement, while the other relates to the sense of time and scheduling.

Consistent with broader cultural norms, the acceptable approach to disagreement varies across nations. In countries where harmony is less valued, power distance is low and individualism is the norm, it is acceptable for disagreement to be openly confrontational. The belief is that energetic debate is positive and that personal relationships between the protagonists in a disagreement need not be damaged by their confrontation over issues. In China, on the other hand, there are important differences in the way disagreement is voiced within a group of insiders, compared with outsiders. Within the group, harmony is a high priority, everyone understands their place, and it is considered rude and inappropriate to be confrontational. Open disagreement is seen as damaging and has a negative impact on the personal relationship between the protagonists. However, the Chinese do make sharp distinctions between "insiders" and "outsiders" and those norms of behaviour only apply within the group with whom you have a relationship. Disagreement with outsiders is not subject to the constraining influence of hierarchy and harmony, and may be confrontational and hostile. (In queues, railway stations, and airports it is not uncommon to see Chinese people screaming at each other at the top of their voices.)

Meyer's final dimension concerns the perceived nature of time and its consequences. The conceptual basis is drawn from the work of the same E. T. Hall who proposed the high-context versus low-context distinction. According to Hall (1983) some cultures – Germany, the Netherlands, the UK and the US – see time as "monochronic". Time is a concrete "thing" to be used. Schedules are taken literally, so that interruptions are a nuisance, deadlines are important and lateness is unacceptable. Other cultures, by contrast, are "polychronic". Appointments are no more than a rough indication of when the meeting might take place, interruptions are accepted, and flexibility valued over discipline.

China's position on the scheduling scale is towards the "polychronic", although not in the relaxed fashion associated with cultures like India, Kenya, or Nigeria. In China, punctuality is a sign of respect and being late for a meeting demands an apology. However, perhaps because everything is in flux, Chinese businesspeople value flexibility over pre-planning and constantly juggle their schedules. Meyer (2014, p.237) quotes one of her interviewees, in a passage that rings very true.

> I've attended dozens of workshops in China, and not one has gone according to plan. Things change the night before: speakers, topics, even venues. But it all ends up working out. Once you understand that the Chinese are extremely flexible, everything works fine if you just do the same.

Guanxi: the one Chinese word every foreigner knows

The analysis thus far has taken a broad view of Chinese culture and identified some of its consequences for business behaviour. There is, however, one phenomenon that above all others is a defining and distinguishing characteristic of Chinese business life – *guanxi*.

The meaning of the Chinese word is close to "connections", and it may be defined as "the set of personal connections which an individual can draw upon to secure resources or advantage when doing business, or in the course of social life" (Davies, 1995, p.155). Such connections are a common feature of most societies. In Russia, a similar concept is known as "blat" (Ledeneva, 2008), while in the Arab world "wasta" also refers to interpersonal connections that can be used to access resources (Hutchings & Weir, 2006). However common it might be elsewhere, in China *guanxi* lies at the very heart of business and social life, as witness one exasperated American joint venture manager's explanation to an academic conference in Nanjing.

> To Chinese managers, *guanxi* is laden with powerful implications. To "*la guanxi*" (literally to "pull" *guanxi*) means to get on the good side of someone, to store political capital with them, and carries no negative overtones. To "*gua guanxi*" (literally to "work on" *guanxi*) means roughly the same but with a more general, less intense feeling and usually carries negative overtones. "*Mei you guanxi*" ("without" *guanxi*) has become an idiom meaning "it doesn't matter". "*Guanxi gao jiang*" (*guanxi* "made ruined") means the relationship has gone bad, usually because of a lack of flexibility of those involved. "*Lisun guanxi*" ("straighten out" *guanxi*) means to put a *guanxi* back into proper or normal order, often after a period of difficulty or awkwardness. "*You guanxi*" ("to have" *guanxi*), which is utterly unlike the American idiom "to have a relationship" means to have access to needed influence. "*Youde shi guanxi*" ("what one does have" or "the one thing one does have" is *guanxi*) is sometimes negative, meaning that one has all the *guanxi* one needs but something else essential is lacking. "*Guanxi wang*" (*guanxi* network) means the whole network of *guanxi* through which influence is brokered. "*Guanxi hu*" (*guanxi* "family") means a person, organization, even government department, occupying a focal point in one's *guanxi* network.
>
> *Guanxi* seems to be the lifeblood of the Chinese business community, extending into politics and society. Without *guanxi* one simply cannot get anything done. Or, what Western managers soon find, things can be done without *guanxi* if one invests enormous personal energy, is willing even to offend even close friends and trusted associates, and is prepared to see such Pyrrhic victories melt away like snow on a hot day while one is off on a business trip or home leave. On the other hand, with *guanxi* everything seems possible.
>
> (MacInnis, 1993, p.345)

Given its centrality to the Chinese business environment, *guanxi* has been well researched and Chao, Chen and Huang (2013) found more than 200 research papers dealing with the concept between 1990 and 2010. In order to understand its implications it is useful first to outline key characteristics of the phenomenon.

Key aspects of the guanxi *phenomenon*

First and foremost, *guanxi* is concerned with relationships between individual people – "personal" or "particularistic" ties. While such relationships may be useful for organizations, and the literature often refers to "organizational *guanxi*", the advantages and liabilities bestowed by *guanxi* reside in the individual. Working with others over an extended period of time can bring individuals together so that they become a *guanxi hu* as MacInnis described, and their collective *guanxi* can be used for the benefit of the organization they work in. However, should an individual leave, their connections go with them, to be used for the former organization only in the context of the leaver's personal relationships with the individuals who remain.

Second, not all relationships between individuals involve *guanxi* in the sense used here. Sociologists divide links between individuals or "ties" into three types (Davies, 1995). First, there are the ties between family and close friends, often referred to as "affective" or "expressive" ties. These ties are an end in themselves for the participants and exchange amongst them is based on need. If a family member needs something, others will give it, without thought of reward for themselves. At the other extreme there are purely "instrumental" ties where the participants are strangers, and their objectives are to gain extrinsic benefits. One-off buying and selling are the obvious examples where exchange is based on the calculation of mutual benefit. I buy water from the supermarket because I believe it is worth the price and the cashier sells it to me because they are employed to do so. We do not know each other and have no relationship beyond the immediate transaction. *Guanxi* is not important in the context of either of these kinds of relationship. However, between the extremes of the family (*jia ren*) and strangers (*sheng ren*) there are acquaintances (*shou ren*), with whom I have "mixed ties". These are the people who are outside my intimate circle but whom I "know" and with whom I will interact in future. I know that they will observe my behaviour and they will make judgments on how I interact with others. In this kind of relationship Confucian principles oblige those involved to show empathy, do favours for each other, help those in need and reciprocate favours. This is the setting in which *guanxi* is important.

As the nature of the "mixed" tie implies, membership of a *guanxi* network requires some kind of original "base" – a pre-existing commonality between the parties (Tsui & Farh, 1997). That may stem from a common birthplace, school, university, military unit or early working experience.

Guanxi involves reciprocal obligation (*bao*), such that if I do you a favour (*ren qing*) you know that you must reciprocate that favour at some future date. Failure to do so would prejudice your place in the network of connections, you would lose "face" (*mianzi*) and others would become less willing to interact with you in the future. For members of a network, their *guanxi* positions can be crudely likened to a set of accounts in which each member has a set of liabilities (the unmet obligations to others) and a set of assets (others' obligations to reciprocate). Network members expect to have their requests for favours from others granted, even if such favours do not adhere to the norms of efficiency or fairness, and they know that they will acquire a future obligation to help the favour-giver, or others nominated by that favour-giver.

Members of *guanxi* networks trust each other and prefer to deal with each other rather than with strangers. Hence, those who are able to join *guanxi* networks that include powerful and wealthy figures are in an advantageous position to access resources, information and position. The use of *guanxi*, however, extends throughout society and is not simply a matter for the rich elite. As MacInnis (1993) put it, without *guanxi* nothing gets done. With it, everything is possible.

Why is* guanxi *so important in China?

Two explanations offer themselves for the importance ascribed to *guanxi* in China, relative to Western societies. The first is to see it as the product of Chinese culture. Confucianism, high context, high power distance and collectivism together mandate a social and moral system where family and small group relationships take precedence over both the individual and society at large. Personal relationships, and harmony, are the basis of the social system and they are so important that *guanxi* are pursued for their own sake. This is a key point which is almost entirely missing from the Western narrative on the issue, because it means that developing and maintaining *guanxi* is a positive moral imperative – a far cry from the almost universal perception in the West that *guanxi* is a "bad thing" associated with corruption. Dedication and commitment to harmony in particularistic relationships is the hallmark of the "gentleman" of Confucian philosophy. The "civilized" Chinese person therefore pays considerable attention to cultivating their personal *guanxi* – giving small gifts, asking after network members' well-being, keeping in touch, responding to requests – for its own sake. Buying officials' favour with red packets stuffed with cash is not the exercise of *guanxi*.

The second explanation sees *guanxi* as a rational response to institutional weakness (Davies, 1995, pp.158–163). In every society, people fulfil specialized tasks and rely on exchanging their personal output with others, in order to acquire what they need. Mutually acceptable money is the most important institution supporting that exchange, so that a professor can give lectures and receive money to spend on whatever he needs. However, the existence of money is not sufficient for the support of exchange because a buyer might refuse to pay or a seller might fail to deliver. In the language of "transaction-cost economics" (Williamson, 1975) there is a threat of opportunism, whereby a transactor cheats by reneging on a deal, or by trying to re-negotiate the terms in their favour when the situation allows it. Hence, exchange needs to be supported by a legal system that establishes protection for property and provides for the enforcement of contracts. China, however, has never had an effective legal system in that sense. Under the Confucian emperors, laws were seen as an inferior substitute for virtue, and the courts were both venal and ready to apply torture in order to determine "the truth". Wherever possible they were avoided. In the Mao era, as in Marxist theory, the law was seen as an instrument of oppression used by capitalists in the class struggle. The legal profession ceased to exist and was replaced by People's Courts, headed by those having "good" proletarian backgrounds and political reliability. Contract law did not exist, being unnecessary in a command economy where all transactions were co-ordinated by the state.

If law-based mechanisms for the support of transactions are not in place, there is little sense of civil responsibility, and no trust in outsiders, how can exchange take place? Minor, one-off spot transactions, are possible, because if the butcher sells me bad meat I can go to a competing butcher and tell my friends about the cheat, thereby costing him future business. That threat acts as a disciplinary mechanism. However, if there is uncertainty about what is being transacted (milk formula for babies sold in 2012 contained poisonous melamine, but mothers could not know that when they bought it), or if there is no competition, or if either side in a transaction cannot go to another partner because they have committed resources to transacting with the specific other partner involved (asset-specificity) it is very risky to deal with someone you do not personally trust.

Hence, *guanxi* provides an alternative mechanism for the support of transactions. In the absence of reliable legal institutions, rational actors will only be prepared to make significant transactions with those they trust. *Guanxi* networks, where people deal with each other over long periods of time, where each person's behaviour is monitored by others, and where harmony and reciprocity are norms, are what Williamson (1991, p.238) referred to as "relational contracting". That is a form of transacting which amounts to "a mini-society with a vast array of norms beyond those centred on the exchange and its immediate processes". From that perspective, *guanxi* is an institution that has evolved to support transactions between individuals who are not part of the same family. It provides a substitute for governance through the legal system.

The "cultural" and "governance" explanations for the importance of *guanxi* are not mutually exclusive, but their relative importance has implications for predictions about the future of the phenomenon, as examined below.

The impact of guanxi *on business performance*

While *guanxi* is fundamentally about relationships amongst individuals (Chai & Ree, 2010), business in China is embedded within those relationships, which may be used on behalf of the organizations for whom the individuals work. However, the impact of *guanxi* on organizational performance has been the subject of contradictory arguments. On the positive side, Luo, Huang and Wang (2012, p.140) describe *guanxi* as "a pervasive relationship lubricant that helps to increase the efficiency and effectiveness of daily business operations". Davies, Leung, Luk and Wong (1995) found that Hong Kong executives valued their Chinese connections as ways to acquire information and resources, and to "smooth transactions". Standifird and Marshall (2000) also emphasized the transaction cost advantages, while others see *guanxi* as "social capital" that gives privileged access to knowledge, opportunities and reputation (Inkpen & Tsang, 2005). Peng and Luo (2000) argued that managers who have personal ties with suppliers are able to secure superior products, that ties with buyers improve customer satisfaction and loyalty and ties with competitors ease collusion. Those arguments suggest a generally positive relationship between the extent and quality of a company's *guanxi* and its performance.

On the other hand, there are potentially negative aspects to the development and use of *guanxi* networks. Most obviously, maintaining personal relationships can absorb managerial time, distracting executives from setting strategy, raising revenues and reducing costs. As every favour done requires a favour in return, those involve additional costs (Chen, Chen & Xin, 2004) and companies may find themselves in a position where they are obliged (for instance) to accept sub-standard components from a supplier to whom they owe a favour (Tsang, 1998). If companies restrict their dealings to others within their employees' *guanxi* networks they may incur higher costs for inputs than necessary. Failure of one firm in a network may lead to "domino" effects on others (Uzzi, 1997) and closed network relationships could lead to collective blindness about major market trends (Gu, Hung & Tse, 2008). As ties with government can be associated with corruption (Guo & Miller, 2010) their use could incur investigation and punishment.

On balance, then, it is not clear whether more extensive membership and usage of *guanxi* networks will have a positive or negative impact on organizational performance. Given that indeterminacy, more than 50 empirical studies have attempted to resolve the issue, reviewed by Luo, Huang and Wang (2012). That leads to a number of conclusions. First, it is useful to make a distinction between *guanxi* involving business-to-business ties, which are horizontal (between peers), and *guanxi* involving business to government officials, which are vertical (between authority and subordinates). The overall results suggest that more extensive use of both types of *guanxi* has positive links with two aspects of organizational performance. The first of these is "economic performance" defined in terms of financial returns, and the second is "operational performance", which refers to a broader range of measures including customer satisfaction and loyalty, new product innovations and productivity and marketing effectiveness. The results further suggest that ties with other businesses have a greater impact on operational performance than on economic performance, while ties with government have a larger effect on economic returns than on operational performance.

These results need to be interpreted with caution because the individual studies on which they are based share methodological problems like a lack of statistical power, doubtful measurement techniques and common method issues. As Peng and Luo (2000) also point out, statistical links do not prove causality and it is possible that good performance "causes" higher levels of *guanxi* as successful firms are more attractive to network participants. On balance, however, the research results do suggest that in the Chinese environment *guanxi* does have a positive effect on organizational performance.

How can foreign firms address the issues raised by guanxi?

If *guanxi* is an important determinant of business success in China, questions arise with respect to how foreign firms should behave in order to secure its advantages. The obvious recommendation is that they should develop their own *guanxi* (Collins & Block, 2007, pp.277–288). However, as the connections involved are particularistic, not corporate, and as they involve the reciprocation of personal favours over time, there are limits on the extent to which that is possible for foreigners. Those who are in China on a short-term basis and who cannot speak the language should probably give up the attempt. Two other approaches suggest themselves. The first is to recognize the ways in which *guanxi* affects business behaviour, and to respond appropriately, without attempting (inevitably inauthentically) to "become Chinese". In negotiations, it is common for Westerners to feel that they are unnecessarily long drawn-out, and that time is "wasted" in eating, drinking and socializing. But in the *guanxi* context the time is not wasted as Chinese counterparts are trying to understand the personal character of their possible future partner. They may also be trying to decide how the business proposals affect the individuals' wider *guanxi* networks. Their thinking may be going beyond the interests of the company they represent, so that the real decision-maker is the network as a whole (Davies, 1995, p.158). Making the necessary investment in time will not admit a foreigner to the Chinese' *guanxi* networks, with all the assets and liabilities that entails, but it will do a good deal to bridge the cultural gap. In the context of on-going business relations, the *guanxi* environment places a premium on flexibility, so that (reasonable) changes to agreements should be acceded to, as the long-term relationship is more important than the immediate transaction. Even if a foreigner cannot truly develop *guanxi*, there is value in spending time and behaving in a way that shows respect to traditions of harmony. Exchanging and receiving (small) gifts, and recognizing that business in China is a personal matter, can lubricate the business process.

The other approach to navigating the *guanxi* environment is to acquire connections from Chinese nationals, by employing them, or hiring them as intermediaries. With respect to employees, Tsang (1998) suggested that companies should carry out "*guanxi* audits" in order to evaluate their connections. As major Chinese companies began listing on foreign stock exchanges, investment banks hired the "princeling" offspring of senior government and Party officials in the hope of securing state-related business through their *guanxi*. However, while it may have been effective in the earlier stages, that tactic has backfired as the US Securities and Exchange Commission investigates the possible conflicts of interest involved.

Given the difficulties associated with acquiring *guanxi* through hiring employees, the most practical approach for foreign firms is to work through an intermediary. At one time, five-star hotel lobbies in China were populated with shady characters proffering *guanxi* for sale to gullible foreigners. More recently, however, the market for intermediation has matured. China has many branches of the world's largest companies in accounting, law and management consultancy, and they are able to help. Boutique consultancies are also common, dealing with specific industries, sectors or nationalities. Choosing an appropriate intermediary requires as much due diligence as the selection of any key service provider, but fellow countrymen and organizations like the national Chambers of Commerce in China provide effective sources of information on which of the consultancy companies have the individuals needed for a particular situation.

Is guanxi *declining in importance?*

In 1998 Guthrie wrote a much-cited article arguing that *guanxi* would decline in importance as China's transition to a market economy continued. On the other hand, it is still a salient feature of the Chinese environment, and Yang (2002) argued that it retains its importance by evolving.

This debate over the future of *guanxi* can be linked to the alternative explanations for its importance. If *guanxi* is important because it supports transactions in the absence of a law-based system, and if a law-based system is being introduced in China, then the use of *guanxi* will decline. On the other hand, if *guanxi* is important because it is a reflection of Chinese culture, and if culture remains relatively stable, *guanxi* will remain important.

Distinguishing between these alternatives is difficult. Taking the efficiency argument first, China's economic reforms have involved significant institution-building and market mechanisms play a much larger role than in the past (Lardy, 2014). That suggests that *guanxi* is being superseded. For example, Chinese people still have very low trust in strangers, which is a key reason for them relying on *guanxi*, and it might be expected that e-commerce would be a failure, because it relies on individuals having confidence in vendors they do not know. In fact, it has been overwhelmingly successful as companies like Alibaba find institutional ways to promote confidence, like escrow accounts that keep buyers' payments secure until they receive the goods they have paid for. These developments would suggest that *guanxi* is becoming less important as formal market institutions develop.

On the other hand, it may be myopic to assume that law-based governance mechanisms are always more efficient, so that they will "crowd-out" less formal systems. *Guanxi* may have some efficiency advantages, especially in respect of adjusting to unforeseen circumstances. America's law-based society is notoriously litigious, and the costs of running the legal system are not trivial. If *guanxi* provides a flexible means by which parties to transactions can accommodate to unforeseen changes, without recourse to law, that may ensure its longevity.

With respect to the argument that *guanxi* is the outcome of Chinese culture, the key issue is the extent to which that culture is changing. The evidence is limited, but there is no compelling reason to believe that Chinese culture has converged on Western nations in respect of its high context, high power distance, collectivist and Confucian nature. When it is recognized that in China, *guanxi* is valued as an end in itself, as an expression of humanness, and not simply for its practical value, then it seems likely that the phenomenon will persist.

A cautionary note on culture

This chapter has described key characteristics of Chinese culture, and their implications for the way business is done in China. However, having emphasized country-level characteristics, it is important to recognize that it would be a mistake to act as if every Chinese person will conform to the stereotype derived from those descriptions. Within any population, there is significant variation across individuals, and in a population as large and heterogeneous as China's there are sub-groups who differ from each other. Individuals are individuals, to be treated as such, and the characteristics of the nations they inhabit are best treated as a part of their background, rather than a possibly unhelpful stereotype.

References

Bary, W., Chan, W-T. and Watson, B., 1960. *Sources of Chinese tradition*. New York: Columbia University Press.

Bell, D., 2015. *The China model: Political meritocracy and the limits of democracy*. Princeton, NJ: Princeton University Press.

Chai, S. and Rhee, M., 2010. Confucian capitalism and the paradox of closure and structural holes in East Asian firms. *Management and Organization Review*, 6 (1), pp.5–29.

Chao, C., Chen, X. and Huang, S., 2013. Chinese *guanxi*: An integrative review and new directions for future research. *Management and Organization Review*, 9 (1), pp.167–207.

Chen, C., Chen, Y. and Xin, K., 2004. *Guanxi* practices and trust in management: A procedural justice perspective. *Organization Science*, 15 (2), pp.200–209.

Cheung, C. and Chan, A. C., 2005. Philosophical foundations of eminent Hong Kong Chinese CEOs' leadership. *Journal of Business Ethics*, 60, pp. 47–62.

Chua, A., 2011. *Battle hymn of the tiger mother*, New York: Penguin.

Collins, R. and Block, C., 2007. *Doing business in China for dummies*. New York: Wiley.

Davies, H., 1995. 'Interpreting *guanxi*: The role of personal connections in a high context transitional economy', in Davies, H. (ed.) *China business: Context and issues*. Hong Kong: Longman Asia, pp.155–169.

Davies, H., Leung, T., Luk, S. and Wong, Y-H., 1995. The benefits of '*guanxi*': The value of relationships in developing the Chinese market. *Industrial Marketing Management*, 24 (3), pp.207–214.

Fisher, W.R., 1985. The narrative paradigm: An elaboration, *Communication Monographs*, 52, pp.347–367.

Gallo, F., 2008. *Business leadership in China: How to blend best Western practices with Chinese wisdom*. Singapore: John Wiley.

Gu, F., Hung, K. and Tse, D., 2008. When does *guanxi* matter? Issues of capitalization and its dark sides. *Journal of Marketing*, 72, July, pp.12–28.

Guo, C. and Miller, J., 2010. *Guanxi* dynamics and entrepreneurial firm creation and development in China. *Management and Organization Review*, 6(2), pp.267–291.

Guthrie, D., 1998. The declining significance of *guanxi* in China's economic transition. *China Quarterly*, 154, pp.254–282.

Hall, E. T., 1976. *Beyond culture*. New York: Doubleday.

Hall, E. T., 1983. *The dance of life: The other dimension of time*. New York: Anchor Books.

Hofstede, G., 1980. *Culture's consequences: International differences in work related values*. Beverly Hills, CA: Sage.

Hofstede, G. and Bond, M., 1988. Confucius and economic growth: New trends in culture's consequences. *Organizational Dynamics*, 16 (4), pp.4–21.

Hutchings, K. and Weir, D., 2006. Understanding networking in China and the Arab world – lessons for international managers. *Journal of European Industrial Training*, 30 (4), pp.272–290.

Inkpen, A. and Tsang, E., 2005. Social capital, networks and knowledge transfer. *Academy of Management Review*, 30 (1), pp.146–165.

Kluckhohn, C., 1961. 'Universal categories of culture', in Moore, F.W. (ed.), *Readings in cross-cultural methodology*. Cambridge, MA: Harvard University Press, pp.89–105.

Lardy, N., 2014. *Markets over Mao: The rise of private business in China*. Washington, DC: Peterson Institute for International Economics.

Ledeneva, A., 2008. Blat and *guanxi*: Informal practices in Russia and China. *Comparative Studies in Society and History*, 50 (1), pp.118–144.

Liu, H., 2009. *Chinese business: Landscapes and strategies*. London: Routledge.

Luo, Y., Huang, Y. and Wang, S., 2012. *Guanxi* and organizational performance: A meta-analysis. *Management and Organization Review*, 8(2) pp.139–172.

MacInnis, P., 1993. *Guanxi* or contract: A way to understand and predict conflict between Chinese and Western senior managers in China-based joint ventures, in McCarty, D. and Hille, S. (eds), *Research on multinational business management and internationalisation of Chinese enterprises*. Nanjing: Nanjing University, pp.345–351.

Meyer, E., 2014. *The culture map*. New York: Public Affairs.

Nesbitt, R., 2003. *The geography of thought*. New York: Free Press.

Parfitt, T., 2012. *Why China will never rule the world*. St John, NB: Western Hemisphere Press.

Peng, M. and Luo, Y., 2000. Managerial ties and organizational performance in a transition economy: The nature of a micro-macro link. *Academy of Management Journal*, 43 (3) pp.486–501.

Standifird, S. and Marshall, R., 2000. The transaction cost advantage of *guanxi*-based business practice. *Journal of World Business*, 35 (1), pp.21–42.

Tsang, E., 1998. Can *guanxi* be a source of sustained competitive advantage for doing business in China? *Academy of Management Executive*, 12 (2), pp.64–72.

Tsui, A. and Farh, J-L., 1997. Where *guanxi* matters: Relational demography and *guanxi* in the Chinese context. *Work and Occupations*, 24 (1), pp.56–79.

Uzzi, B., 1997. Social structure and competition in interfirm networks: The paradox of embeddedness. *Administrative Science Quarterly*, 42 (1), pp.35–67.

Williamson, O., 1975. *Markets and hierarchies: Analysis and antitrust implications: A study in the economics of internal organization*. New York: The Free Press.

Williamson, O., 1991. Comparative economic organization: The analysis if discrete structural alternatives. *Administrative Science Quarterly*, 36, pp.269–296.

Yang, M., 2002. The resilience of *guanxi* and its new deployments: A critique of some new *guanxi* scholarship. *China Quarterly*, 170, pp.459–476.

5

ENTERPRISE REFORM AND CHINESE FIRMS TODAY

Howard Davies

Alternative perspectives on the Chinese firm

Chinese firms feature in very different descriptions of the country's situation. In one of those, the economy is dominated by bloated state-owned enterprises (SOEs) that lose money and resist reform, kept alive by generous support from government. A second perspective sees SOEs as increasingly marginalized in an economy where private companies have become dominant, while a third sees SOEs as flag-bearers for a "state capitalism" that is producing globally competitive corporations, serving the interests of the Chinese state.

There is truth in each of those descriptions. The leadership is open about the problems created by some SOEs. But the country has seen a massive process of "privatization", and Lardy (2014) shows that the private sector has been responsible for most of the growth in output, employment and productivity since 1978. At the same time, the leadership has been priming some SOEs (and some private firms) to be the "tip of the spear" for improved Chinese competitiveness on world markets.

This chapter tries to make sense of this complexity by explaining enterprise reform, and the roles, attributes and performance of different types of Chinese firm in the twenty-first century.

How many firms in China, and of what type?

According to the *China Statistical Yearbook for 2015* (Tables 1–8), the country had 10.6 million "corporate enterprises" in 2014, of which 7.26 million were "private", 1.84 million were "limited liability", 147,251 were "collectives", 145,986 were "shareholding" companies, 130,216 were "state-owned", 119,878 were "foreign-invested" enterprises, 112,076 were "Hong Kong, Macau and Taiwan" firms, 69,767 were "co-operatives" and 21,402 were "joint ventures".

On the other hand, the Chief Economist of the Ministry of Agriculture estimated that in 2003, in the countryside alone, there were 21.9 million "township and village enterprises" (TVEs), employing 137.5 million people and the number was growing rapidly (Liang, 2006).

Confusion about the number of Chinese firms and their types stems from a number of sources. First, the statistical system is underdeveloped. Data collection in the countryside is the responsibility of the Ministry of Agriculture while data for urban settings come from other authorities. The two systems are not integrated, although boundaries between town and countryside are increasingly blurred. Secondly, "enterprises" are categorized in different ways in different reports, definitions change, and some statistics apply only to "above scale" enterprises above a certain size. Thirdly, change has been too rapid for the data to keep up.

Unravelling these complexities to arrive at a definitive number of Chinese firms, divided into meaningful categories, would be a thankless task. It would also miss a key point, which is that firms with the same formal status may differ significantly, and have more in common with firms in other categories. It is more useful, therefore, to understand the process of "enterprise reform".

The "firm" in the command economy

In the command economy, there were no "firms" in the sense of a legal entity, separate from the state, owned by its proprietors, which could decide for itself what to produce, how to produce it, and who to sell it to. The economy was essentially one huge set of transactions coordinated by the authorities, or a single firm with thousands of departments.

With so many departments, those in charge faced a problem of control. In theory, commands could come from the top, with lower level units disaggregating them and passing them downwards while aggregating information and passing it upwards. However, when local officials are self-interested, and better informed of local conditions, they will distort information and hide resources (Milgrom & Roberts, 1992). They could be monitored, but collusion between monitors and monitored would inevitably result. Hence, those at the top have to provide incentives to those lower down to behave properly. That requires four conditions (Davies, 1995, p.138). It should be possible to attribute performance at lower levels to those responsible, and to reward or punish them. There should be boundaries between units, and units should have some autonomy. With those conditions, planners can divide the economy into units, set targets for them, and monitor those targets, without managing the details.

The command economy was, therefore, divided into "units" (*danwei*) or "enterprises". Ownership was vested in "the people" and funds provided by the state. There was no competition for customers, supplies or workers. The explicit objective for each *danwei* was to meet the targets set, while the implicit objective for managers was to develop *guanxi* with the authorities in order to secure more resources and easier targets. Costs, revenues and profits were unimportant, and budget constraints were "soft", meaning that losses were of no concern as a *danwei* could not go bankrupt. Marketing activities were unnecessary as outputs were allocated to users by the plan.

This system helped with the monitoring problem, but provided no incentive to use resources efficiently, meet users' needs, or innovate. There was no concern for costs or quality, the "iron rice bowl" (*tie fan wan*) meant that shirkers could not be dismissed and the system failed to improve living standards. Hence in 1978, the process of reform began in earnest. It has had four components. The first was the introduction of new forms of enterprise in the countryside, the second was the reform of the state enterprises, the third was the rapid expansion of the private sector and the fourth concerned the role of "foreign-invested enterprises".

Township and village enterprises: privatization in the countryside

As China was still a rural society in 1978, the starting point had to come from the countryside. When the "household responsibility system" increased farm production dramatically, surpluses increased and millions of workers became available for redeployment to other activities. That provided the resources for the first round of rural industrialization, which took shape through "township and village enterprises" (TVEs or *xiang zhen qi ye*).

The term "TVE" is usually used to mean any kind of non-farm enterprise in the countryside (Huang, 2008, pp.75–76). However, in the earliest years of the reform era ideological suspicion of private business meant that most were classified as "collective" enterprises under the control of local governments and some observers (Kung & Lin, 2007, for instance) use the term "TVE" in a narrower sense, to mean collectively held non-farm firms in the countryside.

The belief that the TVEs were genuinely under public ownership led to a lively debate on how "the leading force of China's departure from central planning came from market-oriented public enterprises under the purview of local governments" (Kung & Lin, 2007, p.569). Western economic orthodoxy held that collectively owned firms, with ill-defined property rights, soft budget constraints and a lack of owners' incentives, could not be effective vehicles for economic growth and development (Naughton, 2007) leaving an apparent paradox to be explained.

Two answers are possible. First, within the conventional analysis (Davies, 1995, p.146) it can be argued that collective TVEs did yield tangible benefits to "the people around here" as opposed to distant Beijing, which gave them incentives. Managers were held accountable by local governments, which were not squeamish about dismissing them, their budget constraints were "semi-hard" as governments would not finance losses for long periods of time, there was significant competition and wages were much more flexible than in the state sector, which allowed them to recruit talent.

More fundamentally, however, Huang (2008) argues that many of the TVEs, even in the early stages, were not really public enterprises at all. They were openly private and recognized as such by the authorities. By 1996 there were 23.4 million TVEs, 19.6 million of which were family "household businesses", 2.26 million "private run" and just 1.55 million "collective" (Huang, 2008, p.79). The collectives were larger and accounted for 71.4% of TVE employment in 2002, but they were growing more slowly than the private and household firms.

The extent to which the early TVEs were really under local state control, as opposed to "putting on the red hat" and registering as a collective while carrying on private business, is unknowable, and varied from place to place (Unger & Chan, 1999). In some areas, officials did steer economic development through public ownership, and local governments became conglomerates, shifting resources between their collectively owned enterprises in a strategic fashion (Oi, 1992). In others, most famously Wenzhou in Zhejiang, TVEs were almost entirely private from the outset, while in the provinces close to Hong Kong, investors from that city and Taiwan set up the vast majority, which were private "foreign-invested enterprises" (FIEs) rather than public sector TVEs.

This hotchpotch of arrangements supported rapid rural industrialization and the period from 1978 to 1993 was a "golden era" for the collective TVEs. They had political legitimacy at a time when reforms might have been rolled back. Pent up demand provided opportunities for profit, but massive entry into rural industries created competition which forced them to be more efficient than the SOEs. As they focused on revenue growth and job creation (Jin & Qian, 1998), which were national priorities, they were also supported by loans from the state banking system.

However, those circumstances changed. First, the emphasis on revenues squeezed profits, which were necessary for expansion. As they grew into multi-business units, their managers faced increasing stress but their benefits were limited by egalitarian norms and they had no rights to the residual surpluses, which led to shirking and embezzlement (Kung & Lin, 2007, p.574). As a result, they were often technologically backward, they lacked brands, and had little of the expertise needed to participate in a globalizing economy.

Policy changes were also making life more difficult. Central policymakers believed that collective TVEs should focus on supporting agriculture, staying away from other sectors. Bank lending was drastically limited and the policy of "grasping the big and letting go of the small" (*zhua da fang xiao*), implied that TVEs – which were all "small" in that context – should be "let go" by the state.

As a result, the collective TVEs were partly closed and partly privatized. Brandt, Li and Roberts (2005) found that between 1993 and 1998 34.2% of the TVEs in Jiangsu and Zhejiang (rich coastal provinces where collective TVEs had been numerous) had been privatized and 15.4% closed down. Huang (2008, p.131) argues that TVE privatization dated back to the 1980s, especially in the poorer provinces, but there is agreement that by the beginning of the twenty-first century, both farm and non-farm enterprises in rural China had become almost entirely private.

The private nature of TVEs does not mean that they have no links to the party-state. In the privatization process, local governments sold their enterprises to individuals, and many of those were local officials, or their family and friends. Hence, networks of personal *guanxi* connections link the public and private sectors through officials and entrepreneurs who have a foot, or relatives, in both camps. Local governments provide infrastructure and finance, so that sensible private entrepreneurs take care to comply with their requests. Indeed, Xin and Pearce (1996) found that private entrepreneurs made more use of *guanxi* connections with government than did managers in state-owned enterprises (SOEs), because, being outside the state system, they had more need of the informal approach. That is less true today than in the mid-1990s, but the Chinese party-state is still everywhere.

The state-owned enterprise: zombie, national champion or what?

Given that the economy was almost entirely stated-owned less than 40 years ago, and the rhetoric of "socialism with Chinese characteristics" persists, it is not surprising that observers often have the impression that state-owned enterprises (SOEs) remain dominant. That is reinforced by two apparently contradictory strands of commentary. The first sees SOEs as the key barrier to national progress, being inefficient and unprofitable "zombies" that are kept alive by their political connections. The second sees SOEs as the foundation for a type of "state capitalism" where the authorities develop them into "national champions" that can dominate domestic and some global markets. Understanding the process of state enterprise reform, and the nature of the relationship between the central and lower level authorities, helps to explain why both views contain elements of truth.

In the early years of reform, SOEs were given additional autonomy. Under the "contract responsibility" and dual-track pricing systems (Wu & Zhao, 1987) they were still required to deliver quotas to the state at administrative prices, but they were allowed to produce additional outputs and sell them at market prices. Despite those freedoms, SOEs did not see increasing profits in the early years because rising farm prices increased their costs, they were responsible for increasing welfare payments for workers and retirees, and they became subject to competition from the more nimble TVEs. At the same time, they significantly increased their labour forces, the authorities holding them responsible for supporting urban employment. As Duckett (2001) describes in Tianjin, local governments encouraged their departments to set up new businesses, some related to their old functions – public property departments went into real estate – and many not. Most of those new businesses were entrepreneurial, rather than rent-seeking, and local governments were establishing restaurants, department stores and a host of service sector enterprises, not usually associated with officialdom.

These developments meant that the SOEs prevented unemployment but presented an increasing financial problem. They had been financed through soft loans and by 1994 profits were less than half the amount needed just to pay the interest (Lardy, 2014, p.45). The banks were making further loans for the SOEs to pay the interest on existing debts, with no prospect of the principals being repaid.

This led to one of the most important initiatives in the history of reform (Qian & Wu, 2003). In 1993 the 14th Party Congress supported the separation of state-owned enterprises from government and suggested that smaller SOEs be privatized. By 1995 the suggestion had become the policy of "seize the large, let go the small" (*zhua da fang xiao*). As smaller SOEs were privatized or closed, the total number fell significantly, so that industrial SOEs fell from 127,600 in 1996 to 61,300 in 1999 and 34,280 in 2003. Firms were sold to employees through share issues, which converted them to "stock co-operative companies" and many made the further change to limited liability companies, managers often buying controlling shares from the other workers (Lardy, 1998, pp.53–54).

The larger SOEs, which were "seized", remained in state hands but many were "corporatized" by re-organizing them into joint stock or limited liability companies. The managers of such firms are responsible to their boards of directors, but the state retains control through majority ownership, and they are classified as "state-controlled shareholding companies". In 2011 there were about 10,000 such firms in the industrial sector, accounting for 70% of all state firms' output.

Outside the industrial sector there had been around 330,000 traditional SOEs in 1996, falling to 160,000 in 2012. The precise balance between those that were corporatized, privatized and closed is not known, although tens of millions of workers lost their jobs, to be absorbed by the growing non-state sector.

According to Lardy (2014, p.47), by 2012 China had 278,479 state firms, of which 159,644 were traditional state-owned companies, the others being state-controlled shareholding companies. In the industrial sector there were 17,851 "above scale" state firms, 6,770 of which were traditional state-owned, the rest being state-controlled shareholding firms. They no longer dominated the economy, being responsible for 26% of industrial output and 20% of manufacturing in 2011.

Clearly, the portrayal of China as still largely state-driven is incorrect. At the same time, however, SOEs have a crucial influence. Consistent with "seize the large", the authorities took a major step in 2003 with the establishment of the State-owned Assets Supervision and Administration Commission (SASAC), whose central arm took ownership of around 200 of the largest industrial SOE groups. SASAC was given the task of overseeing them, maximizing the value of state assets and reducing the number of centrally controlled groups. By 2015 it had reduced the number to 111. However, as Kroeber (2016) points out, those groups together comprised around 23,000 companies, which is a huge number to oversee. Furthermore, SASAC's control is less than complete. In principle, the companies are corporations, with SASAC owning significant proportions of their shares, through which control can be exercised. However, some groups have not been fully corporatized. Some Ministries continue to assert rights over some groups and half of the groups rank as Ministry-level entities, putting them at the same level as SASAC itself. As the Organization Department of the Communist Party (*zuzhi bu*) appoints the senior managers of the most important SOEs, SASAC is not the all-powerful controlling hand it might appear to be (Lin & Milhaupt, 2013).

Given the small number of groups controlled by the central SASAC, and the much larger number of companies within those groups, some kind of group structure is necessary. Kroeber (2016, p.96) describes a four-level structure as typical, with an unlisted entity controlled by SASAC at the top, a second layer of subsidiaries majority -owned by the top, a third layer of minority-controlled subsidiaries and a fourth set of companies which are not owned by the group but which have significant contractual links.

Most groups focus on a single sector, but they are also networked across related sectors, so that SOEs in steel, for example, have links with others in ship-building and automobiles (Lin & Milhaupt, 2013).

This process of establishing SASAC, and exposing some groups to competition, reduced the number of SOEs significantly, and drove employment in them from 113 million in 1995 to 64 million in 2007. It also improved their financial performance, as their profits rose to 6.6% of GDP in the same period. As the private sector grew rapidly, so the state sector seemed to be in retreat as the major driver of the economy, while simultaneously becoming more efficient.

That "retreat" became less marked after 2008, which some referred to as "the state advances and the private sector retreats" (*guo jin min tui*). It was not really a retreat for the private sector but the number of SOEs did begin to rise after 2010 and employment stabilized. Hu Jintao and Wen Jiabao had statist views, they were lobbied by SOEs, and their response to the global crisis of 2008 was to undertake a huge economic stimulus programme. That involved spending RMB 4 trillion (US$586 billion), which was most easily and quickly channelled through the SOEs, giving them a boost.

Given this shifting background it is difficult to make a balanced evaluation of the SOEs' position in 2017. However, several points are clear.

First, the SOE remains a very significant part of the economy, and the leadership intends it to remain so. Xi Jinping told the Politburo in November 2015 that "the mainstay status of public ownership and the leading role of the state-owned economy must not waver" (Huang, 2016). Out of 92 Chinese firms on the Fortune Global 500 list, 82 were central or local government SOEs. SOE assets were equal to 145% of GDP in 2011 and Kroeber (2016, p.101) estimates that they account for around 35% of GDP.

Second, their performance, circumstances, and relationship to the central state vary enormously. On average, SOE productivity growth has been below that of the private sector, and their return on equity has been much lower than for private firms. Some of these companies, especially those under the aegis of the central SASAC, are protected from competition and are instruments of central state power, should the state choose to use them. In mobile phone services, for instance, the three giants – China Mobile, China Telecom, and China Unicom – account for more than 95% of all revenues for the sector (Szamosszegi & Kyle, 2011, p.38) and the state has not allowed other firms to enter. In principle, competition amongst the three might act as a disciplinary mechanism. However, as Lardy (2014, p.52) points out, the senior executives are appointed by the Organization Department of the Party, and in 2004 their chief executives were swapped over. Wang Jianzhou, Chairman of China Unicom, became Chairman of China Mobile, while Wang Xiaochu of China Mobile became General Manager of China Telecom and Chang Xiaobing of China Telecom became Chairman of China Unicom. Similar reshuffles took place in the state-owned oil companies China National Offshore Oil Corporation (CNOOC), Sinopec and China National Petroleum Corporation (CNPC). Such interventions, and the red telephones connecting senior executives with the government in Beijing, suggest that they are more like departments of the state than independent businesses competing with each other.

This model of the SOE is central to industries deemed strategic – telecoms, defence sectors, aviation, electricity generation, oil and gas extraction, petroleum and petrochemicals. While many of them are listed on international stock exchanges, Szamosszegi and Kyle (2011, p.78) quote their disclosures to make it clear that the interests of the state override those of other shareholders. In the case of aluminium producer Chalco, for instance, there is the statement that:

> The interests of our controlling shareholder (the SOE Chinalco), who exerts significant influence over us, may conflict with ours.

For China Southern Airlines:

> The Company is indirectly majority owned by the Chinese government, which may exert influence in a manner that may conflict with the interests of holders of ADRs, H shares and A shares.

While some SOEs are protected from competition, others are not and even the central SASAC enterprises are not a uniform group. In the steel industry, Ansteel, Baosteel, Sinosteel and Wuhan Iron and Steel are all central SOEs controlled by SASAC but they face increasing competition from private groups like Shagang, from provincial level Hebei Iron and Steel, and from more than 4,000 private firms (Fan & Hope, 2013, p.9).

This diversity amongst SOEs extends further once it is recognized that the central SASAC is mirrored at provincial and local level by sub-national SASACs, whose allegiance is to local government, and that the sub-national SASACs are responsible for perhaps 100,000 SOEs (Mattlin, 2010).

One of the least understood aspects of the Chinese system is that while the country is highly centralized through the party-state, it is also very decentralized (Landry, 2008). Between 2000 and 2011, for instance, local government expenditure rose to 85% of national government expenditures, compared with an average of 32% for OECD countries (Kroeber, 2016, pp.112, 118). Decentralization allows local leaders to follow their own agendas, which include using SOEs under the local SASAC to pursue local objectives. In the vehicle industry, for instance, the central government has sought since 1990 to concentrate production into three large state-owned car makers, with a complete lack of success. China still has more than 100 car assemblers, most of them local SOEs making low-cost, poor quality products. Production provides employment and income for the local governments who support them, and they have been able fend off the centre's "guidance". In the steel industry, the centre seeks to concentrate production in order to have "national champions" who will be internationally competitive, and less damaging to the environment. However, the industry remains fragmented, with massive over-capacity. Local governments have blocked the take-over of their local steelmakers by the central SOEs, and in Hebei the provincial government and its SASAC promoted their own consolidation campaign to the point where Hebei Iron and Steel has become one of the world's top producers, having bought into a dozen private firms.

The steel industry is the foremost example of a sector in which "zombie" firms present a major problem, making losses but surviving through financial support from local governments and the banks. Other major sectors involved are coal, plate glass, electrolytic aluminium, cement, ship-building, petrochemical, photovoltaic and wind power.

Not all zombies are SOEs, but many are, and they represent a challenge for the centre. In May 2016 the *People's Daily* called for their closure, but at the same time output in some zombie sectors, including steel, was increasing and plants that had been mothballed were being brought back into production (Zhou, 2016). President Xi has described "supply-side" reforms as key to the next phase of development, and the rhetoric from the centre, linked to promises made to other countries, is aligned with the zombies' closure. However, the obstacle lies in local governments who depend upon the industries involved. In Shanxi province, for instance, coal is the mainstay of the provincial economy so that the closure of mines would involve the loss of jobs and local tax revenues and a reduction in the local growth rate. Most important, significant unemployment could lead to social unrest and criticism of the Party, which is anathema. Faced with a credible threat of chaos, the centre backs down. While the leadership promised US representatives in June 2016 that they would address the problem of over-capacity, they do not have very powerful levers in place because zombies still provide lifelines for some communities, whose local government will protect them to the full extent of its ability.

In comparison with the SOE job losses associated with the *zhua da fang xiao* initiative of the late 1990s, the numbers associated with zombie firms are small, involving a few million jobs rather than tens of millions. Nevertheless, it will be difficult to find employment in sectors like services and research and development for workers whose skills are in heavy industry, and the central authorities' appetite for a frontal assault on the zombies remains untested.

Overall, in 2017 there are some SOEs that draw on the power of the state and occupy unassailably profitable positions in their protected sectors. Then there are others that are the outcome of a process of merger and consolidation intended to produce efficient national champions with modern management systems and up-to-date technology – an outcome that remains to be seen. There are SOEs that "muddle along" with positive but poor financial returns, and there are a significant number of zombies – including perhaps 300 listed companies – which together have huge over-capacity, suffer significant losses and are kept alive because the authorities fear the consequences of their demise.

Private enterprises and entrepreneurship in China

For centuries, the Chinese have been known for their entrepreneurial spirit. From the Silk Road, to the goldfields of California and Australia, to the Chinese restaurants found in every significant city on earth, the Chinese trader and risk-taker has been everywhere.

That spirit is not easily dampened and Huang (2008, p.62) reports that even during the Cultural Revolution, when being "capitalist" could bring a death sentence, the Mao badges worn by Red Guards were being produced by an entrepreneur from Fujian who raised capital from 36 investors and established 30 small factories!

Nevertheless, in the command economy, private business was not allowed and Huang (2008, p.ix) also recalls that 20 years after reform began, a Shanghai official was surprised that a Harvard professor would be interested in the city's private sector, as it was solely involved in "selling watermelons, tea and rotten apples".

Given that background, it might be expected that private enterprises would be peripheral to the Chinese success story, held back by ideology, the dominance of SOEs and the hostile influence of the authorities. Nothing could be further from the truth, as Nicholas Lardy's (2014) *Markets over Mao* demonstrates. In fact, virtually all of the growth in output and employment since the beginning of reform can be attributable to the private sector, and in 2012 there were 40.6 million "individual businesses" employing 86.3 million employees, and 10.9 million "private enterprises" with 113.0 million employees (Lardy, 2014, p.70). The growth of the urban private sector was particularly rapid in the period of *zhua da fang xiao* when the number of employees in urban registered private enterprises shot up from 570,000 in 1990 to 12.7 million in 2000 and 34.6 million in 2005. That spectacular growth continued so that by 2012 the figure was 75.6 million. The growth in "individual businesses" or *geti hu*, which were restricted to less than 8 non-family employees until 2001, was also dramatic with 6.1 million employees in 1990, 21.4 million in 2000, 27.8 million in 2005 and 56.4 million in 2012. By 2012 private and individual businesses accounted for 35.6% of urban employment (Lardy, 2014, p.83).

Tracing this reversal of fortune for private enterprise provides another example of the idiosyncrasies of China's development. As always, the action began in the countryside rather than the city. Giving responsibility for agriculture back to households led to the establishment of millions of TVEs, described above. Most were either "wearing the red hat" or were overtly private, and by the late 1990s China had a significant class of experienced entrepreneurs. In the cities, the pattern of development was similar. As employment in the urban SOEs declined, their employees, and local government officials were encouraged to "jump into the sea" (*xia hai*) and go into business. Mindful of the dangers posed by the potential unemployment associated with the *zhua da fang xiao* initiative, and conscious of the employment benefits of private enterprise, the SOEs and local governments supported their employees, sometimes in ways that have been little reported. For instance, employees were allowed to leave their jobs to pursue private opportunities, without losing their positions. They were no longer paid a public-sector salary, but they had the right to return to their old jobs at any time, and their pensions were maintained. Hence, the state provided a "safety net" for those willing to *xia hai*. How widespread that practice was is unknown, but from the mid-1990s the policy environment for private firms became much more welcoming. As a consequence, in every sector where barriers to entry are relatively low, private companies have largely replaced the SOEs. That includes most of manufacturing, mining, construction, retailing and catering (Lardy, 2014, p.81).

While most private firms remain small, there were some entrepreneurs whose ambitions could reasonably be described as "megalomaniac", particularly given their initial circumstances. For, as Kynge (2006) points out, a significant number of the earliest generation of entrepreneurs began with nothing, or less than nothing if a criminal record is taken into account.

During the Cultural Revolution millions of young people had been sent to "learn from the peasants". When they returned to the cities in the early 1980s many faced unemployment, especially those with poor education. As a result, the authorities were obliged to allow them to set up small private businesses. The initial pool of private entrepreneurs therefore included many from the bottom of the social pyramid, who could not get "respectable" work in the state sector. That included a number of ex-convicts, the most famous of whom was Mou Qizhong. He left jail in 1979 with no *danwei* to support him and began selling clocks. His major coup was to (somehow) broker a deal on behalf of Sichuan Airlines, whereby 500 train cars loaded with instant noodles, socks and garments were exchanged for four passenger jets from the Soviet Union. For a while his "jets for socks" transaction was hailed as an epic of the reform era and he was lauded as one of the "Ten Best Private Entrepreneurs". However, an unfortunate habit of styling himself as "Chairman Mou" combined with schemes like bringing rain-filled air from India through tunnels under the Himalayas led him into disrepute and by 2000 he was back in jail, convicted of a foreign exchange scam.

Mou Qizhong is the extreme, and many of the early entrepreneurs found sustainable lines of business. Nevertheless, they often shared backgrounds of considerable hardship, which may explain their tenacity, opportunism, and a tendency to conspicuous consumption. Li Xiaohua, spent eight years in frozen Heilongjiang and began illegally selling watches from Hong Kong when he returned to Beijing in 1978. He was sentenced to "reform through labour" but policy had changed on his release and he switched business, selling iced drinks. That was highly profitable but he anticipated entry from new competition and moved on to screening films from Hong Kong and Taiwan. He then acquired the rights to sell hair restorer priced at US$100 per bottle, which he purchased for $US8 (Gayah & Fetscherin, 2009), and bought property in Hong Kong following the price falls after the Tiananmen incident of 1989. Most famously he collected luxury cars and is best known as "Mr Ferrari", having bought the first to be imported, in 1992, numbered A0001.

While opportunism and flamboyance were hallmarks for some early entrepreneurs, there were more focused businesspeople. Shen Wenrong, a peasant farmer with a rudimentary education, predicted in 2000 that there would be a crash in steel prices and that companies that had invested in expensive plants would sink under the costs. He therefore purchased the Phoenix steel plant in Dortmund from ThyssenKrupp, at scrap value (US$24 million). The plant was dismantled by Chinese workers in one year, compared with the three years estimated by the seller, and shipped to Jinfeng. At a total cost estimated to be 60% of that for a new plant, the Shagang steel company acquired a major production facility. That has since been expanded through the acquisition of four other Chinese steel firms, and in 2007 a 90% share in Australian Bulk Minerals, giving it large reserves of iron ore. The Shagang Group currently has 30,000 employees, RMB 150 billion in assets and exports to more than 40 countries (Shagang Group website). Shen Wenrong features at 94th on Forbes China Rich List for 2016 with an estimated net worth of $US1.72 billion.

The list of entrepreneurs who built fortunes through developing large private companies is now a long one, so that the Forbes Rich List for 2016 identifies 251 US$ billionaires in China, second only to the US. (The list does not include members of the leadership, whose wealth is difficult to assess.) Table 5.1 shows the 10 largest private companies in China, by revenue in 2014.

The sources of leading entrepreneurs' wealth are spread across the business landscape from cars to steel to software, minerals, and e-commerce and to describe them all is impractical. There are, however, a number of salient cases, which illustrate important themes.

One of those is Geely, the first private auto company in China. The company was founded by Li Shufu in Zhejiang province, at a time when the central government was unwilling to give permission for new car plants. Nevertheless, local government lobbied Beijing effectively and the private car plant was established, with massive subsidies from the

Table 5.1 China's ten largest private companies by revenue, 2014

Company	*Revenue (RMB billion)*	*Major business*	*Founder*	*Founder's net worth in $US bn*
Suning	279.8	Retail electrical	Zhang Jindong	3.9
Legend Holdings	244.0	Computers	Liu Chuanzhi	Not listed
Shandong Weiqiao Pioneering Group	241.4	Textiles	Zhang Shiping	Not listed
Huawei	239.0	Telecoms equipment	Ren Zhengfei	1.67
Amer International	233.83	Non-ferrous metals, semi-conductors	Wang Wenyin	8.4
Jiangsu Shagang	228.04	Steel	Shen Wenrong	2.15
CEFC China Energy Co. Ltd	203.0	Oil, gas, financial services	Ye Jianming	Not listed
Dalian Wanda	186.6	Hotels, Media	Wang Jianlin	33.9
Zhejiang Geely	158.4	Motor vehicles	Li Shufu	2.3
Vanke	135.6	Property development	Wang Shi	Not listed

Source: China Daily 20 August 2014, Forbes China Rich List (2017).

local and provincial governments. Land was sold to the company at a discount of RMB 386 million, which increased to more than RMB one trillion as its value soared (Ngo, 2008).

Geely began car production in 2002, followed by a listing on the Hong Kong Stock Exchange in 2004. Early models were based around the low-cost Daihatsu Charade, which were followed by brand names like Emgrand, Englon and Gleagle, all of which were withdrawn in 2014, to be replaced by Geely. There were concerns over the safety standards of early models, and the company was sued (unsuccessfully) by Toyota who claimed that Geely was implying that some of its parts had been manufactured by Toyota. Sales in 2014 exceeded 400,000 units but that represented a 24% decline over the previous year, and overseas sales were nearly 50% lower than in 2013 (Geely, 2014). According to the J.D. Power's measure of owner satisfaction in China, Geely ranked 5th amongst local brands and 17th overall, which is not impressive, and it remains to be seen whether Geely will be able withstand the fierce competition from foreign joint ventures with better brand names. However, the company's best known move has been to acquire Volvo Cars from Ford in 2010 and the bankrupt Manganese Bronze (which makes the classic London taxi) in 2013. In May 2016 Geely announced the launch of a $US400 million "green bond" to support the development of a zero-emission version of the re-named London Taxi Company's iconic product. In the meantime, the company has been trying to leverage its ownership of Volvo to develop common platforms for higher price segment cars, setting up a research centre in Sweden.

It is not clear how the Geely story will develop, but it does exemplify important aspects of many large firms in the Chinese private sector. First, the company is closely identified with its founder, Li Shufu, who remains Chairman, and 38th on the Forbes China Rich List, with $US2.3bn. Second, despite the private status of the company, its origins were closely linked to the local state, without which it would not exist. Third, its ability to compete in a very competitive sector remains to be seen, as it has yet to develop a brand name strong enough to command higher margins. Fourth, however, it has been bold and imaginative in its attempt to correct its weaknesses, even if success remains uncertain and industry experts doubt the feasibility of integrating foreign acquisitions (Russo, Tse & Ke, 2009).

The largest private firms in China are huge companies. However, as the Geely example shows, their relationships with the party-state are often very close. The best-known example is Huawei, now the world's largest supplier of telecommunications equipment. Established by Ren Zhengfei, who had previously worked for the PLA, Huawei is supposedly an "employee-owned" and therefore private company, although Huang (2008, p.11) observes that there is no documentary evidence on exactly who owns what. According to the governance statement on the company's website there are just two shareholders – Ren Zhengfei and "the Union", which consists of all shareholding employees. The Union is represented by an elected Representatives Commission.

Ren is said to have told President Jiang Zemin in 1994 that "a country without its own switching equipment is like a country without a military" (Ahrens, 2013, p.5) and the strategic importance of telecoms infrastructure is clear. Given that importance, and the fact that the company has received significant government assistance in penetrating international markets, it is simply not credible that it acts independently of the state and "experts believe that the firm is, at a minimum, dominated by the state or a privately-owned firm which behaves like a state-owned one" (Szamosszegi & Kyle, 2011, p.42).

Of the companies listed in Table 5.1, others have close links to the party-state. CEFC China Energy was established in 2002 and grew stunningly quickly, to be listed in the Fortune Global 500 in 2013, with revenues in excess of 200 billion RMB. Its key business is in oil and gas, in which the state has 92.1% of industrial output (Lardy, 2014, p.77) and the company's "enigmatic" founder, Ye Jianming, is also the Chairman of an NGO that commentators believe is an arm of the PLA's intelligence agency (Chubb & Garnaut, 2013). Legend Holdings, which is the parent of computer giant Lenovo, is part-owned by the Chinese Academy of Sciences, which gives the state a major influence, but Lenovo itself has been structured to behave more like a private firm, and has several foreigners in senior positions. On the other hand, founder Liu Chuanzhi revealed to The Economist (2015) that he himself happens to be the head of the CCP's cell in his company!

Complex links between private business and the state are not unique to China. In every part of the world companies lobby politicians. In China, however, the blurring of the boundaries is particularly marked, and is made more complex by the importance of *guanxi* and the parallel organization of the government and the Party. Dalian Wanda is largely focused on property development, shopping malls, hotels and movie theatres (including the AMC chain in the US), none of which are of central importance to the state, and the company is generally seen as fully private. On the other hand, founder Wang Jianlin is reported to be the son of the deputy director of the all-powerful Organization Department and he told the World Economic Forum in Dalian in 2013 that

> China is a government-oriented economy. No one can say he can run his business entirely without government connections. Anybody who says that he or she can do things alone without any connection with the government in China is a hypocrite.
> (Moore, 2013, p.23)

To summarize on the private sector, China has tens of millions of genuinely private companies that compete with each other and with some of the SOEs. They are mostly small to medium in size, they are profitable, they support investment from their own retained earnings and they have been largely responsible for the growth in output and employment over the past two decades. There are also a significant number of large private firms, whose nature varies from the genuinely private to instruments of state power.

Two kinds of foreign investors: the role of overseas Chinese versus multinationals

From the earliest days of reform, foreign-invested enterprises (FIEs) have been central to China's success, and there have been two distinctly different types. The first to participate were ethnically Chinese investors, mainly from Hong Kong. Their companies were small in size, employing 100–200 workers (Tracy, 1995, p.13) and concentrated in the narrow range of industries which had sprung up in Hong Kong when the city's role as entrepôt was denied it by Communist rule in China. Garments, assembly of watches and clocks, wigs, jewellery, toys and the assembly of electronics, all for export, accounted for most of Hong Kong's industry (Whitla & Davies, 1995). They had developed in Hong Kong because the city's precarious situation in the 1950s meant that entrepreneurs had to find sectors that could be established with a little family capital, and employ poorly educated workers using simple general purpose equipment which could be quickly redeployed if overseas markets shifted.

Hong Kong's manufacturing sector was an anomaly in a city built on trade, and a miracle that flew in the face of the received wisdom of the time. It was focused on small firms manufacturing for export, when exporting was believed to be an activity for large firms. The markets served were far away, geographically and culturally, which could have been an impenetrable obstacle. Small firms could not possibly know what Mrs Smith in the US and Frau Schmidt in Germany wanted to wear. But the problem was solved with Hong Kong's one truly disruptive global innovation. That was the "original equipment manufacturing" (OEM) business model. Hong Kong's entrepreneurs focused on manufacturing whatever their customers asked them to make. There were no attempts to build brands or develop new technology, and no attempts to learn directly what European or North American consumers want to buy. Instead, foreign buyers would come to trade exhibitions in Hong Kong, with their designs for products, which Hong Kong firms would compete with each other to produce. To take the watch industry, for instance, Hong Kong firms produce hundreds of millions of watches per year in China, completely dominating the low-price segment, but there is not one single well known Hong Kong watch brand.

These scrappy competitors had several characteristics associated with the Chinese family business (Davies & Ma, 2003). They were family run, with paternalistic, Confucian, cultures. They competed on cost and speed, were intolerant of slack, and expert at using low quality labour to produce medium quality products. By 1979, their success had brought prosperity to the city and the Hong Kong government interpreted high wages and rents as a problem of "competitiveness". Hence, a government "Diversification Report" that called for Hong Kong manufacturing firms to abandon the OEM model and "upgrade" themselves, spending more on technology and brand names. The timing was spectacularly wrong as in December 1978, Deng Xiaoping had announced the policy of opening up and reform (*kaifang gaige*). Tens of thousands of Hong Kong firms packed up their equipment, drove it over the border and established foreign-invested enterprises. Their OEM business model remained firmly in place.

These FIEs were the engine of China's first industrial revolution. Their OEM model was perfectly aligned with China's advantage in cheap labour and land, and its disadvantage in design, technology and commercial intelligence. They were mainly located in Guangdong province, close to Hong Kong, because their owners preferred to live in the city. Its port was the only efficient way to export goods, and many of the owners had been refugees from Guangdong, who returned to their home towns to work with people they knew. Hong Kong entrepreneurs formed joint ventures with local governments in which the labour, land, buildings and utilities were provided by the Mainland partners and the capital, manufacturing capability and all-important market contacts came from the Hong Kong side. By 1993, out of 167,500 FIEs in China, 136,042 originated in the 'Chinese diaspora' and 106,000 of those came from Hong Kong (Tracy, 1995, p.3). By 2002 Hong Kong's manufacturing industry had an average of 26 employees in the Pearl River Delta area for each employee in Hong Kong (Enright, Scott & Chang, 2005, p.72) and China's manufactured exports were predominantly produced by them.

In the period before Deng Xiaoping's "Southern Tour" of 1992, foreign direct investment into China was dominated by the Chinese diaspora, as Western and Japanese investors remained uncertain. After all, under Mao there had been frequent, often murderous, shifts of policy, and the 1989 massacre in Tiananmen Square had rendered the country an international pariah. However, once it became clear that Deng had overcome opposition to reform, inward foreign direct investment (FDI) rose from US$6bn per annum for 1990–1992 to $US33bn for 1993–1995 (Kroeber, 2016, p.53). In part, that arose from increasing investment from Hong Kong firms, but it also marked the beginning of China as a major destination for investment from Europe, North America and Japan.

This second wave of investment was very different from the first. The companies involved were amongst the largest in the world. They contributed to China's second industrial revolution by developing a much wider range of industries, more capital-intensive and technologically sophisticated than the entrepreneurs from Hong Kong. While many of them were directed towards export markets outside China, there was a significant shift towards serving the Chinese domestic market for machinery and equipment, chemicals and pharmaceuticals, motor vehicles and even consumer goods. This wave of investors brought significant technological development, and management techniques suitable for larger, professionally managed, non-family businesses.

As China continued to grow and entered the WTO in 2001, so it became more attractive as both a domestic market and as a base for manufacturing exports. FDI inflows rose to around US$115bn 2012–2014 (Kroeber, 2016, p.53). Caution is needed when interpreting "foreign" direct investment inflows to China because a large proportion originates in Hong Kong, and as much as a third of that is said to be "round-tripping" whereby Chinese firms divert profits to their Hong Kong subsidiaries, which invest it back into China as "foreign investment". Nevertheless, virtually every major company in the world now has investments in China, being afraid to lose out on the opportunities raised by the world's largest economy.

Foreign firms have played a much larger role in the development of China's economy than in other East Asian countries. They contribute disproportionately to exports, accounting for nearly 60% at the peak in 2005, and for "high-tech" exports that figure was close to 90% (Kroeber, 2016, p.54). While "high-tech" exports are really just foreign components assembled in China, the transfer of technology has been hugely important. In the automotive sector, all of the best quality cars and trucks are manufactured in plants managed by foreign companies with Chinese partners unable to match their standards. Similar comments apply in other areas where production of a world standard product requires management of complex global supply chains. As the private sector develops, this advantage is being reduced, and the FIEs share of exports and "high-tech" production have declined since 2005, although the rapid growth of both has meant continuing absolute expansion.

The last issue to consider with respect to FIEs in China, is the distinction between "foreign-equity joint ventures" (FEJVs) and wholly owned foreign enterprises (WOFEs). In the early wave of FDI into China, virtually all of the FIEs took the form of FEJVs, with local governments as the partner. The nature of that "joint-ness" varied from place to place as in many cases the local governments really acted as a substitute for factor markets, supplying labour, land, utilities and a "red hat", taking no part in management. Most of them, especially in Guangdong, had no interest in "technology transfer" – learning how to make jeans or shoes or assemble watches. They were content to have growth, employment, and tax revenue in their towns. In other places, local governments were more involved in day-to-day management. In any event, in the early stages, foreign investors had little discretion over the form of FIE as the FEJV was effectively mandatory.

Managing joint-ventures, where parent companies control an "offspring", is a difficult way to do business, especially if the parents' interests diverge. That was not so important in the Guangdong/ Hong Kong FEJVs because the Mainland side simply wanted "jobs and incomes here" and the Hong Kong firms were low-technology assemblers whose advantage lay in knowing overseas buyers. In more complex industries, however, the Chinese partners and government have often wanted to acquire the foreigners' technology, and a divergence of interest is central. Hence the WOFE has become the preferred entry mode for many foreign firms (Vanhonecker, 1997). As China edges closer to a "rules-based" economy, foreign investors have more of a real choice between FEJV and WOFE. Nevertheless, if they need resources that are available on the open market, including information, licences, permissions and *guanxi* with state officials, entering through an FEJV remains the only really practical alternative.

What is the Chinese firm today?

Four points emerge from the discussion. First, the population of Chinese firms includes tens of millions of small and medium private enterprises, spread across rural and urban settings and most sectors, which have been driving growth, employment and increasingly exports. Second, there is a group of powerful SOEs that manifest state power but there are also perhaps 300 zombie SOEs who represent a major problem for the leadership, and an unknown number who operate, some successfully, in competition with each other and the private sector. Third, there are some very large private firms, but a significant proportion of them have close, sometimes "enigmatic" links to the state. Hence, China has some state firms that behave like private firms and some private firms that behave like the state. Fourth, China is home to several hundred thousand FIEs, which vary from the descendants of the first wave of Hong Kong investment – in garments, watches, toys and generally low-tech activities – to more recent investors from Europe, North America and Japan who produce most of the nation's more complex products, and a large proportion of its exports.

In 1996 Brown and Porter (p.8) described China's enterprise reform process as "China's relentless move from homogeneity to heterogeneity". Twenty years later, that statement can only been re-iterated.

References

Ahrens, N., 2013. *China's competitiveness: Myth, reality and lessons for the United States and Japan. Case Study: Huawei.* Washington, DC: Center for Strategic and International Studies.

Brandt, L., Li, H. and Roberts, J., 2005. Banks and enterprise privatization in China. *Journal of Law, Economics and Organization*, 21 (2), pp.525–546.

Brown, D. and Porter, R., 1996. Introduction, in Brown, D. and Porter, R. (eds), *Management issues in China: Vol I, domestic enterprises*. London: Routledge, pp.1–9.

Chubb, A. and Garnaut, J., 2013. The enigma of CEFC's Chairman Ye. *Southsea Conversations*, 7 June 2013. Available at https://southseaconversations.wordpress.com/2013/06/07/the-enigma-of-cefcs-chairman-ye/ [Accessed 19 January 2017].

Davies, H., 1995. The nature of the firm in China, in Davies, H. (ed.), *China business: Context and issues*. Hong Kong: Longman Asia, pp.137–154.

Davies, H. and Ma, C. 2003. Strategic choice and the nature of the Chinese family business: An exploratory study of the Hong Kong watch industry. *Organization Studies*, 24 (9), pp.1405–1435.

Duckett, J., 2001. Bureaucrats in business, Chinese-style: The lessons of market reform and state entrepreneurialism in the People's Republic of China. *World Development*, 29 (1), pp.23–37.

Economist, 2015. How red is your capitalism. 10 September. Available at https://www.economist.com/news/special-report/21663334-telling-state-controlled-private-firm-can-be-tricky-how-red-your-capitalism [Accessed 11 July 2017].

Enright, D., Scott, E. and Chang, K., 2005. *Regional powerhouse: The Greater Pearl River Delta and the rise of China*. Singapore: Wiley.

Fan, G. and Hope, N., 2013. The role of state-owned enterprises in the Chinese economy, Chapter 16 in China–US Exchange Foundation, *US–China economic relations in the next ten years: Towards deeper engagement and mutual benefit*. Hong Kong: China–US Exchange Foundation.

Forbes 2017. Forbes Rich List. Available at //www.forbes.com/sites/russellflannery/2016/10/29/2016-forbes-china-rich-list-full-list/#38c487302bae [Accessed 14 May 2017].

Gayah, A. and Fetscherin, M. 2009. Li Xiaohua, in Zhang, W. and Alon, I. (eds), *Biographical dictionary of new Chinese entrepreneurs and business leaders*. Cheltenham: Edward Elgar, pp. 87–88.

Geely., 2014. *New Geely era: Annual report* 2014.

Huang, Y., 2008. *Capitalism with Chinese characteristics: Entrepreneurship and the state*. New York: Cambridge University Press.

Huang, C., 2016. Goodbye Likonomics...hello Xikonomics. *South China Morning Post*, 17 February, p. A4.

Jin, H. and Qian, Y., 1998. Public versus private ownership of firms: Evidence from rural China. *Quarterly Journal of Economics*, 113 (3), pp.773–808.

Kroeber, A., 2016. *China's economy: What everyone needs to know*, Oxford: Oxford University Press.

Kung, J. and Lin, Y-M., 2007. The decline of township and village enterprises in China's economic transition. *World Development*, 35 (4), pp.569–584.

Kynge, J., 2006. *China shakes the world: The rise of a hungry nation*. London: Phoenix.

Landry, P., 2008. *Decentralized authoritarianism in China*. Cambridge: Cambridge University Press.

Lardy, N., 1998. *China's unfinished economic revolution*. Washington, DC: Brookings Institution Press.

Lardy, N., 2014. *Markets over Mao*. Washington, DC: Peterson Institute for International Economics.

Liang, X., 2006. The evolution of township and village enterprises in China. *Journal of Small Business and Enterprise Development*, 13 (2), pp.235–241.

Lin, L. and Milhaupt, C., 2013. We are the (national) champions: Understanding the mechanisms of state capitalism in China. *Stanford Law Review*, 65, April, pp. 697–759.

Mattlin, M., 2010. Chinese state-owned enterprises and ownership control. *Asia Papers*, 4 (6), Brussels Institute of Contemporary China Studies.

Milgrom, P. and Roberts, J., 1992. *Economics, organization and management*. Englewood Cliffs, NJ: Prentice-Hall.

Moore, M., 2013 The rise and rise of Wang Jianlin, China's richest man. *Daily Telegraph*, 21 September 2013.

National Bureau of Statistics of China. 2015. *China Statistical Yearbook 2015*. Beijing: China Statistics Press.

Naughton, B., 2007. *The Chinese economy: Transitions and growth*, Cambridge, MA: MIT Press.

Ngo, T., 2008. Rent seeking and economic governance in the structural nexus of corruption in China. *Crime, Law and Social Change*, (49) pp.27–44.

Oi, J., 1992. Fiscal reform and the economic foundations of local state corporatism in China. *World Politics*, 45, October, pp. 99–126.

Qian, Y. and Wu, J., 2003. China's transition to a market economy: How far across the river?, in Hope, N., Yang, D. and Li, M. (eds), *How far across the river? Chinese policy reform at the millennium*, Redwood City, CA: Stanford University Press, pp.31–64.

Russo, B., Tse, E. and Ke, T., 2009. *The path to globalization of China's automotive industry*. New York: Booz and Co.

Szamosszegi, A. and Kyle, C., 2011. *An analysis of state-owned enterprises and state capitalism in China*. Washington, DC: US–China Economic and Security Review Commission.

Tracy, N., 1995. Transforming South China: the role of the Chinese diaspora in the era of reform, in Davies, H. (ed.), *China business: Context and issues*. Hong Kong: Longman Asia, pp.1–21.

Unger, J. and Chan, A., 1999. Inheritors of the boom: Private enterprise and the role of local government in a rural South China township. *The China Journal*, 42, July, pp.45–74.

Whitla, P. and Davies, H., 1995. The competitiveness of Hong Kong's domestic manufacturing operations, in Davies, H. (ed.), *China business: Context and issues*. Hong Kong, Longman Asia, pp. 37–65.

Wu, J. and Zhao, R., 1987. The dual pricing system in China's industry. *Journal of Comparative Economics*, 11 (3), pp.309–318.

Xin, K. and Pearce, J., 1996. *Guanxi*: Connections as substitutes for formal institutional support. *Academy of Management Journal*, 39, pp.1641–1658.

Zhou, X., 2016. The zombies return. Why are steel firms in China coming back from the dead? *South China Morning Post*, 14 May, p.A6.

6

TECHNOLOGY DEVELOPMENT IN CHINA

Howard Davies

Opposing views on China's technology development

Chinese technology surpassed the West for thousands of years until that lead was lost, for reasons examined in Chapter 1, and two opposing narratives now co-exist on the country's technological development. On the one hand, there is the view that technological weakness is a persistent feature of Chinese society, polity, and culture. In 2014, US Vice President Joe Biden noted that China graduates eight times as many technologists as the US and added "But I challenge you, name me one innovative project, one innovative change, one innovative product that has come out of China" (CNN, 2014). Presidential hopeful Carly Fiorina asserted that "the Chinese can take a test, but what they can't do is innovate. They are not terribly imaginative, they don't innovate, that is why they are stealing our intellectual property" (Time, 2015).

In this view, China is a "copycat" nation, dependent upon foreigners for technological advances, often copied without permission. Chinese research is riven with plagiarism, graduates lack the independence of mind required for invention, and the high power distance, collectivist, Confucian culture condemns the country to perpetual "followership".

On the other hand, the opposing narrative, emphatic inside China but subscribed to by many foreign observers, sees "innovation" as key to the next phase of development. The authorities are pouring resources into a re-vitalized science and technology system, and the green shoots of "indigenous innovation" are seen as emerging in many sectors of the economy.

This chapter evaluates these positions, by addressing two key questions: "Does China need indigenous innovation?" and "Is China capable of indigenous innovation?"

Does China need "indigenous innovation"?

The discussion of technology development in China has been clouded by vague uses of the term "innovation" and it is helpful to begin with definitions.

An "innovation" has novelty and practical value, and "innovation" also refers to the process of producing new and useful things. Innovation is distinguished from invention, in that invention is the creation of a new idea but innovation requires both invention and the process that uses that invention to make something of value.

The requirement that an innovation is new is clear, but raises the question of "new to what?" Something that is truly novel, and has never been implemented anywhere before is a "new to the world" innovation. Most of the literature on technology development uses innovation in that sense. "New" means completely new. However, innovations can also be "new to the market" or "new to the organization". An innovation that was "new to the world" but was then copied into another market will be an innovation that is "new to that market". An innovation that other firms in the market have but that has not yet been implemented by a focal firm will be innovation "new to that firm".

This alternative use of the term "innovation" is widespread in China. Fu (2015), in a book titled *China's Path to Innovation*, has this starting point:

> In the present context, innovation concerns not only novel innovations, but also innovation via diffusion of existing ideas and techniques.
>
> (p.5)

Yip and McKern (2016, pp.3–4) similarly include "ideas which are not new to the world but are new to a country or a company" in their definition of Chinese innovation. In other words, in the Chinese context, innovation includes copying. A cynic might interpret defining "innovation" in that way as evidence of just how deeply embedded the "copycat" mentality is in China. What does need to be recognized is that in the Chinese setting the distinction between "new to the world" and "new to the market" innovation is often not addressed and there is a risk that conclusions and policies which are relevant for one aspect are construed in terms of the other.

With respect to "indigenous innovation", if it is interpreted as "new to the world" innovation, the issue is "does China need to produce its own new to the world innovations?"

A starting point is to note that in 2015, China had a per capita income of around $US7,000, at market exchange rates, or $US12,000 at purchasing power parity. The American figure was $US55,000. That has three implications. First, the world already contains technology that can yield per capita income of $US55,000. Second, if "new to the world" innovation ceased today it would be possible for China to reach the $US55,000 level, simply by adopting technology that already in exists. Third, if the aim is to approach the per capita income level of the US, China does not need to divert resources to the expensive production of indigenously produced "new to the world" innovations. It would be better to direct them towards increasing the stock of technologically superior capital which is already available, in order to implement technologies imported from elsewhere. Even after decades of investment, China's capital per person is much lower than that in the US, which is why output per worker is also only 8% of the US figure (OECD, 2015, p.36).

These points hardly appear in the discourse on China's technology development. It is argued that China needs "innovation", the difference between "new to the market" and "new to the world" innovation is glossed over and it is concluded that the latter is needed, when the arguments really apply to the former. At the same time, observers often refer to the "problem" of "low-hanging fruit" (Rein, 2014), meaning that innovation in the "new to the world" sense is "hampered" by the fact that companies can easily copy from elsewhere. That is a perverse way to frame the issue because the availability of "low hanging fruit" is an advantage. Only if technology development is an end in itself, rather than a means to prosperity, can this be seen as a problem. If low-hanging fruit are to be had it is rational that they should be harvested first and it makes no sense to pass them by in favour of expensive and risky "new to the world" innovations.

While China does not need "new to the world" innovation to continue growing, it undoubtedly needs technological improvement and there are other factors to consider before dismissing the need for indigenous innovation. The first is that governments and companies in other countries may be unwilling to allow the transfer of their technology to China, a prospect reflected in the firmly held Chinese conviction that developed countries seek to contain their development. Second, technology imported from other countries requires adjustment in order to be suitable for Chinese conditions, and the novelty of those adjustments could be "new to the world". Third, there are developmental, political and ideological issues, in that to develop wholly on the basis of imported technology is to remain dependent on foreign innovations, which is deemed strategically inappropriate for a country taking its place at the forefront of world affairs.

From a static economic point of view, diverting resources to home-grown innovation is a misallocation when superior foreign technology is already available at lower cost. However, for those concerned with the long-term development of capability, and for the engineers who make up most of the Politburo, technological inferiority and dependence is a source of major discomfort. Lazonick (2004, p.273) makes the point from the perspective of a Western analyst:

> how can the less developed nations accumulate the innovative capability that will enable them to embark on a cumulative development path so that they can eventually join the ranks of the more advanced nations? Is it necessary for them to follow the learning path that the advanced economies took, and hence forever lag behind? Or, by choosing a different path, can they catch up and perhaps even forge ahead? Do they have to accept a permanently subservient role in the international division of labour? Or can they engage, as all of the advanced economies at certain times and in certain sectors, in "indigenous innovation", a process of making use of technologies transferred from the advance countries to develop superior technologies at home?
>
> Put this way, it is obvious that less developed countries want to choose a strategy on indigenous innovation.

There is rhetoric here, in that "accepting a subservient role in the international division of labour" is essentially the same as implementing the "comparative-advantage-following" strategy, which China's leading economist identified as the basis of the country's success (Lin, Cai & Li, 1996). Nevertheless, a nation that depends upon technology developed abroad can never overtake the originating nations, and could be vulnerable to attempts by them to restrict development. Hence, the argument in favour of "indigenous innovation" (*zizhu chuangxin*) has been well accepted and has become a central element in economic policy.

In 2003, Premier Wen brought together the Chinese Academy of Sciences (CAS) and the Ministry of Science and Technology (MOST) into the Leading Group for the Development of a National Mid- to Long-Term Science and Technology Development Plan (2006–2020). The preamble to the Plan declares that "our country is not an economic power, primarily because of our weak innovative capacity". The policies outlined are designed to change that and involve the mobilization of formidable resources. At the same time they embody conflicting emphases. On the one hand, a key tool for technology development is said to be the import of foreign technology, to be improved upon domestically. One the other hand, the policy required state entities to use domestic technologies, especially in "core infrastructure" like banking and telecommunications. As that involved giving preference in government procurement to domestic products, foreign investors became concerned that it was really a form of trade protectionism, and they lobbied to have the policies softened. Following the visit of President Hu to Washington in 2011 the government de-linked procurement from indigenous innovation, but foreign investors remain concerned (Lubman, 2011).

In summary, China has ample room to grow by continuing to import superior technologies from abroad. In that sense, the indigenous development of "new to the world" innovations is unnecessary. However, dependence on foreigners for technology, and the abandonment of any ambition to "leap-frog" over them is not acceptable in a nation with China's history of humiliation. History matters, and one consequence is the leaders' determination to escape from dependence on foreign intellectual property.

Is China capable of indigenous innovation?

Claims and counter-claims

Diametrically opposing views exist on whether China can independently generate significant technological progress. The argument that the country is capable is built around the assertions that:

a) Chinese firms are facing market pressures to innovate, and are therefore motivated now to participate actively in technology development.
b) China's large market makes domestic innovation particularly profitable.
c) The Chinese government is providing enormous resources in support of innovation, so that the country's science and technology system is becoming more effective.
d) Globalization makes Chinese indigenous innovation more valuable.
e) There is increasing evidence of innovation emanating from domestic companies, both in the strictly technological sense, and in respect of new organizational and business models.

On the other hand, the counter-argument claims that:

a) The continued availability of "low-hanging fruit" in easily adopted existing foreign technology inhibits firms from making investments in domestic innovation.
b) China continues to be dependent on foreign-invested enterprises for much of the technological progress observed.
c) Government intervention is unlikely to be an effective stimulant of real innovation, given the tendency towards unwieldy and ineffective "mega-projects" and the government's inability to identify the most suitable prospects.
d) China's "national innovation system", culture and education system are inhibitive of innovation.
e) Concrete results in the form of successful indigenous innovations are few and far between, representing the exception, rather than the rule.

Balancing the evidence is difficult but can be approached by considering: the resources being devoted to science and technology (S&T) development; the extent to which

Chinese companies need to innovate in order to compete; the overall effectiveness with which S&T resources are deployed, and; the extent to which there are useful outputs from the process. Attention also needs to be paid to the cultural and psychological dimension, in order to consider the nature of personal creativity in the Chinese setting, and its consequences for business.

Government increases the inputs to China's science and technology system

Technology development needs funding and the proportion of China's GDP devoted to R&D has risen from less than 1% in 2001 to nearly 2% in 2012, which remains below the OECD average of 2.4%. Government spending accounts for 30% of the total and much of that comes under the Medium and Long Term Plan for Science and Technology Development (MLTP). In some respects, the MLTP recalls the command economy, with 11 "key" sectors targeted for innovation, eight fields of technology in which 27 "breakthrough" technologies are to be pursued, four basic research programmes aimed at exploring 18 fundamental scientific issues, plus priorities given to energy efficiency, water purification, the dairy industry, genetically modified crops, high speed rail and electric automobiles (McGregor, 2010, p.14). In addition, there are a further 16 "mega-projects" aimed at assimilating and absorbing foreign technologies into another list of priority sectors. Overall, the Plan aims for R&D spending to reach 2.5% of GDP by 2020, of which 15% should be on basic research. Extrapolating from current figures, with a growth rate of 5% per year, that implies total R&D spending in 2020 of $US347 billion.

In order to have the skilled manpower needed to use this increased funding, the universities have been expanded, and nearly 7 million students graduate every year, 40% of them in the science, technology, engineering and mathematics (STEM) subjects most closely related to innovation. More than 400,000 Chinese students are studying abroad and Chinese scholars overseas have been enticed back home with promises of attractive benefit packages and lavish research support.

This dramatically increased input of resources has driven China up the technology rankings in many respects. The country has become a significant player in the production of scientific papers (Zhou & Leydesdorf, 2006). The number of R&D workers rose to 3.7m in 2014, patents granted doubled between 2009 and 2012 to more than a million per annum, scientific articles published more than doubled 2005 to 2010 (Fu, 2015, p.28) and citations increased significantly. Chinese supercomputers are the world's fastest, and China's "high technology" exports dominate sectors like laptop computers and smartphones.

However, while the quantitative indicators for the input of resources to technology development, and the outputs in terms of patents, citations, supercomputers and "high-tech" exports are impressive, the overall effectiveness of those activities is questionable. Nearly 90% of patents secured in China are for "utility patents" or "design patents", as opposed to "invention patents", which are the only category to undergo detailed review. Dang and Motohashi (2015) found that, by subsidizing them, government actually reduced the quality of patents applied for, and patents applied for by domestic firms are less valuable than those applied for by foreigners (Zhang & Chen, 2012). Citation rates have risen but remain below the UK which is a much smaller nation. Almost 90% of science and engineering graduates who study abroad do not return (OECD 2012, p.37) and many of the technologists who returned under the "100 Talents" scheme had not secured tenured posts in Western universities (McGregor, 2010, p.10), implying that they were not first class academic material. Most of China's "high-tech" exports are products that are assembled in China by foreign-invested firms, from sophisticated components imported from elsewhere. Most famously, for an Apple iPhone or iPad, assembled in China by Taiwanese firm Hon Hai, only 2% of the retail value is Chinese content and all of the embedded technology was developed elsewhere.

The problems that arise when governments make huge amounts of money available through administrative channels are obvious, and Chinese scientists have criticized the means by which funding is allocated. Those concerns have been confirmed in several cases. Prof. Chen Jin of Shanghai Jiao Tong University became a poster boy for "indigenous innovation" with his new "HanXin" microchip, until it transpired that the only innovation had been to replace the label on a Motorola chip (Hao, 2006). Shi and Rao (2010, p.1128) wrote that "it is an open secret that doing good research is not as important as schmoozing with powerful bureaucrats and their favourite experts". In 2015, in Guangdong, the provincial government made millions of RMB available for the development of robots. Hundreds of robot companies sprang up, but they were incapable of doing more than buy in the components to assemble simple and essentially useless robots. The government then announced schemes to develop "core technologies" for robots, only to find that industry experts believed that the "core technologies" themselves were already obsolete (He, 2016).

The administrative allocation of funds to technology development creates opportunities for "rent-seeking" whose pursuit may be more energetic than the pursuit of new knowledge. It is impossible to know how much of the government's technology spending has been wasted, and it is possible that the "shotgun" approach of targeting multiple sectors and showering them with funding might pay off. It is also clear that the impressive headline figures for "technology indicators" are over-estimates of China's status in terms of innovation outputs.

The market demand for innovation: are Chinese companies innovating?

While governments play a role in promoting innovation, most of the resources needed are provided by companies. Innovation is expensive and for companies to commit funds they need to believe that it is a requirement for their profitability. Technological "optimists" take the view that Chinese firms are increasingly including innovation in their business strategies for a number of reasons.

The first is the rising cost of labour. Wages have been rising and the country may have reached the "Lewis point" at which transfers of labour from agriculture to higher productivity sectors cease to provide the basis for growth. Furthermore, demographic changes mean that the labour force is no longer growing. As labour becomes more expensive, so Chinese companies may need to change the basis of their competitive advantage. Property prices and rents have been increasing.

A second reason why Chinese firms may need to innovate lies in the increasing inefficiency of a capital-driven economic development process, when the amount of capital needed to produce an additional unit of GDP has been increasing. At company-level, it is increasingly expensive to expand output simply by investing more, so that increasing output through technological improvement becomes a more attractive proposition than in the past.

A third reason why Chinese firms may profit from innovation lies in the increasing importance of the domestic market, particularly the growing middle-class segment and the changing tastes of Chinese consumers. Rein (2014, p.15) suggests that this huge group of consumers is increasingly looking for uniquely Chinese products to fit their increasing national self-confidence. Hence, profit opportunities are to be had by developing innovative products and services tailored to their specific needs.

While these are compelling arguments, they need to be set in context. Chinese wages have been rising at rapid rates, and are higher than in some competing locations for manufacturing, like Vietnam, Indonesia and even the Philippines. However, McKinsey (2015) estimated that Chinese labour costs in manufacturing would still only be $US5 per hour in 2019, compared with $US43 in the US and $US54 in Germany. China's "incremental capital-output ratio" has increased, but the country still has only a fraction of the capital stock per worker in use in the US, so that further investment should still produce good returns. Furthermore, the continued availability of "low hanging fruit" provides an alternative route through which Chinese firms can upgrade their technologies without innovating, except in the "copycat" sense.

Given these arguments and counter-arguments on the extent to which Chinese firms face pressure to innovate it is useful to turn to the evidence on their behaviour. Are Chinese firms innovating or not?

The overall data on companies' spending on R&D shows that it is increasing rapidly, with enterprises responsible for more than 70% of the total spending and 60% of the R&D workers (Fu, 2015, p.19). China's share of the total business R&D spending in the "OECD countries plus China" reached 15% in 2010, compared with less than 1% in the 1990s (Barlow, 2013, p.82) and there are more researchers working in businesses in China than in the whole of the European Union (OECD, 2012).

However, some of the increase in business R&D spending has "resulted mechanically from the conversion of some public research institutes into business entities, often without creating the conditions for them to become innovation-oriented firms" (OECD, 2007, p.31). Of the world's top 1000 companies by R&D spending, only 2% were Chinese, and proxies for the quality of R&D suggest that Chinese firms are far from becoming major players. Only 5% of China's patent applications in 2010 were to patent offices outside China and only 875 patents registered simultaneously in the US, Europe and Japan belonged to Chinese companies compared with 14,000 for the US and 15,000 for Europe. Of the world's top ten firms by "patents with at least one inventor having a Chinese mainland address" only three – Huawei, China Petroleum and China Petroleum and Chemical – were Chinese, the others all being from Taiwan or the US.

There are certainly Chinese companies who are spending large amounts on R&D, the most prominent being the "flagship national champions" – Huawei, Lenovo and Hai'er. However, they are not representative of the industrial sector as a whole, where R&D remains a low priority. In 2015 the World Economic Forum *Global Competitiveness Report* found that respondents rated "insufficient capacity to innovate" as the most problematic factor for doing business in China.

On balance, the evidence suggests that Chinese companies are not generating "new to the world" innovations on a scale that would make the country an innovation leader (Barlow, 2013). There are, however, aspects of technological improvement where Chinese firms are improving their standing in global markets, with less dramatic but effective initiatives. The most important of these has been described as "cost innovation" (Zeng & Williamson, 2007), "efficiency-based innovation" (McKinsey, 2015) or "accelerated innovation" (Williamson & Yin, 2014). Some Chinese firms have been applying scale and their skills in operations and manufacturing to the processes associated with product and process development. In genome sequencing, Beijing Genome Institute (BGI) in Shenzhen has an operation employing thousands of PhD students to make the sequencing of genomes faster and less expensive. The world market for small drones is dominated by Shenzhen-based drone maker DJI, which adopted the practices of the Hong Kong toy industry to dominate the low-cost part of the market, while developing significant new markets for cheap drones. Huawei, the "employee-owned" private company seen as having close links with the state, is the world's largest telecom equipment maker. It spends very significantly on R&D, aiming at 10% of revenues, but achieves market share, especially in emerging markets, with prices that are significantly below the competition, by accepting lower margins, by using cheap Chinese engineers, by using software copied from Cisco, and by providing solutions to customers' problems that do not require them to upgrade entire systems (Ahrens, 2013). Haier, in the white goods industry, recognized that wine storage cabinets are really just refrigerators, so they used scale in refrigerator production to make a substitute which can be sold for 50% of the competitors' price, and distributed it through mass retail outlets instead of connoisseur wine stores (Zeng & Williamson, 2007, pp.103–104). In each of these cases, Chinese firms began by absorbing technology from elsewhere, but then went on to raise volumes, lower costs, and make customer-focused adjustments that give them a competitive, if not a technological, advantage.

A second area in which Chinese firms have made significant improvements to technology developed abroad is in the Internet and e-commerce sector. Baidu copied Google but tailored it to the Chinese setting (including the government's demand for control) and became the dominant domestic search engine. WeChat began as a copycat of WhatsApp but developed an extensive platform around the initial application, which allowed it to outcompete its "parent". Alibaba soundly beat eBay, much to the latter's surprise, as TMall did Amazon. In the e-commerce sector Chinese companies adapted very quickly to the "move to mobile" and have gone beyond "copycatting", to the point where they can legitimately be seen as amongst the world's leaders.

A third aspect of China's "indigenous" innovation has been in respect of business models. In smartphones Xiaomi, founded in 2010, sold more than 60 million phones in 2014, at prices that were only marginally higher than the cost of production. It sees the phones as a means through which more profitable products, particularly those arising in the "Internet of things", will be delivered to its customers. There was a concern that in low-trust China, buyers would not be prepared to pay on-line for goods they feared might not be delivered. Hence, Alibaba introduced an escrow system whereby payment is not made to the seller until the customer receives delivery.

Cost-innovation, efficiency-based innovation, customer-driven innovation and business model innovation are less dramatic technologically than radical and disruptive technological breakthroughs. Nevertheless, they are areas in which China's industrial revolutions have given the country an advantage. How many of the country's companies are actively developing that advantage is not known. There is a "genuine cluster of high technology innovation" in Shenzhen (Barlow, 2013) where a well-developed ecosystem allows ultra-rapid prototyping of new products and new product introduction, and Zhongguancun in Beijing is often described as China's Silicon Valley. How successful they will become, and the extent to which such success will be replicated elsewhere, remains an open question.

The national innovation system in China

While government support and industry involvement are important, the "national innovation system" (NIS) perspective (Lundvall, 1992) suggests that a country's technological performance depends upon a more broadly defined set of institutions within which technological effort takes place. "Institutions" here refers to both "hard" institutions like government policies, research institutes, universities, laws, incentives and regulations and "soft" institutions like culture, psychology and individuals' motivations. As Barlow (2013) points out, perhaps the only economy that has developed a truly effective NIS remains the US, which for decades has been better at new to the world innovation than Europe or Japan. Not only does the US have the world's leading technology companies, venture capital industry, universities and government research initiatives. Perhaps more important, they are embedded in a system of well defended property rights, competition, and a set of values which promotes individualism and acquisitiveness, and does not despise failure.

To expect China to have developed such a system is unreasonable. Nevertheless, the NIS framework is helpful and a joint project between the OECD and the Ministry of Science and Technology (OECD, 2007) used it to arrive at six sets of specific recommendations, which illustrate the depth of the systemic changes needed. They were:

> **The role of government needs to be adjusted** to give more emphasis to market-oriented innovation, to focus on the provision of public goods, and to place emphasis on improving "framework conditions" to support both public and business-oriented innovation.
>
> **"Framework conditions"** include improved enforcement of intellectual property rights, fostering competition, improving corporate governance, opening capital markets to improve access to funding for innovation, innovation-oriented public procurement, and use of standards to support innovation, rather than suppress it.
>
> **Sustained growth of human resources for science and technology** as the number of R&D workers remains low relative to the population size, their quality and efficiency needs improvement, and businesses need to have incentives to invest in training, which is insufficient.
>
> **Improved governance of science and innovation policy**, including separating the MOST's responsibilities for policy making and managing R&D programmes, clarifying the roles of central and local government, strengthening an evaluation culture, and ensuring independent evaluations.
>
> **Adjusting the set of policy instruments** to avoid "high technology myopia" whereby sectors deemed "high-tech" attract disproportionate funding, combat the proliferation of technology initiatives, pay less attention to hardware and more to the "software" needed for an effective innovation system, like general management skills.
>
> **Ensure adequate support for public R&D** by re-assessing the role of public sector and university research, and having a balance between competition-based funding and institution-based funding. While most OECD countries have struggled to make their universities take an interest in applied research, China has the opposite problem in that universities have rushed into doing research directed towards minor short-term problems faced by industry and have neglected the fundamental research which companies which forms the basis for later generations of new products and techniques.

As the OECD/MOST list shows, strengthening the NIS involves fundamental changes to the whole of the Chinese system, without which technological improvements could be hampered. Some caution is required because the OECD is a key supporter of the contested "Washington Consensus", which argues that property rights, fully fledged market mechanisms and privately driven economies are the only way to secure long lasting progress. Nevertheless, the report is a joint effort with the Chinese Ministry and it does suggest that considerable institutional barriers exist to the development of a well-functioning NIS in China.

The place of technology import in China's innovation process

The import of technology from abroad has been at the centre of Chinese technology development since the nineteenth century, and remains so. In the first post-1978 "industrial revolution", the most important channel was through "foreign-invested enterprises" from Hong Kong who moved their manufacturing operations across the border (Tracy, 1995). The technologies involved were simple, involving garment manufacture and the assembly of toys, jewellery and electronics, but they gave employment to surplus farm labour and brought the discipline of factory life to agricultural Guangdong province. More important than technology "per se", they had the market intelligence and links to overseas buyers which allowed the "comparative-advantage-following" development strategy to succeed.

As China has developed, the technologies involved have become increasingly complex and sophisticated. Five main channels for technology import have been used.

The first is through the purchase of foreign equipment embodying more advanced technology. China's imports of machinery and equipment from the US, Germany and other developed countries have been a significant aspect of both industrial revolutions, reaching more than $US700 bn in 2012 (China Statistical Yearbook, 2015)

Provided the recipient Chinese firms have the capability to use imported equipment then the technology transfer is complete upon delivery and set-up. Chinese firms could go further by "reverse engineering" purchased equipment in order to earn how to make it, as did companies in Japan, Taiwan and South Korea. There has, however, been little evidence of that strategic intent. Firms importing equipment have been more concerned to put it into immediate use (Cao, 2004, p.8).

The second channel is the purchase of technological information from companies overseas through contracts like the purchase of licences, patents and copyrights. These have been in the region of 40 billion RMB per annum (Fu, 2015, p.23), 70% of which went to China's Eastern regions, 37% for licensing and 32% for consultancy. Evidence on their effectiveness is limited and it depends heavily on the "absorptive capacity" of the recipient companies. Explicit technological information, which can be made the subject of contractual transfers, often requires "tacit" knowledge if it is to be put into practice so that simply purchasing the information may be inadequate. There is also the concern (Davies & Whitla, 1995, p.194) that technology owners may restrict contractual transfers to relatively obsolete or peripheral items, in order to reduce the possible threat of future competition.

The third channel, which has received most attention, is technology transfer through foreign direct investment, where multinational companies establish production in China and bring the required technology with them. This can enhance technology development in two different ways. First, the foreign-invested enterprises (FIEs) bring higher levels of international competitiveness, productivity and efficiency than domestic firms (Fu, 2015, p.121), which is the result of their superior technology. Secondly, there are "spill-over" effects whereby technology development in domestic firms is enhanced as they learn from FIEs in their vicinity. Buckley, Clegg and Wang (2002) found that there were significant positive spill-overs from non-Chinese FIEs to private domestic firms, though not to SOEs, but that "HKTM" FIEs – from Hong Kong, Taiwan and Macau – did not provide any spill-over benefit except market access. That latter result was further supported by Huang and Sharif (2009) who found no evidence that domestic firms in Guangdong benefited from spill-overs from HKTM, the likely reason being that those firms are concentrated in low technology sectors with simple and mature technologies, about which there is little to learn.

Technology import through FDI can take place either through wholly owned foreign enterprises (WOFEs) or through equity joint ventures (EJVs) with local firms. Their relative merits, from both the Chinese and the foreign firms' points of view, depend upon a complex set of factors. WOFEs provide for greater control of the transferred technology which may encourage foreign firms to transfer more valuable and advanced intellectual property. On the other hand, the Chinese authorities want to see technology in local hands and if success requires deep local connections and *guanxi* with the authorities then an EJV remains the only viable option.

Until the early twenty-first century, technology transfer to China through FDI was limited to FIEs bringing technology into the Chinese setting. However, the government now encourages Chinese firms to "go out" and invest in companies overseas, with the specific aim of acquiring their technology at source. Hence an increasing number of Chinese acquisitions abroad, including high profile cases like Lenovo's acquisition of IBM's computer business, Geely's acquisition of the Volvo car company and Manganese Bronze (which makes London taxis), Haier's purchase of General Electric's appliance business, Tianjin Tianhai's purchase of Ingram Micro, ChemChina's takeover of Pirelli and bid for Syngenta, and Sany's ownership of Putzmeister.

How successful these ventures will be in bringing technology to China remains to be seen. A significant proportion have been by state-owned enterprises seeking to comply with the authorities' drive to go overseas, and those companies may be more adept at pleasing government than making effective use of the technology they access. On the other hand, others are developing into China's first significant multinationals, which could make them highly effective.

The fifth channel for the acquisition of foreign technology is through unsanctioned copying, or intellectual property theft, which has been a focus of contention between China and the developed nations for decades. The Business Software Alliance (2014) estimated that in 2013 74% of the software used in China, by value, was not properly licensed, compared with 19% in North America (and 82% in China in 2007). Fake products, from handbags and watches to pharmaceuticals are easily found in Chinese shops and American cyber security companies report continuous "hacking" from Chinese sources, with half of the private companies surveyed reporting the theft of secrets by Chinese-based organizations (Nash-Hoff, 2016). In May 2013 the US Commission on the Theft of American Intellectual Property (CTAIP) reported that China accounts for 80% of that theft and that "national industrial policy goals in China encourage IP theft, and an extraordinary number of Chinese in business and government entities are engaged in this practice" (CTAIP, 2013, p.3).

What impact this theft has had on technology development inside China is impossible to estimate. The US CTAIP report claimed losses to the American economy in the order of $US300 billion per year, which it described as the "greatest transfer of wealth in history" (p.2). However, there was clearly a political element in the report, and to equate estimated

US losses with China's gains is unlikely to be accurate. The most that can be said is that Chinese firms have learned significantly from the unsanctioned use of proprietary technology owned by others, and they have gained employment and market share as a result. Whether pirating knowledge takes China closer to the technological frontier, or locks the country further into dependence, is a moot point. (It might be also noted that American complaints about IP theft forget that, in the nineteenth century, the US built much of its own industry on stolen British technology.)

Innovation, culture and thinking processes: creativity and the Chinese person

The final set of issues concerns the claim that "China cannot innovate" because Chinese culture, the educational system and ways of thinking are antithetical to personal creativity. Chapters 1 and 4 have explained that the Confucian, Taoist and Buddhist philosophies that have shaped Chinese thinking place emphasis on group harmony, the unreality of the external world and the pointlessness of trying to change it, as opposed to the individualist and more activist nature of Western thought. "Holistic" Chinese ways of thinking, as opposed to "focused" Western thinking (Nesbitt, 2003), cultural characteristics like high power distance, collectivism, "knowing one's place", and paternalistic management can be seen as inhibitive of creativity (Ng, 2001). In a modern version of the "examination hypothesis" some blame is placed on the *gaokao*, which is the terrifying university entrance exam, for which Chinese students routinely spend 70 hours per week studying. The *gaokao* is an important element in China's claim to be a meritocracy, because success is the key to top universities, wealth and power, even for those from poor backgrounds. However, Antonick (2015) quotes a Chinese educator who said of the *gaokao*, "it is basically a cram system. It doesn't really encourage critical thinking, creative thinking or intuitive problem-solving. This partially explains why China is very good at copycatting, but not necessarily good at innovation or creativity."

There are reasons, therefore, to hypothesize that Chinese society produces fewer creative individuals, and that is supported by research findings. Niu and Sternberg (2001) found that American students produced more creative artworks than their Chinese counterparts, which was recognized by both American and Chinese judges. Yi, Hu, Scheithauer and Niu (2013) found that both Caucasian Germans and Asian Germans produced more creative art than Chinese students in Germany and Chinese students in China. However, Niu and Sternberg (2003) also found that Chinese students' creativity could be significantly increased by giving them instruction and guidance, so that its lack may be the result of social expectations, educational and testing practices, rather than anything more innate. Taken together with China's thriving art scene and the evidence that creativity can be improved through training (Scott, Leritz & Mumford, 2004) there is no overwhelming reason to suppose that China's technological development must be limited by its absence.

Conclusions on China's technology development

Conclusions must be tentative, given the dynamic nature of the situation and the country's ability to surprise. Nevertheless, a few key findings can be supported. First, the country's science and technology system does not yet generate a sustained flow of "new to the world" innovations of great significance. Vice President Biden was wrong when he suggested in 2014 that it was impossible to find a single modern Chinese innovation, but his basic point is well taken. In 2007 the Guangdong Association of Invention collected more than 50,000 "votes" on the question "what have been China's most significant modern innovations". Four were identified. Those were: the malaria medication artemisin, found in the 1930s, for which Tu Youyou won the Nobel Prize in 2015; the synthesis of bovine insulin in 1966 by Wang Yinglai; the development of hybrid rice in the 1970s by Yuan Longping; and laser typesetting for Chinese characters in the 1980s. Light-hearted participants could add the invention of the e-cigarette, by pharmacist Hon Lik in 2003, but there are no other globally salient Chinese inventions, and not one has originated from the post-2003 policy "push". When compared with the Chinese historical record, or with Western innovations like the microchip, antibiotics, GPS, touchscreens and the Internet, it is a poor performance. Great ambitions, grand projects announced, billions of RMB spent, millions of patents taken out, and world domination in supposedly "hi-tech" exports are not enough to counterbalance that simple fact. China is still unable to produce an internationally competitive passenger car without foreign assistance, the Chinese air force is reliant on Russian engines for its fighter planes, and it was only in 2016 that the country could provide steel of sufficient quality for the production of ballpoint pens!

At the same time, however, if we focus on "technological improvement", rather than innovation, it is clear that there has been real progress through incremental improvement, usually to technology imported from abroad. The most successful technological improvements to date have been those which are consistent with China's "subservient place in the world division of labour" (Lazonick, 2004) in that they focus on reducing costs through efficiency. Instead of inventing products differentiated by "new to the world" functionalities, Chinese firms have been radically speeding up the mundane process of product improvement. That kind of technical progress is less dramatic than the breakthroughs hoped for by the techno-enthusiasts and the policymakers in the Long to Medium Term Plan. However, they are probably of more value in raising China's prosperity, and maintaining companies' ability to compete internationally. Whether they have been helped or hindered by the technophile propaganda, and the mega-projects which have produced little of value to date, remains unclear.

References

Ahrens, N., 2013. *China's competitiveness: Myth, reality and lessons for the United States and Japan. Case Study: Huawei*. Washington, DC: Center for Strategic and International Studies.

Antonick, G., 2015. Breaking the grip of the gao kao, China's SAT, *Wordplay: The crossword blog of the New York Times*, 31 August. Available at: https://wordplay.blogs.nytimes.com/2015/08/31/mathleague/?_r=0 [Accessed 22 January 2017].

Barlow, T., 2013. *Between the eagle and the dragon*. Sydney: Barlow Advisory Pty Limited.

Buckley, P., Clegg, J. and Wang, C., 2002. The impact of inward FDI on the performance of Chinese manufacturing firms. *Journal of International Business Studies*, 33 (4), pp.637–655.

Business Software Alliance, 2014. *The Compliance gap: BSA global software survey*. June 2014, Washington, DC: Business Software Alliance.

Commission on the Theft of American Intellectual Property (CTAIP), 2013. *The IP Commission Report*, Washington, DC: National Bureau of Asian Research.

Cao, C., 2004. Challenges for technological development in Chinese industry. *China Perspectives*, July–August, pp.2–16.

CNN, 28 May 2014. Available at: http://politicalticker.blogs.cnn.com/2014/05/28/biden-name-one-innovative-product-from-china/ [Accessed 22 January 2017].

Dang, J., and Motohashi, K., 2015. Patent statistics: A good indicator for innovation in China?: Patent subsidy program impacts on patent quality. *China Economic Review*, 35, pp.137–155.

Davies, H. and Whitla, P., 1995. Technology transfers to China: The experience to date, in Davies, H. (ed.), *China business: Context and issues*. Hong Kong: Longman Asia, pp.190–214.

Fu, X., 2015. *China's path to innovation*, Cambridge: Cambridge University Press.

Hao, X., 2006. Scientific misconduct: Invention of China's homegrown DSP chip dismissed as a hoax. *Science*, 312 (5776), p.987.

He, H., 2016. Five Year Plan to transform robotics field, *South China Morning Post*, 7 April, p.B7.

Huang, C. and Sharif, N., 2009. Manufacturing dynamics and spill-overs: The case of Guangdong province and Hong Kong, Macau and Taiwan. *Research Policy*, 38, pp.813–828.

Lazonick, W., 2004. Indigenous innovation and economic development: Lessons from China's leap into the information age. *Industry and Innovation*, 4 December, pp.273–297.

Lin, J., Cai, F. and Li, Z. (1996) *The China miracle: Development strategy and economic reform*. Hong Kong: Chinese University Press.

Lubman, S., 2011. Changes to China's 'indigenous innovation' policy: don't get too excited. *Wall Street Journal*, 22 July. Available at: http://blogs.wsj.com/chinarealtime/2011/07/22/changes-to-chinas-indigenous-innovation-policy-dont-get-too-excited/ [Accessed 22 January 2017].

Lundvall, B., 1992. *National systems of innovation: Towards a theory of innovation and interactive learning*. London: Pinter.

McGregor, J., 2010. *China's drive for 'indigenous innovation': A web of industrial policies*. Global Intellectual Property Center, Global Regulatory Co-operation Project. Washington, DC: US Chamber of Commerce.

McKinsey, 2015. *The China effect on global innovation*. McKinsey Global Institute.

Nash-Hoff, M., 2016. What could be done about China's theft of intellectual property? *IndustryWeek*, Feb 9. Available at: http://www.industryweek.com/intellectual-property/what-could-be-done-about-chinas-theft-intellectual-property [Accessed 22 January 2017].

Nesbitt, R., 2003. *The geography of thought*. New York: Free Press.

Ng, A., 2001. *Why Asians are less creative than Westerners*. Singapore: Prentice-Hall.

Niu, W. and Sternberg, R., 2001. Cultural influences on artistic creativity and its evaluation. *International Journal of Psychology*, 36, pp.225–241.

Niu, W. and Sternberg, R., 2003. Societal and school influences on student creativity: The case of China. *Psychology in the Schools*, 40, pp.103–114.

Organization for Economic Co-operation and Development (OECD), 2007. *OECD reviews of innovation policy: China: synthesis report*. Washington, DC: OECD.

Organization for Economic Co-operation and Development (OECD), 2012. *OECD, Main Science and Technology Indicators*, 2012. Washington, DC: OECD.

Organization for Economic Co-operation and Development (OECD), 2015. *OECD economic surveys: China 2015*. Washington, DC: OECD.

Rein, S., 2014. *The end of copycat China*. Hoboken, NJ: Wiley.

Scott, G., Leritz, L. and Mumford, M., 2004. The effect of creativity training: A quantitative review. *Creativity Research Journal*, 16 (4), pp.361–388.

Shi, Y. and Rao, Y., 2010 China's research culture, *Science*, 329 (5996), p.1128, 3 September.

Time, 26 May 2015. Available at: http://time.com/3897081/carly-fiorina-china-innovation/ [Accessed 22 January 2017].

Tracy, N., 1995. 'Transforming Southern China: The role of the Chinese diaspora in the era of reform', in Davies, H. (ed.), *China business: Context and issues*. Hong Kong: Longman Asia, pp.1–21.

Williamson, P. and Yin, E., 2014. Accelerated innovation: The new challenge from China. *MIT Sloan Management Review*, 23 April, pp.27–34.

World Economic Forum, 2015. *Global competitiveness report* 2015–16. Geneva: World Economic Forum.

Yi, X., Hu, W., Scheithauer, H. and Niu, W., 2013. Cultural and bilingual influences on artistic creativity performances: Comparison of German and Chinese students. *Creativity Research Journal*, 25 (1), pp.97–108.

Yip, G. and McKern, B., 2016. *China's next strategic advantage: From imitation to innovation*. Cambridge, MA: MIT Press.

Zeng, M. and Williamson, P., 2007. *Dragons at your door: How Chinese cost innovation is disrupting global competition*. Boston, MA: Harvard Business School Press.

Zhang, G. and Chen, X., 2012. The value of invention patents in China: Country origin and technology field differences. *China Economic Review*, 23 (2), pp.357–370.

Zhou, P. and Leydesdorff, L., 2006. The emergence of China as a leading nation in science. *Research Policy*, 35 (1), pp.83–104.

7

THE END OF "CHEAP CHINA"?

Matevz Raskovic

The pace of change in China has been so startling that it is hard to keep up. The old stereotypes about low-wage sweatshops are as out-of-date as Mao suits. [...] If cheap China is fading, what will replace it?

(Economist, 2012)

Introduction

In 1978 the average Chinese urban worker received an annual wage equivalent to $US1,004 (Li, Li, Wu and Xiong, 2012, p.57), which meant that Chinese wages were only 3% of the average US figure, and lower than in Thailand or the Philippines. By 2010, wages had risen almost six times to $US5,487, reaching a par with those two countries, and significantly higher than those in India and Indonesia. Since then they have continued to rise by around 10% per year, so that in 2015, in Beijing and Shanghai, the monthly average wage was around RMB 7,000 (China Labour Bulletin, 2017), giving an annual figure of around $US12,000. In terms of average wages, Chinese labour is much more expensive than it has been in the past. On the other hand, according to the Economist Intelligence Unit (2014), hourly earnings in Chinese manufacturing were only $US2.10 in 2012, compared with $US35.7 in the US, and their expectation was that by 2020, Chinese labour costs would still only be 12% of the US figure. Chinese labour has become much less cheap and wages have overtaken those in many other emerging markets, but they remain low relative to the "triad" economies of Europe, North America and Japan.

For decades, cheap labour has been the salient characteristic of "Cheap China", which provided a shorthand description for the country's level of development, its low productivity, the basis for its "competitiveness" and its "subservient role in the international division of labour" (Lazonick, 2004, p.273). Living standards were low. Competing on the basis of low costs, arising from cheap labour and other resources, China became the "factory of the world", particularly after entry to the WTO in 2001 (Trivedi, 2016). The country specialized in products well aligned with its comparative advantage, exporting garments, shoes, simple electrical goods and other low technology items, plus "high tech" goods like smartphones and computers, which were assembled cheaply from expensive components produced in more advanced countries. Product quality was often medium to low, with *Poorly Made in China* (Midler, 2009) being a popular, if exaggerated, expression of Western feelings about many Chinese products.

As China is transforming, that picture is changing fast. Since reform and opening up began, growth has involved trying to close two types of *productivity gap* – the *international* one (by moving towards the international technology frontier) and the *internal* one (total factor productivity-based catch up, urban–rural and regional disparity, manufacturing–service transition) (Jefferson, Hu & Su, 2006). Closing both gaps is essential if China is to catch up with the developed world and reach the millennia-old Confucian ideal of a "moderately prosperous society". This has become a central theme within China's socio-economic transformation and a fundamental issue for political legitimacy under the last two generations of Chinese political leadership, climaxing in Xi Jinping's "dream" of a rejuvenated Chinese nation. "Cheap China" refers to low wages and labour productivity, low industrial productivity and low value added, which are reflected in living standards, disposable income levels, and the accompanying patterns of consumer behaviour. It has less to do with an historically embedded concept of "backwardness" (Ghauri & Fang, 2001, p.308), and is more connected to socio-economic transformation and the underlying sources of the country's current and future competitiveness.

As the Chinese rate of growth slows down, its leadership is looking to replace extensive growth based on greater inputs of labour and capital (Naughton, 2007) with growth based on increases in productivity, and a shift towards the international technology frontier. China also needs to avoid the perils of falling into the "middle income trap" (loss of efficiency-based competitiveness due to rising costs and living standards). This may mean that China will use much of the same "medicine" to help sustain moderate economic growth and will procrastinate in carrying out deeper structural economic reforms; or as Orr (2017) put it: "I see 2017 as a year of running faster and using more effort in traditional ways, to, in the end, travel more slowly."

If it seems that the era of "Cheap China" has passed, the future may be much more uncertain under the "new normal" – balancing lower growth rates with needed structural reforms and growing socio-economic disparities. As Lam, Liu and Schipke (2015) show, China's labour market has shown short-term resilience but long-term resilience depends on the implementation of reforms, particularly in sectors battling overcapacity, and unemployment in some SOEs might raise the rate by about 0.5 to 0.75% percentage points (from around 5% in Q1 2015). Nevertheless, the Chinese government needs to sacrifice short-term stability for long-term "structural transition – such as urbanization and service sector expansion" (Lam, Liu & Schipke, 2015, p.3).

In addressing the end of "Cheap China" this chapter focuses on three issues. First, the nature of the country's international competitiveness and its economic structure relative to other countries at different levels of development. Second, the nature of Chinese productivity growth and the internal productivity gaps (total factor productivity, urban–rural wages, manufacturing–service productivity), which create challenges for the next stage of development. Third, the question of whether China has reached the *Lewis turning point* at which rising urban wages and the exhaustion of surplus rural labour forces economic development to shift away from labour-driven growth and towards greater reliance on capital and technology (Golley & Meng, 2011).

China's competitiveness and structure: international comparisons

Building on Porter's (1990) framework for the analysis of competitiveness, the World Economic Forum (WEF) outlines three main types of national competitiveness. Those are: *factor-driven competitiveness* (as in the early stages of "Cheap China"); *efficiency-driven competitiveness* (as in the later stages); and *innovation-driven competitiveness*. In its Global Competitiveness Report for 2016–2017 WEF (2016) ranks China as 28th out of 138 countries worldwide on overall competitiveness, making it the highest ranked emerging country on the list. Examination of its competitiveness profile shows that while China is currently still at the efficiency-based stage, it is slowly outgrowing it and is trying to build up its human capital (education, innovation capacity, business sophistication) in order to transition towards innovation-based efficiency.

Table 7.1 provides a competitiveness overview showing how China compares to the developed markets of the US, Japan and Korea, as well as the emerging economies of India, Vietnam and Cambodia.

China's overall competitiveness ranking (28th) was most close to Korea's (26th), above India (39th) and well ahead of Vietnam and Cambodia, at 60th and 89th place, which have become new destinations for multinationals seeking cheap labour force (Magnier, 2016). While performance on pay relative to productivity was high (as would be expected of a country competing through efficiency), China also ranked well on R&D spending, government technology procurement, buyer sophistication and customer orientation, suggesting that the country is beginning to pursue more innovation-based competitiveness, focusing on human capital accumulation (Naughton, 2007).

Table 7.2 provides a structural comparison of China's economy with the others and also shows its position between innovation-based countries and those still reliant on resource and efficiency-based competitiveness. China's GDP per capita (at PPP) is far below the developed economies, but four times higher than Cambodia's, and more than twice that in both Vietnam and India, showing a gradual climb towards middle-income status. Agriculture represents 8.6% of China's GDP which is eight times higher than in the US and 3.7 times

Table 7.1 Comparison of China's sources of competitiveness with selected countries (2016–2017)

Rankings (out of 138 countries)	*China*	*US*	*Japan*	*Korea*	*India*	*Vietnam*	*Cambodia*
Overall competitiveness	#28	#3	#8	#26	#39	#60	#89
Nature of competitive advantage*	#43	#18	#2	#21	#36	#92	#97
Pay and productivity (ratio)	#27	#8	#24	#16	#33	#62	#63
Production process sophistication	#44	#9	#2	#22	#45	#91	#117
Capacity for innovation	#45	#2	#21	#30	#39	#79	#115
Quality of scientific research institutions	#40	#5	#13	#34	#36	#98	#123
Company spending on R&D	#25	#2	#4	#23	#28	#49	#84
Gov't advanced technology procurement	#10	#11	#16	#37	#7	#27	#95
Buyer sophistication	#33	#10	#5	#1	#17	#62	#59
Degree of customer orientation	#20	#13	#1	#27	#71	#109	#79
Quality of the education system	#43	#17	#37	#75	#29	#76	#87
Quality of management schools	#61	#7	#58	#63	#43	#122	#128

Source: World Economic Forum (2016): *Global Competitiveness Report 2016–2017*.

**Note:* The "nature of competitive advantage" indicator is part of WEF's business sophistication competitiveness pillar and relates to the level of firms' relative competitive advantage.

higher than Korea, but only half the share of GDP in Vietnam and India, or one third the share in Cambodia. Agricultural employment in China may be overcounted (Jefferson, Hu & Su, 2006, p.7) but, on the official figures, the agricultural sector still employs one third of the work force, which is lower than in Cambodia, Vietnam and India, but very high compared to the US, Japan and Korea.

China's industry value added and manufacturing value added as proportions of GDP are about the same as for Korea, but much higher than in Vietnam or Cambodia consistent with its "factory of the world" status (Trivedi, 2016). China's share of services and services value-added in GDP and, especially, employment still lags behind the developed countries, being close to that for India and ahead of Vietnam and Cambodia. China's share of exports of goods and services as a percentage of its GDP is similar to India, Japan and the US, though far below Korea's export oriented economy. It is also far below the figures

Table 7.2 Comparing China with selected countries: key indicators

	China	*US*	*Japan*	*Korea*	*India*	*Vietnam*	*Cambodia*
GDP growth (annual) 2015[a]	6.9%	2.6%	0.5%	2.6%	7.6%	6.7%	7.0%
GDP per capita (USD current in PPP)[a]	14,450	56,116	37,322	34,549	6,101	6,035	3,490
Agriculture as % of GDP[b]	8.6%	1.1%	1.2%	2.3%	16.5%	17%	26.7%
Industry as % of GDP[b]	40.7%	19.4%	27.7%	37.6%	29.8%	39%	29.8%
Services as % of GDP[b]	50.7%	79.5%	71.1%	60.2%	45.4%	44%	43.5%
% of labour force in agriculture[b]	33.6%	0.7%	2.9%	5.7%	49%	48%	48.7%
% of labour force in industry[b]	30.3%	20.3%	26.2%	24.2%	20%	21%	19.9%
% of labour force in services[b]	36.1%	79,1%	70.9%	70.2%	31%	31%	31.5%
Manufacturing value added as % of GDP[a]	29.7%	12.3%	18.7%	29.5%	16.2%	13.7%	17%
Industry value added as % of GDP[a]	40.9%	20.7%	26.9%	38.0%	29.7%	33.3%	29.4%
Services value added as % of GDP[a]	50.2%	78.0%	72.0%	59.7%	53.2%	39.7%	42.3%
Exports of goods & services (% of GDP)[a]	22.1%	12.6%	17.9%	45.9%	19.9%	89.8%	61.7%
High-tech exports (% of manuf. goods)[a]	25.8%	19.0%	16.8%	26.8%	7.5%	26.9%	0.8%

Source: [a]World Bank (2017): Development Indicators dataset; [b]CIA (2017): World Factbook Online database.

Note: data is shown for the last available year, which may vary between countries and indicators (2012–2016), and may be rounded up.

for Vietnam and Cambodia, whose low value added processing trade export driven economies have welcomed companies fleeing China's rising wages in search of cheaper labour (Magnier, 2016).

Taking these indicators together leads to the question: "is the era of Cheap China over?" As with so many issues in China, the answer is complex.

Breaking down China's productivity: a structural shift towards a productivity imperative

Chapters 2 and 3 have outlined China's socio-economic transformation since the late 1970s and we can draw on Taylor's (2016, p.281) analogy of "an economic miracle, but not an economic mystery" to understand the structure of China's competitiveness and productivity. Naughton (2007) suggests that a simple "Harrod-Domar" model of economic growth in which labour is abundant and fixed capital is the only determinant of economic growth captures a good deal "about the Chinese growth experience" (Naughton, 2007, p.146). Indeed, while the relationship between investment and growth is more complex (Easterly & Levine, 2001), empirical evidence confirms that between 1979 and 2011 China's GDP growth has been largely driven by capital investment (Purdy, 2013). Table 7.3 summarizes the breakdown in China's sources of economic growth between the start of the economic reforms and Xi Jinping's accession to power as the 5th generation of Chinese leadership in 2012.

As shown, the contribution of capital has been considerably larger than the contribution of labour throughout the reform period. Growth in total factor productivity (TFP) – which measures the efficiency with which inputs produce outputs – also made a lesser contribution, which actually decreased after 2002. Nevertheless, until the mid-1990s, Chinese economic growth was actually less dependent on growth of capital and labour than in other East Asian economies, with productivity-based growth being more important than in the "Asian Tigers" (World Bank, 1997). That changed in the early 2000s when China entered the WTO. In a comprehensive overview of the sources of economic growth in China's early reform period (1978–1995), Zheng, Bigsten and Hu (2009) found TFP growth to have been responsible for between 30% and 58% of GDP growth in the period. Hu and Khan (1997) came to a similar conclusion. Nevertheless, as Zheng, Bigsten and Hu (2009) have shown, most of the effects of Chinese reform before the 2008 global economic and crisis have had one time, or at best short-term effects in terms of productivity.

What about China's accession to the WTO in 2001? A meta-analysis of the impact of FDI on Chinese economic growth by Gunby, Jin and Reed (2016, p. 242) shows that "the effect of FDI on Chinese economic growth is much smaller than one would expect from a naive aggregation". While productivity spillovers from FDI have been apparent at regional

Table 7.3 Temporal overview of Chinese economic growth sources

	1979–1989	*1990–2002*	*2003–2012*
Average annual GDP growth	9.7%	10.1%	10.5%
Labour contribution	1.4% pts	0.5% pts	0.3% pts
Capital contribution	7.2% pts	5.7% pts	6.9% pts
Total factor productivity (TFP)	1.1% pts	3.9% pts	3.3% pts

Source: Purdy (2013).

level, the overall national effect has not been as high as previously believed, which is consistent with the large coastal-inland and regional development disparities which are still evident today.

Speaking at the G20 summit in August 2016 in Hangzhou, Xi Jinping re-iterated the need "to adopt an innovation-driven development strategy, deepen structural reforms and increase total-factor productivity, and add new impetus to strong, sustainable and balanced growth" (Official translation of Xi Jinping's speech for the G20 summit in Hangzhou, 2015, p.5). By 2014 the leadership, especially Premier Li Keqiang, was facing low and declining capital efficiency, a declining labour force and potential unemployment due to industrial

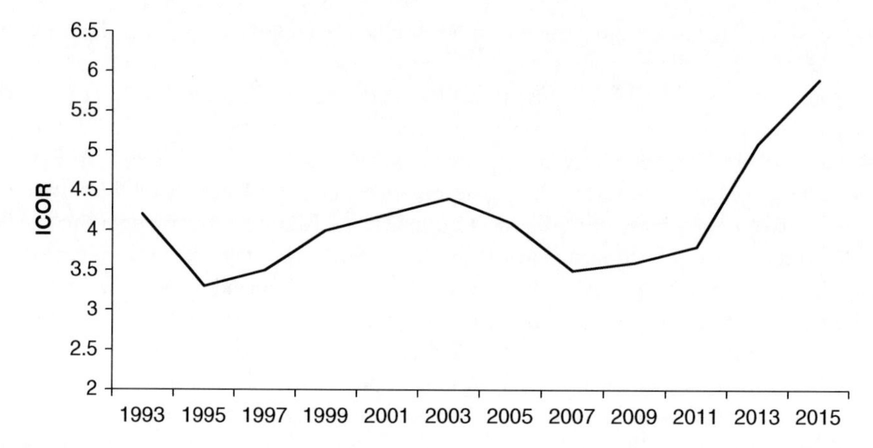

Figure 7.1a China's Incremental Capital Output Ratio (ICOR) (1993–2015)

Source: Goldman Sachs (2016, p.20).

Note: ICOR = incremental capital–output ratio.

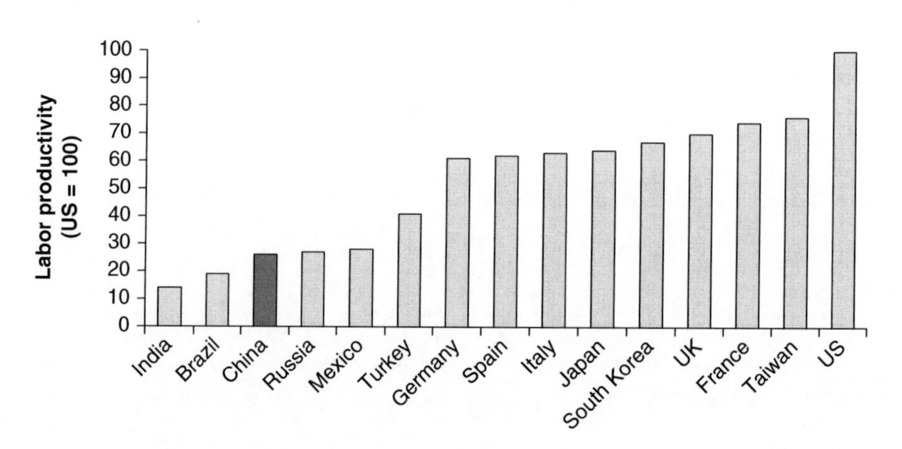

Figure 7.1b China's labour productivity (2015)

Source: Goldman Sachs (2016, p.53).

overcapacity, as well as faltering TFP growth. Figure 7.1a illustrates China's incremental capital output ratio (ICOR) between 1993 and up to 2015, showing the diminishing efficiency of invested capital since 2009. Figure 7.1b compares China's 2015 labour productivity with that of the US and other countries, showing that China's labour productivity is only a quarter (26%) of US labour productivity. Such low labour productivity will continue to be a significant barrier China's its long-term economic growth (Goldman Sachs, 2016).

On the demand side, while consumer confidence remained strong in 2016 and domestic demand grew at around 9%, declining exports and a potential trade war with the US may pose a challenge by reducing total demand and the profits needed to invest in efficiency improvements. If the prospects of a significant rise in capital efficiency are bleak, China will need to boost TFP in order to soften the erosion of its economic growth. Keeping in mind the scenario outlined in the 13th Five Year Plan (2016–2020) with average annual growth of 6.5%, domestic demand is scheduled to growth some 8.5% annually (quite realistic). In order to support that, however, TFP improvement would need to rise from 1.6% in 2015 to 2.5% by 2020 (Goldman Sachs, 2016). That might prove more of a challenge, since compared to, for example, Japan, which has faced similar indebtedness and economic slowdown challenges in the past, China's labour productivity is significantly lower, as are its technological know-how, education level and workforce skills (Goldman Sachs, 2016). Continuing the efforts to build up human capital accumulation and step up structural reforms would provide a boost in China's TFP, which is still much higher than Japan's in the 1990s (Goldman Sachs, 2016). We will return to these challenges again in the last chapter by looking into the future.

The double aspect of China's internal productivity gap

Two other aspects of China's *internal productivity gap* (Jefferson, Hu & Su, 2006), need attention, namely: urban–rural and regional disparities; and the manufacturing–service transition and productivity disparity. Both aspects are connected and have an important regional component.

While regional disparities in China have attracted a lot of attention, most of it has been concerned with either income inequality or economic growth. Regional aspects of productivity have been studied to a much lesser extent (Rizov & Zhang, 2014). However, Jefferson, Hu & Su (2006, p.1) have observed a large productivity gap between agriculture and industry, which persists to this day, despite the attention given by the 5th generation of Xi-Li political leadership to inclusive growth and greater rural development.

> In 2005 the average industrial worker produced more than seven times as much as his or her agricultural counterpart. Moreover, the gap has grown. From 6.1 in 1980, the ratio of industrial to agricultural productivity had shrunk by 1990 to 4.3, but thereafter it grew continuously until, at 7.1 in 2005, it surpassed the 1980 level.
>
> (Jefferson, Hu & Su, 2006, p.11)

Table 7.4 summarizes the regional productivity disparities based on productivity ratios in China calculated by Jefferson, Hu and Su (2006). The ratios use industry in the coastal areas (which is the most productive sector and location) as the reference category. Hence, in 1995, industry in the coastal areas was 4.47 times as productive as agriculture in the same regions. As it shows, the ratios of labour productivity in the industrial sectors decreased between 1995 and 2004 in all three other regions compared to the most developed coastal area. That was not the case with labour productivity in either the agricultural sector or the service sector. Yet, as Molnar and Chalaux (2015) have pointed out, the reason why China's labour productivity improvement has been so low is because most of it came from "within-sector" productivity improvements connected to inward FDI and technology-based mergers and acquisitions. In order to boost labour and TFP, China will need to tap into the "shift effect" of actually moving labour to more productive sectors. Here, the service industry will probably play an important role.

Table 7.5 provides some complementary evidence, with a similar breakdown across the same regional typology for labour, capital and TFP productivity ratios. As it shows, despite convergence in industrial labour productivity between the coastal and other regions, the coastal area was still far ahead in 2004. The biggest industrial labour productivity improvement can be observed for the North Eastern provinces with the productivity ratio to the coastal area dropping from 2.13 in 1995 to 1.39 by 2004. This is not the case when it comes to capital productivity, which was further dragging TFP catch-up of the three other regions compared to the coastal one.

An analysis of regional disparities and productivity from a survey of manufacturing companies for the period 2000–2007 by Rizov and Zhang (2014, p.333) showed that densely populated and highly urbanized coastal areas have the highest level of aggregate

Table 7.4 Chinese labour productivity ratio breakdowns by regions and sectors (1995 and 2004)

Sector/region	*Coastal*		*Northeast*		*Central*		*Western*	
	1995	*2004*	*1995*	*2004*	*1995*	*2004*	*1995*	*2004*
Industry	1.00	1.00	1.32	0.86	1.64	1.48	1.78	1.56
Agriculture	4.47	6.90	3.80	6.94	7.05	10.50	10.22	14.04
Services	1.05	1.50	1.70	1.98	2.24	2.96	2.42	3.67

Source: Jefferson, Hu & Su (2006, pp.11–14).

Table 7.5 Chinese industrial productivity ratio breakdowns by regions between 1995 and 2004

Productivity type	*Region*	*1995*	*2004*
Labour productivity	Coastal	1.00	1.00
	Central	1.66	1.21
	Northeastern	2.13	1.39
	Central	1.73	1.34
Capital productivity	Coastal	1.00	1.00
	Central	1.14	1.15
	Northeastern	1.69	1.55
	Central	1.23	1.29
TFP	Coastal	1.00	1.00
	Central	1.39	1.22
	Northeastern	1.90	1.45
	Central	1.49	1.31

Source: Jefferson, Hu & Su (2006, p.21).

Note: TFP = total factor productivity.

productivity. More importantly, it has also shown that the regional nature of Chinese productivity is affected by policy and structural factors. With regards to urbanization, their analysis points to another interesting aspect: less urbanized rural areas close to large urbanized areas on the coast show higher levels of productivity than medium-sized urbanized cities in mixed areas. The reason for this is that such medium-sized cities are too small to support productivity growth.

Environmental issues are also important in understanding changes in TFP. For example, a study by Zhang et al. (2016) has shown that TFP is overestimated if undesirable environmental outputs are not accounted for. While that is the case for all countries, in China such outputs also help to explain regional productivity disparities. Looking first at TFP changes across regions without adjusting for environmental aspects, for the 2011–2014 period, Zhang et al. (2016) found TFP changes ranging from 7.6% for Eastern provinces, 5.8% for Central and Northeast provinces and 5.3% for Western provinces. Taking the environmental aspect into consideration, TFP changes decreased to 3.9% for Eastern provinces, 3.6% for Central provinces, 3.5% for Northeastern provinces and just 2.1% for Western provinces. Eastern, mainly coastal, provinces have higher non-adjusted TFP not just because of geography, agglomeration, economic advantages, technology and human capital advantages, but also because of a higher level of environmental policies and measures, like energy saving and emission control.

Has China reached its Lewis turning point?

The Lewis turning point derives from the Lewis (1954) model of economic development and refers to the point in economic development when there is "a structural change from an excess supply of labour to one of labour shortage" (Zhang, Yang & Wang, 2011, p.542). That structural change results in rising wages in the industrial sector, which results in a large urban–rural gap (Cai & Du, 2011). Clearly, such a change is central to the narrative of "an end to Cheap China". However, as Cai and Du (2011) and Kwan, Wu and Zhou (2017) point out, there is a great deal of conceptual confusion and mixed empirical evidence on whether China has actually reached that point.

The wave of rural reforms in the late 1970s and early 1980s unlocked a seemingly unlimited supply of surplus rural labour, which was leveraged by China's Hong Kong FDI-driven manufacturing to create a "world factory" competing on labour-intensive production, buoyed by an undervalued RMB (Zhang, Yang & Wang, 2011). However, by the mid-2000s, labour shortages in coastal and urban areas, accompanied by growing wage and income inequality, sparked media-backed questions around the Lewis turning point. Some studies did find evidence that the turning point had been reached in some provinces in the first half of the 2000s (Zhang, Yang & Wang, 2011). However, Golley and Meng (2011, p.555) showed that "despite some evidence of rising nominal urban unskilled wages between 2000 and 2009, there is little in the data to suggest that this wage increase has been caused by unskilled labour shortages". For example, data from the Rural Household Survey shows that only 20% of the rural workforce has actually migrated to the cities, despite the fact that a large majority of that workforce is still "under-employed and earning very low incomes" (Golley & Meng, 2011, p. 556).

Since the 2008 global economic crisis, which significantly decreased export demand for low value-added Chinese products, overcapacity issues and potential unemployment surges have significantly muted the question of whether the Lewis turning point has been reached.

Indeed, it seems that rising labour costs and incomes in China's urban and coastal areas may be less connected to widespread overall labour shortages, and more to do with the lack of certain types of highly skilled worker. "Cheap China" is not over for all Chinese workers. As the government seeks new sources of economic growth, rising rural incomes and maintained levels of income growth in urban and coastal areas should be seen more in the context of China's attempt to become a three-legged economy driven by strong domestic demand (discussed in Chapter 10) and less to do with reaching the Lewis turning point. Kwan, Wu and Zhou (2017, p.1) have, for example, shown that "China [is] in the second stage of transition moving in the direction of full commercialization or the so-called Lewis turning point".

As China adjusts to a new model of development it has to face a series of issues which are more complex than the simple logic of reaching a Lewis turning point or not. Its rapidly aging population may mean "aging before affluence" (Cai & Du, 2011, p.609). That will significantly impact the structure of the labour force, as well as impacting domestic consumption patterns and putting social provision under pressure. Bridging both the urban–rural income gap and the inland–coastal development gap will have structural ramifications that go beyond the simple labour surplus-labour shortage logic and will be shaped by the relaxation or tightening of China's internal migration system, as well as the growing divide in real-estate prices between top-tier and bottom-tier cities. So typical of China and its economy, looking at the issue of the Lewis turning point opens up a series of paradoxes.

Walking a tightrope: labour and manufacturing cost vs. productivity and value added

The issue of labour and manufacturing costs is not only relevant to China, with its export orientation and large share of manufacturing in GDP, but to the whole "Asian Factory" context. That is made up of an intricate regional manufacturing network facilitated by integrating mechanisms like ASEAN. Asia today accounts for almost half of global manufacturing and China alone accounts for close to a quarter (Economist, 2015). Hence, China's transformation into a middle-income society, and its productivity shift, have important ramifications for Asia, its intra- and inter-regional integration, and for trends like global off-shoring, near-sourcing and reshoring for the US and the EU (Thieme & Connolly, 2015).

Official statistics on manufacturing labour compensation in China are scant at both national and provincial levels. There is also a great deal of methodological and conceptual ambiguity about what constitutes labour earnings and, hence, labour costs (EIU, 2014). Fairly solid data exists about urban manufacturing labour, and figures for urban wages are provided in the *China Statistical Yearbook*, which gives the figure of a $US5,487 per annum for 2010 (Li, Li, Wu and Xiong, 2012). However, a large share of China's manufacturing is still linked to town and village enterprises (TVEs) for which there is hardly any data (EIU, 2014). For example, in 2011, some 41 million were employed in manufacturing TVEs, many of which are located in rural areas (especially in Jiangsu, Shandong, Guangdong and Zhejiang provinces). This is much higher than manufacturing employment in urban enterprises (23.6 million) and urban SOEs (39.3 million) (EIU, 2014).

While comprehensive figures for wages and benefits are not available, it is even more difficult to measure changes in labour costs, because they depend upon the balance between increasing wages, guessed to be about 10% per year (China Labour Bulletin, 2017), and increasing labour productivity, which reduces labour cost per unit of output. Two milestones have been important for the wage–labour productivity relationship in China.

The first one is WTO membership in 2001 which created an FIE-led, export-oriented manufacturing boom during which labour productivity significantly outstripped wage growth. Annual wage growth did increase employees' benefits and social security coverage (Long & Yang, 2016) but Zhang and Liu's (2013) study of SOEs and private manufacturing firms between 1998 and 2007 showed that added-value per manufacturing worker grew ten times faster than wages.

The second milestone was the 2008 global economic and financial crisis. It created a significant reduction in demand for exports and was answered by the central government's multi-trillion RMB fiscal stimulus package. That was accompanied by the leadership's commitment to narrow the urban–rural income gap and build domestic demand market buoyed by expectations of significant disposable income increases to drive consumer confidence. Hence, the rate of increase of manufacturing earnings rose quite dramatically, with the increase in nominal GDP, from 2009 onwards, as shown in Figure 7. 2.

After China's accession to the WTO manufacturing labour earnings grew on average 11.9% per year in RMB per hour terms and 14.6% in US dollar per hour terms, given RMB exchange rate in the period. That was, however, much lower than growth in nominal GDP (real growth plus inflation). The biggest gap between wage growth and nominal GDP growth was in 2006 (some 8 percentage points), while the 2009–2011 period shows the effects of the central government's fiscal stimulus package. However, by 2012 manufacturing earnings growth declined to under 10% and again fell below nominal GDP growth, signalling a new era of economic slowdown (EIU, 2014). With the 5th generation Chinese leadership focusing on building a strong domestic market, the EIU (2014) estimates that manufacturing labour earnings will continue to rise in the 2013–2020 period, reaching some 12% average annual growth in RMB per hour terms, while GDP percentage growth will continue to decline and should stabilize around 6.5% per annum. In addition to economic and social policy determinants, China's rapidly aging population should also be taken into

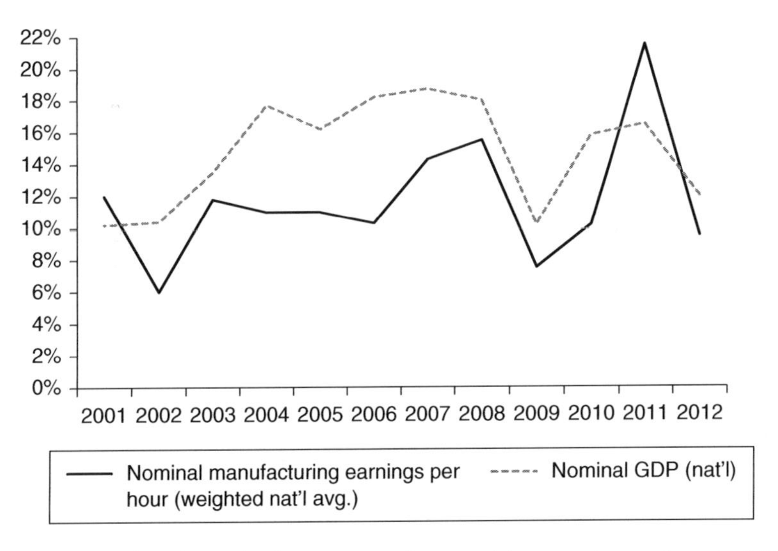

Figure 7.2 The relationship between manufacturing labour earnings and nominal GDP (2001–2012)

Source: EIU (2014, p. 6).

Note: Based on weighted provincial estimates by EIU.

consideration, as a diminishing workforce and the need for more skilled workers will create stronger pressures on labour earnings and manufacturing costs (Thieme & Connolly, 2015). On the other hand, the need to eliminate overcapacity may counter that trend, at least in the short-to-medium term, as workers lose jobs in those sectors.

If the relationship between manufacturing labour earnings and nominal GDP is most relevant for China and its development, the relationship between manufacturing labour productivity and manufacturing earnings shown below in Figure 7.3 is more relevant for foreign multinationals. As Figure 7.3 shows, that relationship changed significantly after 2004. By that time the initial boost in manufacturing labour productivity stabilized (EIU, 2014) and SOE reform produced diminishing productivity gains, consistent with evidence from Zheng, Bigsten and Hu (2009) on the short-term effects of reform processes, and Gunby, Jin and Reed (2016) on the lower than expected long-term national-level gains from inward FDI.

So what implications do these changes have internationally? Higher labour costs and rising energy prices have significantly chipped away at "Cheap China's" manufacturing cost competitiveness. Taking into account exchange rate changes, Goldman Sachs (2016) have estimated that between 2004 and 2015 China's manufacturing cost advantage deteriorated from 86.5% of the US (13.5% cost advantage) to just 97% (a 3% cost advantage). This has prompted many foreign multinationals to shift some of their labour-cost-sensitive manufacturing to countries like Cambodia, Vietnam, Indonesia and the Philippines, as well as to Bangladesh and India, despite their higher levels of risk and poor infrastructure (Thieme & Connolly, 2015).

In the apparel industry, for example, Levi Strauss & Co. entered China early in the 1980s, but by the late 1990s started withdrawing manufacturing from China in favour of countries like Cambodia, probably for cost reasons, despite their claim that the move was based on human rights and labour law considerations.

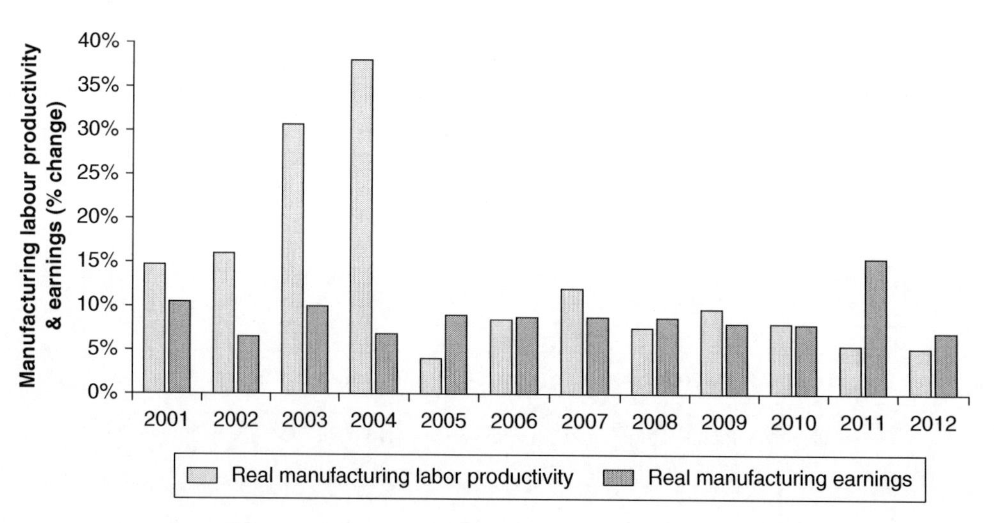

Figure 7.3 The relationship between real manufacturing labour productivity and real manufacturing earnings in RMB per hour (2001–2012)

Source: EIU (2014, p. 13).

However, it is not only rising manufacturing costs that have prompted foreign multinationals to relocate their manufacturing southwards. The costs of logistics and marketing have also increased as have taxes and government regulation (Goldman Sachs, 2016). Nevertheless, China's coastal areas remain important as manufacturing hubs, because their manufacturing ecosystems, logistics and supply chains are much more sophisticated and efficient than those in competing locations (Economist, 2012).

In addition to seeking alternatives in South East Asia, some US and European multinationals have used a combination of "reshoring" and "near-sourcing". Even before the 2016 US presidential election, Sirkin, Zinser and Rose (2013) of the Boston Consulting Group pointed to a growing trend of US multinationals having over 1 billion USD sales bringing back their manufacturing from China to the US, creating between 2.5 and 5 million jobs. While near-sourcing from Mexico may come into question under the Trump presidency, it is increasingly being used by European manufacturers, the Spanish apparel giant Inditex (Zara) being an example. In a reversal of the past, US and European multinationals will continue to shift from sourcing and manufacturing in China to manufacturing for and exporting to China (Thieme & Connolly, 2015).

What implications do these trends have inside China, reflective as they are of higher disposable incomes and growing living standards (addressed in Chapter 10)? Looking at China's manufacturing labour costs, there are also regional differences and convergences stemming from the "Develop the West" strategy. Table 7.6 shows the growth in manufacturing labour earnings for selected provinces both for the 2001–2012 and 2013–2020 periods. In 2000 the gap between the highest (Shanghai) and the lowest (Henan) manufacturing labour costs was 3:1, but by 2012 that had narrowed to 2.4:1 between Beijing and Jiangxi (EIU, 2014).

While many foreign multinationals have remained focused on China's southern regions, others have looked inland. Foxconn, the Taiwanese manufacturer of Apple products, has moved part of its Shenzhen manufacturing/assembly operations to Henan, Sichuan and Guiyang. Hewlett-Packard has moved manufacturing from Shanghai to Chongqing (Economist, 2015).

In terms of China's "going out", the 2013 One Belt One Road initiative proposed by Xi Jinping seeks to facilitate free trade through better land and maritime connectivity. It also seeks to replicate the past success of Korea, Taiwan and Hong Kong, avoiding the "middle income trap" by relocating low-end labour-intensive manufacturing out of China

Table 7.6 Closing the provincial gaps in manufacturing labour costs (average annual changes in % between 2001 and 2020)

Provinces	*2001–2012*		*2013–2020*	
	Highest growth	*Lowest growth*	*Highest growth*	*Lowest growth*
	Henan (17.1%)	Yunnan (10.6%)	Jiangxi (13.7%)	Qinghai (7.4%)
	Inner Mongolia (16.5%)	Guangdong (10.9%)	Guangxi (13.2%)	Shanghai (7.6%)
	Anhui & Tianjin (16.2%)	Fujian & Jiangxi (12.2%)	Fujian (13.1%)	Beijing (7.7%)

Source: EIU (2014, pp.7, 10).

in order to give way to higher value-added manufacturing, inward FDI-based learning and domestic technology development (Huang, 2016).

This has been further complemented by China's "Go Global 4.0" initiative, which aims to go beyond "Go Global 2.0" (SOEs go abroad) and "Go Global 3.0" (Chinese private firms develop overseas operations) but involves the active pursuit of global value chain integration and upgrading (State Council of the People's Republic of China, 2016). On the productivity side, the sophisticated manufacturing ecosystems in the coastal areas have begun a new kind of industrial revolution, seeking to make China one of the top ten most automated nations and to become a top industrial robot nation by 2020 (Reuters, 2016). Such trends, accompanied by a yet more skilled workforce is bound to have long-lasting positive impact on labour productivity, further supported by China's developing upstream strengths in R&D and design, and downstream strengths in marketing and branding.

However, while these trends will impact employment in some innovation-based manufacturing sectors, they are unlikely to have an impact where overcapacity and unemployment loom, while Chinese government appears to favour short-term stability before long-term structural changes.

Conclusion

Following the paths of Korea, Hong Kong and Singapore, China is trying to achieve structural change while re-defining the basis for its competitiveness, in order to move away from "Cheap China" to become a "moderately prosperous society". The words of former Chinese Premier Wen Jiabao are relevant (Harvard Gazette, 2003).

> Since China has 1.3 billion people I often like to make a very easy but at the same time very complicated division and multiplication. That is, any small individual problem multiplied by 1.3 billion becomes a big, big problem. And any considerable amount of financial and material resources divided by 1.3 billion becomes a very low per capita level. And becomes really small. This is a reality the Chinese leaders have to keep firmly in mind at all times. While every benefit is divided by 1.3 billion, every problem is quickly multiplied by 1.3 billion.

What sets China apart from the other "Asian Dragons" is its global economic weight, as well as its political and military importance. As the world's biggest exporter and manufacturer, China is a key player for both the US and the EU. Both have huge trade deficits with China, but increasingly seek to capitalize on its emerging domestic consumer market. While the EU prides itself on being China's chief provider of technology and a key partner in its One Belt One Road initiative, the rhetoric of the Trump presidency in the US raises concerns over trade and military conflict, and has put China into the unexpected position of becoming the vanguard for globalization.

Overall, then, China has graduated from being "Cheap China" in the sense of a low wage producer of low quality and low technology goods, which had no choice but to accept its allotted subservient place in the world division of labour, to a country which has wage levels which exceed that of many other emerging nations, and which is in the process of establishing a new position of influence over the world economic order (Rein, 2012). At the same time, there is a long way to go before wage levels and living standards for all approach the levels of the most developed nations.

References

Cai, F. and Du, Y., 2011. Wage increases, wage convergence, and the Lewis turning point in China. *China Economic Review*, 22 (4), pp.601–610.

Central Intelligence Agency, 2017. *World fact book*. Available at: https://www.cia.gov/library/publications/the-world-factbook/ [Accessed 14 May 2017].

China Labour Bulletin. 2017. Wages and employment. Available at: http://www.clb.org.hk/content/wages-and-employment [Accessed 1 March 2017].

Davies, H. and Ellis, P., 2000. Porter's Competitive Advantage of Nations: Time for the final judgment? *Journal of Management Studies*, 37 (8), pp.1189–1214.

Easterly, W. and Levine, R., 2001. It's not factor accumulation: Stylized facts and growth models. *The World Bank Economic Review*, 15 (2), pp.177–219.

Economist., 2012. The end of Cheap China. 10 March. Available at: http://www.economist.com/node/21549956 [Accessed 11 January 2017].

Economist., 2015. The future of factory Asia: A tightening grip. 14 March. Available at: http://www.economist.com/news/briefing/21646180-rising-chinese-wages-will-only-strengthen-asias-hold-manufacturing-tightening-grip [Accessed 29 January 2017].

Economist Intelligence Unit (EIU). 2014. *Still making it: An analysis of manufacturing labour costs in China*. London: The Economist Intelligence Unit.

Ghauri, P. and Fang, T., 2001. Negotiating with the Chinese: A socio-cultural analysis. *Journal of World Business*, 36 (3), pp.303–325.

Goldman Sachs. 2016. *Walled in: China's great dilemma*. New York and Shanghai: Goldman Sachs, Investment Management Division.

Golley, J. and Meng, X., 2011. Has China run out of surplus labor? *China Economic Review*, 22 (4), pp.555–572.

Gunby, P., Jin, Y. and Reed, W. R., 2016. Did FDI really cause Chinese economic growth? A meta-analysis. *World Development*, 90 (February), pp.242–255.

Harvard Gazette., 2003. Remarks of Premier Wen Jiabao. 11 December. Available at: http://news.harvard.edu/gazette/story/2003/12/harvard-gazette-remarks-of-chinese-premier-wen-jiabao/ [Accessed 7 February 2017].

Hu, Z. F. and Khan, M. S., 1997. Why is China growing so fast? *IMF Staff Papers*, 44 (1), p.103.

Huang. Y., 2016. Understanding China's Belt & Road initiative: Motivation, framework and assessment. *China Economic Review*, 40 (September), pp.314–321.

Jefferson, G. H., Hu, A. G. Z. and Su, J., 2006. The sources and sustainability of China's economic growth. *Brookings Papers on Economic Activity*, 37 (2), pp.1–60.

Kwan, F., Wu, Y. and Zhuo, S., 2017. Surplus agricultural labor and China's Lewis turning point. *China Economic Review* (accepted for publication), doi:10.1016/j.chieco.2017.01.009.

Lam, W. R., Liu, X. and Schipke, A., (2015). China's labor market in the "New Normal". *IMF Working Paper 15/151*.

Lazonick, W., 2004. Indigenous innovation and economic development: Lessons from China's leap into the information age. *Industry and Innovation*, 4 December, pp.273–297.

Lewis, W. A., 1954. Economic development with unlimited supplies of labour. *The Manchester School*, 22 (2), pp.139–191.

Li, H., Li, L., Wu, B. and Xiong, Y., 2012. The end of cheap Chinese labor. *Journal of Economic Perspectives*, 26 (4), Fall, pp.57–74.

Long, C. and Yang, J., 2016. How do firms respond to minimum wage regulation in China? Evidence from Chinese private firms. *China Economic Review*, 38 (April), pp.267–284.

Magnier, M., 2016. How China is changing its manufacturing strategy? *Wall Street Journal Online*. 7 June. Available at: http://www.wsj.com/articles/how-china-is-changing-its-manufacturing-strategy-1465351382 [Accessed 21 January 2017].

Midler, P., 2009. *Poorly made in China: An insider's account of the China production game*. Hoboken, NJ: Wiley.

Molnar, M. and Chalaux, T., 2015. Recent trends in productivity in China: Shift-share analysis of labour productivity growth and the evolution of the productivity gap. *Economics Department Working Papers*, No. 1221, 1–16.

Naughton, B., 2007. *The Chinese economy: Transitions and growth*. Cambridge, MA: The MIT Press.

Orr, G., 2017. What can we expect in China in 2017? *McKinsey & Company Commentary*. January Available at: http://www.mckinsey.com/global-themes/china/what-can-we-expect-in-china-in-2017 [Accessed 15 January 2017].

Porter, M., 1990. *The competitiveness of nations*. London: Macmillan.

Purdy, M., 2013. China's economy, in six charts. *Harvard Business Review Online*. 29 November. Available at: https://hbr.org/2013/11/chinas-economy-in-six-charts [Accessed 16 December 2016].

Rein, S., 2012. *The end of Cheap China: Economic and cultural trends that will disrupt the world*. Hoboken, NJ: Wiley.

Reuters., 2016. China seeks top-10 automation ranking by 2020: robot industry group. Reuters Online, 22 July. Available at: http://www.reuters.com/article/us-china-robots-forecast-idUSKCN102104 [Accessed 30 January 2017].

Rizov, M. and Zhang, X., 2014. Regional disparities and productivity in China: Evidence from manufacturing micro data. *Papers in Regional Science*, 93 (2), pp.321–340.

Taylor, J. B., 2016. The role of the Chinese economy in the world economy: A U.S. perspective. *China Economic Review*, 40 (September), pp.281–285.

Sirkin, H. L., Zinser, M. & Rose, J. (August, 2013). The U.S. as one of the developed world's lowest-cost manufacturers: Behind the American export surge. *BCG Perspectives*. Available at: https://www.bcgperspectives.com/content/articles/lean_manufacturing_sourcing_procurement_behind_american_export_surge/ [Accessed 15 May 2017].

State Council of the People's Republic of China., 2016. Chinese enterprise enter 'Go Global 4.0' era. Available at: http://english.gov.cn/news/top_news/2016/04/11/content_281475325205328.htm [Accessed 29 January 2017].

Thieme, D. M. and Connolly, J.D., 2015. Global manufacturing: The end of China's golden age? *BNY Mellon W-2014-0663*, pp.1–12.

Trivedi, A. 2016. China to world: We don't need your factories anymore. *Wall Street Journal Online*. 18 October. Available at: http://www.wsj.com/articles/chinese-manufacturers-once-needed-overseas-suppliersnot-any-more-1476801578 [Accessed 21 January 2017].

World Bank., 1997. *China 2020: Development challenges in the new century*. Washington, DC: World Bank.

World Bank., 2017. *World development indicators*. Available at: http://data.worldbank.org/data-catalog/world-development-indicators [Accessed 14 May 2017].

World Economic Forum., 2016. *Global competitiveness report 2016/2017*. Geneva: World Economic Forum

Xi, J., 2015. *Official Translation of Xi Jinping's speech for the 2016 G20 summit in Hangzhou*. Beijing: G20 2016 China.

Zhang, X., Yang, J. and Wang, S., 2011. China has reached the Lewis turning point. *China Economic Review*, 22 (4), pp.542–554.

Zhang, J. and Liu, X., 2013. The evolving patterns of the wage-labor productivity nexus in China: Evidence from manufacturing firm-level data. *Economic Systems*, 37 (3), pp.354–368.

Zhang, J., Fang, H., Peng, B., Wang, X. and Fang, S., 2016. Productivity growth-accounting for undesirable outputs and its influencing factors: The case of China. *Sustainability*, 8 (11), pp.1166–1178.

Zheng, J., Bigsten, A. and Hu, A., 2009. Can China's growth be sustained? A productivity perspective. *World Development*, 37 (4), pp.874–888.

8

BEHEMOTHS, SHADOWS AND CASINOS

The financial system

Howard Davies

China's financial markets roil the world

In July 2015, stock markets in Shanghai and Shenzhen fell by 30%, and global financial markets took fright. Federal Reserve Chairman Janet Yellen delayed a rise in US interest rates, attributing it in part to the shock from China, other markets fell, and the media were agog at the "Great Fall of China".

That reaction said more about Western ignorance towards China than it did about China itself. Few media accounts noted that the same markets had risen more than 150% in the 12 months from June 2014 to June 2015 (Lardy, 2015), and the "great fall" still left them with gains far ahead of those in developed countries. More important, few recognized that the connections between Chinese equity markets and the real economy are limited, so that the impact on companies and households was negligible. Equity markets are not a major source of finance for Chinese companies, and only 6% of households have any exposure to them. For the present, they remain highly undeveloped and a playground for retail investors and those who prey on them.

On the other hand, the financial fright of summer 2015 showed that China's financial system now has implications for the rest of the world. It needs to be understood.

The purpose and components of the financial system

In the command economy, household savings were kept low through wage/price setting, so that savings accrued to the state, through the SOEs, and investment was directed by the state. There was no need for a system to gather savings from millions of individuals and companies and direct them into investments determined by millions of others. The essence of a market economy, however, is the de-centralized nature of decision-making. In that setting the financial system has four purposes. The first is "financial intermediation" whereby those who have more income than they wish to spend are able to earn a return on their surpluses, while those who wish to spend more than they have can borrow what they need. Workers save for retirement and purchase insurance to cover unexpected expenses arising from sickness, accident or unemployment. Households take out loans to buy homes and "big ticket" items while companies borrow to acquire premises, machinery and working capital.

The second purpose of a financial system is to direct spending on real investment – in property, plant and equipment and inventory – towards those who will make best use of it. The third is to reduce the risks in the system, by combining risky assets into portfolios whose value will be less variable, and the fourth is to transform short-term assets into funds which can be used to finance longer term projects.

Modern financial systems are a complex nexus of organizations, markets and regulators, which together achieve the system's purposes, with varying degrees of success. The key components are:

- The banks, both "commercial" or "retail" banks and investment banks
- Non-bank financial institutions which perform similar functions to the banks, but are not banks
- The central bank
- Markets for bonds
- Markets for equities
- Insurance companies
- Regulatory authorities.

Table 8.1 shows the distribution of assets across China's formal financial system.

Behemoths: China's banks

China has almost 4,000 banks. However, the sector is dominated by five large commercial banks (LCBs), which own more than 60% of the assets of the banking system (World Bank/IMF, 2011, p.10). They are: Agricultural Bank of China (AgBank); Bank of China (BoC); Bank of Communications (BoCom); China Construction Bank CCB); Industrial

Table 8.1 The structure of China's financial system

Type of institution	*Number*	*Assets (RMB bn)*	*% of financial system assets*
All banks: **of which**	3,639	93,216	87.6
Large commercial banks	5	46,894	44.1
Joint stock commercial banks	12	14,904	14.0
Foreign banks	130	1,742	1.6
Other types of bank: policy; postal; co-operative	2,870	7,893	7.4
Non-bank financial institutions: **of which**	782	13,168	12.4
Insurance companies	125	4,965	4.7
National security funds	1	1,138	1.1
Fund management companies	63	2,520	2.4
Securities firms	106	1,967	1.8
Futures companies	164	192	0.2
Qualified foreign institutional investors	106	297	0.3
Other non-bank financial institutions	213	2,089	2.0

Source: World Bank /IMF (2011).

and Commercial Bank of China (ICBC). If the 12 joint stock commercial banks (JSCBs) are added, together they account for 83% of the sector's assets.

The LCBs are huge. ICBC is the largest bank in the world by total assets and market capitalization, and its IPO in 2006 was the world's largest at that time, to be succeeded by AgBank in 2010. ICBC has assets of $US3.6 trillion in 2015, almost 400,000 employees, 5 million corporate customers and nearly 500 million personal customers. The other LCBs are smaller, but still very large by international standards.

This banking sector has a number of features. First, bank loans are the largest channel for the provision of credit, and bank deposits are households' most important financial holdings. Second, the allocation of finance is still much less "marketized" than the allocation of other goods and services or the allocation of labour. The behemoth banks are listed in Shanghai (A-shares) and Hong Kong (H-shares) but control remains firmly in the hands of the state, usually through Central Huijin Investment, which is the government's investment company (Walter & Howie, 2011). Senior executives of the major banks are all appointed by the Communist Party's all-powerful Organization Department (Elliott & Yan, 2013, p.11) making them agents of the party-state rather than the banks they head.

State control has important implications. First, the general public has total confidence in the banks and believes that bank deposits are fully guaranteed by the government. That implicit guarantee provides trust, which is the foundation for stability, but it can also lead to "moral hazard" where participants take on too much risk in the belief that the government will always bail them out. Second, while they are supposed to operate on commercial principles, the LCBs have been used to provide credit to state-owned enterprises (SOEs), sometimes in situations where commercial judgment would preclude lending. The view that the LCBs are "ATMs for the SOEs" is outdated (Kroeber 2016, p.131). Bad loans they made to SOEs in the 1990s, which reached a frightening third of GDP, were taken off their hands and placed in "asset management companies". The LCBs were then re-capitalized by the Ministry of Finance and directed to focus their business on to healthy companies and consumer loans. As a result, they improved efficiency, the quality of lending has improved and the proportion going to the private sector has risen to around 40% (Borst & Lardy, 2015). Nevertheless, even in 2013, more than RMB 20 trillion in outstanding loans were to the state sector, compared with around RMB 17 trillion to the private sector, and there is scepticism about the declared figure for non-performing loans (NPLs).

Another feature arising from state control has been the availability of "financial repression", as a policy tool. Financial repression refers to a situation in which real interest rates (the rates paid to depositors minus the rate of general price inflation) are negative. Negative real interest rates are in effect a tax on depositors, which transfers resources from them to the banks and the state, which can use them to finance investment. It also gives borrowers access to finance on low interest terms. While many East Asian nations used financial repression as a major instrument of economic development, in China it has been applied sparingly, and in response to changing circumstances. From 1997 to 2003, when the priority lay with keeping inflation under control, real one-year interest rates were around 3%, which is high. There was no financial repression. However, from 2004 to 2013 real interest rates on one-year deposits swung between +3% and –3%, with a mean that was below zero (Kroeber, 2016, p.133). The rationale was that the authorities wanted the banks to re-build their balance sheets by making massive profits, and they wanted cheap credit to fund the massive investment projects that were their response to the global financial crisis of 2008/9.

That increase in spending on infrastructure and residential development was huge even by Chinese standards. When exports to the developed economies began to fall in 2009, and perhaps 20 million workers were laid off, the government launched a stimulus programme valued at RMB 4 trillion or 12% of GDP, which may really have been as large as RMB 11 trillion (Shih, 2010). The stimulus was effective in preventing unemployment, China was relatively untouched by the global crisis, and the country developed the infrastructure that makes America's roads, bridges and railways look hopelessly out of date. At the same time, however, the ratio of debt to GDP shot up so that the figure for the nonfinancial sector rose from about 135% in 2009 to 205% in 2015 (Kroeber, 2016, p.220). The banks were the key providers, SOEs and local governments were the organizations that did the spending, and the stimulus was implemented so quickly, and on such a huge scale, that there are doubts about the quality of some of the loans.

The level of non-performing loans (NPLs) and their consequences is disputed. Local governments have been less disciplined in their spending than the leadership would like, and some industries associated with the infrastructure programme – steel, cement, glass – suffer from overcapacity, pushing prices down, squeezing profits and making it likely that loans cannot be repaid. Hence, some have argued that NPLs are a major problem (Li, 2016). However, official sources report that they have fallen from around 9% of total loans in 2006 to less than 1% in 2013 (Elliott & Yan, 2013, p.14). Lardy (2016) points out that in 2014 and 2015 the banks further reduced the size of their NPLs, and that their coverage ratios exceeded 150%. In any event, he argues, NPLs would be unlikely to trigger a banking crisis because national savings are high, bank liabilities consist largely of deposits, which are "sticky", debt is in RMB not foreign currency, China is a net creditor to the rest of the world, and the authorities could provide instant liquidity to the system by reducing the relatively high reserve ratio of 17%.

Banking crises are rarely predictable and it would be reckless to declare that China is insulated from that possibility. It does, however, appear that a crisis triggered by an avalanche of NPLs is unlikely. While China's banks still have a bias towards the state sector, they are increasingly lending to private firms on truly commercial terms and thereby improving the overall quality of their loan books.

Policy banks and asset management companies

While the LCBs form the core of the banking sector, two other types of institution are important. First, there are three "policy banks". China Development Bank funds large infrastructure projects, like the Three Gorges dam. Export–import Bank of China, provides export credits and concessional loans to developing nations, in support of Chinese-backed development projects, Agricultural Development Bank supports projects in agriculture, water conservancy and rural infrastructure.

Then there are the four asset management companies (AMCs) – China Huarong, China Great Wall, China Orient and China Cinda. When the LCBs were overwhelmed with bad loans in 1999, NPLs equivalent to 15% of GDP were transferred to the AMCs, which took on the role of "bad banks". They purchased more than RMB 2 trillion of bad loans from the LCBs, mostly at face value. In a series of "accounting tricks" (Kroeber, 2016, p.132) the AMCs paid for the NPLs by issuing bonds, which were purchased by the LCBs. Hence, the LCBs replaced NPLs with the bonds of the AMCs. The AMCs were supposed to recover the bad loans over ten years and repay the bonds' principals in 2009.

However, recovery rates were low so the government extended the bonds' duration and spun the worst loans off into separate accounts backed by vague IOUs from the Ministry of Finance (Holland, 2013). Economic growth shrank the relative size of the problem and by 2009 bad loans held by AMCs amounted to less than 4% of GDP and 20% of government revenue. In the mean time the AMCs have transformed themselves into financial conglomerates, "distressed assets" being just part of their business. Huarong and Cinda have been listed in Hong Kong, and Great Wall plans a listing in 2017. In each case part of the burden of the long-standing debts are passed off onto (perhaps gullible?) foreigners, who have taken strategic stakes in the companies. As questions arise again about the level of NPLs, the AMCs stand as an example of the ability of the Chinese authorities to "kick the can down the road" with respect to debt problems, transfer some of the risk to others, and let growth render the problem less intimidating.

Shadows: the informal financial sector

While China's main banks are behemoths, they operate in tandem with the "shadows" of the informal banking sector. As they overlap extensively with the "real" banks they pose important concerns for the effectiveness and stability of the whole system.

Shadow banking is defined as "credit intermediation involving entities and transactions (partially or fully) outside the regular banking system" (Financial Stability Board, 2015). Li, Guo, Kao and Fung (2015) identify four broad types of shadow banking activity. First, there are "bank-related" products – financial instruments sold by the banks, but which are "off-balance sheet" and less tightly regulated. Foremost in this category are "wealth management products" (WMPs) (*licai chanpin*) created by third parties but sold by the banks, often giving the impression that they are part of the formal system. Investors seeking higher returns than the deposit rates paid by the banks find these products attractive because of the higher interest rates and their volume grew to around 9 trillion RMB in 2012. Bank-related products also include: "entrusted loans" where one company lends to another, but does it through a bank, which acts as trustee and earns a fee; "bank-trust" co-operations, where investors place funds with a bank with instructions to use them for a specific investment project, which is implemented by a trust company; and "bank-securities firm co-operations" where five different entities, including two banks, work together to convert a commercial loan which would be subject to regulatory constraints into a form which avoids that regulation (Li, Guo, Kao & Fung, 2015, p.43, explains the convoluted process involved).

The second category of shadow banking in China comprises "non-bank financial institution products", made up of "trust financial products" and small loans from finance companies. The third is "non-financial institution products" made up of private lending, on-line shadow banking, led by Alibaba, and peer-to-peer (P2P) websites, which allow participants to lend to each other. Finally, there are "credit guarantee companies", which guarantee the payment of amounts due to companies, thereby relieving their customers of credit risks.

The shadow banking system is huge. There are no definitive figures, as its very existence stems from attempts to sidestep regulatory processes. However, Yi (2013) puts the figure for 2012 at RMB 30 trillion and it is estimated to have accounted for about 40–45% of all new credit in that year (Li, Guo, Kao & Fung, 2015, p.47). It is also very complex and it changes quickly as technology and the regulations evolve.

Shadow banking has become so important for three reasons. The first is that an economy growing at double digit figures needs a large volume of credit to support spending by both the private sector and local governments, especially in the context of the huge stimulus put in place after 2008/9. Second, government regulations designed to reduce risk have made it difficult for the demand for credit to be fully met through the formal banking system, so that demand has found other sources of supply. As the government keeps deposit rates low and lending rates high, and as it requires the banks to maintain high reserve and deposit to loan ratios, so they cannot meet the demand for credit through their normal operations and they resort to unconventional channels. Third, on the supply side, savers seek higher returns than are available on bank deposits, so there is a willing supply of funds for lending at the higher rates and the higher risk levels which the shadow sector offers.

Several risks arise from the shadow sector. Wealth management products (WMPs) are often highly leveraged in that most of the proceeds are lent out. But WMPs often raise funds on a short-term basis, which are pooled and used to finance longer term projects. As they do not produce returns within the duration of the original WMPs it is necessary for new WMPs to be sold in order to repay the earlier ones. If it proves difficult to sell the later round or if the assets financed by the WMPs – often property – lose value, the banks could face a significant threat. In particular, there is concern that "local government financing vehicles" (LGFVs), set up to evade the requirement that local governments do not borrow money or run deficits, have borrowed in the shadow sector but will be unable to repay. Significant loans have also been made to small and medium enterprises (SMEs) in the export sector that are vulnerable to a decline in exports.

Recognizing these risks, the authorities have taken steps. From March 2013, the China Banking Regulatory Commission (CBRC) required that WMPs be linked to specific assets, and audited, and in December 2013 the State Council called for clarification of the responsibilities of each part of the regulatory system in respect of the shadow sector. The authorities sent warnings to the banks by unexpectedly forcing up short-term interest rates a few times, knowing that would be a threat to those who were relying too heavily on short-term financing. Fundamentally, however, shadow banking happens because the demand for credit is not met through formal channels, despite the presence of willing lenders. If interest rates offered to depositors and charged to lenders were fully marketized, so that credit could be appropriately priced according to the risk involved, the raison d'être for shadow banking would disappear. However, that would imply that loans made to zombie SOEs would have to be made on higher interest terms, or not at all, which would remove an important instrument of control and support. The authorities have made significant moves towards interest rate liberalization, so that in 2013 the floor on lending interest rates was abolished, and in October 2015 the deposit interest rate was also scrapped. However, as Lo (2015) points out, the authorities retain "benchmark" rates, at which SOEs and local governments can access credit, which means that interest rate liberalization does not yet perform the function of directing credit to where it can be best used.

Bond markets in China

Governments and corporations issue bonds in order to raise long-term capital. Bondholders are entitled to a stream of payments, fixed on issue, and to the repayment of the principal on maturity. They can sell them in the period before maturity, so there is a negative relationship between the price of bonds and the interest rate they yield. If government issues a bond at $100 for 5 years, and an initial rate of 5%, bondholders will receive $5 per annum and $100 in 5 years' time. If the bond is sold at a lower price, the $5 represents a higher yield and vice versa. In a smoothly functioning market the price of bonds would rise or fall until its return becomes equal to that available on similar assets.

Bond markets matter (International Capital Markets Association, 2013) because they provide stable sources of funding, they lower the cost of capital by providing competition for bank loans, and they reduce dependence on the banks. Different types of bond allow customization to meet participants' needs, cash flows in and out to be matched, efficient use of working capital and access to international capital markets. They also lead to improvements in governance as many bond purchasers are large institutional investors who demand transparency on the part of bond issuing organizations.

China's bond market, however, remains relatively under-developed, relative to the US. In 2010 the total value of bonds issued was equal to around 50% of the country's GDP, compared with nearly 250% for the US. Most bonds are issued by the "policy banks" (RMB 7.25 trillion in 2012) and the government (RMB 6.7 trillion) with corporate bonds at only RMB 1.98 trillion (Elliott & Yan, 2013, p.20). Most bonds are held by the commercial banks.

Slow development of the bond market can be attributed to a complex regulatory regime, with authority over bond issuance distributed between the People's Bank of China, the National Reform and Development Commission and the China Securities Regulatory Commission. In 2010 they began to work in a more co-ordinated way and to ease issuance of bonds by corporates. The response to regulatory easing was rapid and by 2012 corporate issuance had doubled from the 2008 figure and corporate bonds accounted for 30% of new issues. In May 2014, the State Council called for an increase in corporate financing via bonds and equities, relative to bank loans and that was followed by further dramatic growth. As might be expected, however, that has led to a number of defaults, with ten companies failing to repay in the first five months of 2016 alone (Borst, 2016) and 70 companies cancelling planned issues.

By 2016, China's bond market had become one of the largest, valued at around $US7 trillion (Hughes, 2016), but it faces an uncertain future. Defaults were previously unknown in the Chinese system, and many commentators welcomed them as a "welcome to the real world" for investors and issuers who had assumed that the government would always bail out bond issuers who ran into trouble. Such an injection of realism would certainly benefit the system by allowing the better pricing of risk. On the other hand, if participants have been frightened off, and fear for the security of the market, further development could be hindered for several years.

The insurance sector

China's insurance industry also remains under-developed, with a ratio of premium income to GDP of 3.7% compared with 7.9% in the US and premia per capita of around $US160 compared with $US3,124 in the US (Elliott & Yan, 2013, p.28). Gross premia in 2013 came to RMB 1.7 trillion, which was about 20% of the figure for the US. As incomes have increased, growth has exceeded 16% per annum for the decade up to 2013 (Saldias & Grigalunias, 2014) but some cultural barriers remain, notably the traditional belief that "paying to gain from death and disaster" is likely to bring on the calamity insured.

The industry regulator, the China Insurance Regulatory Commission (CIRC) requires legal entity separation of life and non-life business, and the life sector (which includes health insurance) dominates, accounting for more than 60% in 2013. Within the non-life sector, motor insurance accounts for more than 70% of the premia paid. While there were 68 life and 64 non-life insurers, both sectors are very heavily concentrated with the top three life firms (China Life, Ping An, New China Life) having 54% of the market and the top three non-life (PICC, Ping An and China Pacific) having 65%.

Given the under-penetration of insurance, and the increasing sophistication of the Chinese public, it can be expected that the sector will grow rapidly. However, regulations are complex, change rapidly and are interpreted differently in different parts of the country as the CIRC "crosses the river by feeling for the stones". Hence, growth has been more dependent upon regulatory changes than on market forces (Saldias & Grigalunias 2014, p.14). Foreign firms face different regulations from domestic insurers, who remain dominant, but as regulatory standards gradually approach international levels, there may be more opportunities for foreign direct investment.

Insurance companies are required to invest most of their assets in treasury bonds, local government bonds and deposits, forming an increasingly significant part of the market for those instruments. However, since 2010 the CIRC has allowed them to invest small proportions in riskier assets, again deepening financial markets.

Equity markets: casinos in Shenzhen and Shanghai

The Shanghai Stock Exchange (SSE) was established in 1990 and the Shenzhen Stock Exchange (SZSE) in 1991. Despite being in place for more than 20 years, they still do not play a role comparable to the equity markets in the US or the UK, for a number of reasons.

First, equity markets are not yet a major source of funds for companies, who rely on bank loans (for SOEs) and retained profits (for the private sector). Second, most of the shares traded are of companies that are majority-owned by the state, with relatively small proportions of the total equity being freely traded. As a result, non-state shareholders do not have the kind of rights associated with equity ownership in the US or the UK. They cannot pressure firms to distribute dividends, they cannot organize to replace incompetent executives, and they cannot direct firms to behave in profitable ways if the state decides otherwise. As a result, dividend payments are poor and large institutional investors, who take a long-term view and subject the firms they own to scrutiny, are largely absent from the Chinese equity markets. Furthermore, some types of large investor, like insurance companies and pension funds, who are major players in the US and European equity markets, are either not allowed to invest in equities or tightly restricted in the exposure they are allowed. As a result, most investors in the SSE and SZSE are individuals, many of them elderly people for whom it is a way of whiling away their time – and indulging in the only legal form of gambling allowed. The results can be absurd as in 2016 when a TV soap opera featured characters who had heard that shares in a company called "Red Rock" were about to surge. There was no such company listed, but in the following days shares in companies with similar names surged as naïve investors followed up on the "hot tip".

The SSE and SZSE are also hampered by concerns over the quality of accounting, and by significant fraud and manipulation of retail investors by unscrupulous securities firms. This is a problem for the authorities who would like to see equity markets as additional ways to raise capital for reforming SOEs and other ventures. Perhaps with that in mind they "talked up" the equity markets in 2014/15, describing the situation as the beginning of a "bull run", which retail investors took as a sign that the government would ensure price rises. However, prices in both markets fell by 30% in summer 2015, and the authorities responded in a ham-fisted way by imposing "circuit-breakers", which suspended trading if price falls exceeded a set limit. Such administrative controls tend not to work and they caused panic selling whenever trading was restored. Perhaps more important, the authorities' reputation as a capable technocracy was damaged. It is possible that they deliberately allowed retail investors to take losses as a kind of "investor education", but that seems unlikely. Leaders' angry responses and subsequent search for the "perpetrators" of the stock market crash suggest that was not their intention, and some commentators (Xin, 2016) have even suggested that the real cause of the crash was manipulation by the faction surrounding ex-President Jiang Zemin, seeking to weaken President Xi.

The regulatory framework

In any economy, the regulatory framework is key for the behaviour and performance of the financial system. In China, the State Council is the most senior state body and beneath it, each of the major financial sectors has its own overseer. The People's Bank of China is the central bank, responsible for monetary policy, drafting regulations, accounting standards, managing stability and regulating systemic risk. The Ministry of Finance influences the banks through its ownership stakes through Central Huajin, and the banks are overseen by the China Banking Regulatory Commission (CBRC). Securities firms and stock markets have the China Securities Regulatory Commission (CSRC), the insurance sector the China Insurance Regulatory Commission (CIRC) and the Ministry of Human Resource and Social Security covers the National Social Security Fund.

This system has facilitated rapid growth in the real economy while allowing China to avoid the financial crisis that damaged Western economies in 2008/9. At the same time, however, there are significant concerns both internally and amongst international financial institutions like the World Bank and the IMF, arising from the fact that capital markets are not fully marketized and a large proportion of financial transactions are driven by "regulatory arbitrage" – evading the regulations. In 2013 the Third Party Plenum identified eight significant changes needed in the next phase of reform (Borst & Lardy, 2015), namely:

Establishing fully private banks, which would not have the "implicit guarantee" of government support, and would need to be prudent.

Further develop the capital markets, so that more company financing will come from issuing equity and debt, and less from bank loans.

Establish a deposit insurance scheme, which would replace the dangerous implicit government guarantee.

Create a market-based exit system for failing financial institutions, which would help to replace the implicit guarantee.

Experiment with mixed state and private ownership of the LCBs, as exemplified by BoCom's senior management using their personal funds in 2014 to purchase shares, which might be extended to employee ownership and a reduction in the shares held by the Ministry of Finance.

Further liberalize interest rates, so that SOEs can no longer obtain finance at interest rates below the real value of capital, and households have less incentive to turn to wealth management products in the search for a return on their savings.

Move to a market-based exchange rate for the RMB, so the government can set monetary policy more freely, without the need to "sterilize" currency inflows associated with balance of payments surpluses.

Promote capital account convertibility of the RMB so that investors inside and outside China can freely choose where to place their funds.

Internationalization and convertibility of the RMB

Of all the reforms proposed for the next stage of China's financial development, the most problematic are those concerned with opening the capital account and making the RMB fully convertible at market-based exchange rates. In principle, the authorities have had those goals since 1993. However, the Asian financial crisis of 1997 and the global crisis of 2008/9 involved massive and de-stabilizing international flows of capital, and there is grave concern about what could happen should China "open the flood gates".

The costs and benefits of convertibility are well understood. If the RMB could be freely bought and sold, funds would flow to wherever they provide the best return, adjusted for risk. Chinese households and companies with free funds could place them wherever they thought fit, and banks and companies would have to compete for funds with those in other countries, which would force them to become more competitive. In the longer term, if the RMB becomes more widely used in the denomination and settlement of trade payments, if foreign central banks use it as part of their reserves, and if it provides an alternative "safe haven" to the US dollar, then China could also reap the benefit of "seignorage" whereby the authorities can simply print money and use it to buy goods abroad, knowing that foreigners would happily accept it.

Those gains are systemic, structural and long term, while the disadvantages are more immediate and reduce the authorities' control over the economy. Financial repression has been a useful policy instrument, shifting wealth to SOEs from households, in a system where the latter have limited outlets for their savings. But if households are free to invest their money wherever they choose, they can find positive returns elsewhere and attempts at financial repression would lead to a massive outflow of funds. Convertibility for the RMB denies the authorities a tool that helped them to support the financial sector through levels of bad loans in the 1990s which would have collapsed a more open system. Given renewed concerns over non-performing loans and the level of debt, the authorities are cautious about losing important instruments of control. That caution is heightened by the fact that it is very difficult to predict the net effect of introducing convertibility on the balance of payments. On the one hand, if it were put in place with credibility, so that foreigners believe there would be no reversal, China's growth prospects would make it highly attractive and investment would flow in on an enormous scale. On the other hand, Chinese households and firms have vast holdings of bank deposits which earn low returns even in the absence of financial repression, and they could well be attracted to foreign assets, leading to an equally enormous outflow. Small wonder that in 2015 Zhou Xiaochuan, Governor of the People's Bank of China, said "the capital account convertibility China is seeking to achieve is not based on the traditional concept of being fully or freely convertible" (Wildau, 2015). What that meant is unclear, but there is no reason to suppose that convertibility in the usual sense will be established soon. Whether that is driven by concern over the de-stabilizing effect of sudden huge financial flows, or by the desire to maintain control cannot be known.

Throughout 2016 Xi Jinping emphasized the need to shift to an emphasis on the "supply-side", which seemed to imply that banks, SOEs and the government should accept more market-based discipline, which convertibility would bring. On the other hand, President Xi shows no appetite for losing important levers of control. It seems likely, therefore, that the promise of "convertibility within five years" will be re-iterated, as it has for nearly 20 years, with only gradual progress.

Government and finance

The finance sector in China has grown as explosively as the real economy, through dramatic episodes including the Asian financial crisis of 1997, the bankruptcy of the major banks in the late 1990s and the global financial crisis of 2008/9. The authorities have followed the principle of "crossing the river by feeling for the stones", putting regulations into place step by step, observing the consequences and moving on. For the most part they have been successful, with the exception of the panicky introduction of "circuit-breakers" in equity markets in summer 2015. For decades, they have worked with international institutions like the IMF and the World Bank, to assess progress and learn from international practice. They took a close interest in the Western financial crisis and were gratified to see that the supposedly superior system was riddled with hidden risks, manipulation and moral hazard, which brought it close to collapse. At least two lessons were learned. The first was that the relatively closed nature of China's financial system had insulated it from financial contagion. Hence the extreme caution with which RMB convertibility is being approached. Second, it became clear that in the US Big Finance had captured the government, which the Chinese are determined to avoid. In addition to formal changes to regulations and systems, from time to time leading financial figures find themselves hauled off to answer charges of "manipulation" or "vicious speculation", probably to reinforce the understanding that the Party is in charge. While Goldman Sachs may control the US government (Cohan, 2011) their Chinese equivalent would undoubtedly find its partners enjoying the rough hospitality of the state should they ever attempt to wield similar levels of influence.

References

Borst, N., 2016. China's bond market: Larger, more open and riskier. *Pacific Exchange Blog*. Federal Reserve Bank of San Francisco, 20 May. Available at: http://www.frbsf.org/banking/asia-program/pacific-exchange-blog/china-bond-market-growth-openness-risk/ [Accessed 20 January 2017].

Borst, N. and Lardy, N. 2015. *Maintaining financial stability in the People's Republic of China during financial liberalization*. Working Paper 15-4. Peterson Institute for International Economics, Washington, DC: Peterson Institute.

Cohan, W., 2011. *Money and power: How Goldman Sachs came to rule the world*. London: Penguin.

Elliott, D. and Yan, K., 2013. *The Chinese financial system: An introduction and overview*. John L. Thornton China Center at Brookings Monograph Series No. 6, July, Washington, DC: Brookings.

Financial Stability Board 2015. *Strengthening oversight and regulation of shadow banking*. Available at: http://www.fsb.org/wp-content/uploads/global-shadow-banking-monitoring-report-2015.pdf [Accessed 20 January 2017].

Holland, T., 2013. China's insolvent toxic waste dump Cinda for sale. *South China Morning Post*, 19 August, p.B5.

Hughes, J., 2016. China's bond market on edge. *Financial Times*. 25 April. Available at: https://www.ft.com/content/7246cf2c-0a95-11e6-9456-444ab5211a2f [Accessed 20 January 2017].

International Capital Markets Association. 2013. *Economic importance of the corporate bond markets*. Zurich: ICMA.

Kroeber, A., 2016. *China's economy: What everyone needs to know*, Oxford: Oxford University Press

Lardy, N., 2015. False alarm on a crisis in China. *New York Times*, 26 August. Available at: https://www.nytimes.com/2015/08/26/opinion/false-alarm-on-a-crisis-in-china.html?_r=1 [Accessed 20 January 2017].

Lardy, N., 2016. No need to panic. China's banks in pretty good shape. *Financial Times*, 1 June. Available at: https://piie.com/commentary/op-eds/no-need-panic-chinas-banks-are-pretty-good-shape [Accessed 20 January 2017].

Li, Y., Guo, H., Kao, E. and Fung, H., 2015. Shadow banking and firm financing in China. *International Review of Economics and Finance*, pp.3640–3653.

Li, J., 2016. Chinese banks are set to take on more bad loans as the economy slows. *South China Morning Post*, 5 April, p.B6.

Lo, C., 2015. Here's what interest rate liberalisation means for China. *South China Morning Post*, 9 November, p.B5.

Saldias, C. and Grigalunias, L., 2014. *China's insurance market overview: Characteristics, trends, challenges and opportunities for foreign insurers*. Dagong Europe Credit Rating. Available at: http://www.dagongeurope.com/uploads/news/1403530484commentary-chinainsuranceindustry-24june2014.pdf [Accessed 20 January 2017].

Shih, V., 2010. Local government debt: Big Rock Candy Mountain. *China Economic Quarterly*, 26–32 June. Available at: https://chinaeconomybookdotcom.files.wordpress.com/2016/01/ceq_2010q2_localdebt_shih.pdf [Accessed 20 January 2017].

Walter, C. and Howie, F., 2011. *Red capitalism: The fragile foundation of China's extraordinary rise*. Singapore: Wiley.

Wildau, G., 2015. China's renminbi liberalization leaves capital controls intact. *Financial Times*, 22 June. Available at: https://www.ft.com/content/7727bfec-18a1-11e5-a130-2e7db721f996 [Accessed 20 January 2017].

World Bank /IMF 2011. *China: Financial sector assessment*. Washington, DC: World Bank.

Xin, L., 2016. Lessons behind the China's stock market crash. *China Business Knowledge@ CUHK Blog*, 18 May. Available at: http://www.bschool.cuhk.edu.hk/faculty/cbk/article.aspx?id=43376201 [Accessed 20 January 2017].

Yi, X., 2013. Shadow banking rampant in China. *China.org.cn* January 27. Available at: http://www.china.org.cn/opinion/2013-01/27/content_27775060.htm [Accessed 20 January 2017].

9

ENTRY STRATEGIES FOR THE CHINESE MARKET

Is the joint venture dead?

Matevz Raskovic

> Entry into the Chinese market remains a perplexing phenomenon for most outsiders.
>
> (Yaprak, 2012, p.1216)

Background

As earlier chapters have shown, foreign direct investment into China has played a key role in the country's development. That has involved two "waves" of investment and two very different types of foreign investor. In the first wave, which began in 1979 and continued until Deng Xiaoping's tour of the South in 1992, the investors were predominantly from Hong Kong. The companies involved were small and there were perhaps 100,000 of them (Tracy, 1995). They were concentrated in the small number of manufacturing sectors that had grown up in Hong Kong when the city lost its traditional role as entrepôt, including garments, toys, cheap watches, inexpensive jewellery, wigs and the assembly of electronic components. These companies were export-oriented, having been "born global", and they had a unique business model known as "original equipment manufacture". Instead of developing their own technology, designs and brands, they simply manufactured whatever the overseas brand-owners wanted, at very low cost. They had little technological expertise and put no effort into marketing, making most of their annual sales at industry fairs held in Hong Kong. Their key capability was what Riedel (1974) described as "merchant manufacturing" – knowing where to source and where to sell. This model had served them very well through the 1950s to 1970s but by the end of the 1970s Hong Kong's success had driven up wages and rents, putting their business model under threat. It was fortuitous, therefore, that at the end of 1978 China opened the door to foreign investment and gave these companies access to new supplies of cheap labour and facilities.

These companies first entered China at a time when it was not even clear that foreign investment was legal, and there were no markets on which to purchase labour, land, power, or other facilities. Hence, to operate at all the Hong Kong companies needed to ally themselves with local governments, mostly in the Pearl River Delta area. They therefore formed joint ventures with the local authorities, often from their old homes (*lao jia*) – the towns and villages from which their families had fled in the previous generation. They simply had no choice in respect of entry strategy. However, despite the fact that joint ventures are a particularly difficult form of business operation, with very high failure rates (Li, Li & Liu, 2013), these Hong Kong investors were very successful. There is no evidence that their failure rates were anything like that reported for joint ventures as a whole. That is probably because their Mainland joint venture partners had no interest in managing or controlling day-to-day operations, and were not trying to learn from them in order to become future competitors. Local governments acted as a substitute for markets, giving access to resources, and providing political protection, while the Hong Kong firms had total and undisputed control over what to produce, how to produce it, price it and who to sell it to. Division of the profits was the only area of contention.

The second wave of foreign investment was very different, so that the issue of entry strategy became much more complicated. When it became clear in 1992 that reform was not going to stall, and then when China joined the WTO in 2001, a different kind of foreign investor began to enter China. These were based in the "triad" economies of North America, Europe and Japan. Some were focused on production in China for export, but many were beginning to focus on the Chinese domestic market. They were in more "upstream", technologically complex and capital-intensive industries – vehicle and machinery manufacture, heavy electricals, chemicals, pharmaceuticals. They were much larger on average than the first wave of Hong Kong firms and had recognized brands of their own. For this type of company the choice of entry strategy for China involves a much more complex trade-off than had been the case for the Hong Kong early entrants. This chapter examines that more complex situation.

JVs and WOFEs: joint ventures and wholly owned foreign enterprises

While international business theory focuses on different types of market entry mode, foreign entrants into China need to shift their attention from entry strategies to understanding entry barriers (Niu, Dong & Chen, 2012). They also need to grasp the often paradoxical contextual and institutional factors affecting business in China and tackle the issue of how to deal with their "foreignness", which can be both an asset and a liability (Chen, Griffith & Hu, 2006). For a long time, Sino-foreign joint ventures (JVs) have been the most common approach to market entry into China (Yan & Warner, 2001). Foreign companies seek the help of Chinese partners to enter the Chinese market while their Chinese counterparts have sought to acquire know-how, technology and intellectual property (Niu, Dong & Chen, 2012; Beamish, 1988). Those conflicting motives (Hamel, Doz & Prahalad, 1989) have often spurred "races to learn" between the two sides (Hamel, 1991). As a result, JVs have more than their fair share of tensions and power struggles, and also experience high rates of failure, or strategic mutations (Li, Li & Liu, 2013).

As reform relaxed the legislation mandating JVs (Buckley, 2007), many of them evolved into wholly owned foreign enterprises (WOFEs) (Puck, Holtbrügge & Mohr, 2009). This led to claims that the JV in China was becoming extinct (Vanhonacker, 1997, 2000) and by the late 1990s WOFEs outnumbered JVs (Yan & Warner, 2001). However, despite the trials and tribulations of Sino-foreign JVs, and some high-profile exits by large multinationals, the JV is still not dead in China. Nor has use of the WOFE alleviated many of the institutional and contextual challenges faced by foreign firms. Instead, traditional modes of market entry and business are increasingly complemented and/or replaced by cross-border e-commerce and new kinds of Chinese "outward-for-inward" business. To understand these developments, it is necessary first to examine the historical and institutional factors behind the explosion of Sino-foreign JVs at the start of the reform and opening up process. Then it is possible to look at the benefits and costs of such ventures against the background of conflicting motives, differences in the resource bases of the partners, and the nature of JVs as learning races. That helps to understand success and failure in Sino-foreign JVs, the emergence of WOFEs, and whether WOFEs should be seen as substitutes or complements for the JV in China.

The historical and institutional background

Building on Zhou Enlai's *Four Modernizations* (discussed in Chapter 3), Deng Xiaoping believed in China's need to engage in international ventures in order "to attract foreign technology and expertise in the production of goods in order to satisfy the needs and expectations of the Chinese people" (Salem, 1981, p.74). This can be traced back to his "Twenty Points" policy paper in the mid-1970s, which had criticized China's self-reliance in production, and the rejection of both foreign technology and trade credit (Riskin, 1987). These views had been inspired by Deng's appreciation of the role that foreign investment and technology had played in the success of Japan in the Meiji era and among the "Asian Tiger" economies.

Following Deng's state visit to the US in January 1979, which attracted interest among US companies seeking to enter China, the People's Congress in July passed the Law of the People's Republic of China on JVs Using Chinese and Foreign Investment (the "JV Law"). However, having been closed and self-reliant for decades, China needed a series of new supporting laws on tax, trade, labour and banking (Salem, 1981) and without the accompanying JV regulations, which were not promulgated until 1983, the law had limited effect. Most of the incoming investment in the first years was from Hong Kong, with just a few early US and European JVs, mostly involving contractual relations rather than equity ownership.

Although the first act permitting WOFEs had been passed in 1989, the 1990s saw an explosion of JVs, which were clearly favoured by the state (Yan & Warner, 2001). For example, in addition to special investment ceilings ($US30 million in the coastal areas and $US10 million inland), WOFEs were subject to more stringent approval processes and more frequent reviews, thus providing an institutional barrier (Rosen, 1999). By the mid-1990s, the establishment of guidelines for foreign investment provided a much needed systematic and publicly available framework for the classification of industries into four categories: encouraged; permitted; restricted; and prohibited. It was also an institutional development from "ad hoc" to systematic treatment of all kinds of foreign investments. Nevertheless, while China has made considerable progress and improvements in its processes, it is still the case that:

> From the perspective of a potential foreign investor, China is not wide open. Investment in some sectors is banned, because of both commercial and security concerns; other areas remain difficult to invest in. The flow of investment that would be attracted by such straightforward factors as low labor costs [no longer the case with the end of "cheap China"] is thus heavily influenced by central policy.
>
> (Rosen, 1999, pp.24–25)

Regional differences and China's "Go West" policies mean that the classification of industries varies across regions and localities, providing some leeway for foreign entrants. However, the playing field remains restricted (Prange, 2016).

Sino-foreign JVs: the importance of market entry barriers

In addition to government's priorities (Rosen, 1999), market entry barriers (MEBs) are essential to understanding Sino-foreign JVs. An MEB is any "cost that must be borne by a firm seeking to enter a new industry or market that is not borne by firms already in that industry or market" (Niu, Dong & Chen, 2012, p.69). In the Chinese situation, such costs may vary significantly between domestic and foreign firms in China, as well as across the regions.

A distinction can be made between "structural" (technical) and "behavioural" (strategic) entry barriers (Greer, 1992). Depending on the industry, country of origin may be a strategic barrier, or it can be an advantage (Niu, Dong & Chen, 2012). At the same time, the *guanxi*-driven nature of the Chinese business landscape means that foreign entrants have an incentive to partner in order to lower behavioural barriers and gain much needed market access (Quer, Claver & Rienda, 2010). Table 9.1 illustrates the conflicting preferences of Chinese participants and partners from the "triad" nations in the establishment of Sino-foreign JVs.

Those conflicting preferences are complemented by fundamental differences in expectations between foreign investors and Chinese counterparts entering a JV, shown in Table 9.2, and often referred to as "One Bed, Different Dreams".

Besides the conflicting motives, which are not unusual when firms from developed markets enter emerging markets, JVs in China involve partners whose backgrounds, resource

Table 9.1 Conflicting preferences in Sino-foreign JVs

Foreign investor preference	*Chinese preference*
Small investment	Large investment
Produce for domestic market	Export orientation
Low-level technology/value added	High-level technology/value added
WOFE structure and control	Chinese majority JV
National market orientation	Single market orientation
Gradually phased paid-in capital	Up-front capital injection

Source: Adapted from Rosen (1999, p.29).

Table 9.2 Different expectations of parties entering the Sino-foreign JV

Rank	*Foreign investors' expectations*	*Chinese expectations*
#1	Open Chinese market to products (access)	Adopt advanced production technology
#2	Overcome trade and market barriers	Improve R&D capability
#3	Resource-seeking behaviour (labour costs, materials)	Open more information channels
#4	Expanding home scale and techniques	Allies for international cooperation
#5	Reducing financing risk and sunk cost	Additional (foreign) financing source
#6	Protecting copyright for intellectual products	Increasing firm reputation through famous brand
#7	Reduce capital input and investment	Utilize current and available resources
#8	Access natural resources	Reduce operational risk

Source: Adapted from Yang & Lee (2002, p.101).

bases and capabilities are very different. In comparison with relationships between companies which have similar characteristics, which Jolly (2006) dubs "endogamous" ("marrying in") relationships, such "exogamous" ("marrying out") ventures offer more significant potential for learning

Sino-foreign JVs as economic drivers

As noted above, Foreign Invested Enterprises have played a major role in China's economy and economic development. In the mid-1990s, FIEs (largely from Hong Kong) produced 47.1% of Chinese manufacturing exports and generated about 24% of industrial output in China with an average foreign equity share of 55% (Huang, 2001). Table 9.3 illustrates their role in specific manufacturing industries in China in 1995. As a wider range of foreign investors became involved, the share of FIE exports in total Chinese exports rose to around 2005–2006 with 58%, and then slowly decreased to some 45.9% by 2014 (Morrison, 2015). The role of FIEs was even greater for "high-tech" exports (largely the assembly of electronic components sourced from more developed economies), increasing their share from 79% in 2002 to 82% by 2010. The proportion of industrial output driven by FIEs increased from 2.3% in 1990 to a peak of 35.9% in 2003, settling down at around 26% by 2011. In 2010, FIEs employed about 16% of the urban workforce, or over 55 million (Morrison, 2015).

While the role of FIEs might appear to have diminished in recent years, they have remained important, even after the 2008 global economic slowdown. The overall share of exports in Chinese GDP has been declining (to about 22% in 2016), but the overall share of FIEs in those exports has increased from some 15% in 1991 to the 40% range (45.9% in 2014) (Huang, 2001; Morrison, 2015).

Zhang (1999) outlined three waves/stages of FIE presence in China prior to its 2001 WTO membership. In the first stage (1979–1985), most investment came from Hong Kong as a wait-and-see approach was adopted by most other foreign investors. This was followed in 1986–1991 by a small number of high-investment equity-based Sino-Foreign JVs, including the infamous Danone–Wahaha JV (discussed in the next section). There then followed rapid growth after Deng's 1992 Southern tour, which convinced investors that the reform agenda was not going to be reversed.

Table 9.3 Importance of FIEs in selected manufacturing industries in 1995

Manufacturing industry	*FIE exports to all exports of firms*	*FIE sales to all firm sales*	*Foreign equity shares of FIEs*
Food processing	57.5%	21.2%	57.5%
Garments and fibre products	60.5%	50.8%	63.3%
Furniture manufacturing	75.1%	30.7%	53.9%
Printing and record pressing	79.4%	18.3%	51.7%
Rubber products	53.3%	25.0%	59.1%
Plastic products	77.2%	33.1%	54.4%
Metal products	61.1%	26.6%	59.5%
Electric equipment and machinery	58.3%	21.8%	57.7%
Electronics and telecommunications	94.5%	60.8%	61.0%

Source: Huang (2001, pp.156–157).

Sino-foreign JVs: a foot-in-the-door strategy or smart business?

In addition to low labour costs, the key benefits of a JV in the early years included a mixture of government incentives including tax concessions, import-export tariff exemptions, free land and a wide array of supporting ecosystem infrastructure and services (Yan & Warner, 2001; Zhang, 1999). This was consistent with the resource-seeking motive for internationalization (Dunning, 1993). More recently, while foreign entrants still enjoy (some of) those benefits, their behaviour is now more consistent with market-seeking behaviour (He, Zhang & Wang, 2015). Chen, Griffith and Hu (2006) have also linked differences in behaviour with the "liability or advantage of foreignness". Analysing over 3,000 Sino-foreign manufacturing JVs, they found that resource-seeking behaviour was associated with foreignness being a liability and with labour cost-based competitive advantages, while firms for whom foreignness was an advantage (because of their technology or brand names) were more focused on market-seeking behaviour and higher level of control-focused strategies.

In terms of international business theory, several theoretical frameworks can help explain the motives behind JVs (Kogut, 1988). In the early stage, which saw a higher share of contractual JVs, the resource-seeking behaviour of foreign investors was consistent with a transaction cost logic (Hennart, 1988). Export processing zones and special economic zones (SEZs) translated into significant transaction cost reductions (Tse, Pan & Au, 1997). Sino-foreign JVs tapped into China's pool of low cost labour and enjoyed tax breaks, import–export exemptions, free land and a plethora of supporting services. These benefits helped to offset higher coordination and monitoring costs, as well as dealing with cross-cultural and governance issues, tipping the scale in favour of medium-term inter-firm cooperation over one-firm hierarchies or short-term market transactions. However, large market uncertainty and bounded rationality, as well as high asset specificity and idiosyncratic investments, not to mention opportunistic behaviour, all called for a relationship-based approach, not a transactional one (Lau & Tovstiga, 2015).

In the second stage, when equity joint ventures (EJVs) expanded rapidly, Dunning's (1979, 2001) eclectic paradigm, or the so-called OLI framework, helps to understand the balancing act between ownership (O), location (L) and internalization (I) advantages of MNCs engaging in FDIs. While foreign investors did have technology or brand names, and equity shares in the JV, which provided ownership advantages, and while cheap labour, export processing zones and SEZs provided clear location advantages, the conflicting motives of the two sides impeded the realization of internalization advantages over the medium- and long-term period. Even a strong relationship-based orientation could not offset the benefits of internal organizational hierarchy. For that reason, WOFEs were seen as the better alternative (Vanhonacker, 1997).

Strategic behaviour theory can also help to explain the motives for EJVs and their perseverance alongside the boom in WOFEs after WTO membership in 2001. While having a local partner might increase transaction costs, the strategic behaviour perspective suggests that partnering with a local can bring advantages in dealing with competitors (Kogut, 1988). It can help secure a local distributor, neutralize a competitor by making him a partner, redirect materials and inputs from other competitors, help build dominant standards and design, and deter new entrants. In the dynamic, uncertain and opaque Chinese market, these strategic considerations could be paramount.

Consistent with China's long-term development objectives, the organizational learning perspective (Kogut, 1988) also helps to explain why Sino-foreign EJVs have not died out in spite of the surge in WOFEs. If firms have very different capabilities, and "neither party owns each other's technology or underlying 'comps' [knowledge-based capabilities], nor understands each other routines" (Kogut, 1988, p.323) then learning from each other is required and EJVs work better than WOFEs. This has been often the case, for example, in the food and beverage industry, or in more high-tech industries where local Chinese firms have developed or perfected proprietary technology. At the same time, it explains the downside of such JVs when they become "races to learn" which one side must lose (Hamel, 1991).

Risk is also an issue in the choice between JV and WOFE. In the earlier US JVs, for example, the focus was on political risk (Daniels, Krug & Douglas, 1985), but that evolved into a mixture of overcoming partner-related risks (opportunistic behaviour) and the ramifications of resolving partner disputes. More recently, amidst growing US–China tensions at the beginning of a Trump presidency, the political risk aspect may once again come to the fore.

Table 9.4 provides an assessment of key benefits and drawbacks associated with Sino-foreign JVs.

While equity JVs are a form of strategic alliance where the two partners create a new legal entity, the contractual JV (CJV) is one that does not include the establishment of a separate legal entity. The negotiated control, obligations, and the division of profits are determined in a contract, which may more easily be subject to change and dissolution. CJVs between "foreign" firms and local governments were more popular than EJVs in the first stage of the opening up (1979–1985), which was dominated by Hong Kong firms, but they became less popular after the mid-1980s (Wang, 2007). Most often, CJVs related to contractual manufacturing, assembly and/or buyback operations, typically in labour-intensive assembly operations in southern Guangdong province (Pearson, 1991).

In contrast to CJVs, the establishment of EJVs requires a negotiation process which balances the different owners' preferences through concessions. Those preferences are determined by asset superiority (strong brands, technology) and degree of non-redeployable assets and idiosyncratic investments, which determine the amount at risk. In a study of 4,223 Sino-foreign EJVs in China between 1979 and 1992, Pan (1996) found that advertising intensity, foreign capital input (above requirement), lower level of country risk, longer duration of the EJV, higher cultural distance, higher competitive intensity and coastal location were all associated with a higher foreign share of equity in the JV. The proportion of local partner state-ownership and a higher level of investment had negative impacts on the share of foreign equity.

Failures of Sino-foreign JVs: the Wahaha effect or timing out?

In 1996 the EJV between France's food giant Danone and the Chinese beverage company Hangzhou Wahaha Group was described as a "showcase" Sino-foreign JV (Gielesen, Helsen & Dekimpe, 2012, p.398). The 51% French-controlled JV encompassed a total of 39 different JVs for Wahaha branded drinks and snacks, creating at its height a $US2-billion behemoth and making Wahaha the biggest beverage company in China. A decade later, the French and Chinese partners became entangled into a tumultuous two-year much publicized breakup, with Danone accusing the Chinese partner of opportunistic behaviour and parallel sales of branded products in direct violation of their JV agreement.

Table 9.4 Key benefits and drawbacks in Sino-foreign JVs for foreign investors

Benefits for foreign investors	*Drawbacks for foreign investors*
Institutional and political factors	
• Government support (tax breaks, import/export exemptions, infrastructure, less red tape) • Manufacturing ecosystems and support	• Potential dispute "politization" of disputes • Long and costly dispute resolutions • Impartiality of Chinese courts • Long and complicated JV set-up • High legal costs • Variations in legal enforcement and institutional variations (central-local gov't differences)
Risk factors	
• Overcoming market risks and risk sharing • Risk pooling and risk offsetting • Overcoming behavioural MEBs (*guanxi*)	• Market volatility and opaqueness • Rapid institutional and structural market changes • Potential opportunistic behaviour of partner
Resources and capabilities	
• Resource pooling and complimentary resources • Capability pooling • Decreasing market entry sunk costs	• Exogamous relationship • Non-aligned resource bases • Non-aligned capability bases • Idiosyncratic investments and asset specificity
Marketing and competitive advantage	
• Overcoming LoF • Access to information • Stronger market orientation • Perception of "local" origin and brand presence • Timing and market entry (first mover advantage) • Learning potential • Generation of large sales and profitability • Reducing competition and vertical integration	• Problems of "foreign element" • Less opportunity for joint learning • Limited absorptive learning and technology capacity • Less opportunity for joint knowledge creation • Long-term development of a local competitor • Overreliance on Chinese market as business grows • Need to reinvest profits
Management and governance	
• Access to local talents (competitive costs) • Relationship-based and personal management • Greater diversity • Transfer of managerial know-how	• Mixed-motive dyad and different expectations • Opportunistic behaviour tendencies • Various perceptions and procedural justice issues • Importance of interpersonal relationships and fit • High monitoring costs • Cross-cultural and organizational issues • Constant relationship maintenance • Subsidiary-headquarter tensions • Usually defined time duration

Source: based on Yan & Warner (2001), Daniels, Krug & Douglas (1985), Niu, Dong & Chen (2012), and Yang & Lee (2002).

The Chinese counterpart responded by drawing on Opium war-based historical resentment of French imperialism and stirred up a huge public backlash against Danone in China, which was their most important overseas market (Bu, 2011). Filing over a dozen lawsuits in China and before the Stockholm Chamber of Commerce Arbitration Institute, Danone achieved a "pyrrhic victory" internationally, becoming a "landmark case" for the verification of "western judicial systems in China" (Bu, 2011, p.589). However, the return of the Wahaha trademark to the Wahaha group against a $US450-million compensation to Danone by the Chinese court was seen not only as a de facto victory for the Chinese partner, but also significantly dented Western investors' confidence in dispute resolutions in Sino-foreign cases (Bu, 2011).

The Wahaha case was not an isolated case, or an aspect of the post-1990s JV boom. There has been a resurgence of high-profile cases (Uber's sale to Didi, McDonald's decreasing their share to 20%), which raised the question: are Sino-foreign JVs doomed to the Wahaha effect, victims of political tensions or simply a matter of learning races which have reached their inevitable conclusion?

Success factors for JVs

As they involve two different organizations working together, JV success clearly depends on a wide range of economic, political and managerial contingencies (Child, Davies & Cheung, 2003). The performance of JVs is also often attributed to qualitative factors like the personalities of the leaders, and the match or mismatch of organizational cultures, administrative styles and management philosophy (Yan & Warner, 2001).

Yang and Lee (2002) found that in China at the end of the 1990s political, economic and managerial factors were more important than cultural or societal factors. In terms of political factors, government stability was seen as the most essential. Among the economic factors, market growth and potential, and the continuation of economic reforms were seen as the most crucial. Among the managerial factors, the appropriateness of technology was the most essential factor.

Comparing the market entry success of foreign firms into China and India (n=168), Johnson and Tellis (2008) found higher rates of success in China than in India. Smaller firms, early market entrants and JVs with higher degrees of foreign ownership were more successful. In contrast to expectations, they also found that cultural distance did not play a major role, once other factors were controlled for (managerial practices, level of control). A meta-analysis of 62 empirical papers focusing on foreign firm performance in China by Quer, Claver and Rienda (2010) showed that more relationship-embedded JVs in which partners committed more resources, as well as engaged in stronger cooperation and collaboration were more successful. That is consistent with more recent evidence in Lau and Tovstiga (2015), and also shows that those Sino-foreign JVs that managed to overcome the difficulties caused by differences in their backgrounds had a higher chance of success and long-term survival. Other factors contributing to success were: having more closely related products; using the contractual mode of JV, and; having prior experience in the Chinese market. Consistent with Dunning's OLI paradigm, there was also a strong and positive location effect, showing the positive effect of operating in better developed manufacturing ecosystems of the coastal and urban regions.

Case studies of Finnish firms in China (Zheng & Larimo, 2010) showed that high levels of partner commitment, establishing trust, and higher levels of partner cooperation had a positive impact on Sino-Finnish JVs, as did conflict between the partners, provided there was effective conflict resolution. The latter established a feeling of procedural justice. Both foreign investor bargaining power and higher level of control also had a positive impact on the JV. Similarly, analysing 20 Sino-UK JVs, Wilson and Brennan (2009) found a link between a stronger relational orientation from the side of the foreign investor and JV performance. Trust was seen as essential, but it needed to be accompanied by commitment, cooperation and satisfaction.

Drawing together the various studies, based on different types of sample and widely different methodological approaches, three key findings emerge. The first relates to higher levels of foreign investor control, which provides the foreign investor with the reassurance needed to make larger idiosyncratic investments and to utilize firm-specific assets in the JV. The second relates to stronger levels of foreign investor commitment, which goes beyond invested resources, and which helps to build trust, smooth over potential conflicts and ensure procedural justice. The third relates to overcoming the conflicting motives and "exogamous" nature of the relationship between the partners at the outset, in order that they engage in deeper cooperation and cooperation as the JV takes off and grows.

WOFEs: one bed, one dream

By the mid-1990s, WOFEs gained favour, partly because of relaxation of the legislation on ownership, but also because of foreign investor frustration with the JV (Vanhonacker, 1997). As a means of escaping the "One Bed, Different Dreams" problem, the shift towards WOFEs was not just a matter of control issues and inter-firm relationship frustrations, but also a response to the growing need to respond more quickly and effectively to rapidly changing market conditions and market reforms. WOFEs have the advantage of higher flexibility and control, compared to EJVs. They also help to reduce problems caused by technology spillovers to the partner and issues arising from the excessive focus on short-term profit-maximization in many Chinese counterparts, compared with the more long-term strategic-oriented thinking of foreign investors (Vanhonacker, 1997). Table 9.5 summarizes the key pros and cons of WOFEs relative to EJVs.

The potential drawbacks of WOFEs can be mitigated in several ways. A greater degree of local production and sourcing is beneficial and helps the WOFE offset the perception that it is a foreign "predator". Likewise, a higher proportion of locals in the workforce and the employment of locals in middle and top management positions, is also welcome. Because their "foreignness" directs attention to them, WOFEs also need to pay greater attention to corporate social responsibility and engagement with local stakeholders, especially the government, which can be helped by formally establishing the venture as a joint stock company (Vanhonacker, 2000).

Table 9.5 Pros and cons of WOFEs relative to EJVs

Pros of WOFEs	*Cons of WOFEs*
Foundational requirements	
• Quicker set up (processing) • Lower legal costs • No board of director requirements • Government more interested in what foreign investors bring to China, less with how they do business • Can be combined with EJV (hybrid or umbrella projects)	• Prohibited and restricted for some industries • More complicated registration procedures and bureaucratic burden • Stricter government oversight • Subject to stronger government discretion • May be more politicized

Management and governance	
• Greater control • Greater flexibility • Quicker market responsiveness • Less emphasis on short-term financial performance • Greater control over sourcing and marketing • Promotes greater idiosyncratic investment • More suitable in cases of high headquarter dependence (isomorphism) • May be more appropriate for technical labour	• Lack of local managerial know-how • Lack of local connections • Harder access to materials (pricing) • Lower bargaining power with local stakeholders • Stricter enforcement of existing regulations • More sensitive labour issues • Industrial espionage and huge staff turnover • Local talent recruitment and expat staffing • More sourcing and distribution problems
Competitive advantage	
• Promotes long-term strategic orientation • Facilitates experiential learning • Promotes innovation and technology development • May combine benefits of EJV and WOFE functioning	• Lack of local *guanxi* • Subject to more behavioural MEBs by locals • Perceived as a foreign entity (public backlash) • Harder to win government contracts • Difficult establishment of local alliances
International trade and domestic business	
• Similar restrictions in term of foreign-exchange rules • Greater flexibility with transfer pricing	• Higher export quotas (at least 50%, even 70% for restricted industries) • Generally, fewer/no import tariff exemptions

Source: Adapted from Vanhonacker (1997, 2000), Yan & Warner (2001).

Case studies of Italian firms entering the Chinese market and choosing between JVs and WOFEs showed that smaller firms were more inclined to employ JVs (Bontempi & Prodi, 2009). In terms of specific sectors, WOFEs have been prohibited or discouraged in financial services, the automobile industry and telecommunications and in those sectors firms have no choice (Vanhonacker, 2000). However, where they do have a choice, JVs were preferred for intermediate goods and mature products requiring little protection while the WOFE was preferred for younger products, and for more high-tech and sophisticated products needing greater protection.

Conversion of JVs into WOFEs

Puck, Holtbrügge and Mohr (2009) provide useful insights into how JVs can be transformed into WOFEs. Applying a transaction cost logic and an institutional perspective to organizational decision making, they analysed a sample of 195 Sino-foreign JVs from 13 different countries. They found that higher levels of acquired local knowledge by the foreign investor, and a reduction in external uncertainty, increase the probability of JV-into-WOFE conversion. Greater cultural distance between the foreign investor's host country market and China decreased the probability of JV-into-WOFE conversion, as did having local partners better equipped to deal with local stakeholders. All those findings are consistent with transaction cost logic. On the other hand, in contradiction to transaction cost reasoning, higher asset specificity did not have a positive association with conversion. Consistent with an institutional perspective, their results also show how internal "isomorphic" pressures can initiate JV-into-WOFE conversion. Since many MNCs have a tendency to "isomorphism" – they prefer to do the same things in the same way – they seek to replicate their management from headquarters and they seek greater control of Chinese subsidiaries. Hence, there is a tendency to transform a JV into a WOFE, unless other factors prevail, most obviously Chinese government involvement or regulation.

In many cases the conversion of a FEJV into a WOFE can be seen as a natural process arising from experiential learning and the dynamics of market positioning. It may also arise from changes in managerial style, changes in the firm's ability to acquire the human resources it needs without the aid of a partner, or from market and regulatory changes (Yan &Warner, 2001). It may arise from the dissolution of a JV partnership that has failed, or a wish for greater control and flexibility. In any event, the transition from JV to a WOFE is more likely to be successful if it can be seen as a natural conclusion of the relationship (Vanhonacker, 1997). Coca-Cola and Starbucks have been good examples of amicable transition in which the foreign investors bought out their local partners without public backlash and government outrage (Economist, 2007).

The future of the JV

It is clear that deciding between JVs and WOFEs when entering and operating in China is complex (Vanhonacker, 2000). In many cases, it is not simply an "either/or" decision, but rather a "what now/ what then if" sequence of decisions, which follows a sequential and complementary logic. Chinese institutions change and markets are increasingly liberalized but JVs will continue to be useful in a high-context, *guanxi*-based, opaque and ever fluid environment where local knowledge and connections (Yan & Warner, 2001) have the potential to offset the "One Bed, Different Dreams" problem and potential for messy divorce associated with the JV (Vanhonacker, 1997). Put simply, if a company seeking to do business in China needs resources that are not freely available on a competitive market, it needs a local partner, and it needs to use the JV mode.

For the future, JVs are increasingly taking the form of "JV-WOFE hybrids", which include: JVs with "silent partners", which de facto operate as WOFEs; the combination of WOFE research centres and production with EJV sales and distribution; and EJVs that are designed from their inception to eventually convert into WOFEs. Even without such hybrids and mutations, Yan and Warner (2001, p.21) predict that Sino-foreign JVs will continue to exist for the foreseeable future in niches that are "dynamically defined".

As the Chinese economy becomes less focused on exports and oriented more towards domestic demand, and if China becomes more innovation-driven, new kinds of Sino-foreign JV may emerge to serve the idiosyncratically Chinese consumer. They could be based on less conflicting motives and on relationships between companies who differ less from each other in terms of background, experiences and resources. Instead of having foreign partners with a clear lead in technology and branding, which the Chinese partners seek to acquire from them, to the foreigners' disadvantage, there could be partnerships of equals, seeking to realize mutual advantage. In a reversal of the historic relationship, Sino-foreign JVs could become a vehicle through which foreign firms capture China's domestic branding and innovation potential, or its increasingly skilled technical labour force. In such cases, the two partners sleeping in one bed might well have the same dream.

References

Beamish, P. W., 1988. *Multinational joint ventures in developing countries*. London: Routledge.

Bontempi, M. E. and Prodi, G., 2009. Entry strategies into China: The choice between joint ventures and wholly foreign-owned enterprises: An application to the Italian manufacturing sector. *International Review of Economics and Finance*, 18 (1), pp.11–19.

Bu, Q., 2011. Danone v. Wahaha: Who laughs last? *European Journal of Law Reform*, 11 (3/4), pp.588–602.

Buckley, P. J., 2007. The strategy of multinational enterprises in the light of the rise of China. *Scandinavian Journal of Management*, 23 (2), pp.107–126.

Chen, H., Griffith, D. A. and Hu, M. Y., 2006. The influence of liability of foreignness on market entry strategies: An illustration of market entry in China. *International Marketing Review*, 23 (6), pp.636–649.

Child, J., Davies, H. and Cheung, L., 2003. The performance of cross-border units in China: A test of natural selection, strategic choice and contingency theories. *Journal of International Business Studies*, 34, pp.242–254.

Daniels, J. D., Krug, J. and Douglas, N., 1985. U.S. joint ventures in China: Motivation and management of political risk. *California Management Review*, 27 (4), pp.46–58.

Dunning, J. H., 1979. Toward an eclectic theory of international production: Some empirical tests. *Journal of International Business Studies*, 11 (1), pp.9–31.

Dunning, J. H., 1993. *Multinational enterprises and the global economy*. Harlow: Addison-Wesley.

Dunning, J. H., 2001. The eclectic (OLI) paradigm of international production: Past, present and future. *International Journal of the Economics of Business*, 8 (2), pp.173–190.

Economist. (19 April 2007). Joint ventures in China: Wahaha-haha! *The Economist Online*. Available at: http://www.economist.com/node/9040416 [Accessed 10 February 2017].

Gielesen, K., Helsen, K. and Dekimpe, M. G., 2012. 'International entry strategies', in Shankar, V. and Carpenter, G. (eds), *Handbook of marketing strategy*. Cheltenham: Edward Elgar, pp.391–414.

Greer, D. F., 1992. *Industrial organization and public policy*. New York: Macmillan.

Hamel, G., 1991. Competition for competence and inter-partner learning within international strategic alliances. *Strategic Management Journal*, 12 (1), pp.83–103.

Hamel, G., Doz, Y. and Prahalad, C., 1989. Collaborate with your competitors – and win. *Harvard Business Review*, 67 (1), pp.133–139.

He, X., Zhang, J. and Wang, J., 2015. Market seeking orientation and performance in China: The impact of institutional environment, subsidiary ownership structure and experience. *Management International Review*, 55 (3), pp.389–419.

Hennart, J-F., 1988. A transactions cost theory of equity joint ventures. *Strategic Management Journal*, 9 (4), pp.361–374.

Huang, Y., 2001. 'The role of foreign-invested enterprises in the Chinese economy: An institutional foundation approach, in Chen, S. and Wolf, C. (eds), *China, the United States, and the global economy*. Santa Monica, CA: RAND, pp.147–191.

Johnson, J. and Tellis, G. J., 2008. Drivers of success for market entry into China and India. *Journal of Marketing*, 72 (3), pp.1–13.

Jolly, D. R., 2006. Sino-foreign joint ventures: From exogamy to endogamy. *Journal of Technology Management in China*, 1 (2), pp.131–146.

Kogut, B., 1988. Joint ventures: Theoretical and empirical perspectives. *Strategic Management Journal*, 9 (4), pp.319–332.

Lau, V. and Tovstiga, G., 2015. Exploration of relational factors: Sino-foreign joint venture partnering. *Journal of Strategy and Management*, 8 (2), pp.191–202.

Li, Z., Li, Y. and Liu, C., 2013. Modelling the strategic mutation of international joint ventures: Insights from 494 international joint ventures. *Chinese Management Studies*, 7 (3), pp.470–487.

Morrison, W. M., 2015. China's economic rise: History, trends, challenges, and implications for the United States. *Congressional Service Report*, 21 October 2015, pp.1–48.

Niu, Y., Dong, L. C. and Chen, R., 2012. Market entry barriers in China. *Journal of Business Research*, 65 (1), pp.68–76.

Pan, Y., 1996. Influences on foreign equity ownership level in joint ventures in China. *Journal of International Business Studies*, 27 (1), pp.1–26.

Pearson, M., 1991. *Joint ventures in the People's Republic of China*. Princeton, NJ: Princeton University Press.

Prange, C., 2016. 'Internationalizing to China: Challenges and pitfalls', in Prange, C. (ed.), *Market entry in China: Case studies on strategy, marketing and branding*. Switzerland: Springer, pp.9–16.

Puck, J. F., Holtbrügge, D. and Mohr, A. T., 2009. Beyond entry mode choice: Explaining the conversion of joint ventures into wholly owned subsidiaries in the People's Republic of China. *Journal of International Business Studies*, 40 (3), pp.388–404.

Quer, D., Claver, E. and Rienda, L., 2010. Doing business in China and performance: a review of evidence. *Chinese Management Studies*, 4 (1), pp.37–56.

Riedel, J., 1974. *The industrialisation of Hong Kong*. Tubingen, Germany: Mohr.

Riskin, C. 1987. *China's political economy*. London: Oxford University Press.

Rosen, D. H., 1999. *Behind the open door: Foreign enterprises in the Chinese marketplace*. New York: Peterson Institute of International Economics.

Salem, D. I., 1981. The joint venture law of the Peoples' Republic of China: Business and legal perspectives. *Maryland Journal of International Law*, 7 (1), pp.73–118.

Tracy, N., 1995. 'Transforming South China: the role of the Chinese diaspora in the era of reform', in Davies, H. (ed.), *China business: Context and issues*. Hong Kong: Longman Asia, pp.1–21.

Tse, D. K., Pan, Y. and Au, K. Y., 1997. How MNCs choose entry modes and form alliances: The China experience. *Journal of International Business Studies*, 28 (4), pp.779–805.

Vanhonacker, W. R., 1997. Entering China: An unconventional approach. *Harvard Business Review*, 75 (2), pp.130–140.

Vanhonacker, W. R., 2000. A better way to crack China. *Harvard Business Review*, 78 (4), pp.20–22.

Wang, Y., 2007. Understanding contractual joint ventures in China. *Journal of Chinese Economic and Business Studies*, 5 (1), pp.75–90.

Wilson, J. and Brennan, R., 2009. Relational factors in UK–Chinese international joint ventures. *European Business Review*, 21 (2), pp.159–171.

Yan, D. and Warner, M., 2001. "Sino-foreign joint ventures" versus "Wholly foreign owned enterprises" in the People's Republic of China. *University of Cambridge, Judge Institute of Management Studies Working Paper*, WP 11/2011.

Yang, J. and Lee, H., 2002. Identifying key factors for successful joint venture in China. *Industrial Management & Data Systems*, 102 (2), pp.98–109.

Yaprak, A., 2012. Market entry barriers in China: A commentary essay. *Journal of Business Research*, 65 (8), pp.1216–1218.

Zhang, X., 1999. Foreign investment policy, Contribution and performance, in Wu, Y. (ed.), *Foreign direct investment and economic growth in China*. Cheltenham: Edward Elgar, pp.11–41.

Zheng, X. and Larimo, J. A., 2010. Identifying key success factors for international joint ventures in China: A foreign parent perspective from Finnish firms. *E a M: Ekonomie a Management*, 17 (2), pp.294–301.

10

THE "TWO BILLION SOCKS" SYNDROME

Marketing to China's diverse markets

Matevz Raskovic

> An enterprising Englishman in the 1850s famously said that if he "could add an inch of material to every Chinaman's shirt tail, the mills of Lancashire could be kept busy for a generation." Those mills have since turned to rust, but selling to China and the world's other emerging markets will keep many Western firms busy for years to come.
>
> (Woodall, 2011)

With over 700 million urban consumers and a rapidly rising middle class, China has captured the commercial imagination of Westerners who dream of a vast Chinese market. That fascination isn't just recent, but can be traced back for millennia, to trade along the ancient Silk Road (Studwell, 2003). However, the dream of an alluring Chinese market has led Westerners to ignore a series of complexities and paradoxes (Faure & Fang, 2008), which has often led them into trouble. Too often, they have overestimated the size and attractiveness of the Chinese market, while underestimating its diversity, its sophistication and the local competition. To have a chance of success, Western marketers need to understand China's diversity, the regulatory environment and the fusion of traditional values with elements of Western consumer culture (Hulme, 2014). Even large and well-resourced multinational companies (MNCs), like Home Depot, Best Buy, Ikea, Uber and eBay have found that the cut-throat Chinese market taught them some unexpected lessons. Many have withdrawn, only to see their products, ideas and business models being "pimped up" by savvy Chinese competitors with a better understanding of local customers, more competitive cost structures, better service and government support. This chapter examines the complexities that need to be addressed if the Chinese market is to be understood.

Simple dream, complex reality

Variations in geography and climate, ethnic, cultural, religious and historical differences, coupled with economic and development disparities, mean that China is not a single market but rather a patchwork of fragmented markets and consumer segments (Cui & Liu, 2000). Differences between North and South, the coast and inland, rural and urban, young and old, traditionalist and modern, mass and mainstream, higher and lower-tier cities, all contribute to the existence of many sub-markets within China (Zhou, Arnold, Pereira & Yu, 2010; Cui & Zhu, 1998). Failure to appreciate those differences has caused Western marketers to overestimate the size of the market for their products, to wrongly assess market demand and patterns of consumer behaviour and to formulate ineffective marketing strategies (Cui & Liu, 2000).

An early example is PepsiCo's overestimation of demand at the beginning of the 1980s. Having set up three bottling plants across China, PepsiCo found that not all regions had the "super consumers" who were found on the coast (Cui & Liu, 2000, p.58). Survey data from 1996 showed the household penetration rate of cola products was above 70% in the coastal cities of Guangzhou and Shanghai but only around 50% in the southwest (Chengdu) and northeast (Shenyang) (Cui & Zhu, 1998). More recent survey data by the McKinsey Global Institute (2012) shows that the same pattern persists.

A more recent example is Uber's exit from China in 2016. The American online ride-hailing giant was forced to sell its business to its local arch-rival Didi, despite rapid growth in China's ride-sharing market. In part, that was simply due to fierce competition, which had both companies operating at significant losses. However, it was also due to the fact that local conditions forced Uber to change its "core product". It had to abandon credit card validation upon registering an account, it had to set up servers in China to meet government regulations and it had to enter a partnership with local search engine Baidu in order to have adequate map coverage. It also found local drivers faking trips in order to make more money. By mid-2016 the government implemented nationwide regulations that put "handcuffs" on the whole industry, and also introduced even more stringent regulation and oversight for foreign companies (Kirby, 2016). Uber had little option but to give up, while taking a share in the local winner.

Of all the contrasts that make up the Chinese situation, the gap between rural and urban residents is often seen as the single biggest divide, associated with a large gap in disposable income. That gap is also to be found across cities in different "tiers" and it has profound implications for consumer behaviour. As Chapter 2 has shown, urbanization has been one of the most fundamental forces transforming the Chinese market. In 1985, some 254 million or about one quarter of 1.06 billion Chinese lived in urban areas. By the end of the 12th Five Year Plan in 2015 more than half of China (52%) lived in cities (McKinsey Global Institute, 2006) and the level expected in the 13th Plan is set to reach 60% (Kennedy & Johnson, 2016). Hence, the likely prospect of a billion Chinese urban consumers by 2030, who may drive future global growth (McKinsey Global Institute, 2009). For example, China's passenger vehicle sales were less than 1 million in 2001. By 2016 that had increased to 21 million and the predictions are that by 2018 the figure will be 30 million and as many as 50 million by 2030.

However, as Uber's experience shows, urbanization has also produced a complex system of city tiers, which impacts on consumer behaviour, and also involves substantial regulatory differences. Different cities have different regulations that are better understood and worked around by local firms. Furthermore, in the case of ride-hailing, as in many other industries, the authorities often seek to secure local involvement in foreign enterprises. Hence, ride-hailing firms are urged to merge or co-operate with taxi companies, which usually just happen to belong to the local government or their friends. In order to operate within the (not yet written) "law" Uber needed local, provincial and national regulatory approval (Kirby, 2016).

In addition to differences in regulations across cities, differences in the level of infrastructure development and logistics service also mean that while intra-city delivery or large city-to-city delivery is very efficient, inter-regional or nationwide distribution is still a significant challenge. Rapidly rising labour costs exacerbate that difficulty, as does an exponentially growing e-commerce market which imposes cut-throat profit margins.

Nevertheless, however difficult they can be to reach, Chinese consumers are important and that has been given added impetus by the country's re-structuring and the attempt to introduce a "new normal". In the aftermath of the 2008 global financial crisis and in order to avoid the "middle income trap" (loss of low-cost competitiveness due to rising wages and life style), the current leadership is trying to re-focus from an economy "standing on two legs" (investment and exports) to an economy "standing on three legs" (the third leg being consumption), driven by strong domestic demand. Consumption is scheduled to drive more than half of GDP growth by 2030 (McKinsey Global Institute, 2006).

Social divides and their marketing implications

Deng Xiaoping was content to let "some people get rich first" (Vogel, 2011). However, by the early 2000s Premier Zhu Rongji faced increasing criticism over the widening income gap between urban and rural residents, which was supported by the resident permit system (*hukou*). With roots going back to ancient China (though introduced by the CCP in 1958) the system allows each person to claim benefits like public housing, education, and health care in their registered place of birth/residence and not elsewhere. It therefore provides a "floodgate" for controlling China's internal migration towards the favoured urban areas (Wang, 2010). At the same time, the income gap and the socio-economic disparities it produces are a threat to social stability, eroding the legitimacy of the CPC (Economist, 2001). The fifth generation Xi-Li leadership has therefore called for more "inclusive growth" which is focused on reducing inequality.

According to the Gini coefficient, which measures income inequality, China had relatively low inequality before the 1980s, with a measure around 0.30. That increased with economic reform and approached 0.50 shortly after the 2001 WTO membership. It began to decline after the global financial crisis and further reduction became a priority under the Xi-Li fifth generation of leadership. Even more problematic was the widening urban–rural gap, with urban income exceeding rural income 3.4-fold in 2009, compared to 1.8 in 1996 (Li, 2016). Not only were rural incomes lower, they were also more unequal. In 1978 the rural Gini coefficient stood at 0.21 and the urban at 0.16. By 1999 the rural figure was 0.34 and the urban 0.29.

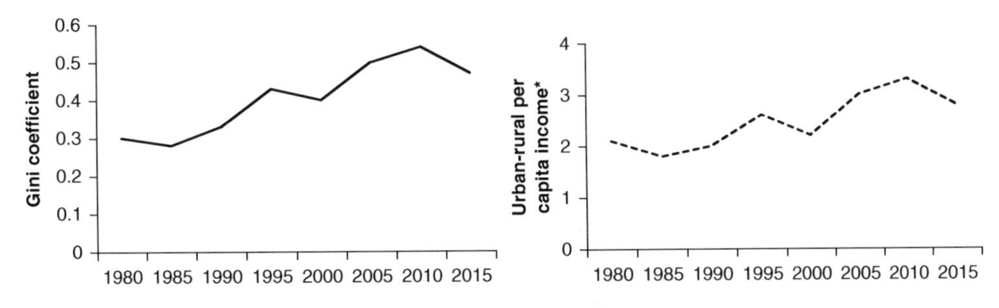

Figure 10.1a China's income inequality (Gini coefficient) and urban–rural income ratio

Source: Stratford & Cowling (2016, p.32).

**Note:* Rural disposable income spliced with net income before 2013.

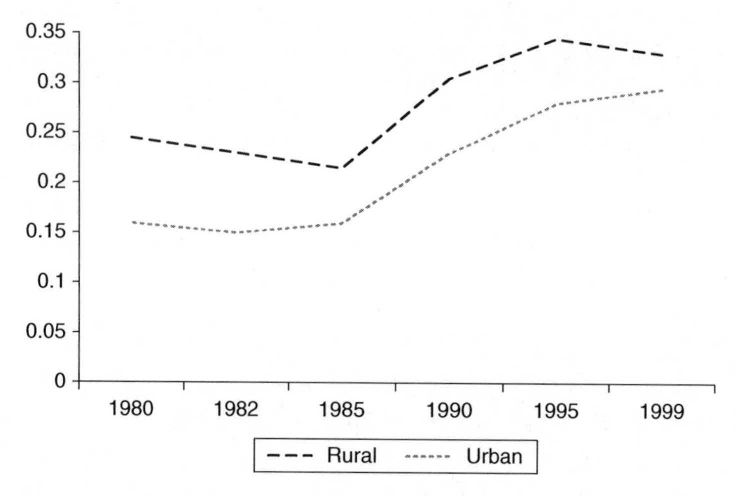

Figure 10.1b China's urban–rural Gini coefficients (1978–1999)

Source: Economist, 2001.

According to Fan, Kanbur and Zhang (2011, p.48) inequality in China has "peaked three times – during the Great Famine, at the end of the Cultural Revolution, and in the current period of global integration". Also important to note is that, "while the urban–rural gap accounts for a large share of overall inequality in the whole period, it is the inland–coastal disparity that has grown rapidly since the late 1970s" (Fan, Kanbur & Zhang, 2011, p.48).

These inequalities have important implications for marketing. In a 2012 consumer survey, a comparison of two clusters of smaller low-tier cities in China showed striking differences in both socio-economic development and consumer behaviour. A cluster in the coastal Hangzhou area having 36 million inhabitants showed 40% higher GDP per capita and a six times higher share of automobile ownership compared to an inland Yangzi delta cluster of some 32 million. It showed a increase of 9 percentage points for willingness to pay for premium products, an increase of 5 percentage points for willingness to pay for advanced technology (within the bounds of affordability), a 6-times higher importance of "emotional benefits" and 2.3-times higher level of brand loyalty towards fast moving consumer goods (McKinsey Global Institute, 2012). These coastal–inland contrasts are accompanied by significant differences in consumer confidence. According to the 2016 McKinsey Consumer Report, 70% of consumers in the southern Xiamen–Fuzhou city cluster expect significantly higher income over the next five years, compared with only 33% in the northern Shandong city cluster.

Geographic and developmental differences are not the only ones impacting consumer behaviour in China. After decades of the single-child policy and with a rapidly aging population, consumer behaviour also differs by demographics. One useful distinction is between "new mainstream consumers" and "mass consumers". While both are part of China's urbanized middle class, new mainstream consumers are younger (half of them less than 35 years old). A majority of them live in tier 1 and 2 cities, mainly in the coastal areas. Compared to mass consumers, who have lower disposable income, are older and live in tier 3 and 4 cities (many inland), new mainstream consumers look more for emotional benefits (consistent with hedonic consumer behaviour), are more willing to pay for premium products and are distinguished by "aspirational trading up". A recent analysis of social stratification and mobility of China by Song, Cavusgil, Li and Luo (2016) identified three determinants of middle-class stratification: income, education and occupation. Of the three, education-based mobility has the most significant impact on both material and culture consumption, particularly if it is accompanied also by occupation and income (the "core" middle class).

Chinese culture, philosophy and consumer behaviour: essentials for marketing

The impact of philosophy

The links between Confucianism and economic development have been well examined since Max Weber's (1951, in English) seminal work. This was complemented by Kahn's (1979) *World Economic Development*, which led to the concept of so-called "Confucian capitalism" – an explanation for the transformation of Singapore, Taiwan, Hong Kong and South Korea in the 1980s and 1990s (Hulme, 2014). Implicit in those analyses is the question of the relationship between Confucianism, consumption and consumerisms, well addressed by Sigurdsson (2014).

While Confucianism emphasized frugality and modesty as key virtues, meritocracy and its material rewards were seen as "generally good", as they provide an incentive for personal moral cultivation. Material wealth was seen as a legitimate source of family and individual well-being. Provided that morality wasn't violated, the pursuit of material wealth was not grounds for moral suspicion (Fan, 2010, p.233). Wealth was even seen as "an expedient tool for improving one's moral development" (Hulme, 2014, p.136).

The concept of *li* (introduced in Chapter 4) provided a direct link between Confucianism and consumption. It prescribed gift giving, food consumption and clothing (Hulme, 2014) as aspects of adhering to ritual. The act of gift giving, in particular, was closely linked to the concept of *renqing*. Translated loosely as "favour", *renqing* was also connected to reciprocity (*bao*) – with both seen as essential elements of *guanxi*-embedded social relations. The importance of gift giving persists today, with lavish gifts seen as signs of commitment to particularistic relationships (Rabkin, 2012).

Mohists (followers of Mo Di) worshipped a divine heaven (*tian*), which would bring "fortunes to the virtuous and misfortunes to those who encroach upon the innocent and the weak", and they resented Confucian *li* manifested through lavish funeral processions and wasteful music performances (Sigurdsson, 2014, p.142). Adopting a more "utilitarian" approach, Mohists' understanding of human behaviour was guided by searching for a balance between the benefits of *li* and the societal harm (*hai*) that it caused. Their utilitarian philosophy also called for consumption to be limited to that which was "immediately useful" and condemning any unnecessary "embellishment" (*ibid.*, p.143).

Daoism was even more antagonistic towards consumerism. While Mohism tried to balance *li* and *hai*, and curtail excessive desires, Daoists wanted to relinquish desires altogether "to realize a calm and peaceful community" (Sigurdsson, 2014, p.144). Like Buddhists, Daoists believed that desires lead humans on a vicious path, fraught with envy and destructive behaviour. While Confucianism and Mohism both supported economic development through a centralized state, Daoism followed a "prosumer" logic whereby people should consume only what they themselves produced (Sigurdsson, 2014).

Impact of culture

The hierarchical nature of Chinese society and its high power-distance have created a status-conscious middle class (Doctoroff, 2013). While Wang (2014, p.2) argues that consumerism might not be "the sole factor in defining cultural and social practices and the attributes of middle-classness [. . . it . . .] is constructed *through* rising consumerism and middle-class consumption of specific commodities". The study of consumerism in modern China should therefore focus less on Weber's socio-demographic determinants of "middle-classness", but more on the examination of life styles and practices (Wang, 2014).

At the beginning of the economic reforms, the Chinese middle class pursued the "Big Four" products – namely: a bicycle, radio, watch and sewing machine – to proclaim their identity. By the late 1980s and 1990s, this was expanded to the "Big Six" – a colour TV, washing machine, refrigerator, music player, fan, and camera. After China's accession to the World Trade Organization and the boom of the Hu-Wen era (2002–2012) a "New Big Four" emerged to include: a car (replacing the bicycle), a smartphone and a computer (replacing hi-fi and TV), and air conditioning (replacing the fan). Home ownership is another key aspect of middle-class identity so that real estate "is the largest consumption item for Chinese middle-class families and has become a symbol of social and economic status for the middle class" (Wang, 2014, p.14).

While conspicuous consumption is undoubtedly a signifier of status amongst middle-class Chinese consumers that does not translate into extravagance across the board. Instead, it has produced an interesting paradox, which Doctoroff (2013) outlines as his "three golden rules" of marketing in China. This first relates to a need for "social status projection" through maximizing public consumption exposure, while at the same time protecting personal wealth through frugal behaviour (Confucianism). That explains why a Chinese middle-class consumer will spend more money on a conspicuous high-class foreign-brand mobile phone, or camera to be "consumed" in public. But at the same time they will buy low cost domestic-brand household appliances since they would be used in private at home. For example, Sony's expensive camera has a large market share in China, but the market share of its expensive TVs is much lower (Doctoroff, 2013).

The Confucian emphasis on self-improvement, combined with a strong utilitarian logic and a need to project one's status, link to the second golden rule – a focus on "externalized product benefits" and looking at products as "vehicles taking you forward in life" (Doctoroff, 2013). In contrast to Western consumers who are driven by intrinsic benefits and hedonism, Chinese consumers want products that "do something" and give them a competitive edge. For example, while shower gels are advertised in the West as relaxing and feel-and-smell-good bathing experiences, in China they become energizing elixirs and youth fountains that give a kick start to your day, keep you fresher and younger-looking (Doctoroff, 2013).

The third golden rule is related to the "need for reassurance" (Doctoroff, 2013). In a market with weak rule of law and consumer protection, combined with cut-throat competition, products and business models need to reassure on a physical level, social and emotional level. Scale and size reassure, which explains Haier's dominant position in household appliances. Positive country of origin also reassures, so that foreign products, particularly European brands, are perceived to be of better quality. Social reassurance relates to the importance of brands in projecting one's status, and the danger of losing face by using the wrong kind of product. It also relates to externalized benefits (i.e. like in the previous example of marketing shower gels). Emotional reassurance is related to specific product categories (education, anything ingested into the body, anything baby or wedding related) and is related to the feelings generated through such consumption. For example, middle-class consumers strive to feed their babies expensive imported (preferably German) baby powder milk, as they believe it will not poison their children (unlike some Chinese brands) and their baby will grow up taller, more handsome, stronger and smarter, gaining a competitive edge in life.

Other aspects are also worth mentioning. For example, loyalty cards providing discounts are widely employed. In trying to protect wealth, showing savviness, and at the same time not "losing face" by appearing to beg for a discount, various levels of VIP cards have made their way into the wallets of millions of Chinese middle-class consumers (Doctoroff, 2013).

Chinese consumers are proverbially price sensitive, which makes them responsive to price promotions. They also tend to haggle and negotiate, particularly in more traditional market places. This tendency stems partly from the need to protect personal wealth and generate "face" through good negotiation skills, but is also connected to the concept of "excess water" (*shui fen*), meaning that consumers need to drive the price down in order to squeeze out the excess water, while sellers need to pad their price. Indeed, the number one factor leading to failure in negotiations with Chinese was the inability to lower one's price (Fang, Worm & Tung, 2008). Packaging is another important marketing element influenced by China's *guanxi*-based culture, since high-end products are often given as gifts. Packaging should look sophisticated, and should also adhere to the choice of specific colours (prosperous red, or imperial gold or yellow) and aesthetic principles (a preference for rounder, less angular shapes). Marketers also need to be careful with regards to language and homophony (the fact that many words sound exactly the same). Coca-Cola, for example is rendered as *ke kou ke le*, which sounds like its English name but also translates roughly as "making one's mouth pleasant" (Xing, 2006).

It is also important to remember that there are considerable regional and generational differences when it comes to the impact of Chinese culture on consumer behaviour. It is better, therefore, for marketers to avoid cultural generalizations that are too sweeping and focus more on appropriate market segmentation, and the corresponding patterns of demand.

Consumer behaviour and patterns of demand

In addition to the regional differences and disparities, Chinese consumers can be grouped into three subsets, namely: rural consumers; traditional urban mass consumers; and urban mainstream consumers (the post-1980s consumer generations). All three groups' ways reflect a changing China.

The overlooked rural consumer

Rural consumers were traditionally believed to be "too poor, too dispersed and too far away to engage with" according to Crabbe (2016). However, with urban markets becoming saturated, e-retail giant Alibaba began to focus growth on China's 600-million rural consumers in 2015. It invested $US1.6 billion in an extensive distribution network, making the rural consumer more reachable. Backed by wage increases and government policy focused on lowering the urban–rural income gap, which subsidized the purchase of household appliances to "stimulate" rural spending, estimated rural consumer spending grew from $US28 billion in 2014 to $US55.5 billion in 2016 (KPMG, 2015) and perhaps as much as $US148 billion by 2020 (Bloomberg, 2016).

Before Internet shopping, significant differences across the marketing mix could be found between rural and urban Chinese consumers, reflecting different values and life styles. Sun and Wu (2004) showed that in 2002, rural consumers were much more price sensitive, less willing to experiment, and less brand conscious. They were twice as inclined to shop alone and "suspicious of mass advertising" (Sun & Wu, 2004, p.248). Being "well-to-do" and "healthy" were the main aspirations of rural consumers, compared with urban consumers who also strove for relaxation, spiritual enrichment, stability and being in sync with nature.

The recent growth of online retailing has changed that, which is why Alibaba has partnered with China Telecom in an effort to increase rural Internet penetration (at 30% in 2015) and equip rural consumers with affordable smartphones (penetration rate about 32% by end of 2015). This has also started to change the pattern of rural consumer behaviour as disposable incomes reach the $US6,000 threshold deemed critical for discretionary consumer spending (KPMG, 2015). As KPMG (2015) points out: "In the past, the rural consumer has often been faced with limited choice of product and been offered low quality goods where price was the main attraction." With close to 80 million rural online shoppers, these consumers now "want to experience brands for the first time and look to buy products that improve the quality of their lives". These shoppers still appreciate a bargain – the right price point is crucial – but are less willing to compromise on quality. As Wang Feng, a sociologist from the University of California at Irvine, points out, rural China's consumer power lies in its youth – "They are the best-ever educated rural youth in Chinese history. Their parents — as migrants or farmers — worked hard, and then they gave the young people the capacity and resources to be able to consume" (Bloomberg, 2016).

China's urban consumers: then, now and tomorrow

China's urban consumers are made up of many different segments. Cui and Liu (2001) identified four distinct groups, based on a Gallup consumer survey in 1997, shown in Table 10.1.

More than ten years later, a study by McKinsey (2012) outlined a similar four-way segmentation of Chinese urban households, as shown in Table 10.2. The share of affluent households is estimated to triple from 2% to 6% between 2010 and 2020, growing from 4.5 million households to around 20 million as shown in Table 10.2. Mainstream consumer households will rise from 6% to more than 50% or from less than 14 million households to nearly 170 million.

While those changes are startling, in the era of the "new normal", with its shift to a greater emphasis on consumption, consumer behaviour has also been transformed. Table 10.3 describes those shifts that began when the Xi-Li leadership assumed power,

Table 10.1 Segmentation of Chinese urban consumers in 1997

	Working poor	*Salary class*	*Little rich*	*Yuppies*
Segment size	55%	25%	15%	5%
Annual income (1997)	≤ 10,000 RMB	≤ 20,000 RMB	≤ 40,000 RMB	> 40,000 RMB
Satisfaction with life	68%	84%	73%	80%
Work hard and get rich	46%	27%	43%	32%
Willing to pay for brands	44%	53%	43%	68%
Prefer foreign goods	22%	24%	28%	48%

Source: Cui & Liu (2001, pp.89, 91).

Table 10.2 Structural shifts in China's growing urbanized middle-class households (2010 to 2020)

	Poor	*Value*	*Mainstream*	*Affluent*
Annual income (household)	< 6,000 USD	6K to 16K USD	16K to 34K USD	> 34,000 USD
% of 2010 urban households	10%	82%	6%	2%
% of 2020 urban households	7%	32%	51%	6%

Source: McKinsey: *Meet the 2020 Chinese Consumer* (2012, p.14).

Table 10.3 A shift towards a new modern Chinese urban consumer under the "new normal"

Yesterday's Chinese urban mainstream consumer	*Tomorrow's Chinese modern urban consumer*
• Pragmatic and price sensitive (fixed budget for purchases, willing to spend energy on bargains). • Trading up and aspirational consumption buoyed by strong future outlook and consumer confidence. • Conspicuous consumption to show social status (before the anti-corruption campaign). • Strong value-for-money orientation. • Planned purchases for large items (low impulse purchase behaviour), but also growing discretionary spending for smaller thrills. • Shift from functional orientation (quality and durability) to emphasis on well-being, user friendliness and emotional benefits. • Growing consumer sophistication. • Growing importance of brands, but overall still dwindling brand loyalty. • Foreign brands and products put on a pedestal. • Conservative consumer at home, consumer innovative in public. • Influenced by social media, word of mouth and store staff. • Still, a predominance of brick-and-mortar shopping. • High savings rate among young consumers, insecure older generation reluctant to spend. • Conspicuous consumption to maintain *guanxi*, dominant male consumerism. • Traditional payment methods and transaction platforms. • Social media and apps used for information gathering and communication.	• Stable consumer confidence, but buoyed by rural consumers and tier 1 urban consumers. • More selective consumer behaviour, shifting from product to services, trading up from mass to premium segments. • Influenced by a quest for greater life balance (health, happiness and experience given priority). • Greater emphasis on family, health, experiences and international travel. Declining relative spending on dinning and food. • Greater heterogeneity among consumer segments (regionally and in terms of demographics). • Diverging consumer confidence paralleled with economic disparity. • Consolidation of preferred brands and increased brand loyalty. • Decline in overall conspicuous consumption as consumers become vary of flaunting their wealth. • Domestic luxury consumption takes a dive, more luxury consumption from international travel or *dai guo* (Chinese living abroad and selling goods to mainland customers). • In mass market local brands gaining market appeal based on stronger value propositions, premium segment still dominated by international brands. • Empowered middle-aged female consumers and less reluctant older generation consumers start spending. • Increased adoption of new payment services (i.e. Alipay), new online retail platforms and new sharing economy services (i.e. Didi's ride sharing app). • Physical stores still attract interest due to "retailment" – combination of shopping, dining and entertainment for the whole family.

Source: McKinsey: *Meet the 2020 Chinese Consumer* (2012, pp.27–33); McKinsey: *The Modernization of the Chinese Consumer* (2016, pp.1–15).

gained momentum in 2015/2016, and which show the emergence of a new type of modern Chinese consumer (MGI, 2016).

McKinsey (2016, p.15) has summarized the shift as follows: "Gone are the days of indiscriminate spending on products. The focus is shifting to prioritizing premium products and living a more balanced, healthy, and family-centric life."

Consumer behaviour and city tiers

Within the Chinese tier system for cities, there are generally agreed to be four tiers, which correspond to their rank and relationship to the government, and which differ in levels of income and in terms of consumer behaviour. Tier 1 cities are the biggest and most important, namely Beijing, Guangzhou, Shanghai and Shenzhen, which are sometimes referred to as "super cities". Tier 2 cities are other large and important urban centres, usually corresponding to provincial capitals, like Hangzhou, Chengdu, Tianjin and Zhengzhou. They have also been called China's "affluent cities". Tier 3 cities are called "satellite cities" and correspond to smaller cities of up to some five million, made of prefectural capitals close to either affluent or super cities. An example would be the prefecture-level city of Jinhua in Zhejiang province with a population of 5 million and within an hour's drive to Hangzhou. Tier 4 cities are urban areas with smaller populations (Keely, 2015).

While growth may have slowed in Tier 1 and Tier 2 cities, where foreign competition is already present and domestic competition is strong, some Tier 3 and 4 cities can offer better growth prospects. They do, however, need to be carefully selected. As Keely (2015) put it: "for every solid Tier 3 bet, there's just one 'maybe' city and four 'stay-away-at-all-costs' cities crippled by pollution, industrial safety concerns, and an over-reliance on mining and commodities." Out of 104 Tier 3 cities only 18 are seen as "promising" and another 19 as "perhaps interesting". Amongst Tier 4 cities, only a handful offer potential growth for Western MNCs over the next decade (Keely, 2015). Nielsen (2013) estimated the consumer market potential of the 16 million Tier 1 city households to be around $US163 billion, twice that of the 38 million Tier 2 households and three times that of the 75 million Tier 3 households.

McKinsey's *Consumer & Shopper Insights: Meet the 2020 Chinese Consumer* (2012) identified different consumer behaviour drivers across the four tiers, for the example of personal care products and services. In Tier 1 cities, product innovation and new product category consumption were the main drivers, while in Tier 2 aspirational trading up was most important, indicating a need for firms to upgrade their product portfolios. In Tier 3 cities consumer behaviour was driven by quantity or purchase frequency increases, while in Tier 4 cities new product category consumption (albeit of a different kind) has also been on the rise, as shown in Figure 10.2.

But have the recent attempts to shift the development model led to significant changes? Many of the Tier 4 industrialized cities are facing industrial overcapacity problems, which may result in increased unemployment, particularly in the North, stifling consumer spending. And many of the urban "pyjama investors" who lost money on the turbulent stock exchanges come from Tier 1 cities, which might have stifled consumer spending. However, any large negative impact on aggregate consumer spending is unlikely (BCG, 2016a). On the contrary, in many ways consumer spending has consolidated and shifted to Tier 1 and 2 cities, where household wealth has been hugely increased by the rise in residential house prices, and where real estate gains hugely outweigh stock market losses (BCG, 2016a). In particular, middle-age female consumers and the post-1980s consumer generations have

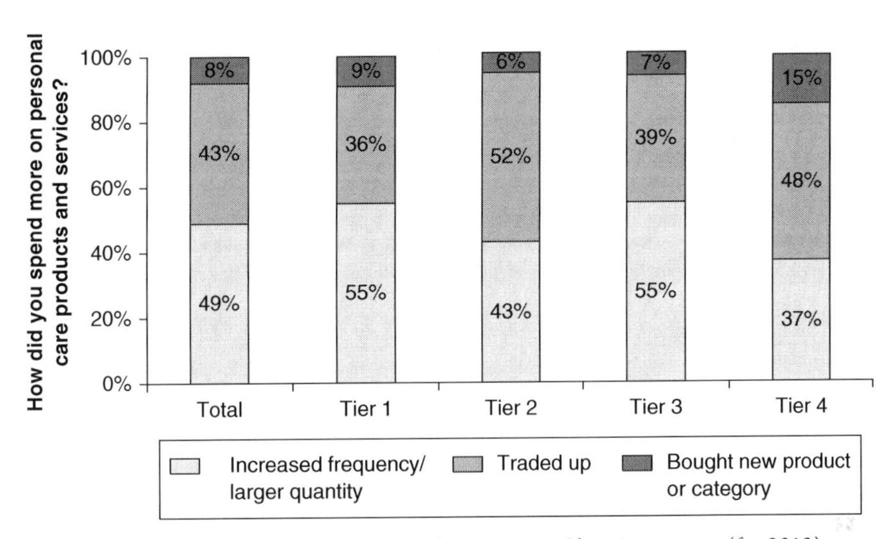

Figure 10.2 Different consumer behaviour drivers across China's city tiers (for 2012)

Source: McKinsey Consumer & Shopper Insights (2012): 2012 Annual Consumer Report, p.15.

emerged as the drivers of spending in top-tier cities. As rural consumer spending also increases it is likely that only the lower-tier cities will see sluggish growth in consumption (KPMG, 2015).

A changing landscape: trends to watch out for

According to the Boston Consulting Group (2016b) the future of China's consumer market will be shaped by three forces: (1) upward socio-economic mobility, (2) a generational shift, and (3) an explosion of e- and m-commerce.

Structural changes in China's middle class

While China's middle class will undoubtedly be a key engine of future economic growth for China and the global economy, it will undergo structural changes which marketers need to be aware of. The biggest shift will be geographic. According to MGI's (2013) projections, while only 13% of China's middle class lived inland in 2002 and 87% on the coast, by 2022 39% will be living inland and 61% on the coast. That will be accompanied by a shift across city tiers. There will be a significant decrease of the share of middle class living in Tier 1 cities (from 40% in 2002 to only 16% by 2022) and an increase of the share of the middle class living in Tier 3 cities (from 15% in 2002 to 31% by 2022). As already noted, while the tier system can be an appropriate framework for understanding the relationship with the central government, marketers shouldn't blindly follow the tier city classification, but look at cities in terms of being "advanced", "developing", "emerging" and "lagging". There will be overlap between the two classifications ("Tier 3" often corresponds to "emerging"), but many cities may be impacted by industrial overcapacity, housing overcapacity and unemployment challenges.

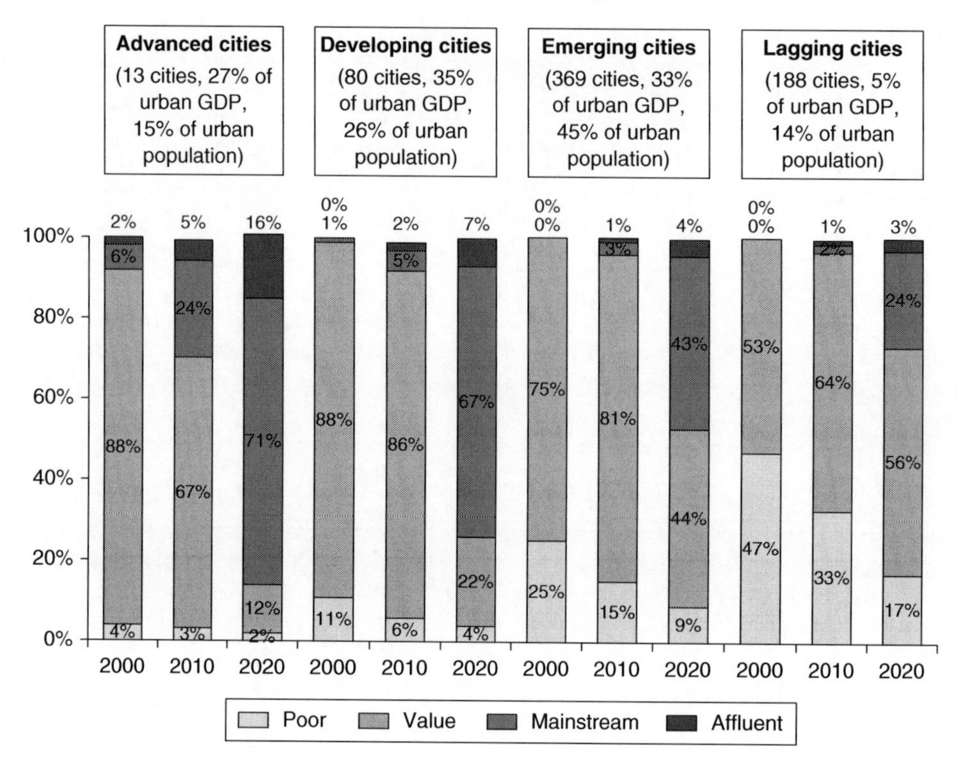

Figure 10.3 Income distribution estimates by city type and household group (2000–2020)

Source: McKinsey (2012): *Consumer & Shopper Insights: Meet the 2020 Chinese Consumer*.

Consumer behaviour and generational shift

In mid-2016, private household consumption remained strong and even if GDP growth fell below 5.5% (well below the government target of 6.5%), China's domestic consumer economy is expected to double and reach $US 6.5 trillion by 2020 (BCG, 2016a). Where will that growth come from? As households linked to the industrial sectors dealing with overcapacity problems will face difficulties, future growth will come mainly from younger generation consumers and emerging city middle-income affluent consumers (MACs) (BCG, 2016a). This might further be accompanied by a consolidation of MACs in Tier 1 cities, buoyed by middle-age female consumers (key for certain product categories – i.e. FMCGs and cosmetics).

The post 1980s generation of younger consumers are "freer" in their spending and are more "sophisticated" consumers (BCG, 2016a). In 2012, they numbered around 200 million. Between 2012 and 2022, the share of their spending is predicted to increase from 15% to 35% of urban consumer spending and they will also be the key driver in rural consumer spending growth (Crabbe, 2016).

This group is confident about its growth in personal income, willing to spend and driven by aspirational trading up – particularly for cosmetics, spirits, hair care, fresh produce, beer, ice-cream and frozen desserts and soft drinks (MGI, 2016). They are also more brand aware and loyal to brands (not just for consumer electronics and personal care, but also for apparel

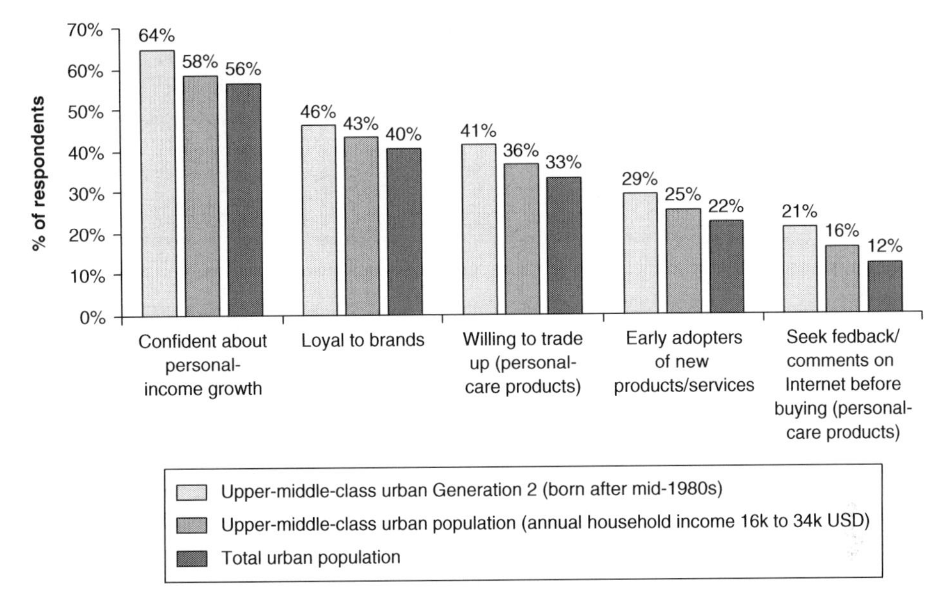

Figure 10.4 Consumer behaviour driven by young-generation consumers in China

Source: MGI (2013): *Mapping China's Middle Class.*

and food and beverage) (MGI, 2016). They prefer foreign brands and niche brands to mass market brands. In the process of their social identity building they are more willing to experiment (consumer innovativeness) and become early adopters of new products and services. They are hyper connected, use multiple social media platforms, shop online (mostly through mobile phones), but will still not completely abandon traditional shopping retailment. They are also more emotional and hedonic consumers, seeking intrinsic and emotional benefits. In terms of their consumer-related values, they will be driven by strong family focus (happiness being less related to being rich, and more to having a happy family), a healthy life, as well as experience and entertainment (especially international travel) (MGI, 2016). If the economy slows down, spending on some products might falter. However, growth in service spending will remain robust (particularly related to leisure and entertainment, international travel and personal care services) (MGI, 2016).

Is China's luxury market dead?

Impelled by status-driven consumption, China's luxury market has seemed robust in the face of global economic and financial crisis. Even amidst global recession, luxury market growth in 2009 and 2010 remained in double digits. Most of that growth came from the four Tier 1 cities and from wealthy households (0.3–10 million RMB of assets) seeking internationally well-known brands (MGI, 2011). However, with Xi's crackdown on corruption (see Chapter 11), the luxury market began to decline. A report by Bain & Co. (2016) showed China's luxury sales of $US15 billion contracted by 2% in 2015 compared to 2014. While luxury spending decreased by 24% in mainland China, Hong Kong and

Macau, luxury purchases made overseas grew by about 10%. Thus, while luxury consumption remains strong, domestic purchases have become replaced by luxury consumption on international travels and by *dai gou* (overseas personal shoppers), accounting for some 38% of luxury consumption in 2015 (Bain & Co., 2016).

E-commerce and m-commerce boom

China's e-shopping bonanza – the November 11 "Singles' Day" – is perhaps the best illustration of the unprecedented e-commerce boom. As online retailers like Alibaba and JD.com increasingly tap into the rural consumer market, logistics seem to be the only barrier to the seemingly unlimited potential of e-commerce. For example, during the 2015 Singles' Day event, more than 680 million parcels needed to be delivered across China clogging the delivery market for weeks (Lau & Su, 2016). In 2016 online retailer Alibaba, reported some $US20 billion in sales, which was 32% larger than in the previous year. This made it by far the biggest online shopping event on the planet, compared to either Black Friday ($US2.7 billion), or Cyber Monday ($US3.1 billion) in the US (CNBC, 2016).

As Figure 10.5 shows, while e-commerce was worth some $US100 billion and represented only 3% of private consumption in 2010, by 2015 it had reached $US600 billion USD and 15% of private consumption. According to Boston Consulting Group estimates, e-commerce is set to further increase three times to 1.6 trillion USD by 2020, representing a

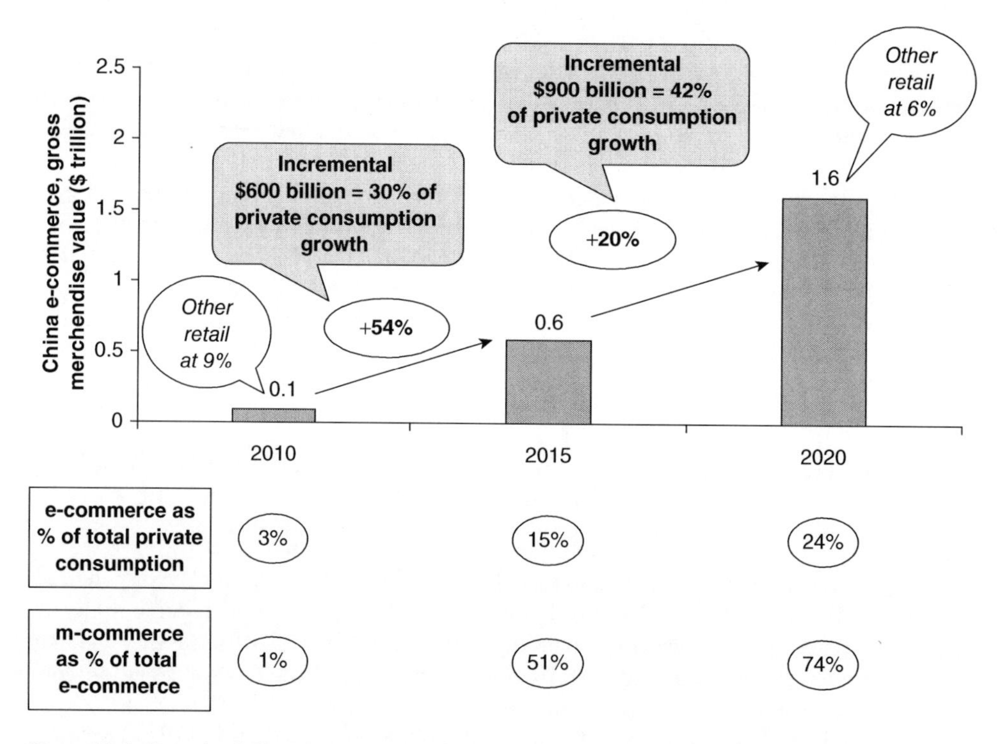

Figure 10.5 Growth of China's e-commerce/m-commerce market between 2010 and 2020

Source: BCG (2016b): *The New China Playbook.*

24% share in total private consumption, with 74% of it driven by purchases through mobile devices. The main drivers behind that trend will be urban post 1980s consumers, middle-income affluent consumers in emerging cities and young-generation rural consumers.

According to a study by KPMG (2016) more than 90% of Chinese consumers have used a smartphone to make an online purchase within the last 12 months, compared to 70% globally. A staggering 49% have made online purchases several times per month within that period, compared to only 28% globally. It is no surprise, therefore, that China's mobile-commerce retail market was worth some $US500 billion in 2016, representing 11% of all retail sales in China and year-on-year growth of 52%.

By 2019 this share is predicted to reach 24% and a value of $US1.4 trillion (KPMG, 2016). A breakdown of the most popular categories purchased online shows a wide variety of goods being bought. Food and groceries, women's apparel, and electronics and computers are the three most common categories. They are followed by men's apparel and books and music, which show higher growth trends for the next 12 months compared to the previous three categories. Cosmetics and skincare, accessories and household goods and appliances are also well represented, while furniture and décor shows one of the biggest intended purchase increases in 2017 (KPMG, 2016). Chinese online consumers are unique in their consumer behaviour. Compared to their Western European peers, they are four times more inclined to use their smartphones to conduct online purchases (KPMG, 2016). While 61% of them look up reviews and recommendations prior to searching for products, 70% them use their smartphone while in physical stores. A staggering 52% provide feedback online and share their experience, compared to only 31% globally. In addition to convenience, price comparison and better services and prices are the main reasons cited for using e-commerce. In terms of payment methods, the most popular are credit cards (79%), Alipay (72%) and WeChat (35%).

These shifts have polarized the Chinese e-commerce market into two distinct sub-groups – "high-speed" and "low-speed" consumers (BCG, 2015). High speed consumers are usually from the middle-income affluent and young-generation groups, they are frequent online shoppers (affluent households are twice as likely as aspiring households to shop online frequently) and they utilize multiple sales channels, both online and in-store. To cater to high-speed online consumers companies need to have good online e- and mobile-commerce platforms, as well as strong in-store brand presence. Excellent customer support is essential. For example, Haier's 24/7 hotline was a huge success factor helping them to secure the market leader position in the highly competitive and price sensitive household appliance market. Special promotions (like Single's day) and frequent customer offers are also important, supported by well-designed loyalty programs. Providing platforms for customers to access others' feedback and to share their experiences is also very important (KPMG, 2016).

The outlook for Western marketers and MNCs

As China changes its development model, the days of double digit income growth, exuberant consumer confidence and status-driven conspicuous consumption in pursuit of personal success defined by wealth might be ending. While middle-income affluent consumers from emerging cities will drive market development for some product categories, as well as experimentation and brand switching, post 1980s consumers are becoming increasingly sophisticated. That in turn will drive different types of consumer behaviour to which Western marketers and MNCs need to adapt. Thus, "the winning strategies of the past are becoming outdated. Greater affluence, a new generation of consumers, and the rise of e-commerce will shift the action to different product categories, branding strategies, and retail channels" (BCG, 2016b).

What implications do these changes hold for Western marketers and MNCs? Well,

> [it] will be more important than ever before for companies to be highly strategic in the way they pick targets. [...] targeting the wrong income segment, playing in the wrong categories, and being underrepresented in the fast-growing online channels will be a formula for slow growth.
>
> (BCG, 2016b)

References

Bain & Co., 2016. *2015 China luxury market study*. Shanghai: Bain & Co.

Bloomberg, 2016. Alibaba and JD.com battle to capture rural China's spending power. Available at: https://www.bloomberg.com/news/articles/2016-11-07/alibaba-and-jd-com-battle-to-capture-rural-china-s-spending-power [Accessed 11 January 2017].

Boston Consulting Group (BCG)., 29 June 2015. A tale of two Chinese consumers. *BCG Perspectives*. Availableat:https://www.bcgperspectives.com/content/articles/center-consumer-customer-insight-globalization-tale-of-two-chinese-consumers/ [Accessed 10 January 2017].

Boston Consulting Group (BCG)., 20 June 2016a. China's consumers stay the (slightly slower) course. *BCG Perspectives*. Available at: https://www.bcgperspectives.com/content/articles/globalization-center-customer-insight-china-consumers-stay-slightly-slower-course/ [Accessed 10 January 2017].

Boston Consulting Group (BCG). 2016b. *The new China playbook*. Available at: https://www.bcgperspectives.com/content/articles/globalization-growth-new-china-playbook-young-affluent-e-savvy-consumers/?chapter=6#chapter6 [Accessed 11 January 2017].

Crabbe, M., 2016. China's 622 million rural consumers just got a lot closer to retailers. Available at: http://www.mintel.com/blog/retail-market-news/chinas-622-million-rural-consumers-just-got-a-lot-closer-to-retailers [Accessed 10 December 2016].

CNBC., 11 November 2016. Singles' day: Alibaba smashes records at world's largest online shopping event. Available at: http://www.cnbc.com/2016/11/11/singles-day-news-alibaba-poised-to-smash-records-at-worlds-largest-online-shopping-event.html [Accessed 11 January 2017].

Cui, G. and Zhu, J., 1998. China's geographic market segment: A preliminary study, in Hung, K. and Monroe, K. B. (eds), *AP – Asia Pacific advances in consumer research: Volume 3*. Provo, UT: Association for Consumer Research, pp.38–44.

Cui, G. and Liu, Q., 2000. Regional market segments of China: Opportunities and barriers in a big emerging market. *Journal of Consumer Marketing*, 17 (1), pp.55–72.

Cui, G. and Liu, Q., 2001. Executive insights: Emerging market segments in a transitional economy: A study of urban consumers in China. *Journal of International Marketing*, 9 (1), pp.84–106.

Doctoroff, T., 2013. *What the Chinese want*. New York, NY: Palgrave Macmillan.

Economist., 31 May 2001. Income distribution in China: To each according to his abilities. Available at the following website: http://www.economist.com/node/639652 [Accessed 8 December 2016].

Fan, R., 2010. *Reconstructionist Confucianiesm: Rethinking morality after the West*. Dordrecht: Springer Verlag.

Fan, S., Kanbur, R. and Zhang, X., 2011. China's regional disparities: Experience and policy. *Review of Development Finance*, 1 (1), pp. 47–56.

Fang, T., Worm, V. and Tung, L. R., 2008. Changing success and failure factors in business negotiations with the PRC. *International Business Review*, 17 (2), pp.159–169.

Faure, G. O. and Fang, T., 2008. Changing Chinese values: Keeping up with the paradoxes. *International Business Review*, 17 (2), pp.194–207.

Hulme, A., ed., 2014. *The Changing landscape of China's consumerism*. Oxford: Chandos Publishing/Elsevier.

Kahn, H., 1979. *World economic development: 1979 and beyond*. London: Croom Helm.

Keely, L., 2015. The problem with ranking Chinese cities. *Fortune* online. Available at: http://fortune.com/2015/12/05/china-cities-tier-system-problem/ [Accessed 7 January 2017].

Kennedy, S. and Johnson, C.K., 2016. *Perfecting China inc. The 13th five year plan*. Center for Strategic and International Studies. New York: Rowman and Littlefield.

Kirby, C. W., 2016. The real reason Uber is giving up in China. *Harvard Business Review*. Available at: https://hbr.org/2016/08/the-real-reason-uber-is-giving-up-in-china [Accessed 8 December 2016].

KPMG., 2015. Harvesting China's rural consumers. Available at: https://home.kpmg.com/xx/en/home/insights/2015/12/harvesting-china-rural-consumers.html [Accessed 10 December 2016.]

KPMG., 2016. *China's connected consumers 2016: A mobile revolution*. Shanghai: KPMG Huazhen LLP.

Lau, A. and Su, M., 2016. China's e-commerce soft spot: Logistics. *McKinsey Quarterly*. Available at: http://www.mckinsey.com/industries/high-tech/our-insights/chinas-e-commerce-soft-spot-logistics [Accessed 8 December 2016].

Li, S. (2016). Income inequality and economic growth in China in the last three decades. *The Round Table – The Commonwealth Journal of International Affairs*, 105 (6), pp.641–665.

McKinsey and Company., 2012. *Consumer & shopper insights: Meet the 2020 Chinese consumer*. Shanghai: McKinsey & Company.

McKinsey and Company., 2016. *2016 China consumer report: The modernization of the Chinese consumer*. Shanghai: McKinsey & Company.

MGI., 2006. *From 'made in China' to 'sold in China': The rise of the Chinese urban consumer*. San Francisco, CA: McKinsey Global Institute.

MGI., 2009. *Preparing for China's urban billion*. Shanghai: McKinsey Global Institute.

MGI., 2011. *Tapping China's luxury-goods market*. Shanghai: McKinsey Global Institute.

MGI., 2012. *Urban world: Cities and the rise of the consuming class*. Seoul/San Francisco/London/Washington, DC: McKinsey Global Institute.

MGI., 2013. *Mapping China's middle class*. Shanghai: McKinsey Global Institute.

MGI., 2016. *2016 China consumer report*. Shanghai: McKinsey Global Institute.

Nielsen., 2013. *China 2014: A new era in consumption*. New York: Nielsen Holdings N.V.

Rabkin, A., 2012. *Scenes from the Chinese consumerist revolution*. Available at: http://nymag.com/thecut/2012/08/scenes-from-the-chinese-consumerist-revolution.html [Accessed 8 December 2016].

Sigurdsson, G., 2014. Frugalists, anti-consumers, and prosumers: Chinese philosophical perspectives on consumerism, in Hulme, A. (ed.), *The changing landscape of China's consumerism*. Oxford: Elsevier, pp.125–150.

Song, J., Cavusgil, E., Li, J. and Luo, R., 2016. Social stratification and mobility among Chinese middle class households: An empirical investigation. *International Business Review*, 25 (3), pp.646–656.

Stratford, K. and Cowling, A., 2016. Chinese household income, consumption and savings. *Reserve Bank of Australia Bulletin*, September Quarter, pp.31–40.

Studwell, J., 2003. *The China dream: The quest for the last great untapped market on Earth*. 2nd ed. New York: Grove Press.

Sun, T. and Wu, G., 2004. Consumption patterns of Chinese rural and urban consumers. *Journal of Consumer Marketing*, 21 (4), pp.245–253.

Vogel, E., 2011. *Deng Xiaoping and the transformation of China*. Harvard, MA: Belknap Press.

Wang, F-L., 2010. Renovating the great floodgate: The reform of China's hukou system, in King Whyte, M. (ed.), *One country, two societies: Rural–urban inequality in contemporary China*. Cambridge, MA: Harvard University Press. pp. 335–364.

Wang, X., 2014. In pursuit of status: The rising consumerism of China's middle class, in Hulme, A. (ed.), *The changing landscape of China's consumerism*. Oxford: Elsevier, pp. 1–22.

Weber, M., 1951. *The religion of China: Confucianism and Daoism*. New York: Macmillan.

Woodall, P., 2011. Hey big spenders. *The Economist: The world in 2012*. Available at: http://www.economist.com/node/21537925 [Accessed 6 December 2016].

Xing, J. Z., 2006. *Teaching and learning Chinese as a foreign language: A pedagogical grammar*. Hong Kong: Hong Kong University Press.

Zhou, J. X., Arnold, J. M., Pereira, A. and Yu, J., 2010. Chinese consumer decision-making styles: A comparison between the coastal and inland regions. *Journal of Business Research*, 63 (1), pp.45–51.

11

ETHICS, CORRUPTION AND SUSTAINABLE DEVELOPMENT

Howard Davies

One of the most fundamental questions to be asked of organizations and individuals is "are their actions morally sound?" This chapter addresses that question in the Chinese context by first examining business ethics, corporate social responsibility and the problem of corruption. It then goes on to examine the extent to which the country is putting a sustainable model of development in place, thereby safeguarding future generations.

Business ethics in China

Alternative ethical perspectives

Ethics maybe defined as:

> The application of reason to elucidate specific rules and principles that determine right or wrong for a given situation.
>
> (Crane & Matton, 2007, p.8)

The rules and principles that arise from this application of reason are usually referred to as "ethical theories". Babson College (2007) has developed a useful framework for ethical decision-making, which builds on the three key schools of thought. The first of these is the "deontological" or "duty" approach, which avers that we have a duty to behave in certain ways, encapsulated in Kant's insistence that we "act only in such a way that (1) you would be willing for the principle of your action to be a universal law, and (2) you treat other human beings with respect." As Romar (2002) points out, that second injunction is also a part of Confucian thinking on moral behaviour.

The second school of thought is the "utilitarian" or "consequences" school, where the injunction is to act in the way which overall does most good or least harm, which implies that some form of cost-benefit analysis can be applied. It also raises the difficult question of measuring one person's benefit or harm against another's. If a course of action leads to a gain for all parties, or a gain for some and no loss to others then it is said to be "Pareto optimal" and an unambiguous overall gain. However, there are many situations where some gain but others lose, so that the Pareto principle does not apply. Burning the Indonesian jungle may lead to higher incomes and employment for poor Indonesians but damage wildlife and impose choking pollution on the rich inhabitants of Singapore. In such situations, it is common to use cost-benefit analysis to try to weigh one set of interests against another, but there clearly could be a clash with the outcomes that would be determined on Kantian grounds.

Despite these difficulties there are many general conventional moral rules – do not steal, lie or cheat, and treat others as you would be treated – which draw their strength at least in part from the "consequences" view. If these rules were not conformed to for most of the time, society would be unable to function at all, hence their overall consequences are positive, even if thieves suffer from punishment while the honest citizen gains.

The third perspective is attributed in the West to Aristotle, but is very close to the Confucian emphasis on the importance of the "virtuous" person, described in Chapter 4. From this perspective doing the "right thing" is the consequence of habitually behaving in ways that allow us to live at peace and in harmony with others. Good decisions and actions will be taken, even when there is limited information, or no time to reflect, by the person who has habituated themselves to diligence, kindness, trustworthiness and tolerance.

Ethical thinking and behaviour is most obviously attributable to individuals, and there is difficulty in attaching it to collective entities and hence to business organizations. Nevertheless, "business ethics" can be defined as "the study of business situations, activities and decisions where issues of right and wrong are addressed" (Crane & Matton, 2007, p.5.); it is a lively field of inquiry, and a good deal of work has been carried out in the Chinese context.

Focusing on business ethics in the specific Chinese context implies making comparisons between the interpretation of "right" and "wrong" in China and in some other location, most notably a rather vaguely defined "West", presumably typified by the US and Great Britain. That can be done, and is useful, provided that the "health warning" of Chapter 4 is heeded, and tendencies in a population are not attributed equally to every member of that population.

Two different sets of issues need to be examined when describing business ethics in a specific situation. The first concerns behaviours that may be considered "good" in one setting but "bad" in another. The second concerns the extent to which local ethical norms are adhered to or breached.

Differences between Chinese and Western ethical norms

There are a least two areas of behaviour where practices that are morally acceptable in the Chinese setting might be considered unethical in the West.

The first stems from the "high context" nature of Chinese culture, the less developed legal system, and the Confucian belief that virtuous behaviour amongst "good" people is a morally superior way to govern affairs. Those cultural traits mean that explicit statements of intent, including contracts, standards and code of practice, are taken less literally than in "low context" cultures. Instead, they are often viewed as general statements of intent, to be amended in the light of circumstances. Hence, it is not uncommon for Chinese businesspeople to feel ethically comfortable with seeking changes to agreements, or deviating from written standards, sometimes to an extent that Westerners can interpret as reneging on the agreement or improper failure to comply.

The second area of difference arises from the Confucian emphasis on the family, the lack of trust and the consequential importance of *guanxi*, also examined in Chapter 4. From the Chinese perspective, an individual has a moral duty to help his family and *guanxi* connections before he helps those with whom he has no such ties. Hence what could be considered "nepotism" or "cronyism" in Western cultures can be seen in China as a laudable effort to help family and friends, and a Westerner's refusal to give them priority as evidence of an immoral lack of care for those who matter most.

This last point raises the question of "is *guanxi* ethical?" which has been addressed very usefully by Dunfee and Warren (2001). In their normative analysis, they identify six ways in which *guanxi* can be ethically problematic. Those are:

- Its use may reduce societal wealth by promoting inefficiency. Not every use of *guanxi* has that effect but the distorting effect on capital markets is presumed to produce an overall negative effect. (Some observers might be less convinced than the authors of the benign nature of capital markets!)
- The few gain at the expense of the many and if the many oppose the use of *guanxi* in that way, it is unethical.
- Use of *guanxi* may violate fiduciary duties, as where an official awards a licence to an insider whose standing is insufficient or a manager in a private company disadvantages its owners by paying too much for supplies purchased from a friend or relative.
- *Guanxi* may run counter to the norms of communities whose interest should be taken into account. While historically, *guanxi* has been accepted, managers dealing with bureaucrats, and foreigners doing business in China, are increasingly important and they may be opposed to the practice, rendering it less acceptable.
- *Guanxi* may violate "hypernorms", which are "manifest universal ethical norms defined as principles so fundamental to human existence that we would expect them to be reflected in a convergence of religious, philosophical and cultural beliefs" (Dunfee & Warren, 2001, p.202). Such hypernorms include rules banning murder, deceit, torture, oppression and tyranny – although definitions of the latter two might well differ from place to place. Specific practices that could breach hypernorms include using *guanxi* to evade regulations protecting safety, the sale of public assets for private gain, and bribery.
- *Guanxi* may corrupt institutions like the legal system by overriding rules that should apply to everyone. (A similar argument is often made by China's leadership in respect of the impact of corruption on the Chinese Communist Party. As the Party's legitimacy stems from its claim to serve the people, corrupt actions, which may or may not be associated with *guanxi*, weaken that legitimacy.)

Overall, Dunfee and Warren (2001) conclude that it is impossible to judge the overall ethical impact of *guanxi* because different forms affect efficiency and the well-being of Chinese people in different ways. Each instance needs to be considered on its particular merits, using a framework proposed by Donaldson and Dunfee (1999) or the list of points above.

Ethical issues in the era of reform

The *guanxi* issue is important and a key point of difference between Asian and Western ethical norms. However, in a setting where incomes have risen exponentially and where institutions, norms and perhaps even culture are changing very quickly, ethical issues are much more extensive. Lu (1997) provides a mid-reform-era Chinese perspective on how thinking about business ethics in China has developed and she identifies the main challenges. "Practical issues" include: the difficulties arising when government takes management responsibility for state-owned enterprises and is both "target and leader" of those reforms: How to have fair competition between state-owned and other firms? How to provide employment without crippling state firms? Who should become richer, how should they become richer, how to help the poor and how should the rich contribute? How to share the burden of social security between the state, enterprises and individuals? In which spheres (like arts, the media and hospitals) should markets be excluded? How to harmonize economic progress with social development?

These are huge issues and Lu (1997, p.1514) goes on to separate issues of corporate ethics and management ethics. For corporates, the salient issues are identified as: the allocation of responsibility for ethical behaviour between enterprises and the government that no longer controls them directly; SOE's responsibilities for welfare provision, and; responsibility for the environment. Three issues are seen as posing ethical "puzzles" for entrepreneurs. The first is product quality – how should enterprises that are honest on product quality cooperate with those that are not? The second is triangular debt – should enterprises accept large debts in order to enter certain markets? The third concerns whether or not an enterprise should assist a partner if doing so would damage the interests of its employees and stockholders?

Progress has been seen on most of these corporate issues and puzzles in the 20 years since Lu's paper was published. Some corporates, though a minority, see themselves as being socially responsible. Responsibility for welfare is increasingly the responsibility of the state, markets, and individuals, rather than the enterprise. Product quality has improved through market pressures and the triangular debt problem was largely resolved by Zhu Rongji's *zhua da fang xiao* reforms. The process of marketization has meant that companies are less likely to assist a partner if it damages their interests – unless that partner happens to be the state. Nevertheless, there remain significant problems in respect of corporate responsibility for the environment.

With respect to the ethical issues facing managers, Lu (1997) identified discrimination between employees, relations between men and women, personal integrity in competitive markets, careerism, and the tension between "good ethics" and "good business" as the key areas of concern. As Chapter 12 shows, the treatment of workers in the huge informal sector often breaches international norms on labour rights and worker protection, which is an important additional concern, and Chapter 2 has described the unfair seizure of land rights from farmers, with inadequate compensation, which is another.

Corporate social responsibility and business ethics in China

The range of ethical problems to be addressed in China is enormous, running from destruction of the environment, to the mistreatment of workers, to the government expropriation of farmers' rights, to the misuse and appropriation of both private and state assets, to product quality issues like the sale of poisoned baby milk and the routine bribery of quality inspectors in factories (Riley 2012).

Cataloguing and assessing such ethical breaches would be an endless and thankless task. What is more useful is to consider China's position with respect to the broad notion of "corporate social responsibility".

Corporate stances on the purpose of an enterprise may be arranged along a spectrum of ethical positions. At one end of the spectrum lies Milton Friedman's (1970) position that the sole responsibility of an enterprise is to make profits within the limits set by the law, and to engage in free competition without deception or fraud. In Friedman's view, using company resources to pursue other objectives is tantamount to stealing from the owners and hence unethical in itself. Deception and fraud should be avoided but issues like safety standards, worker protection and environmental protection should be determined by the law, within which companies should work. It is the law that secures justice and corporate social responsibility is an oxymoron.

Friedman's position, which privileges owners over everyone else involved in a firm, is subject to a number of objections. Why privilege shareholders just because they have put their funds into the firm? They are often able to withdraw it fully and quickly, by selling shares, whereas workers who have put their lives into a firm, and have firm-specific skills, are much less able to extract themselves. What if the law fails to secure adequate justice because rich firms suborn or subvent it? What if firms can avoid the law by moving their legal domicile to less demanding jurisdictions, doing harm for profit wherever they choose?

The Friedman position that shareholders are paramount is largely an Anglo-Saxon stance that is not widely held elsewhere. A different perspective on the purpose of a company is the "stakeholder" perspective, which holds that firms exist to serve their "stakeholders", defined as "those who depend on the organization to fulfil their own goals and on whom the organization depends." The primary stakeholders are owners and employees, so that in Germany and Austria, for instance, the interests of employees are safeguarded by national rules on their inclusion in the decision-making process. As stakeholders also include customers, suppliers and lenders, the stakeholder approach implies that their interests should also be taken into account.

An even broader view on the purpose of the enterprise is that it should be a "shaper of society", which serves not only its stakeholders but also brings about social and market change through visionary leadership and which has less responsibility towards its shareholders. A company like Amazon, which has paid little attention to profits, Google's promise to "do no evil", Alibaba's aim to bring e-commerce to everyone, Uber and Airbnb's disruption of traditional industries and both giants and minnows in Silicon Valley all seem to either fit that description or aspire to it.

These different ethical stances correlate closely with companies' positioning with respect to corporate social responsibility (CSR), so the question that arises is "where do Chinese firms stand on their purpose and hence CSR?" Clearly, the widespread incidents of poor product quality, exploitation of workers, absconding owners and disappointed minority shareholders suggest that there are plenty of firms in China whose real purpose is to enrich the dominant owners and managers, regardless of any other parties' interests, and to the detriment of society as a whole. In 2011 the Chinese Academy of Social Sciences gave 300 large companies an average score of less than 20 out of a possible 100 on their CSR index, and 70% were found to "lack any sense of corporate social responsibility whatever" (Chen, 2011). Irwin (2012) confirms the extent of the problem but also notes a number of key drivers towards increased social responsibility. The first of those is the involvement of foreign companies producing in China, who face pressure from customers and governments at home to meet standards in respect of workers' rights, safety, product quality, the environment and corrupt practices. The second pressure also comes from abroad as Chinese companies sell to, and begin to operate facilities in, countries which demand higher standards. The third driver is the gradual development of civil society organizations, and interest from prestigious Chinese research institutes, who bring CSR issues to the public notice through conferences and publication. Another very important driver is the development of the Internet, through which the public regularly demonstrates its anger at abuses, and which channels the increasing involvement of the post-90s generation, especially on environmental issues. Social unrest arising from abuses is the abiding nightmare of a leadership that needs the "mandate of heaven" to legitimize its position, so that both the 12th and 13th Five Year Plans have given considerable priority to tackling pollution, workers' conditions, product safety and the whole range of CSR issues.

Government concern has also led to a wide range of official initiatives. The Chinese Company Law of 2006, Article 5, requires that companies "undertake social responsibility". Companies listed on the Shenzhen and Shanghai stock exchanges are required to provide information about their CSR contributions. State-owned enterprises supervised by the State-owned Assets Supervision and Administration Commission (SASAC) are subject to guidelines on CSR, as are foreign-invested enterprises and financial institutions.

It is clear that the authorities see the importance of CSR, and understand that it is in their self-interest to pursue it as a support for their legitimacy amongst the common people. However, as with so many issues, their ability to force compliance is limited, especially if that compliance would run against the interest of powerful agents. If a locality depends upon a polluting and dangerous industry which produces unsafe products but provides a major source of local income and employment, the local government is well placed to push back against the centre. Add the general tendency in a "high context" culture to take regulations lightly, plus the ubiquity of *guanxi* relations amongst the powerful, and the ever presence of corruption, and it is clear that deep-rooted change is needed before China becomes a paragon of CSR.

Americans reporting "Death by China" (Navarro & Autry, 2011) and "Poorly Made in China" (Midler, 2009) exaggerate and are a decade out of date on Chinese corporate irresponsibility in respect of the quality of Chinese goods and conditions in Chinese factories. They also underplay the fact that in many cases poor quality goods are produced as a rational response to unreasonably low prices negotiated by overseas buyers. If a Chinese company is asked to produce something for a ridiculously low price they will very often take the order and then do anything they can to wring a margin out of the deal. In those cases, it is difficult to assign all of the blame for corporate irresponsibility on to the Chinese Party. Nevertheless, exaggerations aside, China clearly has a long way to go before it can be said that the majority of companies put serious effort into CSR.

Corruption in China

What is corruption?

Corruption can be defined in several ways. The usual Chinese translation is *tanwu* ("greedy dirt"), which Wedeman (2004, p.897) renders more narrowly as "graft", or *fubai* ("rotten defeat") which is more general. He (2000) identifies the core element of the Chinese official definition as "the use of public authority and public resources for private interests" (*yi quan mou si*). Most definitions of corruption in the literature limit its scope to the public sector by making explicit reference to the "sale by government officials of government property for private gain" (Shleifer and Vishny, 1993, p.599). As that implies corruption cannot take place in private sector transactions, which is manifestly incorrect, the definition adopted here is more general – "the use of office or position to secure advantages to which that office or position does not entitle the holder".

Gong (1997) provides an impressive list of activities considered corrupt in China consisting of: graft; bribery; misappropriation of public property; seeking illicit benefits for relatives and friends; neglecting official duties; nepotism and favouritism; shirking; retaliation; making false accusations and reports; boasting and exaggerating; banqueting at public expense; running unauthorized businesses; profiteering; housing irregularities; living lavishly; improper sexual relations; forming cliques; gambling; whoring; excessive spending on marriages and funerals; superstitious activities; smuggling; selling state secrets; insider trading; real estate speculation; evading taxes; financial fraud; making illegal bank loans; and diverting disaster relief goods. Despite the length of that list it still omits academic plagiarism, cheating in examinations and sexual abuse of women, all of which are rife.

Myers (1989) argued that some of these activities are not really corruption as defined, but should instead be considered "unhealthy tendencies". That is correct, but pedantic, and the long list is useful in providing an overall picture of the range of wrong-doing that is in place.

How corrupt is China?

Whatever the definition adopted, China is a very corrupt country. That much is accepted by everyone from the leadership to the common people – the *lao bai xing* – who suffer most from the predation of corrupt office-holders, whether public or private. Corrupt behaviour is everywhere, from kindergartens and schools, where teachers routinely take bribes (not just apples) to favour (or more strictly monitor) some pupils, to hospitals where *guanxi* and bribes are needed to secure beds and ensure that careless mistakes are not made, to companies where supply contracts and promotions are paid for. Academic fraud, including cheating in examinations, plagiarism, faking research results and putting a professor's name on papers he didn't write are all common. Most significantly it is recognized that corruption is a major issue for the Communist Party itself. It is widely understood that the unrest in 1989, which led to the Tiananmen massacre, was in part attributable to anger at corruption amongst officials, and when Xi Jinping took office in November 2012, he declared to the press that "our party faces many severe challenges, and there are many pressing problems within the Party that need to be resolved, especially problems such as corruption and bribe-taking by some party members and cadres" (BBC, 2012).

One approach to measuring corruption is through the work of Transparency International (2016), which collects survey data on the extent of malfeasance in order to make comparisons across countries. According to their "Corruption Perceptions Index 2016" China ranked 79th out of 176 countries included in the analysis, with a score of 40 out of the possible 100, which would indicate a perfectly "clean" society (Denmark scored highest, at 90). China also ranked 27th out of 28 countries on the 2011 "Bribe Payers Index", which measures the perceived likelihood that companies from each country will pay bribes when operating abroad – only Russian companies scored worse.

Behind such summary rankings lie some quite astonishing figures and individual cases. Liu Zhijun, the Minister in charge of the famously corrupt Ministry of Railways (now abolished), was found to own 350 apartments, have 16 cars and 16 mistresses, before he was sentenced to death, with a reprieve, in July 2013. Zhang Shuguang, Deputy Chief Engineer of the Railways was held to be in possession of $US2.8 billion. Senior energy official Wei Pengyuan had around RMB 200 million ($US33m) hidden in his home, so much that counting it broke four of the 16 counting machines used! (BBC, 2014).

What is additionally disturbing is that all too often the officials found to be involved in corruption are themselves supposed to be responsible for its suppression. The most extreme case was Zhou Yongkang, who had been Minister for Public Security in charge of the police, before becoming a member of the Politburo Standing Committee, which is the highest decision-making body in the country. He retired in 2012 and then was arrested in 2013, convicted of bribery and other crimes that brought him RMB 129 million. He was then expelled from the Party and jailed for life, being the biggest "tiger" arrested to date.

Behind these very high profile cases, of which there are many (Pei, 2016), there are tens of thousands of lesser offenders, spread throughout the system. Nearly 200 chief or deputy chief police officers appeared on a list of offenders in 2011 (Pei, 2016, p.184). The judiciary is heavily implicated, officials' connections with organized crime are well documented, tax officials routinely solicit bribes, regulatory agencies are riddled with dishonesty and the People's Liberation Army has been a playground for corrupt senior officers selling promotions. A report from the People's Bank of China, dated 2008 (and subsequently removed from the Bank's website) estimated that up to 18,000 corrupt officials had either fled abroad or gone into hiding, having made away with an estimated RMB 800 million (Wall Street Journal, 2011). According to Lee (2016), more than 200,000 Party members and officials have been investigated since 2013, with a 99% conviction rate, suggesting total involvement in the millions.

What is the impact of corruption?

Corruption has both economic and socio-political impact. In the economic sphere, some observers have suggested that corruption can actually assist with economic development (Leys, 1965). In an imperfect world, if the bureaucracy is an impediment to growth by slowing down projects and daily business, "greasing the wheels" through bribery could speed up the process and also attract more able people to work in (illicitly) better paid official positions. Furthermore, bribery to get procurement contracts might improve efficiency if the more efficient firms are able to offer higher bribes (Beck & Maher, 1986). After all, the "Asian Dragons" of Korea, Japan and Taiwan were all notably corrupt in the periods of their most dramatic economic development. On the other hand, the "sand the wheels" hypothesis (Meon & Sekkat, 2005) suggests that corruption does not speed up administrative permissions if many of them are required from independent agents (Shleifer & Vishny, 1993). Corrupt officials might be more able but then they are more likely to devise additional distortions to the economy which they can use to enhance their power and income (Kurer, 1993). The argument that firms who are able to offer the most bribes can do so because they are the most efficient fails to recognize that the ability to pay more may arise simply from the willingness to reduce quality and evade standards (Rose-Ackerman, 1997), witness the construction companies which built "tofu" schools in Sichuan, which collapsed killing hundreds of children in the earthquake of 2008.

Given that China has grown at such spectacular speed in the last three decades, the question of whether corruption has made it grow faster or slower is not as important as it might be in countries whose growth is less impressive. Would a less corrupt China have grown at 12% per annum for 30 years instead of 10%? It is possible, but seems unlikely. What is important, and indisputable, is that corruption has socio-political consequences that are potentially very serious indeed. Corruption is a source of inequality and it leads to public anger, especially when it arises from the exercise of *guanxi* by the well-connected. The Chinese Communist Party cannot draw on a democratic mandate for its legitimacy and hence relies on a modern form of the "mandate of heaven" whereby it earns the right to rule by taking care of the people as a virtuous emperor would have done – feeding them, keeping them safe and protecting them from rapacious officials. If they should be seen by the people to fail in that Confucian version of a social contract the resultant social unrest could prove beyond even the Party's considerable capacity to contain. For that reason, the last two generations of Chinese leadership have placed considerable emphasis on the need to rein in official corruption, in terms of bribery and graft and the whole list of "unhealthy tendencies".

What causes corruption?

The causes of corruption can be divided into "structural" and "non-structural" factors. Structural factors are those that arise from the institutional features of China's economy and society, while non-structural factors refer to the impact of the Confucian heritage, general moral standards and other cultural characteristics.

With respect to structural factors, several can be identified. When an economy is subject to government intervention and controls, and official permissions are required to carry out profitable or desirable activities, there are opportunities for "rent-seeking" where officials demand bribes in return for those permissions (Jain, 2001). This will be particularly prevalent when higher incomes are being generated so that companies and individuals can afford to pay the bribes. That has been the situation since reform, and it was exacerbated by the second factor, the "double track" reform strategy (He, 2000, p.248.) For some time, there were two prices for many products – administered low prices for products produced within the plan and higher market prices for additional output. A businessman or official who could acquire goods at plan prices and then illicitly sell them at market prices could make huge profits, and they did.

Third, when institutions are weak and undeveloped, particularly in respect of property rights and the laws determining their transfer from one party to another, there are ample opportunities for the development of "crony capitalism" (Pei, 2016) whereby officials who have "de facto" control of state resources can transfer them to themselves or members of their *guanxi* networks. As Chapter 8 has explained, in the late 1990s, the policy of *zhua da fang xiao* involved closing tens of thousands of smaller state-owned enterprises or transferring them into private ownership, which provided immense opportunities for officials or their relatives and friends to take control of what had been state or collective assets. In this case, the transfer of assets was a part of state policy and the terms on which it took place were not subject to very close scrutiny. The legacy which remains is that officialdom and the private sector are closely entangled in a complicated web of loyalties and commitments which is impossible to unravel.

A fourth structural factor underpinning corruption (He, 2000, p.251) is the inequality between the salaries paid to officials and the incomes earned by others. As public officials' pay fell behind they were driven to illicit sources of income, both for themselves and for their organizations so that the latter could improve welfare for their members and retain them in the public service. When that tactic succeeded and there was little or no punishment, it became widespread, an important part of officials' benefits and deeply embedded in the system.

A fifth structural factor is that lack of experience in the anti-corruption agencies, and the involvement in corruption of their personnel and leaders, meant that the likelihood of being caught and punished was very low. Hence, corruption became a "high reward, low risk" activity.

In addition to the structural factors that have contributed to the level of corruption in China, there are a series of historical and cultural characteristics that also have some explanatory value. In Confucian thinking, virtuous behaviour should be instilled through education and the cultivation of the virtuous character, not through the promulgation and enforcement of laws and regulations, which are given lower status. In a sense, then, Confucius naively "opened the door" to cheating by downplaying enforcement and placing reliance on good behaviour, which is rarely fully manifest. Certainly, his emphasis on giving preference to family and friends over others, and the powerful moral imperative to help "insiders", makes nepotistic behaviour feel less morally bad.

Three other cultural factors are relevant. In a high "power distance" culture, subordinates expect to be under the control of their "superiors" and to accept their subordinate status, which makes it difficult for them to "whistle blow" or to refuse to take part in corrupt activities. The "collective" nature of Chinese culture also deters individuals from taking actions on their own initiative. An individual who feels that "something should be done" may at the same time be concerned for the interests of their group, some of whom may be involved in corrupt activities.

The third cultural factor concerns the general moral climate that has prevailed in China in the reform period. In the Mao era, everyone was poor but relatively equal and the moral climate was one in which material gain was not valued. "Class struggle" was the overriding rhetoric while "serve the people" (*wei renmin fuwu*) was the day-to-day exhortation to the masses. Self-sacrificing behaviour was presented as the ideal to be emulated. In the era of reform, however, that set of values was swept away. Economic development was the priority, and it was accepted that some could become richer than others and at a faster pace. Entrepreneurs and officials who oversaw the most rapid growth were lauded, even if their activities were in part corrupt and self-serving, and the moral certainties of the past were replaced with a crass materialism. As faith in Marx and Mao was lost it was not replaced by any moral compass except the one pointing to personal gain. As a result there was what He (2000, p.254) calls a "decline in the moral cost of corruption". Corruption became more widespread in part because people simply ceased to feel guilty about participating in it.

Can corruption be eliminated: swatting flies and taming tigers or not?

If corruption is attributable to the factors identified, its elimination could be achieved by systematically addressing them. That points to a number of remedies. First, the process of economic reform needs to be broadened so that business activities require fewer of the administrative permissions that provide an opportunity for "squeeze". To some extent that has been carried out gradually over the years, and the dual track pricing system that provided such a cornucopia of illicit incomes is long gone. However, property rights are still not well defined or protected, the laws concerning their transaction remain unclear and compliance with the law is far from universal. There have been eight completed rounds of administrative reform (Wang, 2010) often focused on down-sizing the bureaucracy. However, as the Party bureaucracy and the government bureaucracy are essentially one, full blown administrative reform implies political reform, about which the Party is very cautious. Hence, "the Party also reinforces China's informal politics, clientelism, and authoritarian governing style, making the problem of corruption worse" (Wang, 2010, p.116). Low levels of pay for public servants remain – President Xi's salary is said to be $US22,000 per year (Kuo, 2015) – and the gap between their lifestyles and nominal salaries is enormous, suggesting significant and ubiquitous alternative emoluments, whether in cash or kind.

This analysis suggests that the fundamental sources of corruption have not been eliminated. Nevertheless, over the years the Party has put considerable effort and publicity into "anti-corruption campaigns" aimed at punishing the guilty and improving the moral climate. These have been a feature of the Party's activities at least since 1982 (He, 2000, p.267). For the most part, the earlier campaigns could be described as "short-lived political drama" (Wedeman, 2016) in which there was a good deal of publicity, the arrest of several thousand petty offenders ("flies") and a few slightly more senior officials ("tigers"). Those campaigns then faded away quietly and the perceived level of corruption continued to increase. That does appear to have changed when Xi Jinping took office in November 2012 and made anti-corruption a centrepiece of his policy platform. In December of that year an "Eight-point regulation" was promulgated, with the objective of reducing corruption significantly. By September 2016 an unprecedented 213 "tigers" had been seized, from both civilian and military life alongside an unknown number of "flies", which may have been as high as 500,000 (Wedeman, 2016). Furthermore, some of the "tigers" were at levels in the hierarchy that had previously been believed to be exempt. The most senior were four former members of the Politburo: Bo Xilai (Party Secretary in Chongqing, who had been a member of the Politburo Standing Committee); Zhou Yongkang (previously head of Public Security); Xu Caihou (former Vice Chairman of the Central Military Commission); and Guo Boxiong (also former Vice Chairman of the Central Military Commission.)

Exposure and punishment of officials at the highest level points to a level of commitment to anti-corruption that was hitherto unknown. The anti-corruption drive has also been highly visible in other ways. Expenditure on luxury goods, top brand alcohol and expensive meals fell significantly, and some five star hotels actually applied to be formally downgraded to four star because their clients were nervous about eating and staying there (Areddy & Wang, 2014). After Xi Jinping declared that an appropriate business lunch should consist of no more than "one soup and four dishes" that became the standard. In universities, it used to be common for foreign guests to be invited to a "simple lunch", which featured heavy duty alcohol, expensive seafood, and the attendance of entire departments of professors whose connection to the foreign guest was mysterious or non-existent. That has now been replaced with polystyrene lunch boxes or a visit to the faculty canteen.

There is no doubt that Xi Jinping's anti-corruption campaign is going further and deeper and reaching higher than any of its predecessors. It is also undeniably popular with the mass of the people, which strengthens his position should the "tigers" and "flies" try to strike back. Nevertheless, two major concerns remain. The most important is that arrests and exhortations do little to address the fundamental causes of the corruption that is so deeply embedded in the system. Pei (2016, p.260) goes so far as to argue that

> the emergence and entrenchment of crony capitalism in China's political economy, in retrospect, is the logical outcome of Deng Xiaoping's authoritarian model of economic modernization because elites in control of unconstrained power cannot resist using it to loot the wealth generated by economic growth.

As the Party is unwilling to accept constraints on its power, and will always find it difficult to control its 80 million members, the prognosis is not good, despite current attempts to establish a "super agency" similar to Hong Kong's Independent Commission Against Corruption (Kwok, 2017).

The other concern is that Xi has undoubtedly used the anti-corruption campaign as a weapon against his political rivals. Bo Xilai, in particular, was seen as a rising star and possible competitor for power before he was found to have been involved in widespread corruption and an amazing drama in which his wife poisoned a British businessman. There is also a widespread belief that there is animosity between Xi and the faction around former leader Jiang Zemin, and that some of the arrests have been a part of that ongoing rivalry. Xi has taken steps to acquire a degree of control over the levers of power, which is unprecedented since Deng Xiaoping, and it is unlikely that a coup against him could succeed. Nevertheless, rich and powerful people lose out in the anti-corruption campaign so that nothing can be entirely dismissed in the opaque world of Chinese politics.

Towards sustainable development

The discussion thus far has dealt with the impact of "good" and "bad" behaviour in business on the world in which it is set. In so far as that world has a future, one of the broadest interpretations of "ethical" business behaviour is that it should contribute to "sustainable" development, which can be defined as:

> development that meets the needs of the present without compromising the ability of future generations to meet their own needs.
>
> (World Commission on Environment and Development, 1987, p.16)

In the language of the stakeholder perspective, sustainability includes future generations as stakeholders whose interests should be taken into account.

Given that corporate social responsibility is not yet widely accepted in China, it can be argued *a fortiori* that sustainability has yet to take its place as an observable element of ethical business behaviour. Nevertheless, there are a number of "green shoots" to be found, particularly in the domain of public policy. As Kennedy and Johnson (2016, p.32) point out, the 13th Five Year Plan shows a markedly increased emphasis on protecting the environment, which they attribute to five factors. First, it is natural that as a country becomes richer, its attention turns to the environment. Second, despite the limitations on civil society, China has an active grassroots environmental movement. Third, the Ministry of Environmental Protection has done a lot of work to explain the importance of climate change and environmental protection to the public (though it lacks the authority to enforce regulations). Fourth, the international community has done much to involve China in the discourse on the environment, and sometimes shamed the authorities into yielding on the notion that environmental information is a "state secret" – as when the US Embassy in Beijing took to measuring pollution on the Embassy roof and publishing the results on the Internet. Fifth, and potentially most important in the Chinese system, President Xi takes a personal interest in the environment having been affected by the notorious polluting of Lake Tai in Zhejiang when he was an official there. The *Peoples Republic of China National Report on Sustainable Development* (Ministry of Finance, 2014), compiled by a Leading Group led by Zhang Ping,

Chairman of the National Reform and Development Commission, provides an impressive list of achievements on sustainability in recent years. China has become the world's largest producer of hydropower, wind power and solar energy collection. Water consumption per RMB 10,000 of income fell by more than 50% in 2000–2010. Forest coverage has increased, the poverty rate reduced from 10.2% to 2.8% of the population, disposable chopsticks taxed, and the "Plastic Bag Limit Order" promulgated. The energy requirement per unit of industrial output fell by 26% for enterprises "above a designated size" (p.38), more efficient power stations opened and a "green mining" initiative stepped up.

There is solid evidence to believe that China is making a gargantuan effort at policy level to ensure a more sustainable model of development that will make fewer demands on the environment, be safer for workers and consumers and protect later generations. However, as with so many issues in China, the problems are at least as gargantuan and the need to maintain growth can override the imperative for sustainability. The ability of some sectors and locations to obstruct the good intentions of the central leadership remains.

References

Areddy, J. and Wang, F., 2014. Chinese hotels drop stars in order to score political points. *Wall Street Journal*, 23 January. Available at: http://blogs.wsj.com/chinarealtime/2014/01/23/chinese-hotels-drop-stars-to-score-political-points/ [Accessed 14 February 2017].

Babson College., 2007. *Introduction to the Babson framework for ethical decision making*. Wellesley, NY: Babson College.

BBC. 2012. Full text: China's new party chief Xi Jingping's speech. Available at: http://www.bbc.com/news/world-asia-china-20338586 [Accessed 11 February 2017].

BBC. 2014. China corruption: Record cash find in official's home. 31 October. Available at: http://www.bbc.com/news/world-asia-29845257 [Accessed 11 February 2017].

Beck, P. and Maher, M., 1986. A comparison of bribery and bidding in thin markets. *Economic Letters*, 20, pp.1–5.

Chen, W., 2011. Damage limitation is badly needed. *China Daily*, 11 November. Available at: http://www.chinadaily.com.cn/opinion/2011-11/11/content_14076274.htm [Accessed 10 February 2017].

Crane, A. and Matten, N., 2007. *Business ethics: Managing corporate citizenship and sustainability in the era of globalization*. Oxford: Oxford University Press.

Donaldson, T. and Dunfee, T., 1999. *Ties that bind: A social contracts approach to business ethics*. Cambridge, MA: Harvard Business School Press.

Dunfee, T. and Warren, D., 2001. Is *guanxi* ethical? A normative analysis of doing business in China. *Journal of Business Ethics*, 32, pp.191–204.

Friedman, M., 1970. The social responsibility of business is to increase its profits. *New York Times Magazine*, 13 September, pp.1–6.

Gong, T., 1997. Forms and characteristics of China's corruption in the 1990s: Change with continuity. *Communist and Post-Communist Studies*, 30 (3), pp.278–286.

He, Z., 2000. Corruption and anti-corruption in reform China. *Communist and Post-Communist Studies*, 33, pp.243–270.

Irwin, J., 2012. *Doing business in China: An overview of ethical aspects*. Occasional Paper 6. Institute of Business Ethics. London: IBE.

Jain, A., 2001. Corruption: A review. *Journal of Economic Surveys*, 15, pp.71–121.

Kennedy, S. and Johnson, C. K., 2016. *Perfecting China inc. The 13th five year plan*. Center for Strategic and International Studies. New York: Rowman and Littlefield.

Kuo, L. 2015. Does Chinese president Xi Jinping really earn just $22,000 a year? *Quartz*, 20 January. Available at: https://qz.com/329584/does-chinese-president-xi-jinping-really-earn-just-22000-a-year/ [Accessed 13 February 2017].

Kurer, O., 1993. Clientelism, corruption and the allocation of resources. *Public Choice*, 77, pp.259–273.

Kwok, T., 2017. Can China be the next anti-corruption success story, after Hong Kong and Singapore? *South China Morning Post*, 24 January. Available at: http://www.scmp.com/comment/insight-opinion/article/2065298/can-china-be-next-anti-corruption-success-story-after-hong [Accessed 14 February 2017].

Lee, J., 2016. Why Xi's anti-corruption campaign won't work. *Forbes*, 29 January. Available at: http://www.forbes.com/sites/johnlee75/2016/01/29/why-xis-anti-corruption-campaign-wont-work/#10f7fbf821cd [Accessed 11 February 2017].

Leys, C., 1965.What is the problem about corruption? *Journal of Modern African Studies*, 3, pp.215–230.

Lu, X., 1997. Business ethics in China. *Journal of Business Ethics*, 16, pp.1509–1518.

Meon, P. and Sekkat, K., 2005. Does corruption grease or sand the wheels of growth? *Public Choice*, 122, pp.69–97.

Midler, P., 2009. *Poorly made in China: An insider's account of the tactics behind China's production game*. New York: Wiley.

Ministry of Finance (ed.), 2014 *Peoples Republic of China National Report on Sustainable Development*. Available at http://www.china-un.org/eng/zt/sdreng/P020120608816288649663.pdf [Accessed 14 February 2017].

Myers, J., 1989. Modernization and 'unhealthy tendencies'. *Comparative Politics*, 21 (2), p.196.

Navarro, P. and Autry, G., 2011. *Death by China: Confronting the dragon – a global call to action*. New York: Pearson.

Pei, M., 2016. *China's crony capitalism: The dynamics of regime decay*. Cambridge, MA: Harvard University Press

Riley, C., 2012. How to build a robust due diligence process, Secura Ltd. PowerPoint presentation.

Romar, E., 2002. Virtue is good business: Confucianism as a practical business ethic", *Journal of Business Ethics*, 38 (1/2), pp.119–131.

Rose-Ackerman, R., 1997. The political economy of corruption: Economics, culture and the seesaw dynamics, in Elliott, K. (ed.), *Corruption and the global economy*. Washington, DC: Institute for International Economics, pp.31–60.

Shleifer, A. and Vishny, R., 1993. Corruption. *The Quarterly Journal of Economics*, 108 (3), pp.599–617.

Transparency International. 2016. *Corruption perceptions index* 2016. Available at http://www.transparency.org/ [Accessed 11 February 2017].

United Nations World Commission on Environment and Development, 1987. *World Commission on Environment and Development: Our common future*. Geneva: United Nations

Wall Street Journal. 2011. Report: Corrupt Chinese officials take $123 billion overseas. Available at: http://blogs.wsj.com/chinarealtime/2011/06/16/report-corrupt-chinese-officials-take-123-billion-overseas/ [Accessed 11 February 2017].

Wang, Q., 2010. Administrative reform in China: Past, present and future. *Southeast Review of Asian Studies*, 32, pp.100–119.

Wedeman, A., 2004. The intensification of corruption in China. *China Quarterly*, 180, pp.895–921.

Wedeman, A., 2016. Four years on: Where is Xi Jinping's anti-corruption drive headed? *Hong Kong Free Press*, 25 September. Available at https://www.hongkongfp.com/2016/09/25/four-years-xi-jinpings-anti-corruption-drive-headed/ [Accessed 14 February 2017].

12

MANAGING AND LEADING PEOPLE IN CHINA

Howard Davies

As Chapter 2 explained, labour market reform has freed most employees to search for jobs wherever they choose, and employers are largely free to hire whoever they choose. In that respect, China has become more like Western developed economies. At the same time, Chinese organizations are embedded in a particularly complex and dynamic setting. Industrialization and urbanization are shifting the sectoral and geographical structure of employment, marketization is changing the nature of employing organizations, and globalization is bringing Chinese workers and managers into competition and co-operation with their "foreigner" counterparts, both at home and overseas. Vestiges of the state-owned approach to management co-exist with intensively competitive private management practices and the modern but evolving version of an ancient culture has implications for the ways in which workers and leaders interact. This idiosyncratic setting makes China a vast ongoing "natural experiment" in management and leadership, which this chapter describes.

The unskilled/skilled divide: scarcity amid plenty

In the crude sense, China has a superabundance of workers, with 772 million employed persons in 2014. In the initial period of reform, growth was driven by the voluntary re-allocation of hundreds of millions of under-employed agricultural workers into the industrial sector, which was able to compete internationally through low cost production, achieved through very low levels of wages. Workers were anxious to escape the drudgery of the fields, and they flocked to the factories. Skill requirements and technology levels in the export-focused sectors were rudimentary, and simple "Tayloristic work organization" was the dominant mode of production (Cooke, 2012). Even today, in factories across South China, thousands of (mostly) young women from far-off villages sit for 60 hours per week at moving belts, assembling smartphones, computers and the whole range of China's exports. Line workers wear uniforms of one colour, and share rooms in the factory's dorms, while their supervisors (also mainly women) watch over them directly, wear a different colour of uniform and have slightly less sparse living conditions. Management is rudimentary, but does present some China-specific challenges. For instance, workers often divide into groups according to their places of origin, and there are sometimes bitter rivalries and feuds between the groups, whose spoken native languages can be incomprehensible to each other. In the most extreme example, Uighur workers from Xinjiang were attacked by Han workers in factories in Guangdong province, and the battle spread back to Xinjiang itself where rioting broke out in sympathy with the embattled workers hundreds of kilometres away in the South. Most rivalries are on a smaller scale but managers need to develop ways to deal with them. In some cases, workers are all recruited from the same region, in others line workers, supervisors and managers are each recruited from different areas (senior levels usually being locals) in order to inhibit collusion across the different levels of the managerial hierarchy. In many manufacturing regions, workers from other parts of the country form "hometown associations" (*tong xiang hui*) to protect their fellows from the perceived predations of the locals.

While China's industries have become more sophisticated, especially in the more technologically complex sectors, and wages are much higher than they used to be, the simple Tayloristic model persists in the assembly-for-export sectors, and can be remarkably adaptable. In a Hong Kong company visited by the author, the "products" being produced in South China were digitized files of British Army records from the 1870s and Italian marriage records from a similar era. Copies of the handwritten records were transferred to the company via satellite dishes, and then typed into digital files by several hundred young women, each of whose keystrokes per hour and "off-task" minutes were monitored via computer by the only men in the building, who sat in the computer room at the back. The young women had only primary level education and spoke neither English nor Italian. However, they had been trained using an in-house manual on "Palaeography" – the study of ancient writing – to recognize the specific terms used in the particular documents they were transcribing. Once the files had been digitized they were returned via satellite dish to the client in America. The management system for this "knowledge factory" was essentially identical to that in any Hong Kong or Taiwan-controlled jeans, watch, smartphone or computer factory, using direct supervision and task-focused training to produce a good quality product at low cost using relatively poor quality labour.

The Hong Kong factory model remains in place, but is no longer the only mode of production to be found. The second industrial revolution, dating from the mid-1990s onwards, expanded the range of manufacturing industries to include more complex, capital-intensive and technology-driven sectors, and the service sector began to expand. Foreign direct investment flooded in from Europe, North America and Japan, establishing activities which require greater skills on the part of both front-line workers and the managers who plan, direct and control their activities.

In this more complex environment, there are huge differences in the availability and bargaining power of skilled and experienced workers relative to the unskilled, which have a major impact on the ways in which the different groups are managed. Unskilled workers are still plentiful, if more expensive, and the expected move of a further 200 million rural residents to the towns in the next 15 years implies that they will remain so. There is a general air of anxiety in the factories of the Pearl River Delta every Chinese New Year as migrant workers go home for the festival and employers fear that they will not return. However, there has been no significant difficulty to date and simple actions like offering bonuses to returning workers who bring new recruits with them has been sufficient to maintain the supply. Rising societal expectations, and labour laws, mean that managers treat unskilled workers with more consideration than in the past, but there is little market pressure on them to do so. Skilled managers and technicians, however, are generally in short supply, and at the top end Farrell and Grant (2005) estimated that Chinese firms seeking to expand abroad needed 75,000 internationally capable managers compared with a supply of only 3,000. As a rough generalization, the higher the skill level required, and the more experience is needed, the greater the shortage.

The first salient feature of Chinese labour markets and human resource management in the twenty-first century, then, is the difference in the balance of supply and demand between skilled and managerial workers on the one hand and the unskilled on the other, which is reflected in the ways they are managed, recruited, retained, developed and rewarded.

Recruiting, selecting and retaining workers and managers

The distinction between skilled and unskilled workers overlaps with the divide between the "formal" and "informal" employment sectors. In the informal sector, also referred to as "flexible employment", workers rarely have employment contracts. They work in both formal and informal organizations, including self-employment, and have little access to social security provision, or to the protections supposedly provided by the labour laws. Some of them work full-time, some part-time, some seasonally but they share the same basic lack of protection. As might be expected, definition of the informal sector is imprecise and statistics are difficult to assess. Nevertheless, it is clear that the informal sector in China is huge in both absolute and relative terms. The State Council estimated that 150 million urban workers were engaged in informal employment, making up 20% of urban employment and 58% and 52% in urban industry and services (Cooke, 2012, p.33). Given the informal nature of agricultural employment, and the generally small scale and private nature of industry in the countryside, the proportion of rural workers in informal employment must be very much higher.

It is ironic that in a "socialist" country such a large proportion of workers fall outside the workplace protections of the state. However, the authorities had little option once they had decided in the late 1990s on the policy of "seizing the large and letting go the small" (*zhua da fang xiao*). The closure of many state- and collectively owned enterprises generated job losses in the tens of millions so that rapid re-employment and income creation became an overwhelming priority (Xu, 2009). Having seen how privatization in the countryside had energized production and produced millions of township and village enterprises, the authorities extended what would hitherto have been anathema into the urban setting.

The recruitment of workers in the informal sector is a simple affair. Migrant workers who provide "ad hoc" household services like plumbing, carpentry and electrical work are self-employed and they sit in groups outside apartment blocks, with signs advertising their specialities and phone numbers. Most middle-class households employ at least part-time maids recruited through family and neighbourhood networks. Every town and city has a "labour market" (*lao wu shi chang*) street where employers and workers can advertise their vacancies and skills and make direct contact. The same streets also have employment agencies, run by both private companies and (officially unsanctioned) local governments, which act as intermediaries for employers who cannot participate directly.

For the rural migrants who make up most of the factory and construction site workforce, employment agencies are not the preferred recruitment mechanism, as they are regarded as yet another mechanism for cheating the powerless, and they prefer to use family or personal networks to find jobs. However, in many cases they have no choice because many employers prefer to hire workers from the agencies, as agency employees, so that employer responsibilities fall on the agencies, not on the "real" employer.

This practice of passing employer responsibility on to others is in part an unintended consequence of the Labour Contract Law of 2008, whose purpose was to introduce significant worker protection through social insurance, redundancy pay, less use of "flexible" employment and fines for employer non-compliance. Given its impact on costs, the Law was fiercely opposed by employers, but also by local governments, and even by many workers who feared unemployment and were opposed to making contributions to insurance schemes. The law as passed was a messy compromise but nevertheless many companies seek to bypass its requirements by avoiding formal employment relationships with their workers. In the run up to the law's introduction many companies sacked their long-term employees and then re-hired them on less formal terms. Even China's high tech "flagship" company, Huawei, took that approach. Another tactic is to use workers who are employed by the employment agencies, a third is to rely on verbal agreements and a fourth to make direct "top up" payments to workers in lieu of (and less than) the social security payments that are formally required. In the retail sector, junior sales floor staff in large stores are often not employed by the store itself. Instead, they are "vendor representatives", employed by companies whose products are sold in that retail setting (Gamble & Huang, 2009). Such workers are often non-locals and female, working harder for lower wages and less security than the store's formal local male employees.

As noted in other chapters, local governments often stand in the way of the implementation of central government policies and while they were instructed to stay out of the employment agency business many remain involved through sub-contracting to agencies run by local government officials or their relatives. They also tend to shield local employers from the more expensive requirements of the Labour Contract Law. For unskilled workers, there are really just two sources of meaningful protection. The first is in some small firms owned and managed by workers turned entrepreneurs, whose life experience leads them to accept a degree of accommodation with their employees, as found by Li and Edwards (2008). The second comes through pressure for corporate social responsibility on firms producing for Western brand names. As revelations about poor treatment of workers can be damaging to such customers, they insist that central government labour regulations are met and they audit their contract manufacturers from time to time. Hence, there is an economic incentive to comply with the labour laws, which is not generally in place.

For skilled workers and managers, who are in short supply, the balance of power and the recruitment process is very different. Lu (2008) found that in 82% of loss-making state enterprises the difficulties could be attributed to a lack of management expertise and Arkless (2007) found that 40% of employers surveyed had difficulty in finding suitable senior managers. Expansion of undergraduate university education has done little to relieve the shortage because the 7 million undergraduates graduating each year (China Statistical Yearbook, 2015) are widely held to lack the skills needed to function as junior managers. Justly or not, the post-80s "one-child" generation are often stereotyped as spoiled, dependent, unable to accept hardship but expectant of immediate success, and significant proportions either remain unemployed or take up lower quality jobs. The very brightest of China's young graduates, from Peking, Tsinghua and other top universities, still go to the USA or Europe on graduation, with relatively few returning. In any event, those who do return often lack formal work experience, or the China-specific understanding needed, especially in the service sector. Shortages of technicians and senior technicians are also marked, with the 2006–2010 Five Year Plan identifying a need for at least 7 million technicians and nearly 2 million senior technicians.

Faced with these shortages, companies need to understand the factors that motivate scarce workers and how they can be recruited and then retained. The evidence provides a fairly straightforward picture, where employees are highly mobile and motivated by immediate financial reward, and the prospect of financially rewarding promotion opportunities, rather than the kind of rewards associated with a "high commitment" model of human resource management (Pfeffer, 1998). While Chinese employees do value having good relationships with their supervisors and managers, and being recognized by them for good work (Howard, Liu, Wellins & William, 2007), Chinese culture means that such relationships tend to be particularistic so that reciprocation is with the individual superiors, not the company as a whole. Loyalty to the employing organization is limited (two thirds of technicians in Shenzhen were found to be looking for better positions) and workers with scarce skills "job hop" frequently in response to offers of higher wages or more prestigious job titles.

In response to employees' "transactional" approach to employment and a sellers' market for skills, employers seeking to recruit can do little but offer higher wages, impressive job titles and "poach" workers from their competitors. Networks are used to attract recruits with common social ties, who may be less mobile (Han & Han 2009). In some cases, local industry associations have worked with local government to increase the supply of needed skills and co-operate to prevent poaching, as in the small-scale ship-building industry in Guangdong (Cooke, 2012, p.62) and the foreign-invested firms in Suzhou Industrial Park (Li & Sheldon, 2010). On the whole, however, in-company skills development is inhibited by the prospect of poaching, the supply of skills remains a bottleneck, and it has been left to the state to try to correct the market failure through large scale expansion of vocational and professional training, and by requiring a percentage of companies' wage bill to either be spent on training or remitted to the local government to be spent for the same purpose. However, given limited compliance with the labour laws, and employers' dissatisfaction with the quality of vocational education, it seems unlikely that the skills gaps will be closed in the foreseeable future, which has further implications for China's ability to move up the value chain, emphasize "innovation" and implement the ambitious plan for Manufacturing 2025.

The second key feature of human resource management in China is the prevalence of a highly transactional approach to job seeking and employment on the part of employees in both skilled and unskilled segments of the market. Employers may do what they can to make themselves attractive in terms of their brand as employer and their organizational culture. However, those factors are insignificant if they do not offer high enough starting pay, and in the skilled sector it is difficult to attract and retain employees without offering prospects for rapid advancement, often at speeds that are scarcely justified by the employees' increasing experience and productivity.

Managing for performance in China: can Western approaches be effective?

Simple Tayloristic modes of performance management dominate in the assembly-for-export sectors, where intense competition directs executive attention away from more sophisticated "strategic human resource management" practices (Morris, Wilkinson & Gamble, 2009), and simple HR practices are a good fit with cost-driven competitive advantage. However, both domestic and foreign companies now produce more complex, differentiated and sophisticated manufactures, and the service sector is expanding rapidly. A key issue, then, is whether human resource management practices developed in the higher income and culturally different settings of Europe and the US can usefully be transferred to China.

Two questions can be addressed. First, are companies in China adopting more explicit and formal systems for the management of human resources? Second, are more "commitment-based" approaches to managing people, as understood in Western settings, likely to be effective in the Chinese setting?

In the state-owned sector before reform, human resources were allocated by the planning system and managed through the "three irons" – the iron rice bowl (*tie wan fan*) where everyone's employment was guaranteed, regardless of their performance, the iron wage (*tie gong zi*) where pay was fixed, and the iron chair (*tie jiao yi*) where the state decided who should hold senior positions. Personnel management was mainly concerned with distributing egalitarian pay and benefits, lauding "model workers", maintaining personal records and exhorting workers to participate in whichever mass campaign was the order of the day. Enterprise reform, however, has exposed many of the SOEs to marketization and competition, forcing them to place greater emphasis on performance, and the effective management of people. At the same time, there is undoubtedly organizational inertia, and a significant number of "zombie" firms remain, so that the pressure to perform varies with the individual circumstances of each SOE. As a result, the adoption of HR practices varies widely across the SOE sector. Ding and Akhtar (2001) found that they were less likely to adopt human capital-oriented personnel practices than foreign-invested joint ventures. Sun (2012) found that in a "super-large" SOE – China National Petroleum Corporation – personnel practices were still essentially administrative and rules-bound, largely concerned with payment and records management. On the other hand, Cooke (2012, p.60) quotes a survey finding that SOEs were more likely to have training plans in place than either FIEs or private firms. As the Chinese authorities are determined that SOEs should spearhead the drive to develop globally competitive firms in technologically sophisticated sectors, there is an understanding that the use of human resources is key to that initiative, and there is pressure on at least some SOEs to develop their HR systems.

With respect to the tens of millions of township and village enterprises (TVEs) Ding, Ge and Warner (2004) found that as their governance structures evolved from simple "responsibility" systems through contracting arrangements to joint stock companies, and as the TVEs increased in size, so did HRM functions become more "marketized". Under the responsibility system, few firms had human resource departments, recruitment consisted of hiring from the supply of cheap migrants and training was minimal. In the larger joint stock companies, independent HRM departments were in place, more locals were hired at higher cost, and some attention was paid to training. Nevertheless, even in the largest firms, training was limited for workers, reward systems were largely based on piecework rates, and only the most senior managers gained any significant incentives from the distribution of ownership shares. Kim and Gao (2010) similarly found that in family firms, larger size predicted the establishment of both a formal HR department and the formalization of HR tasks including job specifications, remuneration and performance appraisal.

In foreign-invested enterprises, the adoption of HRM systems also varies. Pope and Meyer (2015) argued that the rise of "global corporate organizations" means that national contexts have become less consequential for multinational corporations in which case foreign-invested firms from Europe, Japan and the US could be expected to simply transfer their HRM systems into the Chinese subsidiaries and joint ventures. The evidence, however, suggests that convergence on a single set of company practices is only useful for technical or operational tasks subject to physical laws. When dealing with local people and institutions, differences need to be introduced (Ma, Chen & Zhang, 2016), and HRM policies like the design of employee incentives cannot simply be "cut and pasted" across international boundaries. On the whole, foreign-invested enterprises in China (especially those from Europe, North America and Japan) do have formal HRM departments and systems but their detailed practices vary from those in their home base, and in the case of joint ventures they need to accommodate the practices of the Chinese partner.

As Wang (2011) points out, the shortage of skilled labour, which is central to China's labour challenges, applies as much to HRM as to other categories of skilled manager. Promotion is often rapid, running ahead of ability, and the profession has not yet had time to develop the skills, the pool of understanding and the sharing of experiences which is central to the HR professional in Europe and North America. It is therefore likely to be some time before systematic and locally appropriate approaches to HRM are in place throughout the economy.

The second key question on managing people in China is the extent to which approaches held to be effective in Western countries can be transferred to a very different cultural and institutional setting. There are many such approaches, but the set of practices referred to as the "high commitment" model of HRM (Pfeffer, 1998) is of particular interest. Central to that model is the "humanist" proposition that organizations will perform best if their employees are personally and psychologically committed to the long-term future of their employer, and a package of HR practices is in place to contribute to that end (Marchington & Wilkinson, 2005). That package includes: employment security; selective and sophisticated hiring procedures; extensive employee training and development; employee involvement in decision-making; empowerment of middle management; self-managed team-working; reduction of status differences, and; higher than average compensation based on performance. There are questions about whether such a universalist model can reliably improve performance even in its original US setting, but it provides a useful model of Western HR thinking against which to compare Chinese practices.

Several factors, economic, institutional and cultural, suggest that the high commitment model may be inappropriate in the Chinese setting. As skilled workers and managers are in very short supply they face multiple opportunities and tend to "job hop" on the basis of short-term financial inducements. Confucian values of loyalty and mutual obligation are overridden by material concerns. For them, employment security is not a concern and they adopt a largely "transactional" attitude to work. For their employers, the cost of extensive training on anything except non-transferable skills can be lost through poaching and turnover, so they hesitate to make such expenditures (Au, Altman & Roussel, 2008). Wang and Wang (2008) found that enhanced career development actually reduced companies' competitiveness, probably because the better trained workers left. Elsey and Leung (2004) found when training Chinese elevator maintenance technicians that workers had no tradition of consciously learning from experience, taking initiative or even understanding the value of high quality standards. The Confucian emphasis on "knowing one's place" and high power distance place value on status differences and tend to make workers compliant and dependent on their superiors, making participative and democratic style management less culturally acceptable. Superiors who have legitimacy are expected to know what to do without conferring with those paid to execute their orders, and those who do confer can be seen as incompetent. Low trust in strangers, and fear of appearing to disagree with the supervisor can make it difficult to elicit honest expressions of opinion, which are a pre-requisite for self-managed team-working. Sophisticated hiring and appraisal procedures are inhibited by the lack of skilled HR professionals to implement them. Perhaps the only element of the high commitment model that fits comfortably in the Chinese setting is compensation based on performance. Bonuses have become a larger proportion of employee compensation in SOEs (Cooke, 2012, p.101) and in the private sector pay and benefits are tightly linked to productivity through piecework systems for line workers and by "rent-sharing" arrangements with managers whereby their pay is directly linked to company financial performance. Such arrangements are not, however, driven by the "humanistic" concerns underlying the high commitment approach, but as means to drive efficiency and pass risk from employer to employee. The overwhelming impression is that Chinese HR practices are tightly aligned with the immediate commercial needs of the employer. Companies do provide accommodation, food, health care and even entertainment, but those are more a means of worker control than a Silicon Valley style employee benefit programme. Companies do sponsor workplace social events and worker welfare, but their basis lies in the expectation of paternalistic behaviour on the part of the boss, and compliance from the workers. Considerations of work/life balance in China are less about creating time for workers to spend with their children and more about helping them to cope with the intense work pressures they are expected to bear on behalf of their employer.

This evaluation seems rather bleak, and like every judgment on China, it needs qualification. Elsey and Leung (2004) found that a planned sequence of action learning did in fact lead to significant changes in the attitudes and behaviour of their elevator technicians, and learning is, after all, a Confucian virtue. Leading companies like Huawei use Western consultancy companies to help them develop their HR policies. Bai and Bennington (2005) found that SOEs in coal-mining, a sector usually seen as backward, were beginning to use more sophisticated performance appraisal methods and Taormina and Gao (2009) found Chinese employees open to performance appraisal criteria put together in consultation with employees. If there is one generalization about China that does not need qualification it is that change can come about with unexpected speed. In so far as traditional values, and the "imprinted" impact of the command economy, are being overtaken, so it may be anticipated that the management of people will also change. It can certainly be argued that the current approach is well adapted to the pursuit of efficiency and low cost in manufacturing, but if the economy is to pivot towards innovation, significant change is required.

Leadership in China

Much of what has been said about managing people in China applies to the issue of leadership. A command economy past, a still-powerful state, hyper-growth, Confucianism, high context, power distance, *guanxi*, collectivism, and low trust combine to create an idiosyncratic setting from which many idiosyncratic leaders have emerged. It has been pointed out in Chapter 5 that some of the most notable business leaders in the first round of private enterprise development were jailbirds for whom there had been no other employment options. China's business leaders have become more respectable over time, but they continue to reflect the society from which they come, combined with their own unique characteristics. Jack Ma Yun of Alibaba, perhaps the globally best known Chinese business leader, emerged from a lacklustre academic career to chance upon the Internet during a visit to America. His failed web search for Chinese beer led to early recognition of an opportunity and then to a single-minded pursuit of the possibilities of e-commerce. The business that was run out of his Hangzhou apartment in 1999 made a $US25 billion IPO just 15 years later. Zhang Ruimin of Hai'er famously overcame the company's SOE mentality by having his employees take sledgehammers to 76 defective refrigerators before embarking on a quality-focused improvement and expansion programme that led the company to the world's largest global share of the white goods market.

China's top business leaders have emerged from many different walks of life: from peasant farmers, to graduates of top universities, to English teachers to soldiers, to Communist Party princelings. There has been no common path to the top and no homogeneous leadership style. It is possible, however, to outline some distinctly Chinese traits. The Hay Group (2007) identified three "unique strengths of Chinese CEOs" in the 37 organizations they examined. Those were: a sense of social responsibility, to which they attributed their success; achieving harmony when dealing with complex business-to-business and business-to-government relationships; and a quest for self-improvement, ranging from self-criticism and Buddhist meditation to the study of English as a means to communicate globally. The Confucian link is obvious, although there is a rather self-serving flavour to those findings. The Hay Group report further noted that Chinese leadership is predominantly "paternalistic", CEOs are less likely to explain their reasoning for decisions, using a "directive" style, while at the same time seeking to assure their people that they care for them, in an "affiliative" style (Hay Group, 2007, pp.5–6). The same report also found that the Chinese leaders in their sample rarely displayed "visionary" styles, with an overall vision and direction, although it is difficult to reconcile that with Jack Ma's laser focus on e-commerce, or Zhang Ruimin's refrigerator-smashing exercise.

Gallo's (2008) review of his experience extends the list of specifically Chinese leadership competences to include *wu*, which refers to a deep all-round understanding of issues utilizing all five senses, *zhong yong*, which is the avoidance of extremes, nationalism, and the indirect expression of views, which is interpreted as thoughtfulness.

These characteristics are clearly consistent with the explanation of Chinese culture in Chapter 4 and Gallo (2008) explains how they further manifest themselves. Chinese leaders place a higher value on courtesy, than on truth, relative to Westerners, as to be expected in a high context culture that values harmony. Trust is in short supply and is personal rather than associated with a person's standing in an organization, so that Chinese leaders take pains to work on their personal links with business partners. They tend to be uncomfortable with the concept of "empowerment" believing that good leaders should be able to tell subordinates what to do, and that empowered subordinates might abuse the implied trust. Collectivist tendencies, especially amongst the older generation, require that attention and respect be given to groups more than individuals. Teamwork is strong within the team itself, but communication and trust across different teams does not come naturally and requires input from the leader. The rule of man dominates the rule of law so that contracts and written plans are regarded as "signposts" rather than concrete commitments. Innovation is viewed with caution, and some leaders still hold to "management by fear" as was practised in the command economy.

Overall, leadership and HRM practices in China reflect their setting, and the country's hyper-rapid growth is evidence that they have not been as dysfunctional as they might appear to Western observers. However, there are two major concerns. The first is that the general shortage of skilled managers extends to the top level and urgently needs to be addressed. The second is whether the people management methods that have proved effective in driving efficiency and low cost will remain suitable for the new economy envisaged by the country's leadership. Can Chinese management methods evolve quickly enough to support initiatives like Manufacturing 2025 and an enhanced level of innovation? The answer is far from clear.

References

Arkless, D,. 2007. The China talent paradox. *China–Britain Business Review*, June, pp.14–15.

Au, A., Altman, Y. and Roussel, J., 2008. Employee training needs and perceived value of training in the Pearl River Delta of China: A human capital development approach. *Journal of European Industrial Training*, 32 (1), pp.19–31.

Bai, X and Bennington, L., 2005. Performance in the Chinese state-owned coal industry. *International Journal of Business Performance Management*, 7 (3) pp.275–287.

Cooke, F., 2012. *Human resource management in China: New trends and practices*. London: Routledge

Ding, D. and Akhtar, S., 2001. The organizational choice of human resource management practices: A study of Chinese enterprises in three cities in the PRC. *International Journal of Human Resource Management*, 12 (6), pp.946–964.

Ding, D., Ge, G. and Warner, M., 2004. Evolution of organizational governance and human resource management in China's township and village enterprises. *International Journal of Human Resource Management* 15 (4), pp.836–852.

Elsey, B. and Leung, J., 2004. Changing the behaviour of Chinese employees using organizational learning. *Journal of Workplace Learning* 16 (3), pp.167–178.

Farrell, D. and Grant, A., 2005. China's looming talent shortage. *McKinsey Quarterly*, No.4. Available at http://www.mckinseyquarterly.com/article_page.aspx?ar=1685 [Accessed 23 January 2017].

Gallo, F., 2008. *Business Leadership in China: How to blend best Western practices with Chinese wisdom*. Singapore: Wiley.

Gamble, J. and Huang, Q., 2009. One store, two employment systems: Core, periphery and flexibility in China's retail sector. *British Journal of Industrial Relations*, 47 (1), pp.1–26.

Han, J. and Han, J., 2009. Network-based recruiting and applicant attraction in China: Insights from both organizational and individual perspectives. *International Journal of Human Resource Management*, 20 (11), pp.2228–2249.

Hay Group. 2007. *East meets West: Bridging two great business cultures*. No.3. 2007. Available at: http://org-portal.org/fileadmin/media/legacy/East_Meets_West.pdf [Accessed 23 January 2017].

Howard, A., Liu, L., Wellins, R. and William, S., 2007. *"The flight of human talent": Employee retention in China, 2006–2007*. Bridgeville, PA: Development Dimensions International.

Kim, Y. and Gao, F., 2010. An empirical study of human resource management practices in family firms in China. *International Journal of Human Resource Management*, 21 (12), pp.2095–2119.

Li, M. and Edwards, P., 2008. Work and pay in small Chinese clothing firms: A constrained negotiated order. *Industrial Relations Journal*, 39 (4), pp.296–313.

Li, Y. and Sheldon, P., 2010. HRM lives inside and outside the firm: Employers' skill shortages and the local labour market in China. *International Journal of Human Resource Management*, 21, (10/12), pp.2173–2193.

Lu, Y., 2008. Human resource development and management in the market economy. *Journal of Hubei University of Economics*, 5 (5), pp.57–58 (in Chinese).

Ma, L., Chen, A. and Zhang, Z., 2016. Task success based on contingency fit of managerial culture and embeddedness. *Journal of International Business Studies*, 47 (2), pp.191–209.

Marchington, M. and Wilkinson, A., 2005. *Human resource management at work*. London: CIPD.

Morris, J., Wilkinson, B. and Gamble, J., 2009. Strategic international human resource management or the "bottom line"? The cases of electronics and garments commodity chains in China. *International Journal of Human Resource Management*, 20 (2), pp.348–370.

National Bureau of Statistics of China. 2015. *China statistical yearbook 2015*. Beijing. China Statistics Press.

Pfeffer, J., 1998. *The human equation: Building profits by putting people first*. Boston, MA: Harvard Business School Press.

Pope, S. and Meyer, J., 2015. The global corporate organization. *Management and Organization Review*, 11 (2), pp.173–177.

Sun, M., 2012. *Employee retention in Chinese state-owned enterprises*. Dissertation submitted to Auckland University of Technology. Available at: http://citeseerx.ist.psu.edu/viewdoc/download?doi=10.1.1.821.4114&rep=rep1&type=pdf [Accessed 23 January 2017].

Taormina, R. and Gao, J., 2009. Identifying acceptable performance criteria: An international perspective. *Asia Pacific Journal of Human Resources*, 47 (1), pp.102–125.

Wang, B. 2011.Chinese HRM in action: An interview with Wayne Chen of Hay Group China. *Journal of Chinese Human Resource Management*, 2 (1), pp.61–68.

Wang, Z. and Wang, S., 2008. Modelling regional HRM strategies in China: An entrepreneurship perspective. *International Journal of Human Resource Management*, 19 (5), pp.945–963.

Xu, F., 2009. The emergence of temporary staffing agencies in China. *Comparative Labor Law and Policy Journal*, 30 (2), pp.431–462.

13
THE CHALLENGE FROM CHINA
How serious?

Matevz Raskovic

Introduction

China's rising wealth and status has led to considerable debate and concern over its impact on other countries, and in particular on the prosperity of the developed nations. In *Death by China,* which is the best-known piece of hostile rhetoric, Navarro and Autry (2011) claimed that China has damaged the US economy by stripping it of manufacturing jobs, through "unfair" competition. Reviews of the book were mixed, and most found a partially reasonable argument to have been obscured by "dramatic overkill" (O'Hehir, 2012) and "xenophobic hysteria" (Adams, 2012). However, in 2017, President Trump appointed Navarro as the head of the new National Trade Council, indicating an American shift towards antagonism in which China is viewed as a mercantilist trader, a rules cheat, and a currency manipulator.

Such a hostile view fits well with populist perspectives, but is not widely held in respect of its specifics. Kroeber's (2016) review of how the Chinese economy got to where it is today marshals the evidence and concludes that "the claim that China's success results from an unusual degree of "cheating" or undermining global economic rules does not stand up to serious scrutiny" (*ibid.*, p.241). American officials themselves admit that China does not meet their criteria for a currency manipulator (Cheng, 2017). Nevertheless, growing US–China tensions are consistent with the "Thucydides trap" (Allison, 2015) where a rising power and an established power naturally come into conflict (Mearsheimer, 2001) and George Soros sees China potentially leading a new *tian xia* (all under heaven) world order that challenges the "Washington consensus" (Callahan, 2008). Others see China's growth as a central part of the transition to a multipolar world (Clegg, 2009) and as the balance shifts from "the West to the Rest', as Ferguson (2011) put it, China has emerged as a role model for many emerging markets and so-called "catch-up" economies (Economist, 2011).

This chapter looks at the challenge from China at two levels. First, at the macro level, it examines China's changing role within global value chains (GVCs), the country's increasing geopolitical influence, and the question of security in the Asia Pacific region. Second, at the industry level, it considers the extent to which Chinese firms are becoming a competitive threat to Western companies.

China's rise in context

China's critics see a manipulative, mercantilist, centrally planned behemoth, growing through subsidized exports, manipulating its currency, and copycatting goods, brands and technology (Tse, 2015). There are elements of truth in that characterization. However, several other factors need to be kept in mind. Exports, and particularly net exports, represent a relatively small part of the Chinese economy (Zhang, 2016). Many of those exports, both "high tech" and low value-added, are produced by foreign companies who shifted production to China in the search for lower cost resources (Huang, 2001), and by private Chinese companies not supported by the state (Kroeber, 2016). China's huge accumulation of foreign currency reserves is as much the result of its high savings ratio and Western firms operating under WTO rules, as it is the outcome of Chinese government manipulation. Navarro and Autry's (2011) focus on the US trade deficit with China fails to recognize that American multinationals are key producers of Chinese exports to the US, and those Chinese exports have a significant "made in America" content (Apple being the outstanding example). It also harks back rather ominously to a similar trade imbalance, where nineteenth-century Britain suffered a similar large deficit. In order to offset that deficit, the British began selling opium to China, whose resistance to the drug trade provided the "*casus belli*" of the Opium wars which plunged China into its century of humiliation and decline (Vogel, 2011).

While some in the US and Europe see China's recovery from that setback as a threat, in the larger scheme of world history the emergence of the "Asian century" is more like a return to an historical balance. In some ways, China's rise signals the decline of Western-type hegemony (Jacques, 2009), which Milanovic (2016) has linked to changes in relative income distribution between the Western and newly emerged Asian middle classes. Ironically, however, it was that hegemony, with its emphasis on globalization, the spread of markets, WTO and international trade, which enabled China to re-emerge as a global economic powerhouse (Lotta, 2009).

While many in the West do see China's resurgence as a threat, others see a more benign mixture of market reforms supporting more inclusive economic institutions and boosting productivity, combined with the power of a centralized political system (Acemoglu & Robinson, 2012).

Also in contrast to the adversarial interpretations, the Chinese leadership under Hu-Wen and Xi-Li have developed the narrative of a "peaceful rise" (Al-Rodhan, 2007), albeit one that differs from a Western democratic model. President Xi's "Chinese dream" of a great rejuvenation (*weida fuxing*) focuses on a strong autocratic state pursuing pragmatic and centrally planned governance, while providing continuously increasing prosperity. Consistent with Chinese culture, the benefits of the collective outweigh that of the individual and China is trying to combine inclusive economic institutions with extractive political institutions (Acemoglu & Robinson, 2012). Nevertheless, observers worry that Xi's emphasis on the consolidation of power points to a new type of economic imperialism and hegemony through more assertive foreign and military policy (Bhattacharya, 2007).

The economics of world order: the limits of zero-sum logic

Central to the debate on whether China's growth threatens other nations is the question of whether global development and trade are "zero-sum" games, where a gain by one party must be matched by an equal loss by the other. Ever since Adam Smith's 1776 *Wealth of Nations* it has been well understood that by specializing and exchanging goods in trade, two countries can both gain (Langdana & Murphy, 2014). There is no zero-sum game. Unfortunately, that understanding has often been lost by businessmen, politicians and analysts who frame international trade relations in terms of "competitiveness" and who confuse competition between countries with competition between companies (Davies & Ellis, 2000). If two companies compete over market share, the result must be zero-sum. But the only meaningful definition of "competitiveness" at country level is "national income per head" (Porter, 1990, p.6). There is no reason at all why an increase in national income for one country must mean a reduction for its trading partners. Quite the reverse. As one grows, it spends more and some of that spending provides additional incomes for its trading partners. However, while both partners in international trade gain overall, the distribution of those gains within each country has often been highly uneven, and the gains tend to be spread thinly across the whole population, while large losses are suffered by a small number, who will be highly vocal in their opposition. To take the specifics of the US–China trading relation, it is estimated that between one and up to five million low-skilled American workers have lost their jobs through trade with China (Gosselin & Dorning, 2015). While a 5 million upper bound may include a series of contributing factors, Acemoglu et al. (2016) have estimated a loss of up to 2.5 million US manufacturing jobs due to Chinese import competition between 1999 and 2011. Yet, one also needs to take into account the positive effects of trade with China on the US economy. Access to cheaper goods from China is estimated to have increased average disposable income of the 320 million-strong US population by up to $US850 in 2015 (USCBC, 2017). As Haft (2015) also points out, every dollar of imported goods from China includes up to 70 cents of US components, technology and know-how. Imports from China also support millions of US service jobs linked to international trade (i.e. logistics, warehousing, shipping) and retail.

Several additional points are important. The first concerns the structure of US–China trade, which is largely one of exchanging complementary types of products, so that the countries are not competing in the same markets, and Chinese sales do not take away from US sales. Second, it is essential to appreciate the importance of Trade in Value Added (TiVA) (OECD/World Bank, 2015), which recognizes that, in the era of complex supply chains, counting the final value of imports as they land can be misleading as an indicator of where incomes are generated. Apple's iPhones and iPads provide the salient example. The phones are designed in California, but assembled by Taiwanese firm Foxconn in China from components made in the US, Korea, Japan and Germany, which account for most of the value. If the actual landed cost were taken into account, every iPhone shipped from China to the US would increase the bilateral trade deficit by several hundred US$. However, the Chinese content of each phone makes up as little as $US5–10, which is the added value of labour assembly in China and Foxconn's profits (Xing & Detert, 2010). Placing a tariff on such imports would in effect be putting a tariff on the American, Korean and Japanese components embedded in the phones, with relatively little impact on China, simply because of the very small component of value added there. China's apparent dominance of some manufacturing sectors, especially in "high-tech" goods, is in fact part of an improvement in the allocation of world resources (Elwell, Labonte & Morrison, 2007), brought about by the ability to separate production into stages, each of which can be carried out more efficiently in a separate location. Imports to the US of goods from China, in which American-made components and design make up a large part of the value, do not represent a threat to US business.

There are also more fundamental structural economic issues that underlie the outcome of trade between nations. Basic macro-economic analysis gives the following equation (Irvin, 2011), which must hold true.

(Saving minus investment) + (Government surplus) = (Balance of trade surplus)

If a nation saves more than it invests (as does China with a very high overall savings ratio of 46% of Gross National Income, see Chapter 14) then it must have a trade surplus and/or a government deficit. As China keeps its government deficit to around 3% of GDP, the country simply must have a trade surplus. Conversely, America has an overall savings ratio of just 19% and invests more than that, so that unless it runs a government surplus, it must have a trade deficit. Americans concerned to reduce the country's trade deficit would be better advised to encourage saving than to try to tackle it through trade reduction measures! Again, China's trade surplus does not represent a threat to Western business, but is the outcome of more fundamental economic forces.

China's trade surpluses do have other repercussions that should not be overlooked. A consequence of high savings and trade surpluses is that the country has accumulated very large foreign exchange reserves (Bonatti & Fracasso, 2013), being the largest holder of US Treasuries until December 2016, when capital outflows took the holdings below those of Japan. That level of ownership of government bonds worries some observers in the US, who fear that it could provide leverage over US policy if the Chinese decided not to lend any further to America, or if they precipitated a sell-off of US government securities, which would push up prices down, interest rates up and possibly de-stabilize the American economy. However, as Miller (2016) notes, $US1 trillion is only a small proportion of the total US debt, most of which is held domestically, and China needs to buy it for a variety of reasons. It needs foreign reserves to finance trade, which is largely denominated in US dollars. It needs them to support the exchange rate, and it needs them in order to "sterilize" incoming currency flows that might otherwise de-stabilize the banking system. As, Scissors and Subramanian (2012, p.174) note, "China's creditor status arises largely from its weaknesses, not its strengths". Its holdings of US securities do not give it significant leverage over the US and do not represent a threat to Western interests.

If the Trump era produces increased government deficits, Chinese ownership of US government debt is likely to increase in absolute terms but decline as a proportion of the total (Labonte & Nagel, 2016). However that plays out, the two superpowers have significant co-dependencies in respect of their imbalances (Bonatti & Fracasso, 2013) and would be foolhardy to attempt to make radical changes, whose consequences would be impossible to predict.

China and the world order: from geopolitics to *tian xia* and international security

Linking tradition and modernity, the ancient concept of *tian xia*, meaning "everything under heaven", has re-emerged as central to China's understanding of world order. Rejecting Western claims to primacy, it seeks to re-affirm China's central position in the world "as a generator of new ideas and norms" (Barabantseva, 2009, p.132). At the physical level, it encapsulates "a particular organization of relationships between people, within families, and among nations" (*ibid.*, p.132). At the metaphysical level, it combines philosophical ideas centred around Confucianism with slogans of national rejuvenation, Chinese dreams and a harmonious society. In terms of geo-politics, *tian xia* is an assertion that China is re-taking its position as the central kingdom in East Asia, with a "Grand Strategy" combining economic, political and military elements (Christoffersen, 1996, p.1067).

Such a stance not only involves putting China's neighbours back in their place as tributary states, but inevitably challenges US dominance in the Asia Pacific region (Solomon, 1994). That raises two issues, the first of which is military. The build-up of the Chinese military over the last decade creates concern in the US, which has acted as a watchdog over the Asia–Pacific region since the Second World War, using its military presence as a hedge (Shirk, 2007). It also challenges the regional balance of power between Japan, Korea, Australia and even India (Cordesman, 2016).

As China becomes the dominant military power in Asia, so the controversy around its military is a mixture of great power tensions and the uncertainty surrounding the statistics on military capabilities and resources. Official Chinese data shows military spending increased almost seven-fold between 2003 ($US22 billion) and 2016 ($US146 billion), consistently outstripping economic growth (Cordesman, 2016). Nevertheless, in absolute terms, China's 2016 military budget was less than a quarter of that of the US ($US622 billion). The build-up of the Chinese military has in part been a matter of modernizing an out-dated system (Bitzinger, 2011) and the country is still heavily dependent on Russia for general procurement and technology development (Cordesman, 2016). In 2016, for instance, it was still incapable of producing a reliable jet engine for its fighter planes (Roblin, 2016). Unless the Chinese military can acquire superiority through the development of "asymmetrical" weapons – unstoppable carrier-killing missiles, or cyber offensives, for instance, its offensive capability remains far behind that of the US.

The second issue, which has an important military component, is China's role in the South China Sea. The build-up of tensions between China and its neighbours involves the dispute over the Diaoyu or Shenkaku islands with Japan, and island and maritime disputes associated with the "nine-dash line" defining China's claims, which also overlap significantly with those of Vietnam, the Philippines, Indonesia, Malaysia and Brunei.

Thus far, the United Nations has ruled in favour of the Philippines' maritime claims against China. However, neither the tribunal that ruled nor the ruling itself have been regarded as legitimate by China, and the Duterte administration in the Philippines has backed away from pressing the claim lodged by its predecessor. China's dispute with Japan has a longstanding and complex background, but China's more assertive role in the South China Sea in general should be seen as a consequence of economic interests and internal Chinese politics (Lee, 2013). In economic terms, more than $US5.3 trillion of trade, and as much as half of all oil and natural gas tanker shipments flow through this "bottleneck" between East Asia and the world, which makes control of it a key strategic objective. That control is rendered even more important by the prospect of large deposits of oil and natural gas on the area's sea bed (O'Rourke, 2016). While geo-politics is key to the importance of the South China Sea, the Xi-Li leadership has also used a more assertive role in the South China Sea as a tool in domestic politics, using it to secure legitimacy as the protector of China's "historical rights", and as a way of keeping the military loyal (Lee, 2013).

In terms of geo-politics, China clearly represents a real challenge to US hegemony in the Asia–Pacific region, and the threat is clear. However, within China's focus on *tian xia*, the emphasis throughout history has always been on maintaining domestic stability, rather than projecting direct power over the region and beyond. If China's domestic interests and continued economic development require that it take action to secure the resources of the South China Sea, there is no doubt whatever that action will be taken. However, it is unlikely that the leadership has any designs for the conquest of its neighbours.

Global value chains and regional production networks: the China effect

The question of whether China represents a threat can also be approached by recognizing the extent of its integration with the global economy, its co-dependence with its trading partners, and the extent to which hostility with those partners would be mutually damaging.

China's "opening up" and its subsequent integration into the world economy has been one of the most important events in world economic history, and one of its most important consequences has been its role in the emergence of global value chains which have "changed the rules of the game" of twenty-first-century globalization (World Economic Forum, 2012, p.13)

A "value chain" is the whole set of activities that add value to a final product from conception and design, to production, to customer delivery and final disposal. "Global" value chains (GVCs) are those in which the value adding activities are widely dispersed geographically. They usually involve multiple firms in various markets and require supporting investment and infrastructure services which are also dispersed (Baldwin, 2012). According to the United Nations Conference on Trade and Development (UNCTAD) (2015) China was ranked 6th in the world in respect of participation in GVCs, well above Japan (51st) or the US (45th). However, it is also clear that China's role in the GVCs has been to process goods imported from elsewhere for export, since the difference in value between merchandise imports and exports is only about 11.2%. It is also clear that China struggles in terms of creating added value, as the iPhone example indicates, because the country operates on those parts of the value chain which add the least value – assembly and manufacturing.

As Chapters 6 and 7 have shown, China is trying to move away from this "subservient role in the international division of labour" (Lazonick, 2004, p.273) as wages and other costs are rising. According to Cui (2007) and IMF estimates, both domestic content and the ability to produce intermediate products have been improving, with rapid expansion in capital goods, equipment and components.

But what effect has China had on GVCs overall? Table 13.1 summarizes the key trade and FDI statistics, which show a massive surge after China's 2001 WTO membership. The relative changes, showing China's global position, are even more impressive. In 2009 China overtook Germany to become the world's largest exporter. In 2012 China overtook the US to become the world's largest trading economy, in terms of exports plus imports. By 2013, China also emerged as the world's third largest outward investor after US and Japan, and

Table 13.1 Trade and investment nexus effect of China (all data in current prices)

	*Imports**		*Exports**		*Inward FDIs*		*Outward FDIs*	
	Value	*% of GDP*	*Value*	*% of GDP*	*Flow*	*Stock*	*Flow*	*Stock*
1990	48.7 bn $	10.7%	60.4 bn $	14.0%	3.5 bn $	20.7 bn $	830 mn $	4.5 bn $
2000	188.4 bn $	18.5%	200.6 bn $	21.2%	40.7 bn $	193.4 bn $	916 mn $	27.8 bn $
2007	1.02 tr $	26.7%	1.34 tr $	35.9%	83.5 bn $	327.1 bn $	26.5 bn $	117.9 bn $
2015	2.32 tr $	18.6%	2.66 tr $	22.1%	135.6 bn $	1.22 tr $	127.6 bn $	1.01 tr $

Source: *Data World Bank Open Data (2017); ** UNCTAD STAT (2017).

the first among emerging markets. In line with its post-WTO status as the "world's factory", China increased its share of global manufacturing value output from 3% in 1990 to 25% by 2015. Today, it produces 80% of global air conditioners, 70% of mobile phones, and 60% of shoes and 40% of the global apparel industry (Economist, 2015).

Since 2010, China has been ranked as the most competitive manufacturing location by Deloitte (2016). The continuing supply of relatively cheap labour has been one of the main drivers but the establishment of support infrastructure, logistics and innovation ecosystems has also been important (WEF, 2016), as witness the electronics manufacturing hub of Shenzhen, China's first Special Economic Zone. These changes have had an impact on the distribution of manufacturing jobs globally. Acemoglu et al. (2016) estimated that some 2 to 2.5 million manufacturing jobs in the US alone have been lost to Chinese import competition between 1999 and 2011. Yet, this is only part of the story, since US manufacturing employment has been decreasing since the 1990s and has continued to decrease even after the dramatic fall in Chinese imports in 2009. It is no doubt that firm-level outsourcing strategies and greater automation also need to be considered.

China has also played a role in the emergence of regional production networks (RPNs) in East Asia. The 2004 China–ASEAN Free Trade Area (FTA) and the currency swap agreement between China and ASEAN countries have proved instrumental in increasing intra-regional trade, which accounted for only 9.2% of Asia's total in 1990, but grew to 51.9% by 2006 (Gruenwald & Hori, 2008). After the Asian financial crisis in the late 1990s, China's WTO membership, and the China–ASEAN FTA, China emerged as the hub for Asia's exports. For example, while China was a net importer from the "newly industrialized economies" (NIEs) and "industrial Asia" in 1990, it became a strong exporter to those countries, and to ASEAN, by 2006. Table 13.2 illustrates that point. Wignaraja (2016) has shown that China increased its share in global production networks from 13% to 25% between 2001 and 2013, and contributed significantly to an increase in East Asia's representation in these production networks from 38% to 48%.

Nevertheless, despite the "decoupling hypothesis" (Athukorala, 2011), East Asia has not become detached from world trade and self-sufficient, but has instead pursued vertical specialization that uses differences in comparative advantage to build a regional product network (RPN) targeting global markets (Gruenwald & Hori, 2008). China's participation in such RPNs has been comprehensive, spanning several industries, including electronics, telecommunication equipment, machinery and the automobile industry (Fung, 2014, p.131).

In terms of foreign direct investment, China has been one of the top three recipients for over a decade. In 2015, it amounted to $US136 bn, which was 7.5% of all global FDI inflows. In terms of stock, China represented 4.9% of global inward FDI in 2015, or 11.2% if Hong Kong is included. China has also became one of the top outward investors, ranking third after the US and Japan. In 2015 outward FDI reached $US128 bn, which was 57% of all outward FDI from Developing Asia and over 8.6% of all global outward FDI

Table 13.2 Emergence of China as East Asia's export hub (share of exports in 1990 and 2006)

Exports from China to . . .	*NIES*	*ASEAN 5*	*Industrial Asia*	*Rest of the world*
1990	−18.4%	1.7%	−3.8%	19.1%
2006	22.8%	4.6%	11.5%	59.7%

Source: Gruenwald & Hori (2008).

Table 13.3 Selected data on Chinese FDIs in the US and Europe in 2015

	Value	*% that are M&As*	*% that are in services*	*% of FDI by SOEs*	*Key industries*	*Most notable investments in 2015*
US	15.7 bn $	89%	64%	16%	Real estate, financial services, ICT, automobile, health & bio tech, entertainment	GE appliances Legendary Entertainment
EU	20 bn $	82%	<30%	65%	Real estate, hospitality, automotive, ICT, business & finance services	Pirelli, Louvre Hotels, Club Med hotels, NXP Semiconductors' RF business

Source: Hanemann & Gao (2016); Hanemann & Huotari (2016).

flows (Hanemann & Huotari, 2016). While the share of Chinese outward FDIs is not yet particularly large globally, resource-seeking Chinese FDI in Africa and Latin America and asset-seeking FDI in the US and Europe has already created apprehension in the West (Meyer, 2015). That has been strengthened by the rapid growth of Chinese outward FDI since the 2008 global economic and financial crisis, with the global share of Chinese outward FDIs quadrupling between 2008 and 2015. Table 13.3 summarizes some of the key features of Chinese FDI in the US and Europe.

Chinese FDIs into the US and EU-28 accounted for 26.5% of all Chinese outward FDI flows in 2015. In both of those markets, the larger share of Chinese FDI is in the form of mergers and acquisitions (M&As), but there is a considerable difference with respect to the industries involved and share of investments by SOEs. While almost two-thirds of Chinese FDI into the US targets service industries and is predominantly driven by private firms (84%), less than 30% of Chinese FDI into Europe targets service industries and the larger share is driven by SOEs (65%). In this regard, Chinese FDIs in Europe seem to pursue stronger strategic asset seeking behaviour than in the US. Ironically, the US seems to be much more critical of Chinese FDIs than the EU.

Chinese firms: are they a threat or not?

As goods manufactured in China take a larger share of global markets, and as Chinese firms increasingly "go out" and establish their operations overseas, the question that naturally arises is whether Chinese companies, state or private, present a competitive threat to Western companies' market shares, at home and abroad. As with so many issues in China, arguments and evidence can be found for opposite views. On the one hand, there are many examples of Chinese firms who have already taken sales from their Western rivals. Some have done so by matching their products to unusual local tastes, like car component maker Zotye who quite shamelessly began to make cars that look rather like expensive foreign brands, including the Porsche Macan, but sell them at a fraction of the price to that segment of the market that cares deeply about the "look" of their vehicle but doesn't mind too much about quality, safety or authenticity. Others, like WeChat (*Wei Xin*), began by copying a Western product (WhatsApp) but then improved on it to the point where it is much superior to the original. Similarly, online retail giant Alibaba began as an Amazon/eBay copy but has created an e-retail empire by offering innovative payment systems that offset the country's general lack of trust, and has established "Single's day" on November 11 as the world's largest online shopping bonanza (as discussed in Chapter 10).

These examples, and China's other "national champions", like Huawei, Haier, Lenovo, Sany, and drone company DJI, all suggest that Chinese firms are becoming a competitive threat to Western firms (Zeng & Williamson, 2007; Tse, 2015). On the other hand, those same few companies feature over and over again in the "dragons are coming" narrative. It can be argued that they are outliers, unrepresentative of the overall picture, and if more Chinese firms are to compete with Western firms who have knowledge-based competitive advantages, then China needs to pursue further structural and institutional changes, and Chinese firms need more international experience.

Why are Chinese firms (still) not a widespread threat to Western firms?

Three key factors suggest that Chinese firms in general pose little threat to Western firms. First, as Chapter 6 has shown, they are still heavily dependent on foreign companies for advanced technology, innovation, and the ability to serve foreign markets. Foreign MNEs have driven most of China's manufacturing-oriented export economy (Huang, 2001). Fetscherin, Voss and Gugler's (2010) review of the research noted that:

- Chinese firms have been dependent on Sino-foreign JVs as a crucial source of learning and competence building.
- China's integration into global value chains, which is a necessity for competitiveness, has been organized by FDI and foreign MNEs.
- While FDIs, especially in SEZs, have had positive spill-over effects on the productivity of Chinese firms, most of those spill-overs remain limited to the region and the industry in which they take place.

Morrison (2015) shows that foreign MNEs were the key drivers behind China's "high-tech" exports, producing 82% of them in 2010, and the share of WOFEs in those exports increased to 67% in the same period, increasing China's dependence, not reducing it, which would be the case if Chinese firms were generally becoming more competent.

The second argument in favour of the proposition that Western firms have little to fear from Chinese companies is that state-owned firms continue to occupy a leading position in many sectors. For them, political considerations take priority over market principles. They enjoy a series of benefits in return for giving the authorities control, scale and employment, so that the performance needed to compete internationally in respect of quality, profitability and innovation is less of a priority (Leutert, 2016). Easy access to financing, permits, and soft-budget constraints make for a relatively easy life, without the necessity of challenging Western firms for market share. The position of the SOEs also means that access to some categories of resource, like export credits and research and development funding, is difficult for private firms, who could be more competitive.

The third reason to doubt that Chinese firms will take market share from their Western competitors is that, despite a partial end to "Cheap China", their competitive advantage is still largely cost-based, and they have very limited international entrepreneurial orientation. Their predominant position is as low margin manufacturers, with limited involvement in the higher margin upstream activities of design (where they simply copy) or the downstream work of distribution (which they leave to specialist firms). Their structures and practices are aligned with efficiency-based advantages, rather than innovation, and cultural characteristics limit their international entrepreneurial orientations (Zhang, Ma & Wang, 2012). Their Western competitors are entrenched in their home markets. They have better marketing capabilities, strong brands, consumer loyalty and control over distribution, supported by positive "country of origin" effects (Alon, Fetscherin & Gugler, 2012; Yu & Liu, 2016). Chinese firms therefore face very significant resource disadvantages relative to Western firms in international markets.

Disruptive dragons at the door?

Despite the overall picture of Chinese firms facing major difficulties in taking market share from Western companies, some observers do see a significant threat emerging. Zeng and Williamson (2007) and Tse (2015) both argue that disruptive Chinese "dragons" are shaking up global competition with new business models. Companies like Alibaba, DJI, Haier, Huawei, Lenovo, Sany, Tencent and Xiaomi are all examples of companies that present credible competition to Western firms inside and outside the Chinese market (Tse, 2015).

Like their Japanese and Korean predecessors, the Chinese dragons first focused on cost innovation where they used their access to low cost resources, and experience with large scale production, to drive costs down to fractions of those incurred by their Western competitors. They then began to adopt more customer-focused innovation, improving design and making frontier level technology available to the mass market at competitive prices. Zeng and Williamson (2007) point out that these companies have taken advantage of a unique confluence of external and internal factors. Of the external factors, "Cheap China's" low-cost workforce and skilled talent provided the needed human capital. Well-developed manufacturing ecosystems, coupled with state support, enabled entrepreneurial innovation-oriented experimentation (WEF, 2016), in an environment where risks can be contained, and companies can realize economies of scale, scope and skill.

The best prepared Chinese companies have benefited from advances in smart manufacturing, specialization, modularization, information technology and other developments, as well as new forms of outsourcing and transportation. They have also started to enjoy the benefits of an increasingly sophisticated domestic consumer base and a rapidly expanding consumer (retail) market (Zeng & Williamson, 2007). Copycat-turned-designer smartphone producer Xiaomi is an example. They began by copying Apple and Samsung but quickly upgraded their designs, while practising cost innovation. Reaching a market capitalization of over 1 billion USD within the first year of foundation in 2010, Xiaomi harnessed scale, increasing market openness, and official support for technology advancement as key drivers in China's market (Tse, 2015).

With respect to the internal factors that have brought success to some of the dragons, Haier illustrates how some Chinese firms have embraced new types of managerial and organizational approaches to foster innovation and entrepreneurship. The company replaced its traditional hierarchical organizational structure with a flat "Platform Innovation Ecosystem" linking autonomous micro enterprises and various types of resource platforms (WEF, 2016, p.18). While maintaining efficiency, Haier has focused on harnessing entrepreneurship, while strengthening their focus on the market and customer through customer-focused innovation. Strong customer support, backed by warranties and scale, provided the necessary reassurance to Chinese consumers (Doctoroff, 2013).

Such new approaches to management have been accompanied by employee incentives focused on innovation and entrepreneurship, as shown in the case of Huawei. The company rose to Fortune 500 status largely by copying Western products and selling at huge discounts. However, in addition to combining imitation with cost innovation, they focussed on the needs of their customers and were able to re-orient themselves towards an "internal management system" where almost half of the workforce focuses on quick innovation, while maintaining autonomy (WEF, 2016, p.19). In 2016, their innovation and customer-oriented foci merge in their 36 world-wide "collaborative innovation centres" where users play a central role. This is accompanied by an incentive system emphasizing "value creation and sharing" (WEF, 2016, p.19), which is unusual (and counter-cultural) in Chinese firms.

The business models of these Chinese dragons are often described as "disruptive" and they have certainly taken market share from Western competitors (Tse, 2015). However, they can also be seen as the latest iteration of the "Cheap China" model. Dawning, for example, created super-computers by replacing expensive high end processors with a much larger number of cheaper low-cost processors while Zhongxing Medical used technology obsolete in the West to produce a low-cost X-ray machine (Zeng & Williamson, 2007). Most of the "disrupters" including Huawei, Haier, DJI (making drones) and Beijing Genome Institute still have low price as their key selling point.

The focus on low price is not just a matter of having access to cheap resources. The best Chinese companies understand their customers well, and they work to meet their specific needs. Haier, for instance, found that rural Chinese customers were complaining that their washing machines became blocked when they used them to clean the dirt from potatoes! Instead of pointing out that the machines were not intended for that purpose, they introduced a model that was capable of washing both clothes and vegetables. While that specific innovation gave them no advantage in advanced country markets, it did put them ahead of foreign competitors in China, who have basically failed in the "white goods" sector. As many Chinese buyers prefer "good enough" products at low prices, to the "best in class" that Western companies produce, Chinese firms have an advantage in their home market as Western competitors need to spend resources to "strip down" their products to make them less expensive, as Bosch found for their vehicle airbags (Tse, 2015, p. 79). That gives the Chinese firms an advantage in their home market, and other emerging nations, but it doesn't always translate into an advantage in the home markets of their Western competitors, so that the challenge they present varies by region.

Haier has also used its low-cost capability and ability to understand consumers to pursue its "loose brick" strategy, whereby it first identifies a market segment in an advanced country that is vulnerable to low price competition. It then dominates that segment, establishing a brand presence and taking out a "loose brick" in the competitors' defensive wall, after which it widens the hole by extending to related product segments. For instance, by studying US college students' living spaces they identified a need for a small refrigerator that could double as a computer table. Having established and dominated that new category, they produced refrigerators specifically designed for offices, sold through OfficeDepot, and others for hotels. They then realized that wine storage cabinets, which had been seen as "high end" products produced by companies like La Sommeliere, were actually just refrigerators. They produced a version that was sold through mass retailers at 50% of the competitors' price, and soon had 60% of the market (Zeng & Williamson, 2007, p.104).

These successes may be seen as a "bottom of the pyramid" orientation (Prahalad, 2004) where products are designed for lower income segments, but it also points to a specific type of dragon entrepreneurial spirit, well illustrated by Jack Ma of Alibaba. That spirit is one of agile opportunism, as illustrated by the rapid development of Taobao and Alipay as a response to eBay's market entry. However, as Tse (2015, p.40) puts it

> Alibaba's strategy is not opportunism pure and simple. Rather, it is a form of opportunism that draws on a vision – one initially based in an awareness of the Internet's potential to link business and people to each other, which has since expanded to include the idea of combining the Internet's reach with the capabilities developed inside Alibaba to enter new areas of business.

The close association of China's most successful firms with their charismatic leaders (see Chapter 12) suggests that the presence of a guiding vision, and the ability to implement it flexibly, is something that the "dragons" have in common with each other and with some of the West's disruptors.

The Chinese "dragons" make it clear that China is capable of producing at least some world-class companies which can out-compete with their Western peers by keeping costs down, identifying hitherto unknown market opportunities and addressing market segments which Western firms see as uninteresting. Some observers see them as "breaking the mould" and becoming the precursors to a wave of Chinese super-competitors. On the other hand, it is now ten years since Zeng and Williamson (2007) warned of the "dragons at your door" and there has been no sign of the Chinese invasion of overseas markets. In 2016 there were 15 Chinese companies in the world's top 100 most valuable brands (BrandFinance, 2017). Of those, seven were in banking and finance, having negligible overseas presence, two were domestic telecoms providers and three were state-owned behemoths – China State Construction, PetroChina and Sinopec. Of the others, one was search giant Baidu, which "beat" Google essentially because it was prepared to submit to state censorship. The only two that remained were Alibaba and "quasi-state" Huawei. Drawing the analogy of eBay as a shark in an ocean and Alibaba as a crocodile in the Yangtze River, Jack Ma once famously said: "If we fight in the ocean we lose, but if we fight in the river we win" (Tse, 2015, p.34). That would appear to be a confession that even the best of Chinese firms has reservations about competing outside its home waters.

So how serious is the challenge from China?

As this chapter has shown, the "challenge" from China can be approached from a number of different perspectives. With respect to trade flows, China's huge surplus with the US arises fundamentally from a structural imbalance whereby Chinese save more than they invest while Americans do the opposite. The challenge for the US is not from China but from its own spending patterns. In general, trade between nations is a positive sum game where both sides gain and that has clearly been the case with China's "rise". Globalization, especially since China joined the WTO, has led to complex and dispersed but highly efficient value chains in which China processes components and raw materials from other countries before exporting them across the world. It no longer makes sense to describe China's exports as simply China's exports. Instead, they represent the sale of US, European, Korean and Japanese designed products and components which are the culmination of a globally co-ordinated production process, whose disruption would reduce the well-being of everyone.

However, framing of the trade issue as one of "competitiveness" points policymakers and businesspeople towards a "blame game", encouraging protectionist measures. Furthermore, the distribution of the gains from trade with China within the rich countries is very uneven, with a small proportion of low skilled workers losing their jobs to China, while every consumer gains from lower priced manufactures. Together with the misunderstanding of trade's determinants, that produces a constituency of the disaffected who perceive China as a threat and who support protectionist measures that could actually cause them further hardship. To them, China is a threat.

The second perspective is that of geo-politics. In that realm, it is clear that China represents a real challenge to the hegemony of the US in the Asia Pacific region, which has held since the end of the Second World War. China has historically regarded the countries of the region as tributaries of the "Middle Kingdom" and is moving to retake its position in that respect (Jacques, 2009). Its military is as yet ill-placed to directly challenge the US, but it is operating closer to home, and if the Chinese economy continues to outgrow the American by 3 or 4% per year, it will not be long before it will be able to do so with some confidence. There are some in the Trump administration of 2017 who see war with China as inevitable, and even look forward to it in the belief that the US must prevail. But they would be wise to be careful of what they wish for and the rest of the world can only hope that the Thucydides trap can be avoided through a gracious American "pivot" back to its home territory. (In 2008 an American admiral was surprised at what he thought was a tongue-in-cheek suggestion from a Chinese admiral that "you take care of East of Hawaii and we take everything to its West!" (Strategy Page, 2008).)

The third perspective on the threat from China concerns the extent to which Chinese firms pose a competitive threat to companies in the developed countries of North America, Europe, Japan and Korea. The conclusion there has to be mixed. Most domestic Chinese manufacturing firms are locked into their longstanding "Cheap China" competitive stance, producing "good enough" products at low cost for the domestic market. That can give them an advantage at home, and in emerging markets, so that in sectors like "white goods" and beer, they have largely seen off the foreign competition. However, in advanced country markets, in sectors requiring complex expertise, like automobiles and aerospace, in products where quality is crucial, and where "foreign-ness" continues to demonstrate sophistication, foreign firms maintain their advantage. As many of China's largest firms belong to the state, and are supported by it, their ability to challenge foreign firms is well established in sectors where state ties are a requirement, as for large infrastructure projects, both at home and abroad. However, their skill sets are ill-suited to more openly competitive settings.

There are a small number of Chinese "dragons" who have taken on the foreign competition and won, showing that it can be done. However, as of 2017, they remain outliers, with just about every breathless commentary referring to the same group of companies – Alibaba, Baidu, DJI, Huawei, Haier, Lenovo, Tencent/WeChat and Xiaomi. Others, like Geely and Sany, have been making bold moves through the acquisition of leading Western brand names – Volvo and Putzmeister – but in those cases the outcome remains undecided. Given China's tens of millions of companies it is inevitable that some emerge from the pack as serious challengers to the world's "best in class". For the time being their numbers are very small.

References

Acemoglu, D. and Robinson, J. A., 2012. *Why nations fail*. London: Profile Books.

Acemoglu, D., Autor, D., Dorn, D., Hanson, G. H. and Price, B., 2016. Import competition and the great US employment sag of the 2000s. *Journal of Labor Economics*, 34 (1), pp. S141–S198.

Adams, S., 2012. Review: Emotions, not economics, guide "Death by China": "Death by China" plays hard and loose with the facts as it examines the trade relationship between the U.S. and China. *Los Angeles Times*, 16 August.

Allison, G., 2015. The Thucydides trap: Are the US and China headed for war? *The Atlantic*, 24 September. Available at: https://www.theatlantic.com/international/archive/2015/09/united-states-china-war-thucydides-trap/406756/ [Accessed 5 March 2017].

Alon, I., Fetscherin, M. and Gugler, P., 2012. *Chinese international investments*. New York: Palgrave Macmillan.

Al-Rodhan, K. R., 2007. A critique of the China threat theory: A systematic analysis. *Asian Perspective*, 31 (3), pp.41–66.

Athukorala, P-C., 2011. Production networks and trade patterns in East Asia: Regionalization or globalization? *Asian Economic Papers*, 10 (1), pp.65–95.

Baldwin, R., 2012. Global supply chains: Why they emerged, why they matter, and where they are going. *CTEI Working Papers CTEI-2012–13*, pp.1–33.

Barabantseva, E., 2009. Change vs. order: *Shijie* meets *tianxia* in China's interactions with the world. *Alternatives: Global, Local, Political*, 34 (2), pp.129–155.

Bhattacharya, A., 2007. Chinese nationalism and China's assertive foreign policy. *The Journal of East Asian Affairs*, 21 (1), pp.235–262.

Bitzinger, R., 2011. Modernising China's military, 1997–2012. *China Perspectives*, 88 (4), pp.7–15.

Bonatti, L. and Fracasso, A., 2013. Hoarding of international reserves in China: Mercantilism, domestic consumption and US monetary policy. *Journal of International Money and Finance*, 32 (February), pp.1044–1078.

BrandFinance, 2017. Global 500 2017: The most valuable brands of 2017. Available at: http://brandirectory.com/league_tables/table/global-500-2017 [Accessed 10 March 2017].

Callahan, W. A., 2008. Chinese visions of world order: Post-hegemonic or a new hegemony? *International Studies Review*, 10 (4), pp.749–761.

Cheng, E., 2017. China's chances of being called a "currency manipulator" appear to have just dropped. CNBC, 23 February. Available at: http://www.cnbc.com/2017/02/23/chinas-chances-of-being-called-a-currency-manipulator-just-dropped.html [Accessed 5 March 2017].

Christoffersen, G., 1996. China and the Asia–Pacific: Need for a grand strategy. *Asian Survey*, 36 (11), pp.1067–1085.

Clegg, J., 2009. *China's global strategy: Towards a multipolar world*. London: Pluto Press.

Cordesman, A. H., 2016. *Estimates of Chinese military spending*. Washington, DC: Center for Strategic and International Studies.

Cui, L., 2007. China's growing external dependence. *Finance & Development Online*, 44 (3).

Davies, H. and Ellis, P. D., 2000. Porter's 'Competitive Advantage of Nations': Time for a final judgement? *Journal of Management* Studies 37 (8), pp.1189–1213.

Deloitte., 2016. *2016 global manufacturing competitiveness index*. London: Deloitte Touche Tohmatsu Ltd.

Doctoroff, T., 2013. *What the Chinese want*. New York: St Martin's Press/Palgrave Macmillan.

Economist. 2011. *A game of catch-up*. Special report: The World Economy, September 2011. London: The Economist Intelligence Unit.

Economist., 2015. Global manufacturing: Made in China? *The Economist Online*. 12 March: Available at: http://www.economist.com/news/leaders/21646204-asias-dominance-manufacturing-will-endure-will-make-development-harder-others-made [Accessed 27 February 2017].

Elwell, C. K., Labonte, M. and Morrison, W. M., 2007. Is China a threat to the U.S. economy? *Congressional Service Report*, RL33604. Washington, DC: Congressional Research Service.

Ferguson, N., 2011. *Civilization: The West and the rest*. New York: Penguin Books.

Fetscherin, M., Voss, H. and Gugler, P., 2010. 30 years of foreign direct investment to China: An interdisciplinary literature review. *International Business Review*, 19 (3), pp.235–246.

Fung, K. C., 2014. Regional and global production networks: the case of China. *Journal of Chinese Economic and Foreign Trade Studies*, 7 (3), pp.126–135.

Gosselin, P. & Dorning, M. (June, 2015). After doubts, economists find China kills U.S. factory jobs. *Bloomberg Politics*. Available at: https://www.bloomberg.com/politics/articles/2015-06-18/after-doubting-economists-find-china-killing-u-s-factory-jobs [Accessed 15 May 2017].

Gruenwald, P. and Hori, M., 2008. IMF survey: Intra-regional trade key to Asia's export boom. *IMF News & Articles: Countries & Regions*, 6 February 2008.

Haft, J. R. (2015). Unmade in China: The hidden trust about China's economic miracle. Malden, MA: Polity Press.

Hanemann, T. and Gao, C., 2016. *Chinese FDI in the US: 2015 recap*. Berlin: MERICS GmbH and Rhodium Group.

Hanemann, T. and Huotari, M., 2016. *A new record year for Chinese outbound investments in Europe*. Berlin: MERICS GmbH and Rhodium Group.

Huang, Y., 2001., The role of foreign-invested enterprises in the Chinese economy: An institutional foundation approach, in Chen, S. and Wolf, C. (eds), *China, the United States, and the global economy*. Santa Monica, CA: RAND, pp. 147–191.

Irvin, G., 2011., Economics 101: Government deficits and national accounting identities. *Social Europe*. 9 June. Available at: https://www.socialeurope.eu/2011/06/government-deficits-and-national-accounting-identities/ [Accessed 5 March 2017].

Jacques, M. 2009., *When China rules the world: The rise of the middle kingdom and the end of the Western world*. London: Allen Lane.

Kroeber, R. A., 2016. *China's economy: What everyone needs to know*. New York: Oxford University Press.

Labonte, M. and Nagel, J. C., 2016. Foreign holdings of federal debt. *Congressional Service Report*, RS22331. Washington, DC: Congressional Research Service.

Langdana, F. and Murphy, P. T., 2014. *International trade and global macropolicy*. New York: Springer Science+Business Media.

Lazonick, W., 2004. Indigenous innovation and economic development: Lessons from China's leap into the information age. *Industry and Innovation*, 4 December, pp.273–297.

Lee, J. T-H., 2013. Not too peaceful: Maritime rifts and governance crises in China. *Indian Journal of Asian Affairs*, 26 (1/2), pp.23–36.

Leutert, W., 2016. Challenges ahead in China's reform of state-owned enterprises. *Asian Policy*, 21 (January), pp.83–99.

Lotta, R., 2009. China's rise in the world economy. *Economic and Political Weekly*, 44 (8), pp.29–34.

Mearsheimer, J. J., 2001. *Tragedy of the great power politics*. New York: W. W. Norton & Company.

Meyer, E. K., 2015. What is "strategic asset seeking FDI"? *Multinational Business Review*, 23 (1), pp.57–66.

Milanovic, B., 2016. *Global inequality: A new approach for the age of globalization*. Cambridge, MA: Belknap Press/Harvard University Press.

Miller, S., 2016. Is it a risk for America that China holds over $US1 trillion in US debt? Center for Strategic and International Studies. Available at: http://chinapower.csis.org/us-debt/ [Accessed 5 March 2017].

Morrison, W. M., 2015. China's economic rise: History, trends, challenges, and implications for the United States. *Congressional Service Report*, RL33534. Washington, DC: Congressional Research Service.

Navarro, P. and Autry, G., 2011. *Death by China: Confronting the dragon – A global call to action*. Upper Saddle River, NJ: Prentice Hall.

OECD., 2015. Measuring trade in value-added. An OECD-WTO joint initiative. Available at: http://www.oecd.org/sti/ind/measuringtradeinvalue-addedanoecd-wtojointinitiative.htm [Accessed 5 March 2017].

OECD/World Bank., 2015. Inclusive global value chains: Joint OECD and World Bank Report. Istanbul: OECD/World Bank Group.

O'Hehir, A., 2012 China's not-so-secret plan for world domination, *Salon*, 21 August.

O'Rourke, R., 2016. Maritime territorial and exclusive economic zone (EEZ) disputes involving China: Issues for Congress. *Congressional Service Report*, R42784. Washington, DC: Congressional Research Service.

Porter, M. E., 1990. *The competitive advantage of nations*. London: Macmillan.

Prahalad, C. K., 2004. The fortune at the bottom of the pyramid: Eradicating poverty through profits. Upper Saddle River, NJ: Prentice Hall.

Roblin, S., 2016. China stole this fighter from Russia: And it's coming to the South China Sea. *The National Interest*, 24 July. Available at: http://nationalinterest.org/feature/china-stole-fighter-russia%E2%80%94-its-coming-the-south-china-sea-17087 [Accessed 5 March 2017].

Scissors, D. and Subramanian, A., 2012. The great China debate: Will Beijing rule the world? *Foreign Affairs*, 91 (1), pp.173–177.

Shirk, L. S., 2007. *China: Fragile superpower*. New York: Oxford University Press.

Solomon, R. H., 1994. Asian architecture: The US in the Asia–Pacific community. *Harvard International Review*, 16 (2), pp.26–29.

Strategy Page (2008) China Discussion Board, 13 March. Available at https://www.strategypage.com/militaryforums/69-30553.aspx#startofcomments [Accessed 8 March 2017].

Tse, E., 2015. *China's disruptors*. New York: Penguin Random House

UNCTAD., 2015. Tracing the value added in global value chains: product-level case studies in China. New York & Geneva: United Nations.

UNCTAD., 2017. *UNCTAD STAT*. Available at: http://unctad.org/en/Pages/statistics.aspx.

USCBC. 2017. *Understanding US–China trade relationship: Prepared by the US–China Business Council by Oxford Economics*. Available at: https://www.uschina.org/sites/default/files/OE%20US%20Jobs%20and%20China%20Trade%20Report.pdf [Accessed 15 May 2017].

Vogel, E., 2011. *Deng Xiaoping and the transformation of China*. Cambridge, MA: Belknap Press, Harvard University Press.

World Economic Forum., 2012. The shifting geography of global value chains: Implications for developing countries and trade policy. Switzerland: WEF.

World Economic Forum., 2016. *China's innovation system: White paper*. Switzerland: WEF.

Wignaraja, G., 2016. Production networks and enterprises in East Asia: Industry and firm-level analysis. Heidelberg: Springer.

World Bank., 2017. *Open data*. Available at: http://data.worldbank.org/.

Xing, Y. and Detert, N., 2010. How the iPhone widens the United States trade deficit with the People's Republic of China. *ADB Working Paper*, No. 257, pp.1–12.

Yu, Y. and Liu, Y., 2016. Country-of-origin and social resistance in host countries: The case of a Chinese firm. *Thunderbird International Business Review*, Early view online. DOI: 10.1002/tie.21873.

Zeng, M. and Williamson, P. J., 2007. *Dragons at your door: How Chinese cost innovation is disrupting global competition*. Boston, MA: Harvard Business School Publishing.

Zhang, L., 2016. Re-balancing in China: Progress and prospects. *IMF Working Paper*, WP/16/183 Asia Pacific Department. Washington, DC: IMF.

Zhang, X., Ma, X. and Wang, Y., 2012. Entrepreneurial orientation, social capital, and the internationalization of SMEs: Evidence from China. *Thunderbird International Business Review*, 54 (2), pp.195–210.

14

WILL IT END IN TEARS?

Howard Davies

Permabears and Panda-lovers

In 2001, when China's GDP was $US1.33 trillion, Gordon G. Chang published a book titled *The Coming Collapse of China*. That was followed in 2007 by Will Hutton's *The Writing on the Wall*, which also predicted that the country could no longer sustain its hectic economic development. At around the same time, James Kynge (2006) was explaining how *China Shakes the World* and Martin Jacques (2009) published *When China Rules the World*.

In a crude sense this debate between the "Permabears", who see China in a constant state of imminent collapse, and the "Panda-lovers", who see a permanently rising power, has been resolved in favour of the latter. It is 16 years since Chang's prognostications and China has not collapsed (although the West nearly did in the 2008/9 financial crisis). China's GDP in 2015 was $US10.87 trillion, second only to the US, and the IMF calculated that China actually became the largest economy in the world in 2014, on the basis of purchasing power parity (PPP).

Success to date, however, does not render the disquiet irrelevant and this chapter examines the concerns for China's future. It first considers whether the country can survive without a pluralist civil society. It then examines whether it can sustain "enough" economic growth, and the extent of progress towards re-balancing the economy. The last part then considers possible "triggers" that might precipitate a national crisis: the burden of debt; "ghost cities" and a property bubble; corruption; the polluted environment, and a trade war with the US. Some of those have been examined in earlier chapters, but it is useful to bring them together before attempting an overall judgment.

Can an authoritarian system survive?

The most fundamental issue for China concerns the sustainability of a country where power is concentrated in a single party-state, with no checks and balances to moderate its actions and support its legitimacy. For many observers, such a system is inherently unstable and they point to China's history of collapsing dynasties and violent transfers of power as harbingers of the future.

Hutton (2007) draws on work by Scott (1998) and Halperin, Siegle and Weinstein (2005) to argue that the top-down "grand vision" organization of economies and societies always fails. High quality economic growth and social stability require that diverse views and interests are represented and have the power to influence policies. Hence, an economy requires market mechanisms, but also needs appropriate non-market institutions to function effectively. Those include the rule of law, protected property rights, independent judiciary and trade unions, freedom of speech, independent media, social insurance mechanisms and a democratic political system where government's legitimacy is drawn from a popular mandate. Without pluralism and room for dissent, there is no way in which the "wisdom of crowds" can operate. The problems caused by "groupthink", and herd behaviour inevitably lead to poor decision-making, inefficiency and eventually decline. As pluralism is always under pressure from public and private monopolies it must be actively protected by a populace that feels it has material certainty. There must also be companies capable of learning, adaptation and innovation, which requires that they have a purpose shared with their employees and stakeholders, supported by powerful processes of justification and accountability.

As China meets none of these requirements, Hutton concluded in 2007 that it was close to its limits and could not grow beyond the development model based on investing in mass-production for export based on cheap labour. To innovate, to compete with multinationals outside China's protected market, and to join the knowledge-based economy requires the installation of pluralist institutions which would undermine the power of the party-state, and which are therefore anathema to it.

This argument that "China needs democracy in order to keep increasing national income" has been accompanied by a conventional political wisdom that as the middle class grows, so the new bourgeoisie will demand greater civil liberties and the introduction of democratic institutions (Mesquita & Downs, 2005). From this point of view, without a fundamental change in the locus of power, the economy will begin to falter, and the legitimacy of the Communist Party will be brought into doubt, leading to civil unrest, a modern version of the withdrawal of the mandate of heaven, and collapse.

These are legitimate arguments, but there are other views. Pragmatically, the predicted economic, political and social collapse has just not happened. China's percentage rate of economic growth has slowed but only after reaching income levels that Hutton considered impossible without systemic change. The leadership of Xi Jinping has seen no loss of control by the Party, quite the opposite, but it is difficult to interpret the Party's tightening of control as a repressive reaction to strident middle-class demands for democracy, because they are hardly evident.

There are more fundamental counter-arguments to the assertion that China will collapse without conventional democratic institutions. In Daniel Bell's (2014) book *The China Model* he points out that societies that seek to be democratic face the problem of how to allow every citizen to have an influence, when systems based on "one man one vote" can be manipulated by demagogues. When Donald Trump and Rodrigo Duterte both won presidential elections, Bell's description of how narcissistic populists can take power by proffering simplistic solutions for complex problems to ill-informed but enthusiastic voters seems prescient. Hutton's argument that effective solutions can only be found through pluralistic institutions generating them from below has a mirror image, which is that allocating too much influence to the grass roots in the selection of leaders and policies also has its problems. The key to effective national governance is to balance the need for popular influence (government by the people) with the need for well-informed and effective policies (government for the people), which requires capable leadership. Bell's assertion is that China's system of political meritocracy, where the leadership is selected on the basis of extensive competition within the Party, is more effective than Western versions of democracy in ensuring the quality of leadership. Prospective leaders, even the "princeling" offspring of Party elders, have to work their way through the layers of government and the economy, running cities, provinces and large state-owned enterprises before being considered by the Organization Department for higher office. Second tier property developers need not apply!

That is not to say that Hutton's arguments about the need to draw on the whole of society's talents are invalid. What is clear is that the Western model often advocated for China is not a panacea. It has problems, even on its home ground, and the search for a balance between government "for" and government "by" the people remains a work in progress.

Empirically, researchers have tested the hypothesis that middle-class citizens demand democracy, as "modernization theory" suggests. Wang (2016) used a sample of nearly 10,000 individuals to address the question "who wants democracy in China?" which was measured through responses to the question "if high economic growth is maintained it is not necessary to improve democracy". The conclusions were telling though not surprising. Approximately half of the respondents demanded more democracy, even if high economic growth is maintained. A significantly higher proportion of Party members were more demanding of democracy than non-members, and there was a hierarchy whereby peasants were less supportive than workers, white collar workers and the self-employed, who in turn were less supportive than intellectuals, private entrepreneurs, SOE administrators and cadres. However, when respondents were asked if they agreed with taking action in the form of mass gatherings, protesting or striking, the results were very different, with Party members and those of middle class and higher status less approving than others. While the Chinese bourgeoisie are in favour of democracy, even when growth is robust, they do not approve of taking action in its support.

It would be complacent to conclude that China will never experience a crisis of legitimacy arising from the lack of democratic institutions, but such a crisis is not imminent. A rapidly growing and home-owning middle class has a lot to lose from instability, and seems to place democracy in the category of "nice to have" but not "worth taking risks for". It is also evident that there is no single model of governance that can be drawn on to ensure a stable future. Bell (2014) makes the case that the Chinese one party system combines political meritocracy at the top, with experimentation in the middle and elements of democracy at the lower levels, thereby providing a system that is both stable and morally defensible. That remains to be seen, but the argument provides a counter-weight to unreflexive statements that the lack of Western style democracy dooms the country to upheaval.

Does China have enough growth and will it be of the right kind?

The central fact of the Chinese experience since 1978 has been spectacular economic growth and its impact on the material well-being and international influence of the nation. That much is undeniable. However, there is still debate on three key questions, namely: "How much growth does China need to maintain social stability?" "How much growth does China really have?" and "How successful are China's attempts to re-balance the economy?"

How much growth does China need?

The most pressing requirement is that growth be sufficient to avoid mass unemployment, absorbing any increase in the size of the labour force, and providing work for the millions of rural residents who continue to stream to the cities. When Presidents Bush and Hu met in 2008, Bush reportedly asked Hu which issue gave him most sleepless nights, to which the unhesitating reply was "unemployment". Nothing (apart from rampant inflation) could be more dangerous to a regime than a mass of workers without jobs, in a society without a strong social security safety net. Putting a number on the required growth rate to provide full employment is difficult. However, with unemployment officially less than 5%, growth thus far has been sufficient to absorb any increases in the labour supply. Furthermore, as the society ages, the population of working age has begun to decline, by almost 5 million in 2015, and a large number of new jobs are no longer needed simply to match a larger labour force. What is required is that new jobs are available in the growing cities and incomes and living standards continue to improve at a rate judged satisfactory by the general public. The 13th Five Year Plan calls for the creation of 50 million new urban jobs, which compares to the 64 million achieved for the period of the previous Plan (Kennedy & Johnson, 2016, p.24), and is a reasonable indication of the official estimate for the numbers required. With a relatively static, even declining, population and workforce, the authorities' expectation of 6–7% growth per year throughout the 13th Five Year Plan should be sufficient to avoid unemployment while providing tangible material improvements year on year.

How accurate are the growth figures?

The question of how much growth China needs leads to the dispute over the real size of the Chinese economy, and its rate of growth (Huang, 2014). Sceptics argue that the national income statistics are inaccurate, and perhaps manipulated, so that the published figures significantly overestimate both the size of the economy and its growth. They also point to the reduction in the growth rate as evidence of China's economic "slow down", which may trigger widespread adverse events, from unemployment and social unrest in China, to declining exports for resource-rich countries like Australia, to falling sales of luxury goods in Hong Kong. Throughout 2016 it was rare to watch a business news programme that did not make at least passing reference to China's "slow down" and its consequences.

There are real reasons to question the accuracy of China's GDP statistics. For many years, annual figures for growth in the previous year were announced in the first few days of January, which is technically not feasible with any degree of accuracy. Prime Minister Li Keqiang said that he himself didn't trust such "manmade" numbers (although he was referring to earlier figures for Liaoning province, which he had governed, not the current national figures (Holz, 2014, p.310)). He argued that a more accurate picture could be had from "hard data" on electricity usage, rail cargo and bank loans.

In principle, the national GDP figure should be consistent with the figures for the individual provinces. However, from 1997 onwards, nearly all provinces were reporting growth rates higher than the national growth rate, and by 2004 the difference between the sum of provincial growth and the national figure was more than 19% (Holz 2014). Given that local government officials have been rewarded and promoted on the basis of their success in stimulating growth, there has been an incentive for them to exaggerate the figures for their regions, and scepticism about the GDP statistics remains in the Western media (Swanson, 2016).

Closer examination reveals a more complicated picture. With the exception of the lunacies of the Great Leap Forward and the Cultural Revolution periods, experts have found Chinese statistics to be "generally accurate and reliable" (Rawski, 1976, p.440) over the long period. There is no doubt that in the late 1990s false reporting at local level became widespread for at least a few years. However, it does not seem to have had a major impact on the national figures, which many Western analysts have found to be reliable. Indeed, as Holz (2014) points out, the supposedly "hard" data that Li Keqiang referred to with approval is much less reliable than it appears because the figures are collected from a set of reporting enterprises which is a declining sub-set of the total. Huenemann (2001), for instance, found that the figure for freight transportation nation-wide stood still at a time when petroleum consumption for transportation was growing at more than 10% per year. The reason was that data on transportation was only available for the declining proportion of the activity carried out by government departments. Similarly, figures for energy use have been poor indicators for GDP as they fail to capture much of the growing private sector, and in any case energy use per unit of national output has been on the decline (Wu, 2012).

GDP figures are of necessity "manmade". They involve collecting data (by sampling) on thousands of goods and services from millions of organizations and households, assigning estimated prices and adding up the total to arrive at a single figure that is somehow representative of the total. To view the result as an accurate metric is a mistake that every student of introductory economics learns to avoid. It certainly makes no sense at all to be sensitive to decimal-point changes in the headline figure. When China's growth rate for 2014 was amended from an estimated 7.5% to a realized 7.4%, and commentators went into full "China slows" mode, they revealed more about the febrile nature of the media than they did about China.

What then can be said about China's recent growth figures and their implications? The first point is a matter of simple arithmetic. When China's GDP grew by a stated 14% from 2006 to 2007, the addition to GDP was $US382 billion. There has been so much growth in the intervening years that a growth rate of just 5% in 2016 would add $US550 billion to the economy ($US367 billion at 2006 prices) and the 6.7% announced added $492 billion at 2006 prices. China added substantially more to GDP in 2015/6 than in 2006/7. Measured in absolute terms, there has been no slowdown. The focus on percentages is reasonable in economies that grow by a very few per cent per year because the base for the percentages grows very slowly, making year-to-year comparisons useful. However, with average growth around 10% the base changes rapidly, so that percentage changes are no longer comparable in magnitude across time. What matters for employment, incomes, spending, savings and imports is the absolute increase in national income, not the percentage, and much of the "China slows" narrative is based on a simple misunderstanding.

The issue of measurement accuracy nevertheless remains. Holz (2014) notes that the National Bureau of Statistics has no independent power over the government units it depends upon for its basic data, that "official GDP values may be rather haphazard" (p.322) and that the complexity and lack of transparency in calculation leaves room for manipulation of the figures at the behest of the leadership. On the other hand, there are simple explanations for anomalies like provincial/ national differences (cross-province activities are often double counted), there is a high level of consistency across different uses of the data and statistical tests found no evidence of actual manipulation or consistent over-estimation of China's growth (Holz, 2014). Some analysts, indeed, have suggested that China's GDP figures may be significant *under*estimates. Rosen and Bao (2015) estimated that the 2008 GDP figures should be raised by 13–16%, for a variety of reasons. First, while the country has committed to using the 2008 version of the internationally accepted System of National Accounts, it has not yet done so, continuing to use the 1993 version, which is known to underestimate activities like services and knowledge intensive work. Second, rapid growth of small firms in employment-intensive, small-firm sectors like wholesale, retail, catering and (especially) property goes under-reported by a system that was not designed to focus on such activities, and third, observers have argued that, for technical reasons, consumption spending in particular is underestimated (Zhang & Zhu, 2013).

Overall, we can conclude that China's GDP figures suffer from the defects inherent to national income statistics everywhere, magnified by the rapid pace and structural nature of the country's economic development. The result is a set of figures that should not be taken seriously to a few percentage points, but is probably not a gross and deliberate upward misrepresentation.

How successful are the attempts to rebalance the economy?

China's critics, admirers and leaders share an understanding that economic development needs to shift away from a model based upon extraordinarily high levels of investment spending, net exports, and manufacturing, and towards a "new normal" more reliant upon domestic consumption, the service sector and technological improvement. If that rebalancing does not take place, the country could fall into the "middle-income" trap of stagnating per capita incomes, or possibly a financial crisis.

Central to the imbalance is China's very high savings rate, amounting to around 46% of Gross National Income, compared with a world figure of around 26% (Zhang, 2016, p.11). Household saving in particular represents nearly 25% of GNI, in comparison with less than 8% world-wide. Such high savings rates reduce spending on consumption as a direct consequence, but they also have implications for the balance of trade and for financial flows. If a country saves more than it invests then it must have a balance of trade surplus and it will have financial inflows to invest abroad. Conversely, as in the American case, a country that saves much less (19% of GDP in 2015 and just 6% for households) will have a trade deficit and will need to borrow from abroad in order to carry out its investments – a point apparently lost on President Trump's economic advisers.

China's savings rate is high for cultural reasons, including the Confucian emphasis on thrift, but it is also a rational response to the institutional setting. Despite the rhetoric of "socialism with Chinese characteristics", China has few of the welfare institutions taken for granted in the capitalist West. Health care has to be paid for, as does education, and only a small proportion of the population are covered by pension schemes sufficient to fully support daily life. The "iron rice bowl" provided by state enterprises is largely a thing of the past, and enterprise reform, along with attempts to reduce over-capacity in some sectors, means that the threat of unemployment is real for some. Hence, Chinese families feel obliged to save, for precautionary reasons. During the period of the one-child policy, which only ended in 2016, they also spent less because they had fewer child-rearing obligations.

Rebalancing the economy therefore requires a reduction in savings, which is followed through into investment, and which will be reflected in a smaller current account surplus. A recent evaluation from the International Monetary Fund (Zhang, 2016) shows that progress has been mixed. The current account surplus has fallen from a huge 10% of GDP in 2007 down to 2–3% from 2013–15, and net exports now make up a very small, sometimes negative, contribution to GDP. Consumption has been growing rapidly, at almost 9% per annum, contributing two thirds of growth in 2015–2016. Nevertheless, investment still accounts for 43% of GDP while consumption is at 38%. It cannot be said in 2016 that very significant rebalancing has yet been achieved. However, there are reasons to suppose that savings will decline further. Continuing urbanization raises consumption, and the population is aging, which will reduce savings. Government spending on health, education and social security in the 13th Plan will reduce government saving directly and weaken the precautionary incentive for household savings. The end of the one-child policy will also tend to support consumption. In the hugely profitable and oligopolistic financial sector, increased competition should reduce profitability and saving. Furthermore, as Chinese households have been saving large proportions of their incomes for decades, they may reach the point where they feel that their bank balances, and improving social security, are sufficient to cover future contingencies so that it is safe to save much less.

Rebalancing is therefore a work in progress, with reasonable but not overwhelming reasons for optimism. When it is recognized that China's capital stock per worker is still much less than that in the US, and that technological improvement requires continued investment in better machinery and equipment, there is still a productivity-led need to maintain high absolute levels of investment, so that a gradual process may be for the better.

Will debt bring the economy down?

In addition to the broad concerns that the Chinese system and pattern of growth is unsustainable, there are a series of triggers that might precipitate a national crisis. The first of these concerns the level of debt, and the associated non-performing loans in the banking system.

According to Kennedy and Johnson (2016, p.5) the figure for total outstanding debt in China grew from 166% of GDP in 2007 to 246% in 2015, held by companies (165%), banks (19%), government (22%) and households (40%). China has a high, and rapidly rising, ratio of debt to national income. It is also clear that a significant amount of bank lending has been made to "zombie" state enterprises suffering from losses and overcapacity and to local governments who are unlikely to be able to repay the loans. They are kept alive financially by the banks who replace unpaid loans with new ones, which in turn are unlikely to be repaid.

Pessimists see this as a harbinger of doom. As credit grows faster than the economy as a whole, so the misdirection of credit increases, into failing state companies, inefficient "white elephant" infrastructure projects, empty residential "ghost cities", and a real estate bubble, none of which will yield the return necessary to repay the debt. Eventually, a string of major defaults is inevitable, putting public trust in the banks at risk and precipitating a full scale global economic crisis (Laing, 2016).

Optimists point to reasons to be less disturbed. First, China has a very high savings rate, which allows it to sustain more debt (Lardy, 2016). The likelihood of households becoming unable to service their mortgage loans, as happened in the US financial crisis of 2008, is close to zero because Chinese properties are purchased with heavy down payments, so that mortgage debt is small relative to valuations. Household saving deposits, at RMB 55 trillion in 2016, are twice the size of their debt and more than half of all households have no debt at all. Second, 95% of the debt is in domestic currency and China is a large net creditor to the rest of the world. There is, therefore, no possibility that economic collapse could arise from foreign lenders refusing to continue credit to Chinese firms, as happened to other Asian firms in the crisis of 1997. Third, banking crises usually begin with problems on the liabilities' side of bank balance sheets but Chinese bank liabilities are mostly retail deposits, which are "sticky" because their owners have few alternative safe "homes" for their savings.

In the unlikely event that a run on the (state-owned) major banks developed, the authorities could simply reduce the very high reserve ratio of 17%, which would instantly increase the banks' liquidity.

If non-performing loans were as high as some of the pessimists believe (and no one believes the official figures of around 2%) there could still be a crisis. However, in recent years the (hugely profitable) banks have been writing off NPLs on a large scale and in 2016 they had around 150% coverage of their reported level. The authorities have experience of re-capitalizing the (then bankrupt) banks in the 1990s by shifting NPLs to the "bad banks" or asset management companies, and only 30% of lending is now to the state-owned sector. As more loan activity is to the private sector on a purely commercial basis, so the banks are better able to absorb the problems associated with the zombies.

On balance, then, the Chinese debt problem is a real concern, which the leadership has recognized must be addressed without delay. However, parallels with the Asian financial crisis of 1997 and the Great Financial Crisis of 2008 are overblown. Provided the economy maintains the rate of growth close to that called for in the 13th Five Year Plan, with a doubling of GDP between 2010 and 2020, there should be ample resources and policy tools available to steer the financial sector away from the abyss.

What about ghost cities and a property crash?

Another concern has been the use of credit to support the over-development of residential property, with millions of square metres of empty apartments, and "ghost cities" thrown up by local governments being left to decay while the loans that financed them go unpaid. At the same time, in apparent contradiction, the prices of residential apartments, especially in the first line cities of Beijing, Guangzhou, Shanghai, and Shenzhen, have risen to the point where they have become unaffordable for many middle-class families. There appears to be simultaneous over-supply and rising prices, which seems to make little economic sense. Here again, it is important to recognize that the Chinese situation is structurally different from that in North America or Europe, in ways that make it inappropriate to draw common conclusions from apparently parallel phenomena.

With respect to over-development, China does have a huge inventory of empty apartments. Residential real estate investment amounted to around 10% of GDP in 2014 and the IMF (2015) reported unsold inventory to be at least 1 billion square metres. An associated phenomenon has been the appearance of apparently empty "ghost cities", leading some analysts to predict catastrophic falls in prices and defaults on debt. That interpretation is exaggerated, for a number of reasons. In the first place, as Towson and Woetzel (2013) point out, the development of new cities has been an integral part of the urbanization process whereby *500 million* people have become newly urban residents. As part of their development plans city governments design new districts to house hundreds of thousands of residents. The apartments are built first as the pre-sales provide funding for other amenities. In the first few years, many remain empty as the purchasers remain in their old homes until the area is further developed. The authorities set up schools, a university and a major hospital, and they instruct state enterprises and government departments to move their offices into the new city. Within a few years, the "ghost city" is as busy as any other urban area. The classic example was the city of Kangbashi, which is a new town in the city of Ordos in Inner Mongolia. As Shepherd (2016) reports, in 2009 the Western media found an empty city and it became a "poster child" for Chinese developmental excess.

However, if the reporters had bothered to ask the local government why the city was so empty they would have found that it was all in the plan. By 2016 the city had a population of 100,000. More than 80% of the homes had been purchased and many of those that remained empty were being kept for their owners' retirement or for their children on marriage. There was no significant downward pressure on prices through oversupply.

There are undoubtedly some "ghost" cities and Wu (2016) reports on Caofeidian in Tangshan city in Hebei province as a current example. They are, however, not typical. As Towson and Woetzel (2013) observe, when a country urbanizes at a breakneck pace it is inevitable that some cities get the balance wrong with too few people, some have too many people (Beijing) and some get it about right (Shenzhen).

Apart from the resurrected "ghost" cities, there are other reasons to be less concerned about the apparent oversupply of housing in China. First, urbanization continues and there will be another 200 million newly urban residents looking for homes in the next 15 years. Second, Hui (2013) estimated that in 2010 more than 60% of households in Beijing were still living in former public housing – which means housing of poor quality, from which they will want to move. Third, the underdeveloped financial system means that residential property is a more important part of households' financial portfolios than it would otherwise be. Households are comfortable in holding apartments empty and nearly half of the more wealthy families do so. Fourth, the gender imbalance created by the one-child policy means that a middle-class boy has little chance of finding a middle-class wife if he does not have a fully paid-for apartment of his own. Before marriage he is unlikely to live in that apartment because he prefers to live with Mum who will cook, shop, clean and wash his clothes. The apartment remains empty but is not on the market and exerts no downward pressure on prices.

This tendency for Chinese households to hold empty properties is difficult to understand for those who live in Europe or North America because in those countries most residences are subject to a significant risk of depreciation if they are not occupied. Roofs can leak, gardens need to be kept tidy and ground level access makes an empty house vulnerable. But Chinese urban residences are almost all apartments in tall blocks. The roof and gardens are taken care of by the management company, there is no ground floor access and entry to the building is watched over by security guards. Hence, there is little concern that the investment may be physically degraded if left empty.

If the oversupply of apartments is less of a problem than it might appear, rapidly rising apartment prices are a real concern, because they might represent a "bubble" whose bursting would precipitate a financial crisis, and because prices are becoming out of reach for many young professionals, on whom the economy depends. As Kroeber (2016, p.79) points out, bubbles are difficult to identify anywhere before the event, more so in China because the housing market has only been in existence since the early 2000s, so there is no long established set of references. While housing market valuations are often assessed by using ratios of house prices to incomes, that has less relevance in China because many households were given their apartments by the state in the privatization process, and they now have a significant legacy value to spend on a new apartment before they have to use their incomes for purchase (for a professor in Beijing that would typically amount to more than a million US dollars). The IMF Country Report for 2015 pointed to "weakness in the housing market" in 2014 (p.36) but since then prices have continued to soar. Average rises in the year to August 2016 were 9.2% across an average of 70 cities, but 31.2% in Shanghai and 23.5% in Beijing. The authorities are concerned, commentators predict a crash and local governments have tried to cool markets by placing restrictions on the purchase of second homes and raising down payment ratios. Nevertheless, the price spiral continues. Couples "divorce" in order that one of them can purchase a "first" home and mortgage loan growth has grown by nearly 90% in a single year to 2016. It is clearly possible that prices could crash significantly as China's richest man, Wang Jianlin, has been predicting. On the other hand, even with the rapid mortgage growth, low loan-to-value ratios mean that householders are not in serious danger of negative equity so that the risk to the financial system is limited to that posed by leveraged property companies, rather than by the general public.

The rise in residential prices has created a major problem of inequity, in that there is one class of home buyers whose families were gifted significant wealth in the privatization, and who can afford to buy in the first-tier cities. Then there is the rest of the population who have to purchase from their salaries and who are effectively priced out of the market. The government has tried to solve it by putting restrictions on the luxury market – which have largely failed – and by encouraging local authorities to develop "social housing" for the less well-off, which has had only limited success. Some cities, like Shanghai, have built social housing in distant suburbs and economically upgraded old properties but most have not, mainly because the central government did not provide enough funding and social housing is not highly profitable.

As a source of considerable discomfort for a large proportion of the urban population, housing prices in the major cities represent a real challenge for the government. The 13th Five Year Plan sets a mandatory target of 20 million units of affordable housing to be produced but whether that will be achieved, or prove sufficient, is an open question.

Will corruption lead to social unrest?

China is a very corrupt country, recognized by everyone from international organizations, to the leadership, to the general public. It extends into every walk of life from schools, where teachers take bribes to favour (or more firmly discipline) selected pupils, to hospitals where bribes are needed to secure beds and ensure good quality care, to the workplace where jobs and promotions are for sale, and to the business arena where contracts are awarded on the basis of side payments. Farmers have tainted milk to fake higher protein content (and poison children), intellectual property and brand names are shamelessly stolen and "tofu" schools are built of inferior materials in order to divert the resources into the pockets of local government officials and contractors. Furthermore, it is often the officials who should be fighting corruption who are themselves deeply involved, as when Politburo standing committee member Zhou Yongkang, who had been in charge of the national security services, was found, with his family and friends, to be in possession of $US14.5 bn.

The key issue here, however, is not how extensive is corruption, or why it arises, but whether its prevalence is likely to lead to unrest and social breakdown. It is certainly presented as an existential threat to the rule of the Party, and in 2011 Premier Wen Jiabao (whose family were reported to be in possession of some $US3 bn by the New York Times) told the National People's Congress that "I think the biggest risk we face is corruption". When Xi Jinping took power in November 2012 one of his first actions was to launch a fierce anticorruption campaign that has touched all walks of life, and that has been very popular with the man in the street, who is hurt most by the inequality of access to opportunity that is caused by corrupt behaviour.

Given that corruption is being tackled in a very public way, with arrests reaching more senior levels than ever before, it is unlikely that popular protest over it will emerge as a serious threat to the party-state. Some observers see Xi's campaign as a means to concentrate power in his own hands, and it has had that effect. However, as it enters a fifth year without abatement, and reaches down to mundane issues like the kinds of lunch that universities can serve to their guests, it certainly also represents a serious attempt to change behaviour across the nation.

Even if corruption were to cause social unrest, which is less likely now than it was ten years ago, the coercive power of the Chinese state is sufficiently well developed to contain it through whatever means it deems fit, which includes extreme violence. There seems, therefore, little reason to suppose that Chinese crowds will take to the streets over that particular issue, although they have done in the past.

Pollution and environmental disaster

While corruption is corrosive of trust, pollution is seriously destructive of people's health. The quality of China's air is so bad that almost half of its people are exposed to levels of PM2.5 that are higher than America's highest threshold (Economist, 2015) and breathing Beijing's air has been described as the equivalent of smoking 40 cigarettes per day. Potable tap water is rarely available, rivers and lakes are full of industrial effluent and sewage, and soils are polluted with heavy metals. Continued dependence on coal as the main source of energy, and the need to heat northern cities where the winter temperature is often more than 20 °C below zero, makes it inevitable that carbon dioxide and sulphates continue to spew into the air, while the huge expansion in car ownership adds damaging fine particles to the mix.

For many years, the public response of the authorities was denial. When four cyclists from the US Olympic team wore masks when riding in Beijing in 2008, they were denounced as insulting the Chinese people and the spokesman for Beijing's environmental protection bureau declared that bringing masks to China was a waste of luggage space (Yan, 2016). They were outflanked, however, by the US Embassy, which began to monitor air quality on the Embassy premises, and publish the results on the Internet. On World Environment Day in 2012 Vice-minister Wu Xiaoqing claimed that the Embassy was unqualified to monitor air quality and its figures were inaccurate, but the Beijing government began to publish its own PM2.5 data – albeit with figures often lower than the Embassy figures.

To some extent, denial remains an aspect of the authorities' response to pollution so that when journalist Chai Jing made a startlingly frank documentary called "Under the Dome", which was released on the Internet in 2015, it was taken down, although not before millions had viewed it (and it remains available on YouTube). Suppression of information continues but on the other hand, the government has made increasingly serious commitments to taking action. The State Council published a grand plan in 2013, thousands of polluting factories have been closed and in December 2016 it was announced that a major initiative to "make the polluter" pay through carbon taxes and fines would be in place from the beginning of 2018.

The key question is whether pollution could be the source of a national crisis. That could arise in two different ways. In the short term, the public could become so concerned that social unrest emerges on a significant scale. In the longer term, the health effects of such extreme levels of pollution on an aging population could massively increase the demand for health care, while simultaneously reducing the economy's productive capacity.

The possibility of social unrest is a real one, as pollution becomes a "top of the mind" issue for many Chinese. Humour is a telling indicator of the public mood, and jokes about pollution abound on the Internet. When a Beijing resident posted "come to live in wonderful Beijing! No need to buy cigarettes, just put your head out of the window and breathe!" a Shanghai citizen riposted, "That's nothing. In Shanghai we turn on the tap and pork soup comes right out." (Thousands of dead pigs had been found floating in the Huangpu river.) Jokes hide the darker side of public feeling, but it is very real. The authorities have noted with concern that the major reason for "mass incidents" (the code for riots and protests) is no longer land seizures but pollution incidents. There has also been a shift in their location from rural settings to the cities, which are infinitely more combustible. Middle-class residents across the country have taken up the "not in my backyard" attitude of many Western households, objecting to the location of potentially poisonous chemical plants in their neighbourhoods. Paraxylene (PX) plants, in particular, have been the source of protests in Xiamen, Maoming and Ningbo, where local authorities have in each case been forced to back down.

Judging whether pollution, and the failure to control it sufficiently quickly, will lead to a social crisis, is difficult. While democracy is seen as "nice to have" but "not worth taking action over" health, particularly children's health, is undoubtedly a higher priority. It is highly likely, therefore, that continued extreme pollution events would lead to significant unrest on the part of the middle class. The state is seen to be taking the problem seriously but at the same time has continued to apply heavy-handed tactics to suppress protests. On one occasion in Chengdu in December 2016 the police arrested a group who were wearing masks, which they chose to interpret as signs of dissent, rather than environmental protection (Yan, 2016). Such actions on a larger scale could create a volatile mix whereby the authorities lose legitimacy by failing to protect the populace from pollution and then further inflame feelings by subjecting them to repression when they protest.

In the longer term, the impact of pollution on the need for health care, particularly with an aging population, could be very significant indeed. Rates of cancer and respiratory disease, in particular, could reach epidemic proportions. Furthermore, if people of working age succumb to environmentally triggered disease, a smaller workforce will have to produce the additional national output needed to radically expand medical services. Whether this can be managed becomes a race between growing national income and resources on the one hand, and a looming health crisis on the other.

Could a trade war with the US trigger a crisis in China?

Before the summer of 2016, the notion that a trade war might break out between China and the US seemed far-fetched. Both countries were gaining from a relationship in which China grew by producing cheap goods for American households and used its surpluses to purchase large amounts of US government securities, thereby allowing the low saving US to spend more than would otherwise be possible. However, Donald Trump built a significant part of his presidential campaign around the idea that China is a currency manipulator and has "stolen" American manufacturing jobs, which would return to the US if tariff barriers were imposed. It therefore becomes necessary to consider whether a trade war with the US could be the trigger for a crisis in China.

As this book went to press, in March 2017, the likelihood of Trump making good on his campaign threat to put tariffs of up to 45% on Chinese goods was difficult to fathom. He did not make good on his threat to (manifestly incorrectly) declare China a currency manipulator on "Day One" of his presidency, and some of his senior appointments seem unlikely to wish to follow that through. On the other hand, the appointment of Peter Navarro, author of *Death by China*, as a senior advisor on trade suggests that he might yet make good on the trade war threat.

If the US did impose heavy tariffs on China, the response would undoubtedly be retaliation, either in kind or by using the power of the Chinese state to reduce Chinese purchases of US products by decree. Other responses could be to make life more difficult for US firms in China, to reduce China's purchase of US government securities, or even to sell part of its huge holdings, making it difficult for the US government to finance its deficit. If a tit-for-tat tariff war broke out, the US could lose as many as 4.8 million jobs (Noland, Hufbauer, Robinson & Moran, 2016), especially in industries like aerospace, where China could simply buy Airbus instead of Boeing. Rising prices would trigger inflation, raising interest rates and uncertainty, and reducing investment. American consumers, especially the poor, would suffer losses in real incomes, and employment could fall by several percentage points.

For China, the impact of such a trade war would also be significantly negative. However, most observers suggest that it would be far less catastrophic than it might have been ten years ago, and that the US needs China much more than the US needs China (Nie, 2016). Increasing reliance on domestic consumption means that exports are less important for employment and net exports make up a much smaller proportion of China's GDP (Zhang, 2016). The US market is slow growing so that China's attention for the immediate future is much more on emerging markets like India, Indonesia and the countries of the "One Belt One Road" initiative. Nevertheless, manufacturing for export is still very important to China, and estimates are that a 10% tariff would reduce exports to the US by 25%, and lead to a reduction in China's growth rate of 1% per annum (Independent, 2017). As that would reduce the anticipated growth rate for the next ten years to around 5.5% it would reduce the country's room to manoeuvre around its other problems, but would not in itself bring stagnation or depression.

So will it end in tears?

The analysis above suggests that an optimistic view of China's future can be supported in that the overall system can probably be sustained, and growth should be enough to provide the space needed for the gradual introduction of a consumption-based pattern of development and the elimination or reduction of problems like debt, housing prices, corruption and pollution. It can certainly be argued that the more breathless predictions of imminent collapse which are found in the Western media are often based on misunderstandings. At the same time, however, it would be foolish to be complacent. If the country faced a "perfect storm" in which growth stumbled and several of the potential trigger events occurred together, there still could be an unhappy ending to the awakening of the dragon.

References

Bell, D., 2014. *The China model: Political meritocracy and the limits of democracy*. Princeton, NJ: Princeton University Press.

Chang, G.G., 2001. *The coming collapse of China*. London: Century.

Economist., 2015 *Mapping the invisible scourge*. 15 August. Available at: www.economist.com/news/china/21661053-new-study-suggests-air-pollution-even-worse-thought-mapping-invisible-scourge [Accessed 23 January 2017].
Halperin, M., Siegle, J. and Weinstein, M., 2005. *The democracy advantage: How democracies promote prosperity and peace*. New York: Routledge.
Holz, C., 2014. The quality of China's GDP statistics. *China Economic Review*, 30, pp.309–338.
Huang, Y., 2014. China's mis-leading economic indicators. *Financial Times: The A-list*. 29 August. Available at: http://carnegieendowment.org/2014/08/29/china-s-misleading-economic-indicators-pub-56499 [Accessed 24 January 2017].
Huenemann, R., 2001. Are China's recent transport statistics plausible? *China Economic Review*, 12 (4), pp.368–372.
Hui, X., 2013. *Housing, urban renewal and socio-spatial integration: A study on rehabilitating the former socialistic public housing in Beijing*. Thesis. Delft University of Technology, Faculty of Architecture, Department of Urbanism.
Hutton, W., 2007. *The writing on the wall: China and the West in the 21st century*. London: Abacus.
Independent, 2017. Goldman Sachs claims Donald Trump trade war would hurt US and Chinese economic growth. Available at: http://www.independent.co.uk/news/business/news/goldman-sachs-donald-trump-trade-wat-us-china-gdp-economy-growth-hurt-a7568486.html [Accessed 28 February 2017].
International Monetary Fund. 2015. *IMF Country Report No.15/234. People's Republic of China*. Washington, DC: IMF.
Jacques, M., 2009. *When China rules the world: The rise of the Middle Kingdom and the end of the Western world*. London: Allen Lane.
Kennedy, S. and Johnson, C. K., 2016. *Perfecting China inc. The 13th five year plan*. Center for Strategic and International Studies. New York: Rowman and Littlefield.
Kroeber, A., 2016. *China's economy: What everyone needs to know*. Oxford: Oxford University Press.
Kynge, J., 2006. *China shakes the world: The rise of a hungry nation*. London: Weidenfeld & Nicolson.
Laing, J., 2016. China's debt addiction could lead to a financial crisis. *Barron's Asia*, 5 November. Available at: http://www.barrons.com/articles/chinas-debt-addiction-could-lead-to-a-financial-crisis-1478322658 [Accessed 24 January 2017].
Lardy, N., 2016. No need to panic, China's banks are in pretty good shape. *Financial Times*, 1 June. Available at: https://www.ft.com/content/5bfb049a-2287-11e6-9d4d-c11776a5124d [Accessed 24 January 2017].
Mesquita, B., and Downs, G., 2005. Development and democracy. *Foreign Affairs*, 84 (5), pp.77–86.
Nie, W., 2016. Why America would lose a trade war with China. *Fortune*, 22 December. Available at: http://fortune.com/2016/12/22/donald-trump-china-trade-war/ [Accessed 28 February 2017].
Noland, M., Hufbauer, G., Robinson, S. and Moran, T., 2016. *Assessing trade agendas in the US presidential campaign*. Peterson Institute for International Economics. PIEE Briefing 16–6.
Rawski, T., 1976. On the reliability of Chinese economic data: discussion. *Journal of Development Studies*, 12 (4), pp.438–441.
Rosen, D., and Bao, B., 2015. *Broken abacus? A more accurate gauge of China's economy*. Washington, DC: Centre for Strategic and International Studies.
Scott, J., 1998. *Seeing like a state: How certain schemes to improve the human condition have failed*. New Haven, CT: Yale University Press.
Shepherd, W., 2016. An update on China's largest ghost city – what Ordos Kangbashi is like today. *Forbes*, 19 April. Available at: http://www.forbes.com/sites/wadeshepard/2016/04/19/an-update-on-chinas-largest-ghost-city-what-ordos-kangbashi-is-like-today/#40e74afd1e08 [Accessed 24 January 2017].
Swanson, A., 2016. The country that tricked the world: The question is how serious are China's exaggerations. *The Washington Post*, 8 January. Available at: https://www.washingtonpost.com/news/wonk/wp/2016/01/08/the-country-that-tricked-the-world/?utm_term=.c927b17e94ec [Accessed 24 January 2017].

Towson, J., and Woetzel, J., 2013. *The 1 hour China book: Two Peking University professors explain all of China business in six short stories*. Cayman Islands: Towson Group.

Wang, C., 2016. Who wants democracy in China? An empirical analysis of Chinese democratization in perspective. *Asian Journal of Social Science Studies*, 1 (1), p.12.

Wu, W., 2016. The city that never boomed. *South China Morning Post*. 23 June, p.B3.

Wu, Y., 2012. Energy intensity and its determinants in China's regional economies. *Energy Policy*, 41, pp.703–711.

Yan, A., 2016. Quick fixes, empty vows and breathtaking inaction. *South China Morning Post*, 21 December, p.B5.

Zhang, L., 2016. Re-balancing in China: Progress and prospects. *IMF Working Paper*, WP/16/183 Asia Pacific Department. Washington, DC: IMF.

Zhang, J. and Zhu, T.2013. *Re-estimating China's Under-estimated consumption*. Working Paper, Social Science Research Network. Available at: https://papers.ssrn.com/sol3/papers.cfm?abstract_id=2330698 [Accessed 24 January 2017].

INDEX